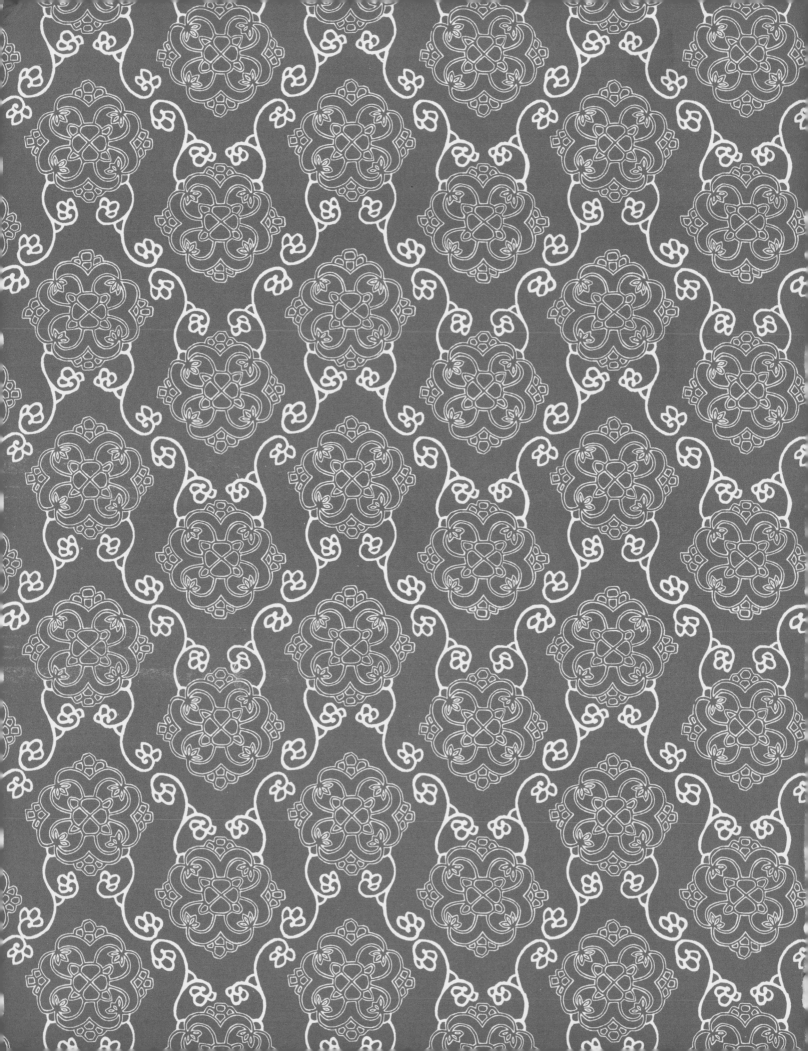

MASTERING THE ART OF CHINESE COOKING

MASTERING THE ART

of

CHINESE COOKING

EILEEN YIN-FEI LO

PHOTOGRAPHS BY SUSIE CUSHNER
BRUSH CALLIGRAPHY BY SAN YAN WONG

CHRONICLE BOOKS
SAN FRANCISCO

Library of Congress Cataloging-in-Publication
Data available.

ISBN 978-0-8118-5933-2

Manufactured in China

Designed by Katie Heit
Illustrations by Steven Noble
Prop styling by Helen Crowther
Food styling by Jee Levin
Typesetting by Janis Reed

10 9 8 7 6 5 4 3 2 1

Chronicle Books LLC
680 Second Street
San Francisco, California 94107
www.chroniclebooks.com

BOOKS BY EILEEN YIN-FEI LO

The Dim Sum Book

The Chinese Banquet Cookbook

China's Food, coauthor

Eileen Yin-Fei Lo's New Cantonese Cooking

From the Earth

The Dim Sum Dumpling Book

The Chinese Way

The Chinese Kitchen

The Chinese Chicken Cookbook

My Grandmother's Chinese Kitchen

In all the world there are only two really great cuisines: the Chinese and the French. China's was created first, untold centuries ago, and is judged to be the greater—when executed by superb chefs. It is the most complicated cuisine; it uses ingredients no other employs; and it is distinctive in that, for the most part, it is cuisine à la minute.

— *James Beard, 1973*

DEDICATIONS

This book is dedicated, as have been all of my books, to my husband, Fred, my careful reader and critic of first, and last, resort, and my love. It is for my children as well, Christopher the Chef, he of the fine palate; Elena the Producer, whose careful list of eating strictures is put on hold when she enters my house; Stephen the Coach, a walking appetite, who adores eating the cooking of others; and my daughter-in-law, Cristina, the Voracious Taster. To them, I add my granddaughter, Elliott Antonia, my "Siu Siu," who sat on my kitchen table and stirred and mixed with me as I wrote. Finally, I give my thanks, my deepest thanks, to Carla Glasser, my agent for many years, who cares about my work.

MASTERING THE ART of CHINESE COOKING

CONTENTS

PART 1

THE MARKET AS CLASSROOM
page 17

PART 2

THE MARKET BECOMES REGIONAL

page 129

PART 3

THE MARKET PARTICULAR

page 235

THE CHINESE MARKET

$\mathcal{M}$y teaching, my cooking lessons always begin in the Chinese market. Heaps of vegetables, familiar and exotic; the pork butchers; the herbalists and their shops comprise my classroom, my laboratory. In them I find recurring veins of discovery. In them I teach and simultaneously I learn. Sometimes when I am at home in my kitchen, my mind focused on the foods I am preparing, my thoughts will suddenly shift to a particular shop, along a particular street, in my Chinatown. I know that the next time I visit that shop I will find the greenest, smallest, most crisp bok choy, the liveliest striped bass swimming in tanks, and mounds of freshly picked lily bulbs and garlic flown in from China.

My mind is ever filled with the memories of a lifetime of cooking, learned and tested, gifts to me from the cooks and chefs, the dim sum artists and the *da shi fu* (kitchen masters), the farmers and fishermen in the many parts of China in which I have lived and cooked. They have given me the permanent legacy of a love and respect for food, its cultivation, and its preparation. It has been my life's work to try to transmit to my students the appreciation I have for the traditions of my native foods.

All of this begins in the market, and my markets are many. Few markets in the world can match the freshness, breadth, and variety of those found in China, and few markets in China can compare to the Qing Ping market in Guangzhou. This unstructured retail space, which snakes its way through a zigzag of tiny alleys, began as an underground free market decades ago when vegetable and fruit growers, fishermen and poultrymen, and the driers and blenders of spices and herbs rebelled against the rigid communes of the Mao Zedong era, which they believed cared more for numbers than for freshness and quality. I have shopped in the Qing Ping market often, and on any morning I have found live chickens and ducks and their eggs; whole pigs, live and roasted; fish swimming in shallow zinc pools; crawling crabs and piles of fresh mussels and clams; and small mountains of vegetables, the dirt of the fields still clinging to their roots. Preserved and pickled foods

fill ceramic barrels. Crude wooden stands and sheds, quickly nailed together, offer fresh herbs that are weighed on tiny bronze scales. This market is a visual and aromatic joy.

Similar markets, less imposing but equally dedicated to the freshness and quality so in demand by the Chinese, are to be found in Beijing. Most of them are movable markets, such as those along streets like Donghuamen and Bai Wan Zhuang and along the edges of Temple of Heaven Park, each determined by the unceasing urban expansion of the Chinese capital. But people will not be denied their morning dumplings, no matter where they have to go for them. Similarly, the unabated growth of Shanghai has seen the repeated upheaval of neighborhood markets, though, again, morning and afternoon shoppers remain undeterred. In Chengdu, Sichuan's capital, the markets are home to the rice-flour dumplings beloved by the locals, and to the special dried

reddish peppercorns that are indispensable to the cooking of western China. Fuzhou markets are a treasure trove of the fine teas and imaginative sweets of Fujian Province, in southeastern China. Regional variety, provincial smells, the foods of tradition—these are the many markets of China.

In Hong Kong, just south of Guangzhou, the rivals to Qing Ping are Sham Shui Po, a sprawling enclave on the route north out of Kowloon toward the New Territories, which border on China proper, and Yau Ma Tei in central Kowloon. I regard them highly, and they are my neighborhood markets when I am in Hong Kong. Sham Shui Po spreads its web among avenues, streets, and tiny dead-end alleys, offering live chickens, ducks, and squabs. Its fish swim in tanks, where they wait to be chosen by housewife or amah, netted, and once approved, bopped on the head with a wooden mallet, scaled, slit, gutted, and then packed into a plastic sack of sea or river water for the

trip home. Yau Ma Tei is a vast, open market, a collection of working pork butchers, chicken pluckers, and fishmongers, with knife sharpeners honing cleavers on rotating stones, next to vegetable and fruit stands and herb growers and driers. On my periodic trips to Hong Kong, I never fail to visit these markets, if only to look at and inhale the sights and smells I remember from my childhood in the markets of Sun Tak Yuen, the district near Guangzhou of my birth.

Because Hong Kong's residents are intensely preoccupied with food and eating, all manner of different markets thrive in this former British colony, now a special administrative region of the People's Republic of China. In Wanchai, near the Royal Hong Kong Yacht Club, a market catering to what was once a lively neighborhood of boat people exists in the remnants of the Causeway Bay Typhoon Shelter. West of Hong Kong Island's Central District lies the Western District, possibly the world's largest collection of

shops selling dried herbs and spices imported from all over Asia. Here, too, are hundreds of dealers who trade in the dried exotica of China's cuisine: shark's fins; very special, very dear abalone from Japan; sea cucumbers; and bird's nests, the saliva-woven homes of Southeast Asian swifts, destined for soups believed to heighten female beauty and prolong youth.

Over the years, these indelible pictures and smells—memories of Chinese-food shopping—have been, and continue to be, carried from China to Europe and to the Americas by immigrants in search of the golden mountain of the West. Nowadays, my memories, both old and new, are constantly refreshed in the ever-changing marketplaces of my adopted country, where Chinatowns, all of them havens for Chinese immigrants, have sprung up in the larger cities.

In San Francisco, all of the necessities for Chinese cooking are found in the shops and kiosks along Powell Street and Grant Avenue, and along Stockton Street, sandwiched between them. The vegetables and fruits, from close-by California farms, are fine indeed, as are Chinatown's fish and meat markets. Its groceries will have the soy of your choice, and the rice wines and black vinegars you will need, and the shop next door will offer carbon- and stainless-steel woks of all sizes. All of this you will find repeated in that sunny-bright enclave of Chinese food just outside of Chavez Ravine in Los Angeles. In Philadelphia the traditional Chinatown hive of shops and restaurants is down-town along Arch Street, and in Boston the live chickens and ducks cackle and quack among the immigrant walk-ups and stores along Beach Street and Washington Avenue.

The new look in Chinatowns is the all-inclusive giant supermarket, found in Chicago along Argyle Street, out in the Arizona desert in Tempe, in the

New Jersey suburbs of New York City, up north in Toronto, and out West in Seattle and Vancouver, all newer settings for Chinese immigrants. Many of these vast stores that consolidate all aspects of Chinese cooking under a single roof—supermarkets that can truly be called *super* markets—dwarf airplane hangers. They offer roasted ducks and pigs and prepare foods of limitless variety to take away. In one, a veritable aquarium of live, edible fish and shellfish swim in individual filtered freshwater and saltwater tanks awaiting nets: striped bass, sea bass, and black bass; flounders and catfish; the grass carp popular in southern China; the yellow croaker favored in Beijing; the yellow eel of Shanghai; and the giant Dungeness crabs from the waters of the western United States. Shelves are piled high with cans from every region of China, with jars and bottles of sauces, wines, vinegars, and pickles.

These huge markets are Chinese versions of that American phenomenon, the big store that has everything. To be sure, they are wonderfully complete, with a wide range of choices, and if a shopper knows what she or he wants and needs, they are time-savers. I use them to advantage; when I need something quickly, and I know exactly what it is, I head to one of these megastores. What they lack, however, is context. They are not, of course, traditional markets of the street, so familiar smells are absent. There is no chatter from buyers haggling with sellers. There is no comparison shopping, no judging of the snow pea shoots, the purple-white eggplants, the *choi sum*, the Tianjin bok choy, the Chinese spinach piled high in front of one sidewalk shop against the same vegetables stocked by a vendor just a few doors away. There are no aged women peeling gingko nuts and selling homemade bamboo leaf–wrapped glutinous rice dumplings on the corner, no careful shoppers picking through baskets of live blue crabs, looking for the fattest. There are no barrels of freshly cooked bean curd, no noodle makers. These big markets are cleaner and brighter, but it is difficult to get a sense of texture through heavy plastic wrappings.

For me, context is all-important. Anyone who hopes to learn to cook in the Chinese way needs to be aware of foods in their purest state possible. It is not sufficient to buy a product you have read about, take it home, and cook it in the way a book says to cook it. Foods should be touched, hefted, smelled, tasted when possible, tested for freshness and crispness with a gentle squeeze. If you will be using sugarcane sugar in a Chinese sweet, pick up a length of the bamboo-like cane, ask a grocer to cut off a small piece, chew it to a straw mash, and you will understand sugarcane. Do not buy a fish lying on a bed of ice if you can avoid it. Buy it live from a tank, have a fishmonger scale and gut it, and then ask to touch it, to smell it. You will instantly understand fish better. To do all of these things, to experience them, go to a Chinese market. It is what I do.

My market is New York City's Chinatown, once two parallel blocks of Lower Manhattan named Mott and Mulberry streets, now a spreading city within a city, a place where hundreds of thousands of Chinese immigrants live and work. New York's Chinatown is irreplaceable as a market and as a piece of history. Before its streets were Chinese, they were where the gangs of New York fought, where the Dutch, Irish, Scandinavians, Italians, and Jews first settled in America before moving on to other parts of the city and to the suburbs. All immigrants bring their culture, their myths, their foods, and their traditions, but no group seems to have accomplished this with more fervor and breadth than the Chinese. I love my Chinatown, as a market, as a place. There are days when its smells remind me of the streets of the Guangdong village of my childhood. Other times I see in it, feel in it, bits and pieces of the China and Hong Kong that I know. Always it is where I begin to cook and to teach.

第一集

PART

1

PART 1
THE MARKET AS CLASSROOM

*M*y classes begin in a market street, of which there are dozens in my Chinatown, in one of the many varieties of food shops. These are centuries-old streets with narrow sidewalks up against venerable tenements, three-story walk-ups of chipped bricks, iron fire escapes, and red stone smooth with age. Some buildings have been refaced, others sandblasted, and still others are as they were left by preceding waves of immigrants. Their ground floors are where change has come. Shops, festooned with signs and awnings dense with Chinese calligraphy, most of them selling fresh and prepared foods, and restaurants, new and old, nestle among storefront Buddhist and Taoist temples. Here a noodle maker, and over there a bean-curd cooker, fashioning what the Chinese, who invented it, call *doufu* and what much of the rest of the world calls tofu. Nearby, under the slanted tin roof of a tiny lean-to that has attached itself to a new bank, a man wearing a New York baseball cap cups his hands as he makes and fries dumplings on a portable steel grill. Chinatown opens early.

I begin early as well because I want my students to see and smell freshness, to begin to experience all aspects of the foods they will first cook with me, then later, I hope, cook by themselves with confidence. I want them to begin to become familiar with, rather than daunted by, the supposed mysteries of Chinese food. "What are we going to make today?" asks one of my students, as we meet a few steps away from shops selling rice wines from Shaoxing and black vinegars from Zhejiang and Guangdong. I am always asked that question, and I find that the asking of it allows me to rein in the impatience, the anticipation, of the class. I tell them what the menu will be, but quickly add that first we have to buy the ingredients we will need. And then the adventure begins, as I attempt to instill in my new students a basic respect for the foods we will be cooking and the importance of precision when buying them.

It is not sufficient to simply buy soy sauce or oyster sauce, bamboo shoots or snow cabbage, red rice vinegar or peanut oil just because particular recipes call for them. I believe that everyone should know something about the properties of these ingredients—some history, some folklore, perhaps a bit of mythology, surely a touch of tradition. I impart this information in bits and pieces and in different ways. We stop at a vegetable and fruit store. "There," I say, pointing to a pyramid of crisp, golden brown fruit, "are Asian pears, usually, incorrectly called, Japanese pears. They actually are Chinese, native to China, and they are called sand pears because of their grainy texture. And these,"—I point to a pile of melons—"are Hami melons." I explain that the oval-shaped, green-skinned fruits are crisp and sweet and have pink-orange flesh like a cantaloupe. They are about the size of a cantaloupe, too, and are particularly prized in China because they are available for only a brief period each summer. I have them touch shiny, finger-shaped Chinese eggplants, some white, some white mottled with pale purple, some deep purple. "These are usually called Japanese eggplants by those who haven't done their homework. They are Chinese."

I walk them in front of a series of similar bulbous stalked vegetables stacked in rows. "These are bok choy," I say. They nod. "Everybody knows bok choy, correct?" More nods. Not so, I say. I show them that bok choy, the most familiar, is white stemmed with green leaves and up to fifteen inches long. Next to it is another bok choy, smaller, with milky white stalks, and are thus called "milk" bok choy, as a reference to infants. Then I gesture toward yet another bok choy, even smaller, about four inches long, and still others that are smaller, no more than two to three inches long. These last two are called baby bok choy. As if all of this was not sufficiently confounding, I point to two other stacks. "That is bok choy, too, Shanghai bok choy and Shanghai baby bok choy." The first is about six inches long and deeper green than bok choy, and the second is about three

inches long. The students' expressions become quizzical. Do we need to know all this? I believe so, and I explain that, although they all are essentially the same vegetable, I have distinguished each one to suggest that when shopping for bok choy, they buy with precision, and for good reason.

Regular bok choy, inherently the sweetest, is perfect for soups and for stir-fries, particularly as a complement to pork and beef. Baby bok choy is tender and sweet and brings its sweetness to soups. Smaller bok choy are usually cooked whole and used as a garnish, and the smallest, also cooked whole in stock, are served as a course of a larger meal or used to dress other dishes. Shanghai bok choy, less tender, is ideal for braising and for soups, but only after first being tenderized in stock. All of this is a tangible lesson in purposeful food buying. As we continue to walk this produce market, I point out *choi sum*; snow peas and their tender shoots, the latter called *dau miu* by the Cantonese and *doumiao* by Mandarin speakers; jicama, the crisp, hard root from America's Southwest that the Cantonese call *sah gut* and which is largely unknown in the north; lotus root and taro root; and fresh, hard red dates, unmatched for imparting sweetness to stocks.

As we shop, I often reach back into my family's beliefs that I absorbed growing up in Guangdong. I tell my students that in my Cantonese village, people often ate the sounds and the symbols of individual foods. I gesture toward heads of Chinese lettuce that resemble romaine heads and that we called *sang choy*, which sounds like the Cantonese for "growing fortune," making it the "good luck" vegetable, and I explain that the lettuces are hung over doorways during the Lunar New Year. Scallions are *chung ming*, which sounds like "always wise"; packages of dried hair seaweed are *fat choy*, a homonym for "prosperity"; and lotus seeds, because of their numbers, ensure every year will bring more sons. All of this helps to illustrate that many vegetables and other foods have homonymic and symbolic meanings, which often vary throughout China depending on regional

dialect and tradition. I point out what I like to call the basic trinity of Chinese cooking—scallions, ginger, and garlic—since virtually every dish has at least one of these and often all three.

I explain that many vegetables native to China that were once little known or unknown in the United States are now, because of the demand from a growing immigrant population, farmed here. Of course, bok choy has been familiar for years, but not green-leaved, green-stalked *choi sum*; hollow-stemmed water spinach; deep green mustard greens; Tianjin bok choy, also known as napa cabbage; chrysanthemum leaves; eighteen-inch-long green beans; yellow and green chives, once grown in Chinatown basements by enterprising immigrants; and so-called hairy beans, small, young, green soybeans eaten as a vegetable, especially in Shanghai.

Once water chestnuts outside of China came only in cans. Now they are sold fresh, still covered with

the dried mud of the mire in which they are grown, but white, crisp, and sweet when peeled. I note that Chinese gourds, such as the round bitter melon and the ridged silk squash, were once rare and are now widely available, as are fresh gingko nuts, and small, deep red beans that are the basis for sweet soups. We will stop back at our grocery to buy the vegetables we will need.

We pause in front of one of the many bakeries that have sprung up in Chinatown in recent years, repositories for the Western-style layer cakes, cupcakes, muffins, and cookies first baked by the Chinese in Shanghai, when its French Concession was dominant. These bakeries also offer glutinous rice flour cakes filled with cooked black sesame seeds and sugar that the Chinese believe will stop their hair from graying. "Before you believe this, however, you should ask my husband," I say. "It hasn't worked for him." I point to another shelf. "Do you see those

Chinese fortune cookies?" I ask rhetorically, then I answer my own question. "Do not think for a moment they are Chinese. I'm not sure where they originated," I go on, "but I do know it was not in China, and I suspect the manufacturers here hire needy English majors from New York University to write the fortunes that paraphrase Confucius."

We stop at the counter of a dim sum parlor to pick up the baked pork buns the Cantonese call *char siu bau* so we can taste them before moving on to a butcher shop, its window hung with long strips of barbecued pork, equally long racks of barbecued pork ribs, glistening roasted ducks, and rows of plump chickens, their skins taut and shiny from being braised with shallots and onions and then hung to dry.

Inside the long, brightly lighted market are rows of whole, freshly killed chickens and their many separate parts, all resting in refrigerated glass display cases. I point out that the cooked ducks and chickens in the window and their fresh refrigerated uncooked counterparts are part of the poultry continuum that has existed in China for seven thousand years. Chickens have been domesticated in China for that long and have been valued not only for their meat, but also for their eggs. In China, I tell my students, chickens are not only fried and roasted, the preparations with which they are most familiar, nor are they eaten breaded and battered in the style of U.S. fast-food restaurants, but they are smoked, boiled, braised, stir-fried, and cooked with noodles. They are minced, sliced, or diced and put into soups, dumplings, and rice or wrapped in lettuce leaves. Even old, tough roosters have value. They are simmered for hours and the resulting rich broth is drunk as a health tonic. Such adaptability is highly regarded, even venerated, I explain, and the chicken is regarded as a symbol of rebirth, an edible manifestation of the phoenix, the bird of myth that arose from its own ashes.

The skins of the refrigerated chickens vary in color from white to yellow to dark charcoal gray, the latter known as black chickens. "Why the different colors?" I am asked. I pose the question to the man behind the display case. "Chickens are like people," he answers, grinning. "Some are light. Some are dark. Some are medium." In that market stop, I also always point out that just as the Chinese have raised chickens for seven thousand years, they have raised ducks for at least three thousand or quite possibly more of those years. This includes not only the best-known breed, the Peking duck, but other breeds as well that are variously roasted, boiled, smoked, and salted.

Later we will go to a wonderful poultry-only market, where fresh chickens, quail, squabs, and ducks lie side by side on refrigerated shelves. It also carries the black chickens we have just seen, fancifully called *juk suh chi,* or "bamboo silk chickens," by the Cantonese. They have "black" skin, bones, and meat and are cooked for as long as eight hours in a process known as double-boiling, which calls for steaming them over boiling water in a closed porcelain container. The liquid they produce is considered a health-giving tonic, and the meat is never eaten. Freshly killed ducks—both farm raised and wild—are for sale, sitting next to dozens of fresh duck eggs. "What are the differences between a duck and a chicken egg?" I am asked. Duck eggs are generally larger and rarer and more commonly salted or preserved.

Back in the long, well-lighted meat market, we move on. I point out that it is important to remember that when the word "meat" is used in the study of Chinese food, it refers always to pork. Historically, lamb and beef were eaten in northern China, but pork was, and is, the meat of most of the country. Pork and its uses are as unlimited as its carefully butchered cuts. I point out a grand display of pork in a refrigerated case: pieces of pork stomach, boned pork feet, loaves of coagulated pork blood, pork shoulder, sliced pig's ears, pork intestines, pork liver, fresh and cured pork belly (the latter, Chinese bacon), pork ribs, pork loin, pork chops, pork shin meat, fresh ham, pork shanks, chunks of pork butt for stew, spare ribs, pork hocks, pig's tails, pork tongue, pork kidneys, pig's uterus, pork neck bones, pig mouth meat, and strips of pork fat for rendering into lard. Amid all of these items, sitting like a pile of lace, are layers of pork caul, stomach membrane that Western cooks use as casings for ground meat or for wrapping meat to keep it moist as it cooks, which the Chinese prefer to render because it makes a particularly fine, delicate cooking fat.

Whole pigs, cooked and not, hang in the butcher's window, and inside the shop, barbecued pig's heads are for sale, their cheeks, ears, snout, and tongue in place. In much of China, I tell my class, a roasted suckling pig—a tiny fellow, no more than twenty to twenty-five pounds that has been carefully turned over an open fire until its skin crisps into virtual parchment—is an esteemed banquet dish. It is the prized skin that is served. Although not on display, such roasted pigs are for sale as well, I explain, but they must be special ordered. The only part of the pig not for sale as food is its whiskers—hard, pliable bristles that make fine hair brushes.

I take my students through the varieties of Chinese pork sausages known as *lop cheong,* thin uncooked sausages that are utterly delicious when steamed with rice or vegetables. They are made of coarsely ground pork, pork studded with pork fat, or pork mixed with pork liver or duck liver and are light red when they are not laced with soy sauce and dark red when they are. I tell them that if in the future they find they like these coarsely ground sausages, they should ask for Hong Kong style, and if they prefer smoother-textured sausages, they should request Canadian style.

As we weave our way through the Chinatown streets we stop to buy such necessities as soy sauce, sesame oil, oyster sauce, white and red rice vinegars, and rice wines. We do not buy pickled ginger, pickled

chile peppers, or chili sauce, though jars of all of these are for sale, because we will be making them ourselves.

We pick up some fermented black beans, fresh garlic and ginger, and some white peppercorns. I mention that when pepper is called for in Chinese cooking, white pepper should be used. Traditionally, black pepper was rarely used in China, though in recent years it has been an occasional ingredient, primarily in Hong Kong, for cooking beef and veal, the latter a meat known only in China's large cities. Near the peppercorns and the packets of vegetable starches are boxes of monosodium glutamate, the infamous MSG. "Are we going to use this?" I am usually asked, a question I welcome because it gives me a chance to preach a bit. "No, we will not be using MSG," I say. "It is nothing but a temporary enhancer, a small jolt of sodium, a salt. It is unnecessary if you cook with good ingredients, good stocks, good oils, and patience."

Fish abound in Chinatown. They are displayed on sidewalk stands atop mounds of shaved ice; often stacked in refrigerated cases following flights from Asia, Canada, and South and Central America; and housed live and swimming about in glass holding tanks. These fresh- and saltwater tanks hold a variety of netted live and farmed fish, including such familiar types as *wan yue,* a Cantonese favorite similarly called *wan yu* in Mandarin; *dah tao yue,* or big head carp, another Cantonese favorite; the so-called buffalo fish or grass carp; silver carp; striped bass and cod from Atlantic waters; catfish from Southern farms, striped bass from the Midwest, and tilapia flown in live from Mediterranean farms. There are porgies; yellow croakers and yellow perch; bluefish and butterfish; yellow eel; black bass; flounder and sole; and odd, small, irregular fish that look exactly like rough stones, thus their Cantonese name, *sak*

tao, or "stone fish." Lobsters from the Atlantic are live, and so are shrimp from the Gulf of Mexico and fat Dungeness crabs from the Pacific.

It is a swimming bounty and always a source of amazement to my students, many of whom I like to say think of fish only as "white rectangles on ice, no head, no tail, no fins, no skin, no bones, no taste." Conversions come easily, I have found, after they have steamed their first fish. We buy two sea bass and stop to pick up some shallots and mustard greens. "Do they have shallots in China?" I am asked. "And mustard greens?" I answer yes to both questions.

We stop in at a bean curd factory where soybeans, or *wong dau* in Cantonese and *huang dou* in Mandarin, are processed into firm, soft, or custard-like cakes and then sit in their cooking milk, waiting to be sold. I point out the round grinders where soaked, skinned soybeans are ground into a wet powder to which a gelling agent is added to create textured bean curd cakes. And what is being made in those huge steel woks behind the barrels of bean curd? Cakes, I tell the class, of fermented rice, which are being steamed into elastic, doughy offerings for dim sum parlors.

LESSON 1
CREATING A CHINESE PANTRY

中國調味品

CREATING
A CHINESE
PANTRY

The first day of shopping is complete, though there will be others as our lessons progress. As I have led my class from shop to store to market to maker through Chinatown's main streets and twisting alleys, I have repeatedly impressed on them the need to exercise care as they shop. I have demonstrated that food labels on Chinese products can be confounding adventures. Although it is true that more and more products from the vast Chinese table have become familiar, and that many foods once deemed exotic and unapproachable are now commonplace, there has also been a proliferation of brands and exercises in fanciful packaging. Which soy? Which sesame oil? Why? Which rice, Texas or Thai jasmine? Why? The inventories often seem endless. However, I test them all, and when I find a particular product to be superior, to be closest to the taste of tradition, I recommend it by name.

Having said that, I still strongly advise a careful reading of labels. Are these dried strands considered noodles or sticks or threads? Are these wrappers meant for spring rolls, for wontons, for American-inspired egg rolls, or for enclosing flavored raw vegetables in the Vietnamese manner? The manufacturers of prepared Chinese foodstuffs are an imaginative lot, so I cannot overstate the need to read labels with attention to every detail on them. I also suggest that when you are shopping for a particular food, you carry along a photocopy of the Chinese calligraphy for that food. I am careful in my classes, careful in my writings, to include the Chinese characters for any food products—canned, bottled, jarred, or fresh—that you will need. Show the shopkeeper the calligraphy. Point and say you want that, only that, and you will be given exactly what you need.

Almost invariably, the product names, ingredients, and brand names on food packages and tins are in English and occasionally in romanized Cantonese. This is a natural circumstance because nearly all of the Chinese who migrated to the United States and Canada, Britain and Western Europe, even to Latin America and the Caribbean in the past—and even today—were from Guangdong and other parts of southern China. They carried their foods with them, and when they settled in their new homes, they made certain their foods continued to follow them.

By necessity, we have come to identify Chinese products by the English and romanized Cantonese spellings on their packaging. Indeed, it is rare to find packages labeled with pinyin spelling, the official system of romanizing Mandarin, China's national language. However, I have included pinyin equivalents where they appear on packaging.

I have also taken particular care to describe the provenance of products—the province, region, city, or ethnic group. Hong Kong is a good example. Since 1997, it has been a unique place in China, with its own governor and elected governing body, and it will remain so until 2047. Many foods are prepared and packaged in Hong Kong, and when I am describing a food that originated there, I note Hong Kong as the source.

Before going on, let me repeat again how important it is to secure the products I describe if you hope to meet with success in the kitchen. Proper buying will help to make proper recipes. These, then, are the foods we have shopped for so far, the first steps in creating a Chinese food pantry:

竹筍 BAMBOO SHOOTS. These pale yellow spears are the young beginnings of bamboo trees. In the past, fresh bamboo shoots were unavailable outside of Asia. Nowadays they are sold in many Chinese groceries, though they are often tough and fibrous and must be boiled for use. Imported, already cooked, canned bamboo shoots are quite good, with those labeled "winter bamboo shoots" or "bamboo shoots, tips" the most tender. I prefer the ones in large chunks, so they can be cut as desired. In some shops, canned shoots are sold loose by weight. These shoots and the shoots in cans you open at home will keep in water to cover in a closed container in the refrigerator for 10 days to 2 weeks, if you change the water daily.

荳腐 BEAN CURD, FRESH. This is the most common form of bean curd and is typically sold in 2½- to 3-inch square cakes, in packages and sometimes loose. The slightly firm, custardlike cakes, known as *doufu,* are made from ground soybeans cooked in the liquid, or "milk," they exude. Buying individual cakes is preferred over purchasing packages that contain several cakes or a single large block. Bean curd has little taste of its own. Its versatility lies in its ability to absorb the tastes of the foods with which it is cooked. Store it in water to cover in a tightly closed container in the refrigerator for up to 10 days, changing the water daily. Japanese brands, sold as "tofu," are packaged in large sizes, up to 16-ounce cakes, and are sold in three distinct textures: soft or silken, firm or medium-firm, and extra-firm. Medium-firm is closest to the Chinese variety, and I favor it. Chinese bean curd is occasionally labeled "tofu" as well, or as *daufu,* the romanized Cantonese. Bean curd factories also sell a bean curd custard. It has the texture of a classic egg custard and must be eaten fresh. The Chinese eat it with sugar syrup as a snack or atop a mound of rice with a drizzle of soy sauce.

南乳 BEAN CURD, RED WET PRESERVED. These are cubes of reddish bean curd, fermented with salt, wine, and red rice. They are packed in jars or crocks and are labeled either "wet bean curd" or "red wet bean curd." The cakes, which are not spicy despite their fiery color, are used as an ingredient in

braising and barbecuing recipes for their taste—which is intense and assertive with salt and wine—and for their color. Once a container is opened, any unused cakes must be refrigerated. They will keep in their closed crock or jar for at least 6 months.

南乳汁 **BEAN CURD JUICE.** A relatively new ingredient, this bottled "juice" is a boon to Chinese cooking. It is a mixture of fermented red wet bean curd liquid, rice wine, red rice, salt, and sugar—ingredients traditionally used separately to flavor and color foods—and is from the same fertile part of east-central China below Shanghai that produces Shaoxing wines (see page 365). Once opened, it should be refrigerated, where it will keep indefinitely.

麵豉 **BEAN SAUCE.** A Cantonese staple, this thick puree is made from the soybeans that remain after soy sauce is made. The fermented beans are mixed with wheat flour, salt, and sugar, resulting in sauce that also contains bits of beans. The sauce comes in jars, labeled either "bean sauce" or "ground

bean sauce," which means the beans have been mashed. This latter sauce also tends to be saltier. I prefer the former. Jars labeled "yellow bean sauce" or "brown bean sauce" hold the same beans made into the same sauce. Once opened, the sauce will keep for up to 6 months in the refrigerator.

芽菜 **BEAN SPROUTS.** There are two varieties. The more common, mung bean sprouts, are white and plump and have a decided crunch. The second, soy bean sprouts, are also white, but they are longer and have a yellow soy bean at the tip. Both types are sold fresh by weight in Chinese markets and are widely available. They are stored the same, too, in the refrigerator in plastic bags punched with holes. They will keep for no more than 2 days, after which they will begin to turn brown and to soften.

粉絲 **BEAN THREAD NOODLES.** These needle-like threads, also called vermicelli bean threads, cellophane noodles, or simply bean threads, are made by moistening, mashing, and draining

mung beans and then forming them into thin, white strands. They come dried, in 1-pound packages, divided into bundles usually weighing 2 ounces each. Avoid other large packages of irregularly shaped sheets and long, thin, rough sticks made from soybean, both of them beige and mistakenly labeled "bean thread" (see Bean Curd Sticks, page 138).

 BLACK BEANS, FERMENTED. These fragrant black beans, preserved in salt, usually come packed in cardboard containers or plastic sacks. Although typically labeled "fermented," some cardboard packages are labeled "preserved beans," or, inexplicably, "dried black beans," which they are not. Look for beans lightly flavored with ginger and orange peel, which I prefer. Always rinse off the salt from the beans before using. They will keep in a tightly sealed container in a cool cupboard for up to 3 months.

BOK CHOY. The best-known Chinese vegetable, bok choy, literally "white vegetable" because of its white bulbous stalk, is grown throughout China and other parts of Asia. Its crispness and inherent sweetness make it particularly versatile. Although often referred to as Chinese cabbage, the vegetable's deep green leaves above a white stalk bear no resemblance to a cabbage. Bok choy comes in various sizes, from as long as 15 to 18 inches to as small as 2 to 3 inches. There are even bok choy sprouts. They are all the same vegetable, and the size of the head dictates how it is used, whether as a primary ingredient or as a garnish. Bok choy will keep for 2 days in the vegetable drawer of a refrigerator. Kept longer, its leaves gradually turn yellow and its flavor diminishes, so use it at its freshest.

BOK CHOY, SHANGHAI. Generally smaller than bok choy, and with pronounced bulbous stalks, Shanghai bok choy is called the "greenish-white vegetable" by the Chinese. The description is apt, for its stalks are not as white as those of bok choy and its leaves are not as deep green. If you want Shanghai bok choy, simply ask for it by that name; the grocer will understand you. It also comes in different sizes, but its color makes it recognizable.

Shanghai bok choy is stored the same way you store regular bok choy and for the same amount of time.

BOXTHORN SEEDS. Also known as "wolfberries," these tiny, red, raisinlike dried fruits of the boxthorn shrub have a faint, mildly sweet flavor and are generally used for stocks and in soups. Because the Chinese believe these fruits are restorative and contribute to eye health, they are available not only in groceries, but also in herbal shops. The shrub itself is useful as well. Its leaves are added to stir-fries and soups or are scrambled with eggs, and its twigs are used to make soups or infusions that are believed beneficial to bone strength in the elderly.

CHILES. Small, slender fresh chiles, deep red and about 1½ inches long, were once imported exclusively from Thailand. Most still are, but others, grown elsewhere, including domestically, are now sold in Chinatown markets. Chiles from Thailand remain my preference, however, because they deliver a unique quality to dishes. Although they are quite hot, they impart a pleasant heat that lingers in the mouth. They are also dependable in terms of the numbers used to achieve the desired hotness. Store them in a container lightly covered with plastic wrap in the refrigerator for up to 10 days. Do not seal the container, or the chiles will deteriorate. For recipes that call for dried chiles, such as my Hot Pepper Oil (page 55), you can dry the fresh chiles, which I prefer, or you can purchase them already dried, but make sure they are dried Thai chiles. Whole dried chiles will keep in a tightly closed container in a cool, dark place for at least 6 months.

CHILI SAUCE. This bottled sauce is a mixture of vinegar, chiles, salt, and often cornstarch and artificial coloring. There are many brands, some of which are adequate. However, it is best to make your own, which we do on page 58.

CHINESE CHIVES. Also known as "garlic chives," Chinese chives are more pungent and flatter and wider than Western chives, though they are the same deep green color. Yellow chives are the same vegetable, but they are deprived of the sun as they grow, which makes them a pale yellow. Although both green and yellow chives have an essential taste of garlic, the yellow is more delicate. Once yellow chives were an underground industry, literally, grown in Chinatown basements by newly arrived immigrants. Nowadays both green and yellow chives are widely available and are sold fresh by weight. Do not use the familiar Western chive in their place. Its taste differs, and your recipe will reflect that difference.

CHOI SUM. This is the most familiar spelling for this vegetable, though its first character is often spelled *choy* or *tsoi* when romanized into Cantonese. The leafy vegetables with thin stalks are all green, from their large outer leaves to their smaller inside leaves to their light green stalks. The stalks, after their hard ends are trimmed, are crisp and sweet. *Choi sum,* like other leafy vegetables, tends to lose its sweetness as it ages. Its leaves become yellow and it sprouts small yellow flowers, so eat it as fresh as possible. It will keep for no more than 2 days in the vegetable drawer of a refrigerator.

CINNAMON. Two kinds of cinnamon are available in the markets, one the descendant of the original cinnamon bark from Sri Lanka known as Ceylon cinnamon, and the second the so-called Chinese cinnamon from the bark of the cassia tree, though the two are related. At one time, vast cinnamon forests covered large areas of Hunan, but they no longer exist. The aromatic sticks of rolled bark, brown and hard, are one of the ingredients in five-spice powder and are used in long-cooked stews and soups. Stored in a tightly sealed container, the sticks will keep at room temperature for up to 6 months, but they will gradually lose their fragrance.

CLOUD EARS. When dried, these fungi, which grow on decaying branches, look like small, round chips and vary from brown to brown-black. When soaked in *hot* water, they soften, glisten, and resemble flower petals. At one time, they were used interchangeably with tree ear fungi, also known as wood ears, a black fungus that grows on wood as well. However, tree ears are larger and tougher than the small, tender cloud ears, so although either may be used in recipes, I prefer cloud ears for their softer, more delicate nature. Store cloud ears in a closed jar in a cool, dry place. They will keep indefinitely.

CORIANDER. This aromatic leaf is called fresh coriander to distinguish it from its seeds, the spice. It is also called Chinese parsley, though it is similar only in appearance to parsley, and cilantro in Southwestern and Mexican cookery. Fresh coriander, which is used as both a flavoring ingredient and a garnish, has an intense smell and imparts a distinctive taste. In the past, it was found only in Asian and Latin American groceries, but it is now widely available. Ideally, you should use it as soon as possible after purchase, so that its bouquet can be appreciated, but it may be refrigerated in a vegetable drawer for up to 1 week.

CURRY. As used in China, particularly in Hong Kong, Guangdong, and other parts of the south, this is a powder, originally introduced from India. There are, to be sure, many brands of curry powder, but based on my testing of many of them, I recommend Roland brand curry powder from Madras. Its ingredients are turmeric, coriander seed, cumin, chile, fennel seed, fenugreek, cassia, clove, curry leaf, garlic, and salt. Stored in a tightly sealed jar, the powder will keep at room temperature for up to 6 months, though it will gradually lose its fragrance.

DRIED SCALLOPS. These disk-shaped, dried sea scallops, known in Cantonese as *gawn bui* and in Mandarin as *gan bei* but romanized to *conpoy*, are quite special in China. The best are dried naturally in the sun and range from ¼ inch to 2 inches in diameter. The largest can command as much as one hundred dollars a pound in herbal shops and food markets. Dried scallops are quite hard and must be soaked in hot water or steamed until softened before using. Once they are soft, they are usually shredded and added to other preparations. Store dried scallops in a sealed plastic container in the refrigerator for up to 6 months.

EIGHT-STAR ANISE. Also called simply "star anise," these are the tiny, hard, eight-point star fruits of the Chinese anise tree, with a flavor more pronounced than that of aniseeds. They will keep in a tightly sealed jar at room temperature for up to 1 year, though they will gradually lose their intensity.

FIVE-SPICE POWDER. Known in China as "five-fragrance powder," this seasoning can be made from a mixture of any five of the following ingredients: star anise, fennel seed, cinnamon, clove, ginger, licorice, nutmeg, and Sichuan peppercorn. Different mixtures abound, though anise and cinnamon dominate. The pungent ground powder is used sparingly in dishes that call for strong flavors. If you have your own grinder, I suggest you concoct your own five-spice powder (page 103).

GINGER. This gnarled, knobby root—actually a rhizome—is often referred to as gingerroot. When selecting ginger, look for large, thick pieces with smooth outer skins because a wrinkled and rough skin indicates age. One of the most important foods in Chinese cooking, ginger imparts an intense, distinctive flavor and should be used sparingly. Its strength depends on how it is prepared, which is why I am careful to specify whether it should be peeled or unpeeled, lightly smashed or not, sliced, julienned, minced, or shredded. It will keep in a heavy, brown paper bag in the refrigerator for 4 to 5 weeks. Some Chinese markets stock yellowish ginger, imported from China. In addition to its distinctive color, its taste is hotter than the more familiar beige ginger. Young ginger, which is slightly pink and has thin, smooth skin and crisp flesh, is also available. It is often called "spring ginger," a misnomer because it is available throughout the year. It is actually regular ginger that is harvested when young to ensure its characteristic crispness and mild flavor.

GINGER PICKLE. Usually made from young roots, thinly sliced, mixed with vinegar and sugar, and jarred, ginger pickle is available under many commercial brand names. Most of them are adequate, but you can make your own ginger pickle (page 57) with relatively little effort and excellent results.

HOISIN SAUCE. This thick, chocolate-brown, sweetened sauce is made from cooked soybeans, garlic, sugar, and chiles. Some brands add a little vinegar to the mix, others thicken it with flour. Too often, this sauce—famous as an accompaniment to Peking duck—is called plum sauce, which

it is not. Hoisin comes in jars and large cans. If jarred, it should be refrigerated once you have opened it. If bought in a can, transfer it to a jar after opening and refrigerate. It will keep for up to 3 months.

 HOT BEAN SAUCE. This Sichuan condiment of chiles, salt, cooked soybeans, and sesame oil is used as a flavoring for stir-fried dishes and as a sauce ingredient. In the past, stores carried a Taiwanese product that mixed mashed fava beans and ground chiles and called it "horse beans," a label rarely seen these days. What you will see are jars labeled "hot bean sauce," "hot bean paste," or simply "bean sauce." Some labeled "bean sauce" add the word "Sichuan" to show the area of production. All are essentially mixes of soybeans and chiles, but some add flour, some sugar, some sesame oil, some garlic. This is an instance where it is essential to shop with a photocopy of the Chinese characters for the sauce in hand. Nor should this spicy condiment be confused with sweet Cantonese bean sauce (see page 138). Once opened, the sauce should be stored in the refrigerator, where it will keep for up to 6 months.

 HOT PEPPER OIL. Several brands of hot oil are on market shelves, but I have found many of them are based on inferior oils. Once again, I prefer that you make an ingredient yourself, this time a hot oil with a peanut oil base (page 55). As you will discover, it is not difficult, and there is a bonus: A by-product of your effort will be a deposit of oil-soaked red pepper flakes for using in other recipes.

 JICAMA. Widely raised in China and elsewhere in Asia, this sand-colored, bulbous root vegetable has sweet, crisp white flesh that can be eaten raw or cooked. Called *sah gut* by the Cantonese, it is a good substitute for water chestnuts. Uncut jicama will keep in a brown paper bag in the refrigerator for 3 to 4 days. Peeled and sliced jicama will keep in a closed plastic bag in the refrigerator for 3 to 4 days.

 MUNG BEAN STARCH. White dried mung beans, their green skins removed, are ground into a starch that, like all Chinese starches, is referred to equally as a powder and a flour. This

is the starch that was in our kitchen when I was a child, and it is the starch I was most familiar with when cooking in China. What makes it particularly desirable is its capacity to impart a glistening finish to whatever food to which it is added. Only in recent years has mung bean starch become widely available in Chinese markets. I use it as I do cornstarch, to thicken sauces and to give them body, to marinate meats, and to coat foods before frying. Sauces made with cornstarch are typically thinner and have less body than those made with mung bean starch.

MUSHROOMS. The mushrooms used most often in China, and collectively called *gu,* are native black mushrooms. Almost never sold fresh in Chinese markets, they come dried in boxes and cellophane packs. They vary from black to dark gray to speckled gray and black, and their caps range from about ¾ inch to 3 inches in diameter. These mushrooms must always be soaked in hot water before use—usually for 20 to 30 minutes, depending on the recipe—and their stems removed and discarded. The dried mushrooms will keep indefinitely in a tightly sealed container at room temperature or, if in a humid damp climate, in the refrigerator. Shiitake mushrooms, known as *dong gu,* have been eaten throughout China since the T'ang Dynasty. Other dried mushrooms include flower mushrooms, with deep, wide ridges in their caps. Although essentially the same species as black mushrooms, flower mushrooms are thicker, meatier, and more expensive and are so highly regarded that they are often given as gifts. Also popular are small straw mushrooms, which are native to southern China and Hunan; have an elongated, domed cap; and are most often sold canned. Once opened, straw mushrooms will keep in a closed container in the refrigerator for about 1 week. Finally, the so-called chicken leg mushrooms are bulbous and meaty and have almost no cap. They are raised in Canada with spores from China and are usually sold fresh. They lend themselves to cooking with other foods and are long-lived. Wrapped in paper towels and placed in a plastic bag, they will keep in the refrigerator for 10 days to 2 weeks.

OILS. Peanut oil is the preferred oil for Chinese cooking, not only because it contributes to a healthful diet, but also for the nutty flavor it imparts to food. However, since many people are allergic to peanut products, I can suggest canola, corn, or soybean oil equally as an alternative. Do not be tempted to use olive oil for Chinese cooking. Its aroma and consistency are incompatible with Chinese foods.

OYSTER SAUCE. This is a viscous liquid comprising oyster extract, salt, and often caramel for color. It is made by boiling large amounts of fresh oysters to arrive at a thickened "soup," to which the salt and caramel, and occasionally sugar and flour, are added. I have been told that at one time dried oysters were used in its preparation, but I have found no evidence of that method. Oyster sauce is a highly prized seasoning, virtually indispensable to the Cantonese cook, and used more and more by cooks throughout China. Its role is to enhance existing flavors and to impart a rich brown color. This sauce is also well regarded by Buddhists because the oyster (along with the clam and mussel) is permissible in their vegetarian diet. Once a bottle of oyster sauce is opened, it will keep in the refrigerator for up to 2 months. Many brands are on the market, not only from mainland China and Hong Kong but also from domestic sources. I recommend Hop Sing Lung brand from Hong Kong.

PEPPER. All references to pepper refer to ground white pepper only. Black pepper came into use late in China, and only recently has it come to be used with any regularity, and then usually in Hong Kong and Shanghai.

PRESERVED EGGS. These processed duck eggs are most commonly referred to as thousand-year-old eggs, or *pidan* in Mandarin and *pei dan* in Cantonese. To make them, raw eggs are usually covered with a paste of salt, tea leaves or an infusion of tea leaves, ground rice husks and whole husks, and a preservative—sodium carbonate (lye water)—and left to cure for fifty-eight days. The curing time is precise. Fewer days will result in weak preservation, and more days will yield hard eggs. When the eggs are ready, the shell will have turned a mottled gray, the white will have become a black-brown gelatin, and the yolk will be a deep, dull green. Preserved eggs were once shipped around the world in big, brown earthenware crocks. Nowadays they are packaged, usually six to the box, and labeled "preserved duck eggs." Although produced throughout China, the eggs from Fujian Province are generally considered the best. They are eaten as a condiment, cold and sliced, and served accompanied by pickled ginger slices. They should not be confused with the salted duck eggs that are cured in a salt solution and eaten with congee (page 93).

 PRESERVED MUSTARD. To make preserved mustard, usually labeled *mui choi* and called *maichai* in Mandarin, mustard plants are cooked, then preserved in salt and sugar, and finally dried. They are dull brown and pliable and come packed in plastic bags labeled "preserved mustard" or "salted mustard." Salt crystals are often visible through the packages, but they do not affect the vegetable. Quite versatile, preserved mustard is used in stir-fries, in steamed dishes, and in soups. It should be stored in a sealed jar at room temperature and will keep for at least 6 months. The longer it is kept, the darker it becomes. Before using, open the leaves and carefully rinse away the salt.

 RED DATES. These deep red fruits, members of the buckthorn family and also known as jujubes, are usually sold dried in 1-pound plastic sacks labeled either "red dates" or "dried dates." They come both pitted and not—though I prefer the latter for their superior taste and fragrance—and are usually soaked in hot water for 20 to 30 minutes, depending on the recipe, before using. They are steamed and used in stocks, steamed together with chicken, or added to clay pots, savory soups, or sweet soups of lotus seeds and red beans. Once the package is opened, transfer the dates to a covered jar and store them in a cool place, where they will keep for about 6 months. In recent times, fresh red dates have been turning up in Chinatown markets. They are oval, hard, and their exteriors are red to mottled yellow. Fresh red dates are used the same way as dried dates and can be eaten raw. They will keep in an open bowl for up to 5 days. Later, as they age, they redden and become dry and wrinkled. They will dry thoroughly in about 3 weeks. Once dried, store them as you would purchased dried dates.

 SALTED TURNIP. Made by blanching, salting, and drying sliced white turnips, this preserved root vegetable is sold in plastic packages labeled "salted turnip." They are also sold loose by weight. A versatile preparation, it's used as a pickle or

condiment and as an ingredient in soups and stir-fries. Once the package has been opened, store the salted turnip in a jar in the refrigerator for up to 3 months.

 SAUSAGES. Uncooked sausages have a long history throughout China, appearing in the wall murals of excavated Han Dynasty tombs. In Cantonese they are called *lop cheong,* and in Mandarin *lachang.* They are traditionally made of coarsely cut pork, pork fat, and pork liver. But over the years, their makeup has varied. These days you will find sausages of pork and pork fat, of pork and pork liver, and of lean ground pork. Even chicken *lop cheong* are made, as are sausages of duck liver. In some shops, the sausages, in casings, are strung together in pairs and are sold loose by weight. Or they are sold, without strings, in 1-pound vacuum-sealed packages. Once imported from China, they are now also made elsewhere in Asia, in the United States, and in Canada, and the quality is generally good. They must be cooked before eating and are commonly steamed, stir-fried, diced and added to rice, or sliced and added to soup. They will keep in the refrigerator for about 1 month, and in the freezer for up to 2 months.

 SESAME SEEDS. These small seeds are either black or white, roasted or raw. Black sesame seeds, both raw and roasted, are customarily used as a decoration or as an ingredient in the preparation of sweet pastry fillings or sweet soups. Roasted and raw white sesame seeds are generally used in dumpling fillings, as garnishes, or in the making of sweets. Sesame seeds are typically sold in plastic bags of 4 ounces to 1 pound and are occasionally sold loose. They can become rancid quickly if left at room temperature, so transfer them to a tightly capped container and store in the freezer for up to several months.

 SESAME OIL. This highly aromatic oil made from toasted sesame seeds has a defined nutlike fragrance. I use it to flavor sauces and marinades or as a dressing. It easily burns if used in direct cooking. Because it is a heavy oil, it should never be used in stir-fries, despite what you may have seen or read. Once opened, sesame oil will keep, tightly closed, at room temperature for up to 4 months.

SESAME SEED PASTE. A mix of ground white sesame seeds and soybean oil, this fragrant paste, sold in jars, is smooth and has the consistency of peanut butter and a pronounced sesame taste. Sesame seed paste is used in the Middle Eastern kitchen as well, where it is known as "tahini." I do not recommend using tahini, however, because it is too thin and its taste and fragrance are weak when compared to the Chinese product. After opening, store sesame seed paste in the refrigerator. It will keep for up to 6 months.

SHRIMP. These days, shrimp can be found live in Chinatown markets. By all means, buy them if they are available, as they have a wonderful natural sweetness. Otherwise, shrimp come cooked or uncooked, both fresh and frozen. I recommend against using cooked shrimp. When buying raw shrimp, always look for gray ones. They have a more cohesive texture than pink ones, which fall apart, especially when used in fillings. (In fact, most Chinatown markets do not even carry pink shrimp because their Chinese customers will not buy them.)

Shrimp are sold in boxes or packs, or they are displayed loose on ice. Some frozen uncooked shrimp are available split and deveined but with their shells intact. These are variously labeled "easy peel shell on" or "quick peel" or "shell on." I find they can save you time, but again be sure you always buy gray ones. Shrimp are typically graded by size and by count per pound. The sizes are usually imaginatively labeled "medium," "large," "extra large," or "colossal." To ensure you purchase the correct size for the recipes, I have provided both the weight and the count per pound. See page 75 for instructions on the proper way to clean shrimp.

SICHUAN PEPPERCORNS. These staples of Sichuan Province are neither hot nor true peppercorns. They are reddish, mild, emit a faint aroma of nutmeg, and impart a faint tingling sensation to the tongue. Nor are they solid like peppercorns; rather, they are open and are sometimes called flower peppercorns. Store these spices as you would peppercorns. Some recipes call for ground Sichuan peppercorns, which cannot be purchased. You must grind them yourself using

a spice grinder, a mortar and pestle, or by placing them in a bowl and smashing them with the end of the wooden handle of a cleaver (see page 46). Stored in a cool, dry place in a covered jar, whole peppercorns will keep for up to 6 months and ground peppercorns will keep for up to 2 weeks.

絲瓜 **SILK SQUASH.** This unusual, deep green, zucchini-shaped gourd, which can range from 1 foot to 3 feet long, has pronounced ridges running along its length. Also known as Chinese okra or luffa squash, it is a sweet vegetable, pure white inside its green skin, soft, and excellent in soups. The squash will keep in a plastic bag in the refrigerator for up to 1 week.

雪裡紅 **SNOW CABBAGE.** Similar to collard greens, this green, leafy vegetable is a favorite in Shanghai. It is called snow cabbage these days, but in earlier times it was called "red in snow," because it was said to grow best, and was ideally harvested, with the first snowfall. It is never eaten uncooked. Most often, it is water-blanched (see page 63) and salted and then cut up for use in soups, with noodles, in stir-fries with meats, or in dumplings. Most famously, it is stir-fried with so-called hairy beans, which are immature (green) soybeans—a Shanghai classic usually served as an appetizer. Snow cabbage comes in small cans labeled "snow cabbage," "Shanghai cabbage," or "pickled cabbage." It is even sometimes still labeled "red in snow," so carry your Chinese calligraphy when shopping.

荳苗 **SNOW PEA SHOOTS.** These tender tips of the vines on which snow peas grow are called *dau miu* in Cantonese or *doumiao* in Mandarin. Both translate as "begin to grow," which perfectly describes these young shoots. They are quite sweet when cooked, and the Chinese have eaten them happily for centuries. They are best prepared as soon as possible after purchase, as they tend to toughen in storage.

黃荳 **SOYBEANS.** Probably the richest source of protein in the world, soybeans contain twice the protein of the same weight of beef, carry more iron than the same weight of a beef liver, and are richer in digestible calcium than an equivalent amount of milk. They are also a highly versatile food, yielding not only the bean itself, but also soybean sprouts, soy sauce, bean curd in all of its forms, and soy milk. In China, the whole pods are boiled in salted water, and then the beans are removed and eaten as a snack or as a popular appetizer in Shanghai.

 SUGARCANE SUGAR. These blocks of caramel-colored sugar come wrapped in plastic or loose in crocks and are sold by weight in Chinese and other Asian markets. They are made by boiling sugarcane extract, which is then recooked to thicken it, and then cooked a third time until it becomes very thick and viscous, honey yellow, and is free of impurities. It is spread in a layer and then cut into blocks.

 TAPIOCA STARCH. Made from cassava root, this finely milled starch is used as the basis for dumpling doughs and sweets and for dusting or coating foods before cooking. Also known as tapioca flour, it is also used as a thickener for sauces, giving them a slightly gelatinous quality and giving the foods they are served with a desirable gloss. The starch will keep in a tightly covered container in a cool cupboard for up to 1 year.

TIANJIN BOK CHOY. This is a vegetable of many names. Often called Tianjin cabbage, Tientsin bok choy (the old spelling of its home city), or celery cabbage, it is also known familiarly as napa cabbage. There are two varieties of this very white, green-tinged vegetable—one with a long stalk, and the second rounder and heavier. The latter is the one most often called by its native city name; it is also the sweeter of the two, and my preference. At its best in late spring and summer, it should be kept in a plastic bag in the refrigerator for no more than 3 or 4 days, after which small, black marks begin to appear on the stalks. I suggest eating it as soon as possible after purchase. Heads range from 3 to 8 pounds, and some grocers will cut the larger heads to accommodate shoppers.

 TIGER LILY BUDS. Also called golden needles, these elongated, reddish-brown lily buds are dried, traditionally in the sun. The best buds are soft and pliable; have a sweet aroma; and when cooked, particularly in soups, give off a faint

sweetness. When dry and brittle, they are too old. Sold in packages, they will keep for at least 6 months in a tightly covered jar in a cool place.

 WATER CHESTNUTS. These bulbous, purple-brown tubers, about 1¼ inches in diameter and 1 inch thick, grow in the beds of still, muddy water. Despite their name and their appearance, they are not nuts. They are the roots of bulrushes. Peeling the tough brown skin is rather laborious, but once done, the rewards are great. The meat of the water chestnut—white, crisp, juicy, and sweet—is delicious, even when eaten raw. Canned water chestnuts are a barely adequate substitute. If you cannot find fresh water chestnuts, I suggest using jicama (see page 33) in their place. So versatile is the water chestnut that it is even transformed into a starch or flour for sweet cakes. As they age, they soften, lose their sweetness, and become quite starchy. Unpeeled, with the remnants of mud still on their skins, they will keep in a brown paper bag in the refrigerator for 7 to 10 days. Peeled, washed, and dried and put into a covered container, they will keep for 2 to 3 days.

 WONTON WRAPPERS. Called *wonton pei* by the Cantonese, these thin, pliable wrappers, also called skins, made from wheat flour, come stacked 60 to 80 to the package (depending on thickness), and are found in the refrigerated section of markets. The wrappers, made with or without eggs, measure 3 by 3¾ inches, and come dusted with cornstarch. They can be used as is, trimmed into circles as wrappers for dumplings, or cut into strips and deep-fried as noodles. They are labeled "wonton skins," or "wonton wrappers." If you see the Chinese characters for the word "glass," or *bor lei pei* in Cantonese, on the package, it means the skins are so thin you can see through them. The traditional skins of Hong Kong are also thin, and some packages are labeled "Hong Kong" to indicate they contain thin skins. Wrappers made without eggs are labeled "Shanghai wonton skins" or "Shanghai wonton wrappers." The skins will keep in their packaging in the refrigerator for 3 to 4 days. Frozen, they will keep for up to 3 months. Usually you will use about half of a package at one time, so you may want to divide packages on purchase and freeze half for later use. (For more information on wonton wrappers, see page 116.)

VINEGARS AND WINES

Before concluding this initial foray into the Chinatown markets, I always make it a point to devote significant time to talk about two necessities—neither of which is usually included in a discussion of Chinese cooking. When I talk about Chinese vinegars and wines, I usually receive puzzled looks. Awareness comes with smelling and tasting, particularly the intense, aromatic Chinkiang vinegar, which is much like Italian balsamic, and Shaoxing wine, which is much like a sherry. (In markets, you will also see wine bottles labeled "Shao-Hsing," a common romanized Cantonese spelling.) I use them frequently in marinades and sauces and as ingredients during cooking.

When I show my students aged Shaoxing wines, some of them of historic lineage, many in decorative ceramic crocks with one-hundred-dollar price tags, there is astonishment. When I point out the vintages of these rice wines, acceptance of their quality grows. "It tastes like sherry" is a usual comment. Shaoxing does indeed taste like a medium sherry. I warn them against buying any of the so-called cooking wines that abound in Asian markets, for they are invariably poor, and I repeat for them my father's dictum, offered nightly, it seemed, as I was growing up. As he sipped his cup of dinner Shaoxing, he would say, "If you cannot drink it, do not cook with it."

VINEGARS. There are various vinegars in China, most of which are rice based. They can be white, which becomes pale yellow as they age; pinkish red, after being tinted with fermented red rice, and recently more like the color of traditional wine vinegar; or black and thick. The latter is Chinkiang vinegar, the aristocrat of all Chinese vinegars. Historically, the best vinegars have come from the province of Shanxi, in China's west, and Zhejiang, once known as Chekiang, below Shanghai. Chinkiang vinegar, from Zhejiang and made from fermented glutinous rice, is essential to many dishes. Some aged Chinkiang vinegars are so highly prized in China that they are handed down from generation to generation. During World War II, many refugees reportedly fled their homes carrying only a few pieces of clothing and their family vinegar pots. There are several good brands imported from China, and I cannot recommend a particular one. If you cannot find Chinkiang vinegar, you can use a commercial unaged balsamic vinegar in its place. There is another, less common, black vinegar—also based on rice—to which other vinegars, sugar, and ginger have been added. It is labeled "sweet vinegar" and is used to make a deeply rooted traditional Cantonese dish of boiled eggs, pig's feet, and ginger, which women eat to rebuild their systems after giving birth. In fact, the Cantonese call this sweet vinegar *tim ding tim cho,* which translates as "vinegar to drink after a son is born."

White vinegars and red vinegars are essentially the same, except for their color, with the red vinegar used primarily as a colorant. Some are made from rice and some from sorghum, labeled "rice vinegar" and "grain vinegar," respectively. You can substitute a grain-based white distilled vinegar for either type.

**酒
類** **WINES.** In China, wines are not thought of as they are in the West. All drinkable alcohols are considered generically wines, or *chiew,* which is how they are most often labeled, though you will occasionally see *jiu,* the romanized Mandarin equivalent. Thus, there are wine *chiew,* spirits *chiew,* liqueur *chiew,* and beer *chiew.* In China's long history of wines, one *chiew* stands out—the rice-based Shaoxing—that is made in the same region as Chinkiang vinegar. Hundreds of wines come from the more than eight hundred wineries in the Shaoxing area. A cooked mash of glutinous rice is mixed with yeasts and clear water and permitted to ferment in pottery crocks. As the wines age, they change from yellow to pale amber to the color of brandy. Aged from 3 to 10 years, they vary in quality. I use Supreme Hua Tiao Chiew, the most respected brand from Shaoxing. The amber wine is an indispensable addition

to marinades and sauces. If that brand is unavailable, look for Shaoxing Far Chiew, a generic term much like Burgundy. Or, in the absence of a Chinese product, use a medium-dry sherry such as an amontillado. (For information on Shaoxing wines for drinking, see page 365.)

I also use white rice wine in some recipes. Kiu Kiang brand, which translates to "new mountain," is usually available. But any white rice wine will do. Other spirits are also looked on as superior *chiew,* but the most famous label is Mei Kuei Lu Chiew, produced in Tianjin in northern China, southeast of Beijing. Its name translates as "rose dew," and it is a special spirit based on sorghum, with the addition of a liquor made from soaked rose petals. It is similar to an eau-de-vie and is often drunk as an aperitif, yet it is exceptionally fine for cooking, too. It is widely available. If you cannot find it, a fine gin will substitute nicely.

COOKING UTENSILS

厨
具
和
厨
藝

At this point, we have gathered our first group of basic Chinese ingredients. But before leaving Chinatown, I insist that my students visit a store, one of only a few, that is a treasure trove of Chinese cooking equipment. All of the shops are called, simply, hardware stores by their proprietors. We walk into one and the questions come. What sort of wok is best? Which should I have? Should I have more than one? Which steamer should I buy? Which knives, and how many? Spatulas? Ladles? The number of Chinese cooking tools is not large, but it is important to buy well and to equip yourself properly, so that when you begin to cook, you will have the best and most suitable in hand. I begin each time in a particular aisle, its floor piled high with woks.

WOK. As perfect an all-purpose cooking pot as exists, the wok is ingrained in Chinese culture and has remained basically unchanged for thousands of years. First made of iron, later of carbon steel, and still later of other metals, the wok has a concave shape that places its round bottom directly into the flame of a stove, permitting the fire to envelop the bowl, making it an ideal cooker. When made of carbon steel, it is essentially perfect. It conducts heat almost instantaneously, and although neither a pot nor a pan in the conventional sense, it functions as both. Its shape permits food to be stir-fried—tossed quickly with small amounts of oil—so it cooks through but does not absorb oil. The wok also works equally well for braising and deep-frying and is ideal for blanching, sauce making, dry roasting, steaming, and smoking.

The most useful carbon-steel wok, which I recommend not only to my students, but to everyone, has a diameter of about 14 inches. It costs little, and when properly seasoned, it behaves like a nonstick pan. The more it is used, the more seasoned it becomes, and the less oil you need for cooking in it. I own more than two dozen woks, and all but two of them are carbon steel. I still have, and still cook with, the first carbon-steel wok I bought after coming to the United States, a wok now forty-five years old. Various cast-iron and stainless-steel woks are available today, and for a short while, there were aluminum woks, too, but these are now rarely seen.

None of these woks performs as well as the carbon-steel wok, and all should be avoided except for specialized functions. Cast iron is too heavy and unwieldy, and though often used in restaurants, is unsuitable for home use. Stainless steel conducts heat unevenly, which means foods can burn, though a stainless-steel wok is good for steaming purposes.

Nor do I recommend woks coated with nonstick finishes, which make it impossible to control the heat effectively and can be damaged by direct, intense heat. A flat-bottomed wok is not a good choice because foods cannot be whisked smoothly through it. Electric woks are essentially useless because of their relatively small size, and because, as with coated woks, there is no way to control the heat successfully.

A new carbon-steel wok arrives with a thick, sticky oil coating to preserve and protect it. Once cleaned of this coating and seasoned, it will last for many years. To clean it, submerge it in extremely hot, soapy (liquid detergent) water and rub the inside with a sponge. Next, scrub the outside with steel wool and cleanser and rinse the wok well. To season it, place it still wet over a high flame and dry with a paper towel to prevent instant rust, then discard the towel. With the wok still over the flame tip a teaspoon of oil into its bowl and rub the oil over the entire interior surface with a clean paper towel. Repeat the process until the paper towel is free of any trace of black residue. The wok is now ready for use.

A new wok absorbs oil until it is properly seasoned, and once seasoned, very little oil is needed to cook in it. After the first washing to remove the coating, detergents should never be used in the bowl. Instead scrub the wok in extremely hot water with a stiff-bristled wok brush. Then, rinse it and place it over a high flame to dry quickly while rubbing it with a paper towel. Following the first 15 to 20 uses, reseason the bowl by rubbing a small amount of oil over the surface with a paper towel. Continue to do this until the towel shows no trace of darkened color, and the bowl of the wok is shiny and dark. Use the wok with all of its specially designed tools.

 WOK COVER. A flat-domed cover, 12 to 13 inches in diameter, that nestles into the wok, permitting it to be covered and used for stewing, steaming, or smoking. The covers are made of either stainless steel or aluminum and have a handle on top.

 WOK BRUSH. This oar-shaped, wood-handled brush has long, stiff, thick bristles. It is used in very hot water, without detergent, to scrub food residue from the bowl of the wok.

 WOK RING. A ring that fits over a stove burner and holds the base of the wok firmly over the flame. Although usually made of stainless steel, carbon-steel rings are also available, and they can be notched with metal shears to fit any burner configuration. It is what I do.

 SPATULA. Long-handled, shovel-shaped spatulas fashioned of hammered carbon steel or stainless steel are used primarily for tossing and stirring foods in the wok when stir-frying. Carbon-steel spatulas become seasoned with use, and I prefer them, but they have become something of a rarity these days; a stainless-steel version serves nicely.

 LADLE. This stainless-steel spoon has a large, cup-shaped bowl and a long, hollow metal handle with a wood insert at the end. Ladles come in various sizes, but one that is 15 inches long with a bowl 4 to 4½ inches in diameter is a good all-purpose size.

 STRAINERS. Two types are useful for Chinese cooking. One is a circular steel-mesh strainer attached to a long handle of split bamboo, with the strainer ranging from about 4 inches to 14 inches in diameter. The most useful size is 10 inches in diameter. The second type combines a long, hollow metal handle with a rather large, sturdy, shallow stainless-steel bowl perforated with round holes. I recommend the 10-inch strainer size for this type as well. The steel-mesh strainer is perfect for draining foods after removing them from stock or oil. The perforated-steel strainer is ideal for lowering foods into hot liquids and removing them with confidence.

 STEAMERS. Many suitable steamers are available. The most traditional is made of bamboo and consists of a circular frame with a woven-bamboo mesh base and a shallow-domed woven-bamboo cover. Bamboo steamers come in various sizes, but those measuring 12 to 13 inches in diameter nestle perfectly in the bowl of a standard-size wok. Foods rest on the mesh bottom and steam passes upward from the boiling water in the wok through the mesh into the food. These steamers can be stacked as many as three high, and different foods can be steamed simultaneously. This is my preferred steamer.

You can also find stainless-steel steamers that fit into the wok as nicely as their bamboo counterparts do. Some of these steel steamers have removable bamboo-mesh bases. Other steamers, also tiered, are made of aluminum. Steaming in aluminum tends to blacken the metal, so I recommend against aluminum steamers.

Also available are stainless-steel steamer sets consisting of a base pot (usually 8-quart capacity), two stackable tiers with mesh base or bases perforated with holes, and a cover. The bottom of one tier can be removed so that large foods can be steamed. Steel basket insets that fit into pots—good for steaming asparagus, corn, clams, and the like—are available as well.

 CLEAVER. A complete collection of Chinese cooking tools requires a cleaver. They come small or large, heavy or light, with a stainless-steel blade or a carbon-steel blade, a wooden or a metal

CLEAVER TECHNIQUES

CHOPPING

CUBING

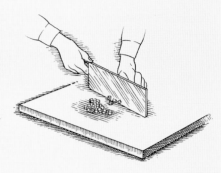

MINCING

DICING

SHREDDING

SLICING

PEELING (WATER CHESTNUT)

POUNDING WITH CLEAVER BLADE
TO BREAK FIBER

MAKING A PASTE WITH CLEAVER
HANDLE, MASHING

handle, imported from China or manufactured domestically. I recommend one in particular, which should be sufficient for all of your needs: a wood-handled cleaver with a balanced steel blade that is perfect for cutting, slicing, chopping, and mincing. It is made by Dexter and it weighs 11 ounces with a stainless-steel blade or 12 ounces with a carbon-steel blade. I cannot recommend too highly the stainless-steel Dexter cleaver, a truly professional knife suitable for nearly every cutting task.

A cleaver can be used for all of the cutting functions of a Western chef's knife, including slicing, dicing, mincing, and cutting into julienne or matchsticks. The difference lies in shredding.

In China, shredding, except when done with the hands, is most precise. Many foods are shredded before cooking, particularly for stir-frying. When shredding hard vegetables such as carrots, ginger, and other roots, you first cut the vegetable into ⅛-inch-thick paper-thin slices, and then you cut the slices into very fine lengths. With meats, the process is basically the same. When shredding raw meat, it is a good idea to place it in the freezer for about a half hour. It will firm up and be easier to cut into fine shreds.

鉆
板 **CUTTING BOARDS.** The number of cutting boards available seems endless. Which to use? My preference, above all, is a board made of a hard-rubber-like composition. It is dull, sand-colored, and comes round and square and in various sizes. It is the cutting board of choice, not only among Chinese cooks, but also among many Western chefs. Its most important property is that it does not dull knife blades. It is also dishwasher friendly. Wooden cutting boards, butcher blocks, and laminated compressed bamboo cutting boards are also good choices. I do not recommend using the white plastic cutting boards so widely available because they tend to dull knives easily.

CHOPSTICKS. Finally, no set of Chinese cooking and eating utensils would be complete without chopsticks. Chopsticks of various sizes, shapes, and materials abound. Decoratively, they can be made of ivory, jade, silver, and ebony, teak, and palisander woods. An old story told over many centuries provides me with a personal bias toward ivory chopsticks: An emperor, told that contact with poisoned foods would cause ivory chopsticks to blacken, always had his official taster use ivory chopsticks when testing. Now, I do not expect to be poisoned, but I like the story, and I always eat with ivory chopsticks. Long bamboo chopsticks with flat ends are more practical and are most like traditional Chinese chopsticks. The shorter types, with pointed bottoms, are better suited to sticking into food than to grasping it properly, and white plastic chopsticks make eating work, rather than enjoyment. Think bamboo or ivory.

Always use bamboo chopsticks for cooking. They are perfect for mixing, for turning foods while deep-frying, or for loosening cooked foods, to mention just a few uses. I do not recommend so-called cooking chopsticks because they are too long and awkward to use. Bamboo chopsticks are strong, resist warping, and are highly durable. I have chopsticks in my kitchen that I have cooked with for more than twenty years.

{ PART 1 }

LESSON 2
A COLLECTION OF BASICS

A COLLECTION
OF BASICS

We now have the prepared ingredients we bought in the markets, foods that we will be using repeatedly as we make the recipes in the coming pages. But my first lesson is on how to make a group of basic preparations—foods, stocks, and oils—that we will also use again and again as our lessons progress.

TRADITIONAL COOKED RICE

|| 4½ TO 5 CUPS ||

 Rice is known as *mi* (or *mai* in Cantonese) when raw and *fan* when cooked. It has been said, much too often, how difficult it is to cook rice, to make *fan,* expertly.

This is not at all the case. To the contrary, it is easy to make cooked rice—to make perfect, fluffy, separate grains. What follows is a foolproof method for cooking rice that can accompany many, if not most, of the preparations in this book, particularly the stir-fries. For the best result, I prefer so-called old rice—that is, rice that has been lying about in sacks for extended periods—because it absorbs water more readily than new-crop rice, which makes it easier to cook. Also, the older the rice, the greater the yield.

1. Add 2 cups extra-long-grain rice to a pot of cold water. Wash the rice by rubbing it between your palms, then discard the water. Do this three times, then drain the washed rice well. Add fresh water to the rice and allow it to rest for an hour before cooking. Use 1⅞ cups (15 ounces) water for 2 cups rice. These precise measures are foolproof. Too much water will make the rice too soft, and too little water will yield hard kernels.

2. Begin to cook the rice, uncovered. Place the pan over high heat and bring the water to a boil. Stir the rice with chopsticks or with a wooden spoon and cook for about 4 minutes, or until the surface water is absorbed. Even after the water is no longer visible, the rice will be quite hard. Cover the pan, reduce the heat to the lowest setting, and cook for about 8 minutes more, stirring from time to time.

3. Turn off the heat and loosen the rice with chopsticks or a wooden spoon. This will help retain fluffiness. Cover the pan tightly until ready to serve. Just before serving, stir and loosen the rice again. Properly cooked rice will not be lumpy, nor will the grains stick together. Instead, they will be firm and separate. The rice may be kept hot, in the pan, in a warm (150°F) oven for an hour without drying out.

RICE: THE NATIONAL STAPLE

Rice is a staple in most of China. It was once rare in the north, where it was second to wheat, but nowadays northerners eat large amounts of rice as well. For many Chinese, rice is the core of nearly every meal. Vegetables, meats, and fish are served with rice, rather than the reverse, the case in the West. Short-, medium-, and long-grain varieties are grown in China, with extra-long-grain rice the most widely used.

The Chinese distinguish between long-grain rice and extra-long-grain rice, with the length of the latter about four times its width. These slender grains are considered more elegant and have a particularly pleasing bite when cooked. When shopping in the United States, extra-long-grain rice grown in Texas and elsewhere is a good choice. Fragrant, extra-long-grain rice from Thailand, called jasmine rice, is also excellent. Medium-grain rice, which is eaten by people who prefer softer kernels, is not as widely available, and much of the harvest is milled into rice flour (powder) for making sweet or savory cakes.

Short-grain rice tends to soften as it cooks, and its grains adhere into clumps. This is the rice favored in Japan and, to a large extent, in Taiwan. I use it, together with short-grain glutinous rice, in congee. Glutinous rice, also known

RICE

as sweet rice or sticky rice, comes both short grain and long grain, and both are sticky when cooked. Because the grains are sticky enough to be molded, glutinous rice is often used in stuffings, dumplings, and cakes. It is also popular in Southeast Asia, where it is ground into a flour for making sweet pastries.

In most of China, but particularly in rural areas, rice is usually eaten three times a day. In Guangdong, eating rice even has its own vocabulary: To eat rice in the morning is to *sik fan,* afternoon rice is *n'fan,* evening rice is *mon fan,* and *siu yeh,* literally "cooked midnight," describes rice eaten as a late-evening snack. Rice is prepared in many different ways: cooked in water, steamed, boiled, fried, in porridge-like congee, for dim sum, in stuffings, in pastries, as fresh rice noodles, as sweet or savory steamed cakes, wrapped in bundles, and steamed in lotus leaves.

Rices of various colors are grown in China as well. Red rice, cultivated extensively in the south, is used mainly as a coloring agent. Black rice, usually long grain and glutinous, also grown in the south and often labeled "black sweet rice," is generally fashioned into sweets or fermented to make vinegar. So-called brown rice is simply rice that has been only partially milled to permit its brown chaff to remain.

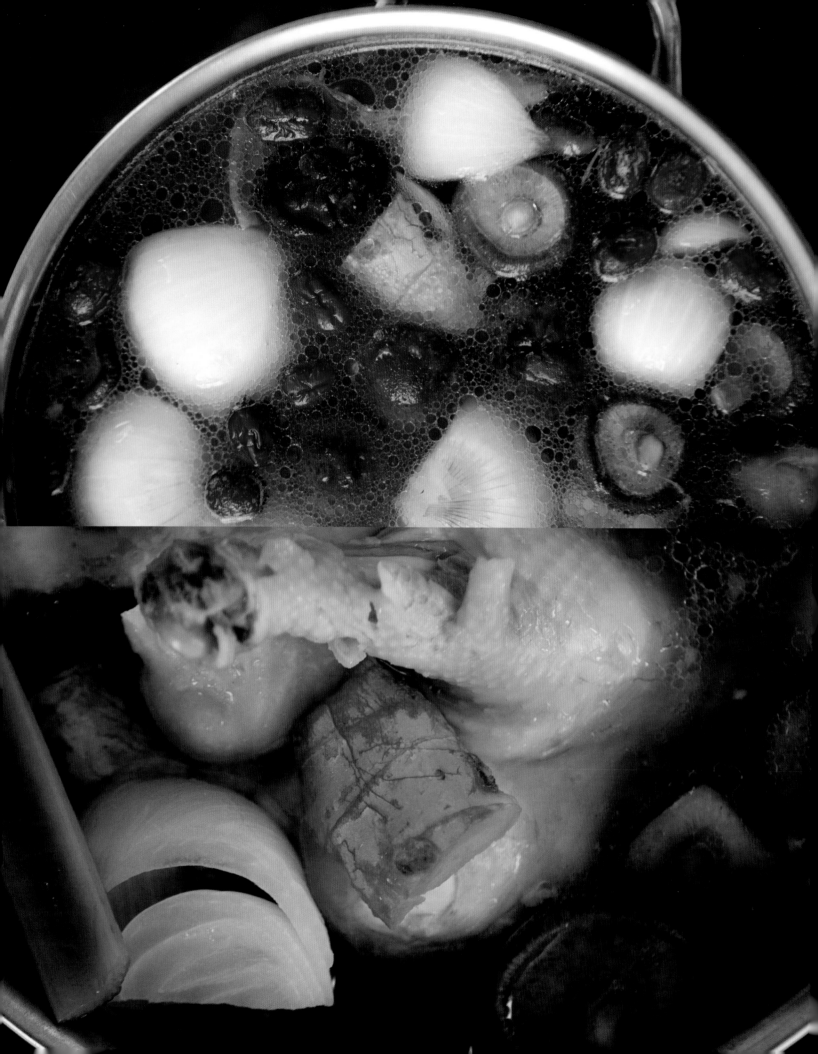

TWO BASIC STOCKS

上湯

With the exception of rice, there is nothing more basic to Chinese cooking than stocks. A stock is the foundation for a well-prepared sauce, soup, or stew and is often used for steaming, blanching, or poaching. Much of the intensity and depth of flavor in a dish begins with stock. It is essential to use specific stocks for specific dishes because of their individual flavor bases. Here are two of my stocks.

VEGETABLE STOCK

‖ MAKES ABOUT 4 QUARTS ‖

INGREDIENTS

5 quarts water

1 ½ pounds carrots, cut crosswise into thirds

3 ½ pounds onions, quartered

1 ½ pounds scallions, cut crosswise into thirds

1 ½ pounds fresh white mushrooms, cut into thirds

12 celery stalks, cut crosswise into thirds

8 ounces fresh coriander sprigs, cut into 3-inch lengths

12 ounces fresh red dates, or ½ cup dried red dates, soaked in hot water to cover for 30 minutes and drained

⅓ cup boxthorn seeds, soaked in hot water to cover for 10 minutes and drained

8 ounces fresh ginger, unpeeled, cut into 3 equal pieces and lightly smashed

¼ cup Scallion Oil (page 56)

1 cup fried scallions from Scallion Oil (page 56)

¼ cup fried garlic from Garlic Oil (page 56)

2 ½ tablespoons salt

1. In a large stockpot, bring the water to a boil over high heat. Add all of the ingredients, cover the pot, and allow the water to return to a boil. Reduce the heat to a simmer, adjust the cover so it is slightly cracked, and simmer the stock for 5 hours.

2. Turn off the heat and let the stock cool in the pot. Strain the stock through a fine-mesh strainer into clean containers to store for later use. Cover the containers and refrigerate for up to 5 days, or freeze for up to 3 months.

CHICKEN STOCK

‖ **MAKES ABOUT 5½ QUARTS** ‖

INGREDIENTS

12½ quarts water

2 whole chickens with giblets (about 8 pounds total), cleaned (see sidebar) and each bird quartered

4 pounds chicken wings

8 ounces fresh ginger, unpeeled, cut into 3 equal pieces and lightly smashed

6 whole garlic cloves, peeled

1 bunch scallions, cut crosswise into thirds

4 onions, quartered

4 ounces fresh coriander sprigs, cut into 3-inch lengths (about 1 cup)

½ cup fried onions from Onion Oil (page 56)

½ cup boxthorn seeds, soaked in hot water to cover for 10 minutes and drained

3 tablespoons salt

---

1. In a large stockpot, bring 4 quarts of the water to a boil. Add the chicken quarters, giblets, and wings and allow the water to return to a boil. Boil for 2 minutes. This will bring the blood and juices to the top. Remove the pot from the heat and pour off the water. Run cold water into the pot to rinse off the chicken and then drain into a colander.

2. Place the chicken parts and the giblets back into the pot. Add the remaining 8½ quarts water and all of the remaining ingredients. Cover the pot and bring to a boil over high heat. Reduce the heat to a simmer, adjust the cover so it is slightly cracked, and simmer for 5 hours. Using a Chinese ladle, skim any residue from the surface as the stock simmers.

3. Turn off the heat and let the stock cool in the pot. Strain the stock through a fine-mesh strainer into containers to store for later use. Cover the containers and refrigerate for up to 5 days, or freeze for up to 3 months. A thin layer of fat will form on the surface of the refrigerated or frozen stock. Leave it in place until you are ready to use the stock, then skim it off with a large spoon just before using. Most of the taste will have gone from the chicken to the stock, but you still may wish to nibble on the meat. Enjoy.

‖ **HOW TO CLEAN A CHICKEN** ‖

HOW TO CLEAN A CHICKEN

Place the chicken in its wrapping in the sink. Unwrap it and discard the wrapping. Run cold water over the outside and inside the chicken. Remove any membranes and fat from the cavity. Take care to clean the body cavity thoroughly.

Sprinkle 2 tablespoons of salt on the breast side of the chicken and rub it thoroughly into the skin of the breast, thighs, legs, and wings. Turn the chicken over, sprinkle 2 tablespoons of salt over the entire back, and rub it thoroughly into the skin. Run cold water over the chicken to rinse away the salt and wash the chicken. The skin at this point will be very smooth and clean.

Put the chicken in a colander placed over a bowl to drain for several minutes.

Meanwhile, wash the sink and the work space well with soap, bleach, and water. Finally, wash your hands and then dry the chicken with paper towels. It is now ready to use.

FOUR FLAVORED OILS

In recent years, there has been a marked increase in flavor-infused oils available to cooks. Some taste adequate, and the others weak. With their popularity has come a spate of manufacturers who suggest they have essentially invented the genre. They have not.

Flavored oils have existed in China for more than two thousand years. Long before the peanut made its way to China in the 1600s and became the prime source of cooking oil, oils were pressed from sesame seeds, grape seeds, and even turnips.

I use peanut oil as the base for my infused oils because it is receptive to other flavors,

absorbing the scents of whichever vegetable or spice it is wedded to by heat. These flavored oils imbue dishes with subtle tastes: the emphasis on inherent flavors, not on alteration.

Use a wok to make these oils, rather than another pot, because the simple act of heating the oil helps to season the wok. Another plus gained from this process is that the fried scallions, onions, and garlic used for these oils can be stored separately and added to stocks, soups, sauces, marinades, and stir-fries. The hot pepper flakes used in making hot oil should be stored in the oil for subsequent use.

HOT PEPPER OIL

|| MAKES ABOUT 1 CUP OIL AND PEPPER FLAKES ||

INGREDIENTS

½ cup hot pepper flakes (see sidebar)	⅓ cup sesame oil
	½ cup peanut oil

1. For this infused oil to be a success, the pepper flakes must be very hot, which is why I specify dried Thai chiles for making the flakes. Heat a wok over high heat for 20 seconds. Add the sesame oil, peanut oil, and pepper flakes and stir. Reduce the heat to medium and cook for 2 to 3 minutes, or until the oil is very hot, but not boiling.

2. Turn off the heat and let cool to room temperature. Pour the oil, including the pepper flakes, into a sterilized glass jar and close tightly. Allow the oil to rest for 10 minutes and

then it can be used. The oil will keep at room temperature for up to 1 week or refrigerated for up to 3 months. The longer the oil is stored, the hotter it will become.

|| **HOW TO MAKE HOT PEPPER FLAKES** ||

HOT PEPPER FLAKES

Look for dried Thai chiles, sold in 4-ounce packages (about 3 cups before grinding), or dry your own chiles. Place the dried chiles in a food processor and pulse for 1 to 1½ minutes, or until ground into coarse flakes. You should have about 1½ cups flakes. Store in a tightly closed jar in a cool, dark place. They will retain their strength for at least 6 months.

SCALLION OIL

|| MAKES 1½ CUPS OIL AND ABOUT 2 CUPS
FRIED SCALLIONS ||

INGREDIENTS

2 cups peanut oil	4 large bunches scallions (1¼ pounds total), cut into 2-inch lengths and white portions lightly smashed

1. Heat a wok over high heat for 30 seconds. Add the peanut oil, then the scallions. Bring the oil to a boil, reduce the heat to a simmer, stirring occasionally, for 20 to 30 minutes, or until the oil turns golden brown.

2. Turn off the heat. Strain the oil through a fine-mesh strainer into a heatproof bowl and allow to cool to room temperature. Set the fried scallions aside to cool. Pour the cooled oil into a sterilized glass jar and close tightly. The oil will keep at room temperature for 1 week, or refrigerated for up to 3 months. Transfer the fried scallions to a plastic container, cover, and refrigerate. They will keep for up to 3 months.

ONION OIL

|| MAKES 1¼ CUPS OIL AND ABOUT
1¼ CUPS FRIED ONIONS ||

INGREDIENTS

1¾ cups peanut oil	1 pound onions, very thinly sliced (4 cups)

1. Heat a wok over high heat for 30 seconds. Add the peanut oil and onions, and cook for 7 minutes, stirring and turning the onions often to prevent burning and to ensure even browning. Reduce the heat to medium and cook, stirring often, for 15 minutes more, or until the onions turn light brown.

2. Turn off the heat. Strain the oil through a fine-mesh strainer into a heatproof bowl, pressing the onions with a ladle as they drain. Allow the oil to cool to room temperature. Set the fried onions aside to cool. Pour the cooled oil into a sterilized glass jar and close tightly. The oil will keep at room temperature for 1 week, or refrigerated for up to 3 months. Transfer the fried onions to a plastic container, cover, and refrigerate. They will keep for up to 3 months.

GARLIC OIL

|| MAKES 1¼ CUPS OIL AND ABOUT
1½ CUPS FRIED GARLIC ||

INGREDIENTS

1½ cups peanut oil	2¼ cups thinly sliced garlic (about 3 heads)

1. Heat a wok over high heat for 30 seconds. Add the peanut oil and garlic and stir. Reduce the heat to medium and allow the oil to come to a boil. Reduce the heat to low and cook for 10 minutes, stirring once every minute, or until the garlic turns light brown.

2. Turn off the heat. Strain the oil through a fine-mesh strainer into a heatproof bowl and allow to cool to room temperature. Set the fried garlic aside to cool. Pour the cooled oil into a sterilized glass jar and close tightly. The oil will keep at room temperature for up to 1 week, or refrigerated for up to 3 months. Transfer the fried garlic to a plastic container, cover, and refrigerate. It will keep for up to 2 months.

SOME CONDIMENTS

Two of the more common condiments used in Chinese cooking are ginger pickle and chili sauce. Both, as I have noted, can be bought in jars and bottles. However, I believe that a good deal of their intensity is lost in commercial processing, so it is best to make your own.

GINGER PICKLE

‖ **MAKES ABOUT 2½ TO 3 CUPS** ‖

This pickle has many uses. It is a delicious snack. It is an appetizer, an ingredient, and a garnish. Use young ginger, which is recognizable by its thin skin, creamy-white interior with a pinkish cast, and the green shoots that protrude from its exterior.

INGREDIENTS

1 pound young ginger	¾ teaspoon baking soda
4 cups water	

MARINADE

6 ½ tablespoons white rice vinegar	⅔ cup sugar
	1 teaspoon salt

---

1. Wash the ginger thoroughly to remove its thin outer bark, but retain its thin skin. Cut the ginger into ⅛-inch-thick slices, retaining the shoots.

2. In a large pot, bring the water to a boil. Add the baking soda, which will dissolve immediately. Add the ginger and allow it to boil for 45 seconds. Remove the pot from the heat, run cold water into it, and then drain the ginger into a strainer. Return the ginger to the pot, run cold water into the pot again, and then drain again. Return the ginger to the pot, add cold water to cover, and let rest for 10 minutes. Drain the ginger.

3. To make the marinade: In a large bowl, combine all of the ingredients and stir well to dissolve the sugar and salt.

4. Add the ginger and mix well. Cover and refrigerate for at least 24 hours before using, and then serve cold. The pickled ginger will keep in a tightly closed jar in the refrigerator for up to 3 months.

HOMEMADE CHILI SAUCE

‖ MAKES ABOUT 2 CUPS ‖

 More brands of chili sauce and hot pepper sauce are on the market today than anyone can possibly count. They come from around the world, are of varying degrees of hotness, and many of them contain preservatives and other additives. Make your own chili sauce and it will be both free of preservatives and as hot as you want it. You can use any fresh hot red chiles you like, but I have had great success with fully ripe red jalapeños. The more mature they are, the more intense the heat. Do not use green jalapeños, which is what is more commonly found in the market. If red ones are not available, the same amount of hot red cherry peppers will do nicely. You can vary the amounts of salt, sugar, or vinegar according to taste.

INGREDIENTS

1 pound red jalapeño chiles, stems removed

2 tablespoons water

1¾ teaspoons salt

1½ tablespoons sugar

2½ tablespoons white rice vinegar

---

1. In a pot, combine the chiles, water, and salt over high heat until the chiles begin to release their liquid. Reduce the heat to low, stir the chiles, and cook, uncovered, for 15 to 20 minutes, or until the chiles soften.

2. Turn off the heat and let the chiles cool.

3. Transfer the contents of the pot to a blender, add the sugar and vinegar, and blend until a smooth puree forms. Use the sauce immediately, or transfer it to a storage container, cover tightly, and store in the refrigerator for up to 4 weeks, or in the freezer for up to 6 months.

STEAMED DRIED SCALLOPS

‖ MAKES 4 WHOLE STEAMED SCALLOPS OR ABOUT ¼ CUP SHREDDED SCALLOPS ‖

 Dried scallops are a costly delicacy that are traditionally slowly dried in the sun, which accounts for their golden color, their dried texture reminiscent of tiny stalks, and their expense. They are used sparingly but effectively to enhance other dishes, from stocks to stir-fries. I use them steamed for their distinctive, pungent taste. Dried scallops are prized ingredients, seldom found in noodle parlors and in expensive restaurants. The Chinese will eat a few foods no matter their price. Dried scallops are one of them.

INGREDIENTS

2 quarts boiling water

4 dried scallops, the diameter of a quarter

2 teaspoons Shaoxing wine

2 tablespoons Chicken Stock (page 54)

½-inch-thick slice ginger, peeled and lightly smashed

1 tablespoon Scallion Oil (page 56)

---

1. Bring the water to a boil. Place the scallops in a steam-proof dish. Add the wine, stock, ginger, and scallion oil, distributing evenly. Put the dish in a steamer set over the boiling water, cover, and steam for 40 minutes. The scallops are done if they fall apart into shreds when prodded with chopsticks.

2. The scallops can be used immediately, or they will keep in a tightly covered container in the refrigerator for 7 to 10 days.

This is the condiment of choice throughout China, north and south, east and west. A staple of Chinese cooking for three thousand years, soy sauce is made by fermenting soybeans, wheat flour, water, and salt, a process that originated in China and was later adopted by the Japanese.

The best soy sauces are fermented naturally in the open air, under the sun. Others are the result of factory fermentation. Light and dark varieties are available. The light soys are usually taken from the tops of soy sauce batches as they ferment in earthenware crocks, and the darker soys come from the bottoms. I prefer soy sauces from China, particularly from Hong Kong, and from Canada. They are markedly better than those produced in the United States and Japan, many of which lack a defined flavor, are thin, and are occasionally too salty. The fermentation formula for most Chinese soy sauces is 90 percent soybeans and 10 percent flour. Japanese soy sauces are customarily 50 percent each soybeans and flour.

Dark soys are labeled "dark" or "black," and "double dark" or "double black," with the so-called double sauces darker and thicker. There is even a thicker and darker "pearl" sauce available. Molasses is added to some dark soys to darken them further and give them more texture. Dark soys are best for imparting rich color to a dish. Light soys are often labeled "pure bean," "light," or "thin." The Chinese often refer to light soys as "fresh sweet," which connotes that they tend to enhance the flavors of the other ingredients being cooked.

**SOY
SAUCE**

**LIGHT SOY
SAUCE**

**DOUBLE
DARK SOY
SAUCE**

Look for Yuet Heung Yuen brand, once brewed in Hong Kong and now only brewed in British Columbia. The company's light soy is labeled "pure bean" and its double dark soy is labeled "(C) soy." The other brand I favor is made in Hong Kong's New Territories by the Koon Chun Sauce Factory. Its light soy is labeled "thin," and its double dark is labeled "double black." Another sauce I like to use includes pureed mushrooms for additional sweetness. It is manufactured in China by Pearl River Bridge brand and is labeled "mushroom soy."

I specify a particular soy sauce for each recipe. I cannot stress too strongly how important it is to procure the soy sauce indicated. What you use will affect how the food looks and tastes. But if I call for double dark soy and you cannot find it, you can use dark soy. If dark soy is unavailable and the only bottles your market carries are labeled "soy sauce," then you can use one of them, but expect the taste to differ from what was intended.

Soy sauces impart richness and body to foods. They are used as ingredients in dishes, sauces, and marinades and as a dip. I also often combine different types to yield different effects, tastes, and colors. In general, the Chinese use soy more sparingly than Westerners do, many of whom pour large amounts of it over their food. Refrain from this. Soy sauce is delicate, and using it to excess destroys its subtlety.

Most soy sauce comes in bottles, and occasionally in cans. Always store the bottles tightly capped and at room temperature. They will keep for up to 6 months.

LESSON 3
STIR-FRYING

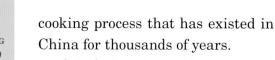

STIR-FRYING

Our basics are now in place, so we begin cooking in earnest. A word to keep in mind as you begin is *ts'ui*. It does not have a concise translation, but essentially it means food cooked so its essence is preserved, its texture is respected, its freshness retained. It describes food that is cooked to the precise point of doneness, no more.

Stir-frying perfectly illustrates the concept of *ts'ui*. It is a quick process and, when done properly, foods are never overdone, their fabric is never destroyed, their taste remains sharp and in focus.

Yet, as I watch a televised demonstration of an alleged Chinese stir-fry, I see the "teacher" drop pieces of chopped vegetables into a wok, follow these with slices of meat, and then with dollops of some jarred sauces. Next, he flashes a spatula through the mixture, exploding with ecstasy as he moves, and finally, he scoops the mix onto a plate, where its appearance is applauded by a wowed audience. However, what I have seen is not a stir-fry, but rather a caricature of a

cooking process that has existed in China for thousands of years.

Stir-frying is cooking prepped foods quickly and in a natural progression. No cooking method possesses the drama of the stir-fry, with foods being whisked about the bowl of a wok with a spatula, quickly passing through cooking oil, all in a continuous, rhythmic motion as flame curls up around the curve of the wok. The Chinese phrase for this is "wok air," or *wok qi* in Mandarin and *wok hei* in Cantonese, and it means the proper amount of heat is being used to cook a food to its point of maximum flavor. Basically, the object of stir-frying is to cook foods so they retain their nature, their beauty, and their nutritional value.

Before the stir-frying begins, all of the foods must be cut to the sizes indicated, all of the marinades must be complete, all of the sauces mixed. And everything must be placed next to the wok, so each addition can be tipped into the pan at the precise moment the recipe directs. The best stir-fried foods retain their nature even as they absorb the heat from the fire.

When ready to stir-fry, heat the wok for the precise time specified. At this point, add the cooking oil, again, a precise amount, and use a spatula to coat the walls of the wok with the oil. The oil is ready to receive foods when a wisp of white smoke rises from it. Or, test the temperature by dropping a slice of ginger into the hot oil. When it turns light brown, the oil is ready.

When cooking vegetables, I usually add a bit of salt to enhance their flavor. With almost all stir-fried preparations, I also add garlic and ginger, in specified amounts. All of the vegetables must be cut uniformly into the sizes indicated. Hard and firm vegetables, such as carrots, string beans, bamboo shoots, *choi sum,* and cauliflower, require longer cooking. Softer vegetables, such as bok choy, lettuce, bell peppers, celery, chives, and scallions, require less cooking. If the vegetables are very wet, pat them dry, or they will not stir-fry properly. In some cases, they should be water-blanched to remove moisture, a process explained on page 63. But if they are too dry, you may have to sprinkle a few drops of water into the wok to create steam.

Meats and poultry are cut into uniform sizes as well. Place them in the hot, oiled wok in a single layer, cook them for the specified time, then turn them over and mix briefly so they cook evenly. How seafood is stir-fried varies. Arrange shrimp in a single layer and cook exactly like a meat. With crabs and lobsters, you may have to cover the wok for a time so the heat penetrates the shells and their meat. Clams, oysters, and mussels are usually blanched to open them before stir-frying.

Whatever ingredients you are stir-frying, they should be mixed in a continuous motion, generally back and forth, almost a crisscross pattern. This ensures the food remains in the center of the wok where the heat is most intense and it guarantees it will cook evenly.

╟ COOKING ON AN ELECTRIC STOVE ╢

A gas range is preferable for cooking Chinese food, particularly stir-fries, because of the height of the flame and the intensity of the heat it provides. However, I know that many people live in apartments or houses equipped with electric stoves. I have devised a technique for obtaining high heat, as well as the necessary variances in heat, using an electric range, and I teach it with success. I use two electric burners, side by side, on the cook top. Turn one to its highest setting and allow it to heat for 10 minutes. After 5 minutes, turn the second burner on to medium. Place the wok on the burner set on high heat and allow it to heat for 1 to 1½ minutes, or until the wok is very hot. Add the cooking oil, coat the wok with it, and allow to heat until a wisp of white smoke appears. The cooking process can now begin. Place the food in the wok. If it cooks too quickly or appears about to burn, move the wok to the burner set to medium heat. Go back and forth between the burners as necessary. Once you become accustomed to this process, you will cook Chinese food successfully on an electric range.

電
爐

COOKING
ON AN
ELECTRIC
STOVE

STIR-FRIED SHANGHAI BOK CHOY

‖ MAKES 4 TO 6 SERVINGS ‖

上海白菜

I have selected this lovely vegetable for my first stir-fry for its inherent crispness, which must be preserved as it is cooked and served. Shanghai bok choy, its stalks light green, its leaves dark green, is a distinct type of bok choy. It is said to have been first grown around Shanghai, thus its name. And in truth, as I was growing up, I don't recall seeing it in Guangdong. Although it is similar to all other types of bok choy, it is prized because once it has been blanched to soften and then cooked in its sauce, it takes on a pleasant sweetness. A head of Shanghai bok choy weighs about 4 ounces, or 4 heads to the pound. If their sizes are similar, other types of bok choy can be cooked using this recipe.

INGREDIENTS

SAUCE

½ cup Vegetable Stock (page 53)	1 teaspoon white rice vinegar
1 tablespoon oyster sauce	1 tablespoon cornstarch
2 teaspoons Shaoxing wine	1 teaspoon sugar
1 teaspoon dark soy sauce	¼ teaspoon salt
	⅛ teaspoon white pepper

2 pounds (8 heads) Shanghai bok choy	2 teaspoons salt
6 cups water	¾ teaspoon baking soda (optional)
1-inch-thick slice ginger, peeled and lightly smashed	

3 tablespoons Onion Oil (page 56)

1. To make the sauce: In a small bowl, mix together all of the ingredients and reserve.

2. To water-blanch the bok choy, first remove most of the outer leaves, then quarter each head lengthwise. Wash the pieces well under running cold water to remove any sand and grit. Repeat twice, then drain well. (I have included specific washing directions here because the shape of the vegetable and its dense character can cause grit to cling.)

3. In a pot, bring the water to a boil over high heat. Add the ginger, salt, and baking soda (if using). When the water returns to a boil, add the bok choy and return to a boil. Immediately turn off the heat. Run cold water into the pot, and then drain off the water. Run cold water into the pot again, drain well, and reserve the bok choy and discard the ginger.

4. Heat a wok over high heat for 45 seconds. Add the onion oil and, using a spatula, coat the wok with the oil. When a wisp of white smoke appears, add the bok choy. Stir-fry for 4 minutes, or until hot. Make a well in the center of the bok choy, stir the sauce, and pour it into the well. Stir for 2 to 3 minutes, or until the sauce bubbles and thickens. Turn off the heat, transfer to a heated dish, and serve.

WATER-BLANCHING

Water-blanching is simply plunging foods into boiling water, an invaluable process for many cooking preparations. Why the process is used depends on what is being water-blanched. In general, boiling water helps to remove some of the water naturally present in foods. In the case of meats and poultry, it also removes blood residue. When water-blanching vegetables, I usually add ginger, salt, and baking soda, or sometimes only ginger. The baking soda helps to tenderize the vegetables and set their bright color, and the salt and ginger help to flavor them. I especially appreciate how the baking soda sets the color, and I know a number of French chefs who must appreciate it as well, as I have seen them use the same technique in their kitchens.

Bok choy, Tianjin bok choy, *choi sum*, Shanghai bok choy, fresh mushrooms, mung bean and soybean sprouts, and lettuce are among the vegetables that benefit from water-blanching to remove excess water. It also helps tenderize the stems of broccoli and cauliflower.

出水

WATER-
BLANCHING

To water-blanch vegetables, bring the water to a boil, add the ingredients—baking soda, salt, and/or ginger—specified in individual recipes, and then add the vegetable. Most vegetables are immersed in the boiling water for only seconds, then removed. Others, such as *choi sum* and pea shoots, are blanched longer because they are tougher, so check the timing in each recipe carefully. Often, to ensure there is no carryover cooking, I immediately plunge the vegetables into an ice-water bath to stop the cooking. Other times, I halt the cooking by running cold water into the pan. Which method I use depends on how long the vegetable was immersed and how it will be used. If it will be going directly into a cooking process, such as a stir-fry, I generally cool it by filling the pan with running water. I use the ice-water bath, which stops the cooking more quickly, for vegetables that will be used later or are more fully cooked during the blanching, such as the *choi sum* in the stir-fry on page 65. I drain all of the blanched vegetables well before using them.

STIR-FRIED HAIRY BEANS WITH SNOW CABBAGE

|| MAKES 6 SERVINGS ||

雪菜炒毛豆

The hairy beans in this recipe, which are actually immature soybeans, take their name from their slightly fuzzy exteriors. They serve as examples of the versatility of the soybean, which is used as a vegetable, a sauce, a curd. This recipe is my introduction to the basic soybean, which, like all stir-fried vegetables, should have bite after it is cooked. Imported from China, these hairy beans are quite tender, and are usually sold shelled and loose in 1-pound packages in the freezer section of markets. This recipe is a favorite in Shanghai, where it is customarily served as an introductory dish to a meal, to awaken the appetite. The beans are traditionally stir-fried with snow cabbage, which is sold in cans in pieces ¼ inch to 1 inch long, depending on the manufacturer.

INGREDIENTS

1 pound hairy beans (shelled young soybeans)

3 tablespoons Garlic Oil (page 56)

3 garlic cloves, lightly smashed

1½-inch-long piece ginger, unpeeled, lightly smashed

1⅓ cups well-drained snow cabbage, cut into ¼-inch pieces

¼ teaspoon salt (optional)

1. Allow the beans, if frozen, to come to room temperature. Heat a wok over high heat for 30 seconds. Add the oil and, using a spatula, coat the wok with the oil. When a wisp of white smoke appears, add the garlic and ginger and stir briefly until the garlic turns light brown. Add the beans and stir-fry for 2 minutes, or until they are very hot. Add the snow cabbage and stir-fry for 1 minute. Taste and add salt if needed. Reduce the heat to medium and stir-fry for 4 minutes, or until the beans and snow cabbage are hot and well mixed.

2. Turn off the heat, transfer to a heated dish, and serve.

CHOI SUM IN OYSTER SAUCE

‖ MAKES 4 SERVINGS ‖

There is no English equivalent for this tender, all-green vegetable, with its sweet stalks and leaves. Its name translates as "heart of the vegetable," an apt description. Like the recipes for Shanghai bok choy on page 62 and for hairy beans on page 64, I regard this recipe as an introduction to an otherwise unfamiliar vegetable, and also like those vegetables, when cooked properly, it will retain its crisp texture. *Choi sum* abounds in southern China. Its tender stalks, and the small stems at intervals up the stalk supporting tiny green leaves, are traditionally cooked with aromatic oyster sauce. Its large, tough outer leaves, and the equally tough stalk ends, must be trimmed away before stir-frying, and are often used to make soup.

1. To make the sauce: In a small bowl, mix together all of the ingredients and reserve.

2. To water-blanch the *choi sum*, first strip off the outer leaves, and then trim off the tough end of the stalk. To test the texture, stick a fingernail into the base of each stalk. It should be crisp, but the nail should penetrate.

3. In a large pot, bring the water to a boil over high heat. Add the ginger, salt, and baking soda. When the water returns to a boil, add the *choi sum* and cook for 1 minute, or until it turns bright green. Turn off the heat and immediately plunge the *choi sum* into ice water to halt the cooking. Drain well, discard the ginger, and dry the stalks.

4. Heat a wok over high heat for 30 seconds. Stir the sauce and pour it into the wok. Stir the sauce until it begins to bubble, add scallion oil, mix well, then add the *choi sum*. Stir-fry for about 2 minutes, or until the *choi sum* is hot and well coated with the sauce.

5. Turn off the heat, transfer to a heated dish, and serve.

INGREDIENTS

SAUCE

2 tablespoons oyster sauce	1 teaspoon sugar
2 tablespoons Vegetable Stock (page 53)	Pinch of salt
1 teaspoon dark soy sauce	Pinch of white pepper

2 pounds *choi sum* (to 1 pound after trimming)	2 teaspoons salt
2 quarts water	¾ teaspoon baking soda
½-inch-thick slice ginger, peeled and lightly smashed	

2 tablespoons Scallion Oil (page 56)

LONG BEANS WITH ROASTED SESAME SEEDS

|| MAKES 4 TO 6 SERVINGS ||

芝
蔴
荳
角
This recipe, like those that precede it, illustrates the textures of foods—the chewiness of the beans, the bite of the roasted sesame seeds. Sesame seeds, both white and black, are widely used in Chinese cooking for their taste, texture, and aroma. Here, they nicely complement the crispness of the beans. Long beans, which are uniquely Chinese, are basically string beans with pods that can grow up to 2 feet long. Once scarce, they are now widely available. However, if you cannot find them, string beans can be used in their place.

INGREDIENTS

1 tablespoon white sesame seeds	3 tablespoons minced shallots
2 ½ tablespoons Scallion Oil (page 56)	12 ounces long beans, or string beans, ends trimmed and cut into 2-inch lengths
½ teaspoon salt	

1. First, dry-roast the sesame seeds. Heat a wok over high heat for 20 seconds. Add the sesame seeds and stir. Reduce the heat to low and stir the sesame seeds for 1½ to 2 minutes, or until they release their aroma and become light brown. Turn off the heat, transfer the seeds to a small dish, and reserve.

2. Heat the wok over high heat for 30 seconds. Add the scallion oil and salt and, using a spatula, coat the wok with the oil. When a wisp of white smoke appears, add the shallots. Stir and cook for 2 minutes, or until the shallots release their aroma. Add the beans and stir-fry for 4 to 5 minutes. If the wok begins to dry out, dip your hand into water and sprinkle it into the wok. This will create steam and help to cook the beans. The beans are done when they become bright green.

3. Turn off the heat and transfer the beans to a heated dish. Sprinkle with the roasted sesame seeds and serve.

|| DRY-ROASTING ||

DRY-ROASTING

Dry-roasting is a simple process in which foods, such as various spices, sesame seeds, or peanuts, are placed in a dry wok over heat and roasted until they release their aroma and usually take on color. The temperature and the timing will vary with what is being dry-roasted and how it will be used. For example, sesame seeds are generally roasted for 1½ to 2 minutes over low heat, and a spice, such as Sichuan peppercorns, might be cooked longer, or not, depending on its use. Rice that will be used as a coating for meat, as in the recipe for Steamed Beef and Roasted Rice (page 186), is also dry-roasted, to draw off its moisture.

CHICKEN WITH CHICKEN LEGS

‖ MAKES 6 SERVINGS ‖

鷄肥菇炒鷄胸肉

This stir-fry demonstrates, as will others, the importance of placing food in the wok in progression from soft to hard, an order that ensures all of the ingredients will be cooked properly. The "chicken legs" in this recipe are uncommonly large (about 5 inches long and 4 to 7 inches in diameter) bulbous mushrooms shaped like chicken drumsticks and with barely visible crowns, thus their name. Believed to have originated in western China, they are now cultivated in Canada and are no longer rare in Asian markets in the United States. They have a pleasantly chewy texture and, when combined with other foods of different textures, they are indeed a treat, as you will discover in this basic stir-fry.

1. To make the marinade: In a bowl, mix together all of the ingredients. Add the chicken strips and turn to coat. Let rest for 20 minutes.

2. To make the sauce: In a small bowl, mix together all of the ingredients and reserve.

3. Heat a wok over high heat for 40 seconds. Add 2½ tablespoons of the peanut oil and, using a spatula, coat the wok with the oil. When a wisp of white smoke appears, add the ginger and salt and stir to mix for 30 seconds. Add the onions and stir to mix for 1 minute. Add the carrots and stir to mix for 30 seconds. Add the bamboo shoots and stir-fry for 1 minute. Add the water chestnuts and stir-fry for 1 minute. Add the mushroom and stir to mix for 1 minute. Turn off the heat, transfer the vegetables to a bowl, and set aside. (As you can see, this is a very rapid stir-fry, and its success depends on timing and some clock watching, rather than visible changes in color or texture. It is the kind of recipe that becomes instinctive after you have made it several times.)

INGREDIENTS

MARINADE

1 tablespoon oyster sauce	1 teaspoon white rice vinegar
1½ teaspoons light soy sauce	1 teaspoon sugar
1½ teaspoons sesame oil	¼ teaspoon salt
1½ teaspoons Shaoxing wine mixed with 1 teaspoon ginger juice (see page 70)	Pinch of white pepper
	2 teaspoons cornstarch

12 ounces boneless, skinless chicken breasts, cut into strips 2½ inches long by ¼ inch wide and ¼ inch thick

SAUCE

½ cup Chicken Stock (page 54)	1 teaspoon sesame oil
2 tablespoons oyster sauce	1 tablespoon cornstarch
1 tablespoon Shaoxing wine	1 teaspoon sugar
1 teaspoon light soy sauce	¼ teaspoon salt
1 teaspoon white rice vinegar	Pinch of white pepper

4½ tablespoons peanut oil	64 fresh water chestnuts, peeled, julienned (about ½ cup)
1½ tablespoons peeled and minced ginger	1 chicken leg mushroom (about 5 ounces), cut crosswise into ¼-inch-thick rounds, then cut into ½-inch-wide strips
Pinch of salt	
2 cups tightly packed julienned onions	
¼ cup julienned carrots	1½ tablespoons minced garlic
½ cup julienned bamboo shoots	1½ tablespoons Shaoxing wine

Continued . . .

. . . continued

4. Wipe the wok and spatula with paper towels. Heat the wok over high heat for 30 seconds. Add the remaining 2 tablespoons peanut oil and, using the spatula, coat the wok with the oil. When a wisp of white smoke appears, add the garlic and stir briefly. Add the chicken and its marinade and spread the strips in a single layer. Cook for 1 to 1½ minutes, or until the strips turn white along the edges. Turn the strips over, mix well, and stir-fry for 1 minute longer, or until they are totally white.

5. Drizzle in the wine, adding it along the edge of the wok, and mix well for about 30 seconds to finish cooking the chicken. Add the reserved vegetables and stir to mix thoroughly. Make a well in the center of the mixture, stir the sauce, and pour it into the well. Stir to mix well for 1½ to 2 minutes, or until the sauce thickens and bubbles.

6. Turn off the heat, transfer to a heated dish, and serve.

║ HOW TO MAKE GINGER JUICE ║

GINGER JUICE

Peel a piece of ginger. Using a small single-panel handheld grater, grate the ginger into a small bowl, then pass the grated ginger through a garlic press. A piece of ginger about 1¼ inches square will yield about 1 teaspoon juice.

║ HOW TO PREPARE FRESH ║ BAMBOO SHOOTS

BAMBOO SHOOTS

Most bamboo shoots are sold canned. If you find fresh shoots, they are not difficult to prepare, and the result is worth the effort. Remove all of the outer husks from each shoot until you reach the tender, cream-colored core. Place the shoots in a pot, add water to cover, and bring to a boil over high heat. Lower the heat to keep the water at a steady simmer. If the shoots are round and tender, simmer them for about 7 minutes. If they look a bit tough, simmer them for up to 20 minutes. In both cases, test them with a knife tip for tenderness. Turn off the heat, run cold water into the pot, and then drain off the water. Let the shoots cool to room temperature. Use immediately, or store in an airtight container in water to cover, changing the water daily, for up to 10 days.

STIR-FRIED CHIVES WITH SCRAMBLED EGGS

|| MAKES 4 SERVINGS ||

 I cannot emphasize enough the need for foods to complement one another in a stir-fry—or in any dish. This perfect illustration of Shanghai home cooking is quick and easy to make. When you contemplate this dish, think chewy, intensely flavored chives and fluffy, seasoned scrambled eggs. This is a traditional lunch dish, ideal for serving at a brief noon meal. Flat Chinese chives are notable for their straightforward garlic flavor, which blends well with the eggs. Be sure to dry them thoroughly before adding them to the wok.

INGREDIENTS

6 extra-large eggs

3 tablespoons peanut oil

⅜ teaspoon salt

Pinch of white pepper

2 ½ cups cut-up fresh Chinese chives (½-inch lengths)

1. In a bowl, beat the eggs with 1 tablespoon of the peanut oil, ¼ teaspoon of the salt, and the white pepper until blended. Set aside.

2. Heat a wok over high heat for 30 seconds. Add the remaining 2 tablespoons peanut oil and ⅛ teaspoon salt and, using a spatula, coat the wok with the oil. When a wisp of white smoke rises, add the chives and stir-fry for 1 to 1½ minutes, or until they turn bright green. Stir the beaten eggs, pour them into the wok, and stir-fry softly to scramble the eggs and mix them thoroughly with the chives, cooking them to your preferred doneness.

3. Turn off the heat, transfer to a heated dish, and serve.

SHREDDED PORK WITH BEAN SPROUTS

|| MAKES 4 TO 6 SERVINGS ||

Here is another recipe that illustrates how utilizing different cooking times when stir-frying ensures you will preserve the natural textures of the ingredients. The pork must cook alone for a bit, then the briefly blanched bean sprouts are added, so they emerge together, but with their individual characters intact. This is a classic example of Cantonese home cooking, a satisfying mix of textures and tastes, of marinated pork and crisp mung bean sprouts, enhanced with fried onions.

INGREDIENTS

MARINADE

2 teaspoons oyster sauce

1 teaspoon light soy sauce

1 teaspoon Shaoxing wine

1 teaspoon sesame oil

¾ teaspoon white rice vinegar

1 teaspoon mung bean starch

¾ teaspoon sugar

¼ teaspoon salt

Pinch of white pepper

4 ounces pork loin, shredded (see Cleaver discussion, page 45)

SAUCE

3 tablespoons Chicken Stock (page 54)

1 tablespoon oyster sauce

1 tablespoon Shaoxing wine

1½ teaspoons light soy sauce

1 teaspoon sesame oil

1 teaspoon white rice vinegar

1 tablespoon mung bean starch

1 teaspoon sugar

¼ teaspoon salt

Pinch of white pepper

Continued . . .

. . . continued

4 cups water	12 ounces mung bean sprouts, ends removed
1-inch-thick slice ginger, peeled and lightly smashed	
2 ½ tablespoons Onion Oil (page 56)	1 tablespoon Chicken Stock (page 54), if needed
1 tablespoon peeled and minced ginger	½ cup fried onions from Onion Oil (page 56)
2 teaspoons minced garlic	½ cup julienned red bell pepper
1 tablespoon Shaoxing wine	

1. To make the marinade: In a small bowl, mix together all of the ingredients. Add the pork and turn to coat evenly. Let rest at room temperature for 20 minutes.

2. To make the sauce: In another small bowl, mix together all of the ingredients and reserve.

3. To water-blanch the bean sprouts, in a pot, bring the water and ginger slice to a boil over high heat. Add the beans sprouts and stir for 6 seconds. Immediately turn off the heat. Run cold water into the pot, then drain off the water. Run cold water into the pot again and drain well. Discard the ginger and allow the sprouts to dry for 10 minutes.

4. Heat the wok over high heat for 30 seconds. Add the onion oil and, using a spatula, coat the wok with the oil. When a wisp of white smoke appears, add the minced ginger and stir briefly. Add the garlic and stir briefly. Add the pork and its marinade, spreading the pieces in a single layer, and cook for 1 minute. Turn the pork over and stir for 1 minute longer.

5. Drizzle in the wine, adding it along the edge of the wok, and mix well. If the pork sticks, add the stock, and mix well. Add the fried onions and stir well to mix. Add the reserved bean sprouts, mix well, and then stir to mix for 1 minute. Make a well in the center of the mixture, stir the sauce, and pour it into the well. Stir to mix well for about 1 minute, or until the sauce thickens and bubbles. Add the bell pepper, mix well, and stir-fry for 1 minute, or until well blended.

6. Turn off the heat, transfer to a heated dish, and serve.

NOTE: Mung bean sprouts have a high water content. Even after they have been water-blanched, they will produce residual liquid in the finished dish. Do not be concerned by this excess liquid.

PORK SICHUAN WITH CHILI SAUCE

|| MAKES 4 TO 6 SERVINGS ||

 This is my adaptation of a traditional Sichuan stir-fry. Customarily, this preparation is flavored with Sichuan hot bean sauce, which gives the dish its heat. I make it with my own chili sauce. The reason? Subtlety. As you eat the dish, you aren't hit with a blast of heat with each mouthful. Rather, the heat from the chili sauce accumulates and builds pleasantly on the palate.

1. To make the marinade: In a bowl, mix together all of the ingredients. Add the pork and turn to coat. Let rest at room temperature for 30 minutes.

2. To make the sauce: In a small bowl, mix together all of the ingredients and reserve.

3. Heat a wok over high heat for 30 seconds. Add 1½ tablespoons of the peanut oil and, using a spatula, coat the wok with the oil. When a wisp of white smoke appears, add the ginger and salt and stir briefly. Add the shallots, stir, lower the heat to medium, and stir-fry for 1½ to 2 minutes, or until the shallots soften. Raise the heat to high, add the red and green bell peppers, and stir to mix well. Add the water chestnuts, stir to mix, and stir-fry for 1 minute. Turn off the heat, transfer to a bowl, and reserve.

4. Wipe the wok and spatula with paper towels. Heat the wok over high heat for 20 seconds. Add the remaining 2½ tablespoons oil and, using the spatula, coat the wok with the oil. When a wisp of white smoke appears, add the garlic and stir briefly. Add the pork and its marinade and spread the pieces in a single layer. Cook for 1 minute, or until the strips turn white along the edges. Turn the pork over and mix well.

5. Drizzle in the wine, adding it along the edge of the wok, and mix well. The wine will create steam and the meat will cook immediately. Add the reserved vegetables, stir to mix well, and cook for 1 minute. Make a well in the center of the mixture, stir the sauce, and pour it into the well. Stir to mix well for about 1½ minutes, or until the sauce thickens and bubbles.

6. Turn off the heat, transfer to a heated dish, and serve.

INGREDIENTS

MARINADE

2 tablespoons peanut oil	1 teaspoon light soy sauce
1½ tablespoons egg whites, lightly beaten	1½ teaspoons cornstarch
2 teaspoons Shaoxing wine	1 teaspoon sugar
1 teaspoon white rice vinegar	¼ teaspoon salt
	⅛ teaspoon ground Sichuan peppercorns (page 37)

12 ounces pork loin, cut into strips 2 ½ inches long by ¼ inch wide and ¼ inch thick

SAUCE

⅓ cup Chicken Stock (page 54)	2 teaspoons light soy sauce
1 tablespoon oyster sauce	1½ teaspoons white rice vinegar
2 teaspoons Homemade Chili Sauce (page 58)	1½ teaspoons sesame oil
	2 teaspoons cornstarch

4 tablespoons peanut oil	1 cup julienned green bell peppers
1 tablespoon peeled and minced ginger	6 fresh water chestnuts, peeled and julienned (about ½ cup)
¼ teaspoon salt	1 tablespoon minced garlic
⅓ cup ¼-inch-dice shallots	1½ tablespoons Shaoxing wine
1 cup julienned red bell peppers	

HUNAN HOT-AND-SPICY SHRIMP

|| MAKES 4 TO 6 SERVINGS ||

 The chefs of Hunan are fond of hot oils and use them skillfully. Hot oils and hot peppers not only provide heat, but also season, balance, and complement, which are the criteria I stress when teaching this dish. These spicy-hot ingredients are particularly common in western China because many preparations are preserved, and hot pepper and oils can mask the taste that comes with preservation. The pepper flakes used to make the hot oils are even more intensely flavored than the oils.

INGREDIENTS

1 pound large shrimp
(40 count per pound)

SHRIMP COATING

2 tablespoons lightly beaten egg whites	1 tablespoon mung bean starch
2 tablespoons peanut oil	1 teaspoon sugar
2 tablespoons Shaoxing wine	½ teaspoon salt
	Pinch of white pepper

SAUCE

5 tablespoons ketchup (see facing page)	1½ teaspoons pepper flakes from Hot Pepper Oil (page 55)
1 tablespoon oyster sauce	1½ teaspoons sugar
2 teaspoons white rice vinegar	¼ teaspoon salt
2 teaspoons light soy sauce	

¼ cup peanut oil	½ cup ¼-inch-dice shallots
1 tablespoon peeled and minced ginger	1½ tablespoons Shaoxing wine
1 tablespoon minced garlic	

1. Peel the shrimp, leaving the tail segments intact, then devein and clean them (see facing page).

2. To make the shrimp coating: In a bowl, mix together all of the ingredients. Add the shrimp and turn to coat. Refrigerate for 30 minutes.

3. To make the sauce: In a small bowl, mix together all of the ingredients and reserve.

4. Heat a wok over high heat for 30 seconds. Add the peanut oil and, using a spatula, coat the wok with the oil. When a wisp of white smoke appears, add the ginger and stir briefly. Add the garlic and stir briefly. Add the shallots, stir to mix, and lower the heat to medium. Cook for 2 to 3 minutes, or until the shallots soften. Raise the heat to high, add the shrimp and their coating, and stir to mix. Spread the shrimp in a single layer and cook for 1 minute, or until the shrimp begin to turn pink. Turn the shrimp over and mix.

5. Drizzle in the wine, adding it along the edge of the wok, and mix well. Stir the sauce, pour it over the shrimp, and mix well. Stir-fry for about 1½ minutes, or until the shrimp are well-coated and the sauce begins to bubble.

6. Turn off the heat, transfer to a heated dish, and serve.

‖ HOW TO CLEAN SHRIMP ‖

This method applies to all of the frozen, thawed, or otherwise raw uncooked shrimp called for in the recipes in this book. It does not apply to live shrimp. Peel and devein the shrimp and place them in a bowl. Add salt, in a ratio of 2 teaspoons salt per 1 pound shrimp. Using your hands, mix the salt into the shrimp for 1 minute. A bubbly foam will appear on the shellfish. Pour cold water into the bowl, and rub the shrimp to rinse the salt off them. Pour off the water. Repeat the rinsing step twice, to ensure the salt is completely rinsed off. Drain the shrimp in a large strainer placed over a bowl, and then dry them with paper towels. They are now ready to use.

HOW TO CLEAN SHRIMP

KETCHUP

‖ KETCHUP IN CHINA ‖

Once a common import stocked on Asian market shelves in the United States, and now found only on occasion, Chinese ketchup is made from tomatoes, vinegar, and spices like its popular Western counterpart. Its use differs, however. In China, ketchup is used as a coloring agent, and nowadays some cooks even use tomato paste in its place. Look for Koon Yick Wan Kee brand ketchup made in Hong Kong.

Some food scholars believe that ketchup originated in China. In southern China, on the island once known as Amoy and today called Xiamen, cooks use a flavoring mixture of fish essence and soy sauce they call *keh chap,* that could be, as has been suggested, a precursor. It is a piquant thought.

CLAMS STIR-FRIED WITH BLACK BEANS

‖ MAKES 4 SERVINGS ‖

This is a familiar Cantonese classic—one that has survived its trip from China to the West relatively unscathed. Often, however, foolish shortcuts are taken. For example, the clams and sauce are cooked separately and the sauce is simply poured over them. Of course, this doesn't flavor the clams, making the method unacceptable. A fine dish like this, no matter how familiar, should be cooked properly, according to tradition, which is what is done here.

INGREDIENTS

2 quarts water	30 medium-size clams, scrubbed with a stiff brush to remove sand and grit

SAUCE

⅔ cup Chicken Stock (page 54)	1 teaspoon sesame oil
1½ tablespoons oyster sauce	1 tablespoon mung bean starch
1½ teaspoons dark soy sauce	1 teaspoon sugar
	Pinch of white pepper

3 tablespoons peanut oil	3 tablespoons fermented black beans, rinsed twice and well drained
2 tablespoons peeled and shredded ginger (see Cleaver discussion, page 45)	1 tablespoon thinly sliced fresh coriander leaves
2 tablespoons julienned garlic	1 tablespoon thinly sliced green scallion tops

---

1. Pour the water into a wok and bring to a boil over high heat. Add the clams and allow the water to return to a boil. This will take 4 to 5 minutes. The clams will begin to open. Move them about with a spatula to help the process along. As they open, remove them to a waiting dish, to prevent them from becoming tough. Continue until all of the clams have opened (discard any that do not open). Set the clams aside. Discard the water and wash and dry the wok and spatula and reserve.

2. To make the sauce: In a small bowl, mix together all of the ingredients and reserve.

3. Heat the wok over high heat for 40 seconds. Add the peanut oil and, using the spatula, coat the wok with the oil. When a wisp of white smoke appears, add the ginger, garlic, and black beans and stir to mix well for about 1 minute, or until the garlic and black beans release their fragrance. Add the clams and stir to mix for 2 minutes. Make a well in the center of the clams, stir the sauce, and pour it into the well. Stir constantly for about 2 minutes, or until the sauce thickens and the clams are thoroughly coated with the sauce.

4. Turn off the heat and transfer to a heated dish. Sprinkle with the coriander and scallion and serve.

A SIMPLE FRIED RICE

|| MAKES 6 SERVINGS ||

 Here is one of my time-honored family recipes, an everyday dish of fried rice with green peas. There will be other, more elaborate fried rice recipes as our lessons continue in Part 2, but this is the most basic use for cooked, or leftover, rice. It traditionally relies on fresh peas for its flavor, though nowadays flash-frozen peas are nearly as good as fresh. The peas, together with the seasoning mix, give an elegance to this simplest of dishes, commonly found in nearly every home, rural or urban.

This final recipe again illustrates how important it is to have all of the ingredients for a stir-fry at hand before you begin cooking so the frying can proceed without interruption. All of the ingredients for this dish can be prepared up to 3 hours in advance of cooking.

INGREDIENTS	
SAUCE	
2 tablespoons oyster sauce	1 teaspoon sugar
2 tablespoons light soy sauce	¼ teaspoon salt
1 tablespoon Shaoxing wine	Pinch of white pepper
5 cups cooked rice (page 50), at room temperature	4½ tablespoons peanut oil
	½ teaspoon salt
1 cup fresh or frozen green peas	Pinch of white pepper
2 cups water, if using fresh peas	2 teaspoons minced ginger
	2 teaspoons minced garlic
5 extra-large eggs	½ cup ¼-inch-dice shallots

1. To make the sauce: In a small bowl, mix together all of the ingredients and reserve.

2. Place the cooked rice in a bowl. Using your hands, break up any lumps and reserve.

3. If using fresh peas, pour the water into a small pot and bring to a boil over high heat. Add the peas and boil for 1 to 2 minutes, or until they are tender. Drain and reserve. If using frozen peas, allow them to thaw, then drain well and reserve.

4. In a bowl, beat the eggs with 1 tablespoon of the peanut oil, ¼ teaspoon of the salt, and the white pepper.

5. Heat a wok over high heat for 30 seconds. Add 2 tablespoons of the peanut oil and, using a spatula, coat the wok with the oil. When a wisp of white smoke appears, add the beaten eggs and scramble with the spatula for about 1½ minutes, or until medium-firm. Turn off the heat and transfer to a plate. Cut into small, coarse pieces, and reserve.

6. Wash and dry the wok and spatula. Heat the wok over high heat for 20 seconds. Add the remaining 1½ tablespoons peanut oil and, using the spatula, coat the wok with the oil. When a wisp of white smoke appears, add the ginger and stir briefly. Then add the garlic and stir briefly. Add the shallots and the remaining ¼ teaspoon salt, lower the heat to medium, and cook for 2 minutes, or until the shallots are translucent. Add the peas, raise the heat to high, and stir and cook for 2 minutes, or until very hot. Add the rice, stir to mix, then lower the heat to medium, and stir and mix for 3 minutes, or until the rice is very hot.

7. Raise the heat to high, stir the sauce, and drizzle it over the rice. Stir constantly for about 2 minutes, or until the rice is evenly coated with the sauce, about 2 minutes. Add the eggs and stir and mix for about 2 minutes, or until all of the ingredients are blended.

8. Turn off the heat, transfer to a heated dish, and serve.

LESSON 4
STEAMING

STEAMING

Steaming foods preserves their natural flavors, moistens them, restores them. Leftover foods that have shrunk expand when exposed to penetrating steam, breads become fresh, and dried-out cooked rice becomes moist and fluffy.

Steaming is, in every respect, a restorative process that makes foods glisten. It is a historic method of Chinese cooking that stretches back through the centuries to when there were no ovens and all food had to be cooked on the top of a brick stove over a wood fire, with woks as the steaming vessels.

There are two ways to steam foods in the Chinese manner. The first is traditional: About 2 quarts water is brought to a boil in a wok, and a circular bamboo steamer (see Steamers, page 45) is placed above the boiling water. A steamproof dish (tempered glass or porcelain) holding the food to be steamed is placed in the steamer (or sometimes the food is placed directly on the base of the steamer), the steamer is covered with a woven bamboo lid, and the food is steamed for a specified time.

When you put the bamboo steamer in the wok, it must be above—not touching—the water. Once you cover the steamer and begin to steam, take care to have a kettle of boiling water on hand to replenish any water that may evaporate. You can stack up to three steamers, as the boiling water will create enough steam to cook the foods in all three tiers simultaneously.

It is possible to steam in a wok without a bamboo steamer, too. Bring the water to a boil in the wok, place a large cake rack over the water, and set the heatproof dish holding the food on the rack. Cover with the wok lid and steam for the specified time.

You can steam in a tiered metal steamer (see Steamers, page 45) as well. The pot holds the boiling water, steamproof dishes holding the foods are placed on the tiers, and a lid tops the pot. To steam large foods, or foods that require long cooking, a metal clam steamer can be used the same way as a metal steamer.

I prefer bamboo steamers because I find they retain heat better. However, whichever setup you use—bamboo steamer and wok, cake rack and wok, or tiered metal steamer—the steaming times will be the same. Steel steamers are easier to care for than bamboo ones. You must brush bamboo steamers with soap and water to remove food residue and spills, then allow them to dry thoroughly before storage. Drying bamboo steamers well is essential. If they are stored wet or even damp, mold can develop.

TEMPERING

This process is as old a Chinese cooking tradition as steaming itself. Before porcelain, glass, or even Pyrex dishes can be used for steaming foods without fear of cracking, they must be tempered. Tempering can be done quickly, and it ensures long-term safety: Place a small cake rack in the wok and stack the dishes to be tempered on the rack. Pour water into the wok to cover the dishes and cover with a wok lid. Bring the water to a boil and boil for 10 minutes. Turn off the heat and let the water cool to room temperature. The dishes are now fully tempered.

TEMPERING

Once you have tempered the dishes, they do not need to be tempered again. You can even store foods in these dishes and then put them directly in the steamer.

Some observers suggest that it is not necessary to temper Pyrex dishes because the glass is tempered by definition, and this is true for Pyrex vessels that will be used in an oven. But it has been my experience, and the experience of several of my students, that Pyrex can crack during steaming. Thus, it is a good idea to temper your Pyrex dishes along with your porcelain ones to provide that measure of assurance and safety.

STEAMED BLACK MUSHROOMS

‖ MAKES 40 MUSHROOMS, OR 8 TO 10 SERVINGS ‖

Black mushrooms are highly regarded throughout China, and a dish of steamed black mushrooms is almost always offered as a symbol of honor to a respected visitor. It is traditionally eaten as a first course or as a course in a banquet of many dishes.

But these mushrooms are also one of my basic preparations. I use the mushrooms as ingredients in other recipes, such as Hunan Pearl Balls (page 193) and Braised "Pork" with Black Mushrooms (page 298). However, I also enjoy eating them as they are. Here, I prepare them the classic way, with chicken fat, but you can substitute 3 tablespoons peanut oil, though the flavor of the finished dish will not be as intense.

INGREDIENTS

40 dried black mushrooms, about 1½ inches in diameter

4 scallions, cut into 2-inch lengths

2½ ounces raw chicken fat, cut into 4 pieces

1-inch-thick slice ginger, unpeeled, lightly smashed

1 cup Chicken Stock (page 54)

2 tablespoons Shaoxing wine

1½ tablespoons double dark soy sauce

2 teaspoons sugar

¾ teaspoon salt

---

1. In a bowl, soak the mushrooms in hot water to cover for 30 minutes. Drain, rinse the mushrooms thoroughly, and then squeeze out the excess water. Remove and discard the stems and place the caps in a steamproof dish.

2. In a bowl, mix together the scallions, chicken fat, ginger, stock, wine, soy sauce, sugar, and salt. Pour the mixture over the mushrooms and toss well.

3. Place the dish in a steamer, cover, and steam for 30 minutes.

4. Turn off the heat and remove the dish from the steamer. Discard the scallions, chicken fat, and ginger, then toss the mushrooms gently in the remaining liquid. Let cool to room temperature. The mushrooms can be served at this point, preferably at slightly cooler than room temperature. Or, cover them tightly and refrigerate for 4 or 5 days. To freeze the mushrooms, transfer them and their liquid to an airtight container and freeze for up to 2 months. Thaw and allow them to come to room temperature before serving or using in another dish.

STEAMED GRASS CARP

‖ MAKES 4 TO 6 SERVINGS ‖

 Because steaming preserves the freshness and natural flavors of fish, most Chinese prefer to eat their fish steamed—particularly the city dwellers of Guangzhou and Shanghai. Fish for steaming are always bought live, which is why I buy my fish in Chinatown—where grass carp, striped bass, sea bass, and many other types are pulled still swimming from large tanks. To eat a perfectly steamed fish is to taste the sea or the pond. The grass carp, a freshwater fish also sometimes identified as buffalo fish, has a long, thick body and white flesh and steams beautifully. It can weigh as much as 8 pounds or as little as 3 pounds. I recommend against steaming the smaller whole carp because they contain many small bones. It is better to steam a fat, meaty, center-cut section from a large grass carp.

1. To make the marinade: In a small bowl, mix together all of the ingredients and reserve.

2. Make sure all of the scales and membranes have been removed from the fish, then wash and dry it well. Place the fish in a steamproof bowl and pour the marinade over it, coating it well.

3. Prepare a wok for steaming using a cake rack (see page 79). Place the dish with the fish on the rack, cover, and steam for 8 to 9 minutes, or until a chopstick slides easily into its flesh. It is then done.

4. Turn off the heat. Pour the scallion oil over the fish and sprinkle with the scallions and coriander. Remove the dish from the wok, and serve the fish in its cooking dish.

INGREDIENTS

MARINADE

2 tablespoons light soy sauce

2 tablespoons white rice wine

1½ teaspoons sesame oil

1 teaspoon white rice vinegar

2 tablespoons peeled and shredded ginger (see Cleaver discussion, page 45)

¼ teaspoon salt

Pinch of white pepper

Center-cut section from large grass carp, at least 1½ pounds

2 tablespoons Scallion Oil (page 56)

¼ cup finely sliced scallions

1½ tablespoons finely sliced fresh coriander leaves

‖ USING INFUSED OILS ‖

INFUSED OILS

My infused oils—Scallion Oil on classic steamed carp or Onion Oil on steamed sea bass—enhance both the flavor and fragrance of dishes. The custom of finishing a steamed fish with boiled peanut oil is an old one in China. My infused oils, which are also boiled, continue that tradition, but with added taste.

STEAMED SEA SCALLOPS

|| MAKES 4 TO 6 SERVINGS ||

 Scallops are common along China's eastern coast, particularly in the South China Sea off Hong Kong, where they are prized for their whiteness and their firm texture. Usually they are served steamed in their shells, with their orange roe intact. Such scallops are common in Europe, too, but are only infrequently seen in the United States. If you find scallops in their shells with their roe attached, snap them up.

INGREDIENTS

12 sea scallops, each
1 inch thick and 1½ inches
in diameter

SAUCE

2 tablespoons white
rice wine

1½ teaspoons white
rice vinegar

1½ tablespoons light
soy sauce

2 tablespoons Scallion Oil
(page 56)

1 teaspoon sesame oil

2 tablespoons minced white
portion of scallions

1 tablespoon peeled and
minced ginger

1 teaspoon sugar

Pinch of white pepper

1. Place the scallops in a steamproof dish.

2. To make the sauce: In a bowl, mix together all of the ingredients. Pour the sauce over the scallops.

3. Place the dish in a steamer, cover, and steam for 3 to 4 minutes or until the scallops become white and firm. Do not oversteam them, or they will toughen.

4. Turn off the heat, remove the dish from the steamer, and serve the scallops in their cooking dish.

STEAMED SEA BASS WITH SHREDDED PORK

║ MAKES 4 SERVINGS ║

 Sea bass, like grass carp (see page 82), are generally found swimming in the tanks of Chinatown fish markets. They are usually small because the fishmongers also sell to restaurants, which typically like to steam the larger fish. Steaming, as I have noted, is the preferred way for cooking whole live fish. But if you are unable to find a live fish, fresh flounder, sole, or red snapper will do nicely for this recipe.

INGREDIENTS

1 whole sea bass, 1½ pounds, purchased live, then cleaned by the fishmonger

MARINADE

2 tablespoons light soy sauce

2 tablespoons white rice wine

1 tablespoon peanut oil

1½ teaspoons sesame oil

1 teaspoon white rice vinegar

2 tablespoons peeled and shredded ginger (see Cleaver discussion, page 45)

¼ teaspoon salt

Pinch of white pepper

4 ounces pork loin, shredded (see Cleaver discussion, page 45)

1 tablespoon sesame oil

1 teaspoon light soy sauce

½ teaspoon sugar

2 tablespoons Onion Oil (page 56)

¼ cup finely sliced scallions

---

1. Make sure the fishmonger has removed all of the scales, gills, viscera, and membranes from the fish. Rinse the fish well inside and out, then dry well. Place in a steamproof dish.

2. To make the marinade: In a small bowl, mix together all of the ingredients. Sprinkle the marinade evenly on the inside and outside of the fish.

3. In another small bowl, mix together the pork, sesame oil, soy sauce, and sugar. Sprinkle the mixture over the fish, and let rest for 10 minutes.

4. Prepare a wok for steaming using a cake rack (see page 79). Place the dish with the fish on the rack, cover, and steam for 12 to 15 minutes, or until a chopstick slides easily into the flesh of the fish.

5. Turn off the heat. Pour the onion oil over the fish and sprinkle with the scallions. Remove the dish from the wok and serve the fish in its cooking dish.

NOTE: If a metal dish is used for holding the fish as it steams, the steaming time will be reduced by half.

LESSON 5
POACHING IN A WOK

白灼

**POACHING
IN A WOK**

Cooking with water has been a characteristic of Chinese cuisine for thousands of years. Using vessels of bronze, iron, or pottery, the Chinese have boiled, blanched, steamed, and simmered. They have cooked water-based soups, sprinkled water into hot woks to create steam to moisten foods, and plunged foods into water of varying temperatures to begin or to halt cooking.

They have also poached foods in water in a wok in both familiar and unfamiliar ways, demonstrating the unmatched versatility of this cooking vessel. I teach wok-poaching early in my classes because of the many subtleties that are easily achieved with the method. Pots are used to poach foods as well, especially smaller amounts. But the wok is preferable when you are cooking a larger amount, or when the shape and appearance of the food, such as a whole fish, is important.

Vegetables, seafood, meats, and poultry are generally poached in boiling or simmering water or stock, or sometimes in liquid to which wines or spirits are added.

Poached foods are believed to be easy to digest, and eating them, particularly vegetables, has a cooling, balancing effect on the body. In other words, it produces a yin effect, as opposed to the yang, or heat, that results when deep-fried foods are eaten. Yin versus yang—my elders preached that philosophy to me when I was young, and I continue to believe it.

Poaching can be a final cooking process, as is the case with the shrimp on the facing page, or it can be a preliminary cooking step, en route to a finished dish. Often food is poached only until it is partially cooked, then it is stir-fried or cooked by another method to completion. In this case, stock, which contributes a measure of its concentrated intensity to the food, is typically the poaching liquid.

Poaching is a simple process, but as with all aspects of Chinese cooking, precision is paramount, especially with regard to the cooking times specified in individual recipes.

LIVE SHRIMP POACHED IN ROSE PETAL DEW

|| MAKES 4 SERVINGS ||

 This delicate and elegant preparation is Chinese poaching at its best. The inherent sweetness of live shrimp is enhanced by the flavor of the rose petal liquor added to the poaching ingredients. Once rare in the United States, live shrimp are now available in many Chinese and other Asian markets and from fishmongers of quality. Live shrimp do not have to be deveined, as they are naturally clean (see note).

INGREDIENTS

DIPPING SAUCE

2½ tablespoons Vegetable Stock (page 53)	1 tablespoon Scallion Oil (page 56)
1½ tablespoons light soy sauce	1 tablespoon finely sliced scallions
1 tablespoon Mei Kuei Lu Chiew (see Wines, page 41)	

3 cups water	1 pound (about 20) large live shrimp
1-inch-thick slice ginger, peeled and lightly smashed	
3 tablespoons Mei Kuei Lu Chiew (see Wines, page 41)	

1. To make the dipping sauce: In a small bowl, mix together all of the ingredients. Divide among 4 small sauce dishes and reserve.

2. Pour the water into a wok and bring to a boil over high heat. Add the ginger and allow the water to return to a boil. Add the wine and allow the liquid to return to a boil. Add the shrimp, and allow the liquid to return to a boil. Poach the shrimp for 2 minutes, or until they curl and turn bright red. Using a Chinese strainer, remove the shrimp from the wok and hold over a bowl to allow the excess liquid to drain away.

3. Transfer to a heated dish and serve with the dipping sauce.

NOTE: This dish is best when made with live shrimp. If you cannot find them, use raw shrimp in split shells, called "easy peel" (see page 37). Devein them and clean them as directed on page 75, but do not peel away their shells. Then cook the shrimp as directed and serve with the dipping sauce.

PONG PONG POACHED CHICKEN

║ **MAKES 4 SERVINGS** ║

The name of this classic poached chicken dish—particularly popular in western China, Hunan, and Sichuan—is derived from its method of preparation. After the chicken is cooked, it is pounded with a rounded, bat-size, wooden dowel, similar to an elongated rolling pin. The chicken is struck with the stick to break its fibers. The term *pong pong* refers to the dowel, the process, and the sound the wood makes when it hits the chicken. A rolling pin can stand in for the dowel. When you see a dish described as "hacked chicken" on a menu, this is what is meant. Classically, once the fibers of the chicken are broken, the meat is hand-shredded.

1. To poach the chicken, place the chicken breasts and all of the ingredients for the poaching liquid in a wok and bring to a boil over high heat. Lower the heat to medium, cover the wok, and simmer the chicken for 25 minutes, turning the breasts over halfway through the cooking time. After 25 minutes, turn off the heat and let the chicken rest, covered, in the liquid for 15 minutes. At this point, the flesh should be white and opaque throughout when cut into with a knife. Remove the chicken from the wok and refrigerate it, covered, for 3 hours.

2. To make the sauce: As soon as you turn off the heat, remove ¼ cup of the hot poaching liquid to a bowl, add the sesame seed paste to it, and stir to dissolve. Then add the soy sauce, sesame oil, vinegar, wine, pepper oil, scallions, garlic, ginger, sugar, and salt and mix well. Reserve at room temperature.

3. Remove the chicken from the refrigerator. Remove the skin and bones from each breast (see note). Place the chicken meat on a cutting board, and hit it with a rolling pin to break down its fibers. Then, tear the meat into shreds by hand.

INGREDIENTS

2 bone-in, skin-on whole chicken breasts, 1 pound each, rinsed thoroughly and drained

POACHING LIQUID

6 cups water

4 scallions, cut in half crosswise

1-inch-thick slice ginger, peeled and lightly smashed

2 garlic cloves, peeled but left whole

1 tablespoon sugar

2 teaspoons salt

SAUCE

¼ cup poaching liquid

3 tablespoons sesame seed paste

2½ tablespoons dark soy sauce

5 teaspoons sesame oil

1½ tablespoons Chinkiang vinegar

1 tablespoon Shaoxing wine

2½ teaspoons Hot Pepper Oil (page 55)

5 tablespoons finely sliced scallions

2½ teaspoons minced garlic

2½ teaspoons peeled and minced ginger

2½ teaspoons sugar

¾ teaspoon salt

2 cups shredded iceberg lettuce

4. In a large bowl, toss the shredded chicken with the reserved sauce, coating the chicken well. Spread the shredded lettuce on a platter, mound the chicken on top, and serve.

NOTE: The skin and bones from the poached chicken breast, the remaining poaching liquid, and the poaching ingredients will provide a rich base for making a chicken soup. Return the skin and bones to the liquid in the wok, cover, leaving the lid slightly cracked, and simmer for 30 minutes. Turn off the heat, strain the liquid, and use immediately, or transfer to a container, let cool, and refrigerate for up to 5 days, or freeze for up to 3 months.

SNOW PEA SHOOTS POACHED IN CHICKEN STOCK

|| MAKES 4 TO 6 SERVINGS ||

Snow pea shoots were a delicacy in China, long before they were "discovered" by chefs in the West and subjected to all manner of unsuitable preparation. In Chinese and Asian markets, these tender shoots with their delicate tendrils have been available for years, and traditionally they were cooked with only garlic. Their pods, the more familiar snow peas, are usually included in stir-fries. I have found that the best way to prepare these slender shoots is to poach them.

INGREDIENTS

2 quarts water

½-inch-thick slice ginger, peeled and lightly smashed

1¼ pounds snow pea shoots, tough leaves and tough bottom portions of stems removed (about 1 pound after trimming)

1 tablespoon salt

¾ teaspoon baking soda (optional)

POACHING LIQUID

3 cups Chicken Stock (page 54)

½-inch-thick slice ginger, peeled and lightly smashed

½ teaspoon salt

1 tablespoon fried garlic from Garlic Oil (page 56)

2 tablespoons Garlic Oil (page 56)

---

1. To water-blanch the pea shoots, in a wok, bring the water to a boil over high heat. Add the ginger, salt, and baking soda (if using). When the water returns to a boil, add the pea shoots and blanch for 45 seconds to 1 minute, or until they turn bright green and are tender. Turn off the heat. Run cold water into the wok, then drain off the water. Run cold water into the wok again, drain well, and reserve the pea shoots and discard the ginger.

2. To poach the snow pea shoots, wash and dry the wok. Place the stock, ginger, salt, and fried garlic in the wok and bring to a boil over high heat. Add the pea shoots, stir to mix well, and allow what is now a soup to return to a boil. Add the garlic oil and stir to mix well. Lower the heat to medium and cook for 2 to 3 minutes, or until the shoots are very tender.

3. Turn off the heat and transfer the shoots and soup to a heated tureen. Serve the shoots and soup in individual bowls.

LESSON 6
CHINESE COOKING IN A POT

中式煲菜

**CHINESE
COOKING IN
A POT**

Not all of the food cooked in China is stir-fried or otherwise prepared in woks, as is often implied. Pots—large and small, shallow and deep—are used as widely in China as they are elsewhere. Historically, cooking pots in China were of cast iron, bronze, brass, or sand clay (more on the latter on page 141). Later came pots of carbon steel, and later still, pots of stainless steel dictated by the nature and size of the traditional Chinese kitchen stove.

Stoves were permanent, embedded and brick-walled, with concrete-slab tops, into which round holes of different sizes were cut. The fires beneath the holes came from burning wood or charcoal. Larger amounts of food were cooked in woks, usually of cast iron, that were nestled into the biggest holes in the stove tops. Pots were usually reserved for smaller food portions, such as for cooking rice and rice congee, for soups and stews, and for braising.

I grew up cooking in that kind of kitchen. It was not until I went to Hong Kong that I saw, and cooked on, a metal stove using steel pots. My first collection of steel pots and pans was a gift from my new in-laws on my arrival in the United States. I recall burning a few foods as I began using them, but I became used to them and quickly came to treasure them. I still have those pots, more than forty years later, and I use them.

You'll need some good-quality stainless-steel pots and a dependable cast-iron frying pan to cook some of your Chinese foods. To begin our session of cooking Chinese foods in pots, we begin, logically, with breakfast, and with that centuries-old morning food, congee, a preparation that can be as inventive as you like, as long as you prepare the basic congee properly and take no shortcuts with its accompaniment. Following this lesson, we continue our discussion of Chinese cooking in a pot with a close look at braising.

CONGEE

粥
類

Congee is generally understood to be a rice gruel, or porridge, eaten at breakfast, usually with other foods added for taste, texture, and/or interest. Historically, however, congees were made from many foods, including wheat, barley, sorghum, millet, tapioca, or even corn, sometimes mixed with rice, sometimes alone. Congees date from the Zhou Dynasty (about 1000 B.C.), when they were thick, softly cooked grain gruels, imaginatively flavored with such additions as pears, lily buds, chrysanthemums, ginger, ginseng, lotus, mint leaves, or sugarcane, as well as medicinal herbs.

Universally known by the Cantonese term as *jook*, or "soft rice," congee is considered today, as it has been for centuries, a nourishing, filling, energy-instilling breakfast for young and old, rich and poor. More often than not, it was part of my childhood breakfast. Babies are raised on it, and the elderly favor it for the ease with which it can be digested. It is so popular that hundreds of congee recipes exist, some with savories and some with sweets added. A cookbook published in Shanghai lists more than five hundred recipes for congee.

Over the years, congees have grown in popularity and esteem. Nowadays, they are no longer reserved only for breakfast, but are viewed as valued preparations of rice suitable for lunch and dinner as well. And it seems there is no limit to what can be used in a recipe, from various fish, meats, vegetables, condiments, and spices to complementary stocks.

WHITE CONGEE

白
粥

This congee, known as *bak jook* in Cantonese, is what most of China eats for breakfast. The word *bak* means white, which connotes purity. In other words, this congee arrives at the table plain, with nothing added, though some condiments are usually mixed into it at the table.

INGREDIENTS	
¼ cup short-grain rice	8 ½ cups water
½ cup glutinous rice	

1. Put both rices in a large pot, preferably nonstick, and add cold water to cover. Wash the grains by rubbing them between your palms, then pour off the water. Repeat twice, then drain the rice in a strainer.

2. Return the washed rice to the pot, add the 8½ cups water, and bring to a boil over high heat. Reduce the heat to medium-low, cover the pot, leaving the lid slightly cracked, and cook, stirring occasionally to prevent the rice from sticking to the pot, for about 50 minutes, or until the rice thickens to a porridge-like consistency.

3. Just before the congee is done, heat a tureen by pouring boiling water into it, then drain. When the congee is done, turn off the heat, pour the congee into the tureen, and serve.

Here are some typical condiments for serving with plain congee. They should be placed in separate dishes and arranged in an arc around the base of the tureen at the table.

SALTED EGGS

Salted eggs, which the Cantonese call *ham dan*, can be prepared from either duck eggs or chicken eggs. Duck eggs are bigger and have harder shells and bigger yolks. To approximate their size with chicken eggs, use jumbo eggs. The curing time for duck eggs is 30 days, and for chicken eggs is 3 to 4 weeks.

The eggs are cured in salted water. In a plastic container, stir 1½ cups salt into 2¾ cups water. Not all of the salt will dissolve. Some will remain at the bottom of the container, but the water will still be very salty. Add 10 eggs to the salt solution, making certain they are totally immersed and adding water if necessary. Place a smaller plastic container top on top of the eggs to cover them and weight them down. Cover the container tightly and keep it in a cool, dark place for the specified curing time. When the eggs are ready, the yolks will be hard, and the whites viscous. To test if the chicken eggs are ready, I remove an egg from the solution after 3 weeks and boil it for 15 minutes, then taste it to see if it has an intense salt flavor. If it doesn't, I leave the remaining chicken eggs in the salt solution for up to 1 week, the timing depending on how salty the tested egg was.

When the eggs are ready, remove them from the salt solution, place them in an egg carton or other container, and refrigerate them for future use. They will keep for at least 6 weeks. Just before serving, hard-boil the eggs, 15 minutes for chicken eggs and 20 minutes for duck eggs, then cool them by running cold water over

咸蛋

SALTED EGGS

炸花生

FRIED PEANUTS

炸麵

FRIED NOODLES

them in the pot. To serve with congee, peel them and cut into quarters.

In the past, *ham dan* were imported from China in ceramic crocks. They arrived covered with a paste of salt, water, and ashes from burnt rice husks and were cured but not cooked. During transit, their yolks became hard red-orange balls, though their whites remained viscous. These days they come packaged, six to a box, labeled "salted duck eggs," and they are cooked and hard. I do not recommend them. There are domestic versions as well, but they tend to be too salty. Make your own.

FRIED PEANUTS

Heat a wok over high heat for 40 seconds. Add 5 cups of peanut oil. When a wisp of white smoke appears, add 8 ounces (about 1½ cups) skinless raw peanuts and stir and cook them for 2 to 2½ minutes, or until they turn light brown. Turn off the heat, remove the nuts from the oil with a Chinese strainer, and rest the strainer over a bowl to allow the excess oil to drain. Serve peanuts at room temperature.

FRIED NOODLES

Brush the cornstarch dusting off 8 ounces of wonton wrappers and cut the wrappers into ½-inch-wide strips. Lift and shake the wrappers with your fingers to loosen and separate the strips. Heat a wok over high heat for 40 seconds. Add 5 cups of peanut oil. When a wisp of white smoke appears, add half of the strips, immersing them in the oil. Stir the strips to ensure they fry evenly for 1 to 1½ minutes, or until they are light brown. Remove them with a Chinese strainer and drain on paper towels. Repeat with the second half of the noodles. Serve at room temperature.

YIN AND YANG EGG CONGEE

‖ MAKES 6 TO 8 SERVINGS ‖

中國調煮實習菜譜

INGREDIENTS

4 Salted Eggs (page 93)	4½ tablespoons Garlic Oil (page 56)
4 preserved eggs (page 35)	3 scallions, finely sliced
White Congee (page 92)	
Salt, if needed	

1. Hard-boil the salted eggs as directed, then cool, peel, and cut into ½-inch dice. Peel the preserved eggs and cut into ½-inch dice. Reserve all of the eggs.

2. Meanwhile, make the congee as directed, stirring it often to prevent sticking as it thickens. After the congee has cooked for 30 minutes, add all of the eggs and stir to mix well. Cook the congee for 20 minutes longer, or until it has thickened. With the heat still on, taste the congee to see if the salt of the eggs is sufficient to flavor the congee. If not, add salt to taste.

3. Add the garlic oil and stir to mix well. Add the scallions and mix well. Turn off the heat, transfer the congee to a heated tureen, and serve.

NOTE: I prefer this congee as cooked, but you may want to add either Fried Peanuts or Fried Noodles (page 93).

PRESERVED EGG AND SHREDDED CHICKEN CONGEE

‖ MAKES 6 TO 8 SERVINGS ‖

INGREDIENTS

White Congee (page 92)	12 ounces boneless, skinless chicken breasts, cut into strips 2½ inches long by ¼ inch wide and ¼ inch thick
3 preserved eggs (page 35)	

MARINADE

1 tablespoon oyster sauce	1 teaspoon sugar
2 teaspoons light soy sauce	½ teaspoon salt
1 tablespoon Shaoxing wine	Pinch of white pepper

¼ cup finely sliced scallions	1 cup Fried Noodles (page 93)

1. Begin cooking the congee as directed in the recipe.

2. Meanwhile, peel the eggs, cut into ½-inch dice, and reserve. Place the chicken in a bowl.

3. To make the marinade: In a bowl, mix together all of the ingredients. Pour the marinade over the chicken, mix well, and let rest at room temperature while the congee cooks.

4. After the congee has cooked for 30 minutes, add the diced eggs and stir to mix well. Cook for 15 minutes longer. Raise the heat to high. Add the chicken and its marinade, stir well, and bring the congee to a boil. Turn off the heat.

5. Transfer to a heated tureen, sprinkle with the scallions, and serve with the fried noodles.

MASTERING THE ART OF CHINESE COOKING

猪
蝦
粥

PORK AND SHRIMP CONGEE

|| MAKES 6 TO 8 SERVINGS ||

INGREDIENTS

12 ounces boneless lean pork butt in a single piece

POACHING LIQUID

3 cups water

1 onion, about 8 ounces, quartered

1-inch-thick slice ginger, peeled and lightly smashed

3 scallions, cut crosswise into thirds

2 teaspoons salt

White Congee (page 92)

8 ounces (about 20) large shrimp (40 count per pound)

MARINADE

1 tablespoon Shaoxing wine

1 teaspoon light soy sauce

1 teaspoon sugar

½ teaspoon salt

Pinch of white pepper

1. To poach the pork, place the pork in a pot and add all of the poaching liquid ingredients. Cover and bring to a boil over high heat. Reduce the heat to low, adjust the lid to leave it slightly cracked, and poach the pork for 45 minutes, turning it over halfway through the cooking time. Turn off the heat, remove the pork, and discard the poaching liquid. When the pork is cool enough to be handled, cut it into julienne and reserve.

2. Meanwhile, begin cooking the congee as directed in the recipe. This will take 50 minutes. While the congee is cooking, prepare the shrimp. Clean the shrimp (see page 75) and place in a bowl.

3. To make the marinade: In a small bowl, mix together all of the ingredients. Pour the marinade over the shrimp, toss to mix, and let the shrimp rest at room temperature while the congee cooks.

4. Five minutes before the congee is ready, raise the heat to high. Add the reserved pork and stir to mix well. Allow the congee to return to a boil. Add the shrimp and their marinade and stir well to prevent sticking. Bring the congee back to a boil. When the shrimp curl and turn pink, indicating they are cooked, turn off the heat.

5. Transfer to a heated tureen and serve.

NOTE: I recommend that no prepared condiments be added to this congee, except for a bit of soy sauce and perhaps some finely sliced scallions.

RICH AND NOBLE CONGEE

‖ MAKES 4 SERVINGS ‖

 Unlike traditional congees, this congee is made with already-cooked rice. Custom dictates that this particular congee be made not only from cooked rice, but from leftover cooked rice. I am not certain about the origin of the dish, but it probably originated either in Fujian or in the neighboring Chaoshan region of eastern Guangdong, home of the Chiu Chow people (see page 218), where cooks traditionally make congees from cooked rice. The reason for its name? It was once accepted that having rice left over from a meal was evidence the family was wealthy and had plenty—that the rice was not a rice of the poor but of the rich or noble. Fanciful chefs in Hong Kong made this a congee of status.

INGREDIENTS	
4 Chinese sausages (lop cheong)	1 or 2 frozen lobster tails in the shell (about 1 pound), thawed
MARINADE	
1 tablespoon oyster sauce	1 teaspoon light soy sauce
2½ teaspoons sesame oil	1 teaspoon white rice vinegar
2 teaspoons white rice wine mixed with 1 teaspoon ginger juice (page 70)	1¼ teaspoons sugar
	Pinch of white pepper
2½ cups cooked rice, preferably leftover	1 cup water
	Salt
3 cups Chicken Stock (page 54)	

1. Place the sausages in a steamproof dish, place in a steamer, cover, and steam for 10 minutes. The sausages should become a deep red and shrink slightly. Allow the sausages to cool, then cut them into ⅓-inch dice. Reserve.

2. Shell the lobster tails, dry the meat with paper towels, and cut into ½-inch dice. Place in a bowl and reserve.

3. To make the marinade: In a small bowl, mix together all of the ingredients. Pour the marinade over the lobster, turn to coat, and reserve.

4. Place the cooked rice in a blender, add 1½ cups of the stock, and blend on low speed for 1 minute, or until the rice has a grainy consistency (called "sand" by the Chinese to describe how it should feel). Transfer the rice to a large nonstick pot. Add the remaining 1½ cups stock and the water and stir to combine well. Add the sausages and mix well. Turn on the heat to low, cover the pot, and cook for 5 minutes, stirring often to prevent sticking. Uncover the pot, raise the heat to medium, and stir for 5 to 7 minutes, or until the congee boils. Add the lobster and its marinade and mix well. Bring the congee back to a boil. Taste and adjust the seasoning with salt, if needed.

5. Turn off the heat, transfer to a heated tureen, and serve.

BRAISED MUSHROOMS IN OYSTER SAUCE

|| MAKES 40 MUSHROOMS, OR 8 TO 10 SERVINGS ||

 This mushroom preparation is a companion of sorts to my recipe for Steamed Black Mushrooms (page 81). Like the steamed mushrooms, this recipe is a basic preparation that can be eaten as is or in combination with other foods. The ideal size for these mushrooms is 1 inch in diameter, which is important because they are intensely flavored with oyster sauce and are meant to be eaten whole, rather than cut.

INGREDIENTS

40 dried black mushrooms, about 1 inch in diameter

1½ tablespoons peanut oil

1-inch-thick slice fresh ginger, peeled and lightly smashed

6 garlic cloves, peeled and lightly smashed

2 ounces raw chicken fat, cut into 4 equal pieces, or 2½ tablespoons peanut oil

3 tablespoons Shaoxing wine

4½ tablespoons oyster sauce

1 tablespoon double dark soy sauce

2 teaspoons sesame oil

2 teaspoons sugar

Pinch of white pepper

1 to 1¼ cups Chicken Stock (page 54)

Salt

1. In a bowl, soak the mushrooms in hot water to cover for 30 minutes. Drain, rinse the mushrooms thoroughly, and then squeeze out the excess water. Remove and discard the stems and reserve the caps.

2. Heat a pot over high heat for 20 seconds. Add the peanut oil and heat for 20 seconds. Add the ginger and garlic and stir until the garlic releases its fragrance. Add the reserved mushrooms and stir to mix. Add the chicken fat and stir to mix. Add the wine, mix well, and cook for 1 minute. Add the oyster sauce, soy sauce, sesame oil, sugar, and white pepper and stir together, making certain the mushrooms are well-coated. Add 1 cup of the stock, stir to mix well, and allow the mixture to come to a boil.

3. Reduce the heat to low, cover the pot, leaving the lid slightly cracked, and cook at a low simmer for 30 minutes, or until the mushrooms acquire a glaze. Stir the mixture occasionally to make certain it does not stick to the pot. If the liquid is almost absorbed, add the remaining ¼ cup stock and mix well.

4. Taste and adjust the seasoning with salt, if needed. Turn off the heat, transfer the mushrooms and their braising liquid to a heated dish, and serve. Or, let cool to room temperature, cover tightly, and refrigerate for up to 1 week. The mushrooms and their liquid can also be frozen for up to 2 months. Thaw and allow to come to room temperature before using.

|| **BRAISING** ||

BRAISING

Braising in China is similar to braising elsewhere in the world: Foods are simmered in seasoned liquids or in sauces for varying lengths of time, depending on the particular food. Cooking times for vegetables, such as for the braised mushrooms, are generally shorter than for meats. When a food is cooked gently for a relatively long time, such as braising a large cut of meat, the Chinese call the process long-cooking.

Throughout the lessons in this book, I will demonstrate various aspects of braising, from cooking mushrooms to such unusual creatures as abalone (see page 240) and sea cucumbers (see page 243) to the classic seasoned pork shoulder of Shanghai (see page 311). Cooking in a clay pot (see page 141), a traditional method of Chinese braising, will also be part of our repertoire. For now, I will introduce the process.

TIANJIN BOK CHOY WITH BRAISED MUSHROOMS

‖ MAKES 4 TO 6 SERVINGS ‖

 Tianjin bok choy, familiarly known as napa cabbage, is widely available in markets. A ubiquitous vegetable in the Chinese kitchen, it is found in dim sum dumplings, stir-fries, soups, and in cool dishes, such as this preparation. Considered a salad by the Chinese, this dish can be eaten either as the first course of a larger meal or as a main course of a small family dinner.

INGREDIENTS

1½ pounds Tianjin bok choy	2 teaspoons salt

MARINADE

3 tablespoons white rice vinegar	2 teaspoons sesame oil
2 tablespoons liquid from Braised Mushrooms in Oyster Sauce (page 98)	3 tablespoons sugar
	Pinch of white pepper

20 braised mushrooms (page 98), julienned	2 tablespoons julienned Ginger Pickle (page 57)
¼ cup julienned carrots	

1. Separate the stalks of the bok choy and cut crosswise into ¼-inch-wide pieces. Place the bok choy in a bowl, add the salt, and toss well. Let the bok choy rest for 45 minutes, then drain off the water and squeeze the bok choy pieces to rid them of any remaining moisture.

2. To make the marinade: In a large bowl, mix together all of the ingredients.

3. Add the bok choy, mushrooms, carrots, and ginger pickle to the marinade and mix thoroughly. Refrigerate for at least 6 hours, or preferably overnight to allow the flavors to blend more fully. Serve chilled.

LONG-COOKED PORK BELLY WITH PRESERVED MUSTARD

‖ **MAKES 10 SERVINGS** ‖

 This pork dish is equally well known and important in Beijing, Shanghai, Suzhou, Hangzhou, and Guangzhou and is a particular specialty of the Hakka, who are Han Chinese believed to have migrated from northern China to the south centuries ago (see page 218). It is called *meicai kourou* (or *mui choi kau yuk* in Cantonese) and involves a two-method cooking process that calls for long-cooking, or braising, followed by steaming in a wok. The cut used is pork belly (fresh bacon), which is called *wu hua rou* (or *ng far yuk* in Cantonese), literally "half meat, half fat." When it is cooked, some remarkable kitchen chemistry occurs: The fat appears to still be intact, but it has actually run out of the pork into the braising liquid, and what is left is basically an illusion. When you bite into it, it dissolves in the mouth, and the flavors of the dish combine pleasantly. There is even a version of this dish called *Dongpo rou*, named for celebrated Hangzhoua poet Su Dongpo, active during the Northern Song Dynasty (960 to 1127). This is perhaps the only occasion on record in which having one's name attached to pork belly is considered an honor.

INGREDIENTS

5 ounces preserved mustard	2 quarts water
3 pounds fresh pork belly with skin intact, in one piece	1 cup mushroom soy sauce
6 ounces sugarcane sugar, broken into small pieces	¼ cup Mei Kuei Lu Chiew (see Wines, page 41)

---

1. Separate the stalks of the preserved mustard, open the leaves, and rinse well 4 times to remove any sand and the preserving salt.

2. In a large pot, place the preserved mustard; the pork belly, skin side down; and the sugar. Pour in the water and bring to a boil over high heat. Add the mushroom soy sauce and stir well. Add the *chiew*, stir well, and allow the liquid to return to a boil. Reduce the heat to low, cover the pot, leaving the lid slightly cracked, and cook at a low simmer for 5 hours total. After the first hour, turn the pork belly over. After the second hour, turn the pork belly again. After the third hour, turn the pork belly once again, and then cook for the final 2 hours with the skin side up. At this point, the pork belly will be tender, and its fat layers will be translucent.

3. Turn off the heat and transfer the pork belly and the preserved mustard to a large plate. Allow to cool to room temperature, then cover and refrigerate for at least 8 hours, or up to overnight. Cover and refrigerate the cooking liquid.

4. Remove the preserved mustard from the plate and cut crosswise into ⅛-inch-wide strips. Arrange the mustard pieces in a bed on a steamproof dish. Cut the pork belly crosswise into ½-inch-thick slices. Assemble the slices, skin side up, on top of the mustard. Spoon 1 cup of the cooking liquid over the slices to give them a dark coating (see note).

5. Place the dish in a steamer, cover, and steam for 30 minutes. Turn off the heat, remove the dish from the steamer, and serve the pork in its cooking dish.

NOTE: The leftover sweet-and-salty cooking liquid can be used to add flavor to sauces or soups. It will keep, refrigerated, for 2 to 3 weeks.

LESSON 7
THE BARBECUE

燒
烤

**THE
BARBECUE**

In China, to barbecue is to cut meats—most often pork—in specified ways, coat them with a marinade, and then cook them over an open fire of wood or charcoal. When I was growing up in China, we seldom barbecued meats at home because we had no indoor oven. Most often, we bought meats already cooked in the market, where they were prepared in huge, wood-fired brick ovens. Only occasionally did we cook them at home, in a portable open-topped red-clay stove that stood in the open air just beyond our kitchen door. When we wanted to barbecue, we would light the coals or the wood in the portable cooker, spear marinated meats on a long metal fork, and roast or barbecue them by holding the fork over the fire. It was very tiring.

This custom gave its name to the popular dish known as *char siu* in Cantonese or *chashao* in Mandarin—literally "fork over fire"—or barbecued pork, which is made from long, wide strips of pork and is most commonly found in Guangdong and in Cantonese enclaves elsewhere. A second Cantonese phrase, *siu jeu,* is used for a whole pig roasted over a fire until the skin is crisp, glistening, and golden brown. You often see these pigs hanging in windows of Chinatown butcher shops and restaurants. If you buy a piece of one of these whole pigs, you are buying *siu juk.*

Before you begin to make barbecued pork, a word about color: Most of the barbecued pork you see hanging in shop windows and restaurants is red. Once, these meats were colored with red vegetable dye. Nowadays, they derive their color from liquid of ground red rice or from the liquid of red wet preserved bean curd, available in bottles labeled "bean curd juice." The color is for presentation only and does not affect the taste.

When I make barbecued pork, it has a slight red tinge after roasting. But this comes from a combination of soy sauce, honey, and a bit of the red wet preserved bean curd mashed with its liquid.

BARBECUED PORK

|| MAKES 10 TO 12 SERVINGS ||

 This tasty, sweet, pungent pork can be sliced and eaten hot or cold as a first course, or it can be sliced or diced and stir-fried with vegetables or noodles. It is also a popular filling for steamed or baked pork buns (pages 277 and 280).

INGREDIENTS

5 pounds boneless lean pork butt, in one piece

MARINADE

¾ cup honey

¼ cup double dark soy sauce

¼ cup light soy sauce

¼ cup hoisin sauce

3 tablespoons oyster sauce

3 tablespoons Shaoxing wine

3 cubes red wet preserved bean curd, mashed with 1½ tablespoons of its liquid

1½ teaspoons five-spice powder (see sidebar)

½ teaspoon salt

¼ teaspoon white pepper

---

1. Cut the pork along its length into strips 1½ inches wide and 2½ inches thick. With a small knife, pierce the meat at 1½-inch intervals to help tenderize it.

2. To make the marinade: In a large bowl, mix together all of the ingredients. Add the pork strips and turn to coat. Refrigerate, uncovered, for 4 hours, or cover and refrigerate overnight. Occasionally, turn the pork in the marinade.

3. If the pork has marinated overnight, it should be removed from the refrigerator 30 minutes before cooking. Preheat the broiler for 20 minutes. Line a roasting pan with heavy-duty aluminum foil. Lay the pork strips in a single layer in the pan. Pour the marinade from the bowl over the pork. Place the roasting pan under the broiler about 4 inches from the heat source. Broil, basting

the meat with the marinade 5 or 6 times and turning the meat over 4 times at even intervals over 30 to 50 minutes. If the marinade in the pan begins to dry out, add a little boiling water. To test if the pork is ready, remove 1 strip from the pan after 30 minutes and cut a slice from it to see if it is cooked through.

4. When the meat is done, turn off the broiler, remove the pan from the oven, and let the pork rest for 10 minutes. If it is to be served as is, slice the pork and serve it with some of marinade from the pan. If it is to be used at a future date, allow it to cool to room temperature, cover, and refrigerate for 4 or 5 days. It can also be frozen for up to 2 months. Allow it to thaw to room temperature before using.

|| FIVE-SPICE POWDER ||
MAKES 6 TABLESPOONS

 There are various brands of five-spice powder on the market, all of them adequate, some better than others. As with many of the Chinese basics, you will be better served if you grind your own.

FIVE-SPICE POWDER

8 eight-star anise

4 cinnamon sticks, 2½ inches long, broken into small pieces

30 whole cloves

1 teaspoon Sichuan peppercorns

2 teaspoons aniseeds

Heat a wok over high heat for 30 seconds. Add all of the spices and stir to mix together. Lower the heat to medium and dry-roast the spices for 3 to 4 minutes, or until their fragrance rises. Regulate the heat as needed to prevent burning. Turn off the heat, transfer the spices to a bowl, and let cool completely.

Pour the cooled spices into a spice grinder or a blender and process to a coarse powder. Transfer the powder to a jar with a tight-fitting lid and store at room temperature for up to 3 months.

BARBECUED PORK RIBS

|| MAKES 12 RIBS, OR 4 SERVINGS ||

 This Cantonese preparation is found, at least in name, in almost every traditional restaurant in southern China and throughout the West. It is a legacy of immigrants. In Guangdong, these ribs, like barbecued pork (see page 103), were rarely made at the home because of the absence of indoor ovens, and by habit and tradition, they are still usually purchased. They are quite simple to make, however, and easy to enjoy.

INGREDIENTS

1 rack pork spare ribs,
4 pounds (12 ribs)

MARINADE

6 tablespoons honey

2½ tablespoons hoisin sauce

2 tablespoons oyster sauce

2 tablespoons double dark
soy sauce

2 tablespoons light
soy sauce

2 tablespoons Shaoxing
wine

2 tablespoons red wet
preserved bean curd liquid
or bean curd juice

¼ teaspoon white pepper

1. To prepare the ribs, remove the flap and extra fat from the rack of ribs, then, with a sharp knife, score the ribs all over. Line a roasting pan with heavy-duty aluminum foil. Place the ribs in the pan.

2. To make the marinade: In a small bowl, mix together all of the ingredients. Pour the marinade over the ribs. Using your hands, rub the marinade into the ribs. Cover the pan and refrigerate for at least 6 hours or up to overnight, basting the ribs with the marinade from time to time. Remove from the refrigerator at least 1 hour before cooking.

3. Preheat the broiler for 20 minutes. Place the roasting pan under the broiler 4 inches from the heat source. Broil the ribs, basting them twice and turning them over twice, for 30 to 40 minutes. If the marinade in the pan begins to dry out, add a little boiling water to it. To test for doneness, pierce the thickest part of the rib rack. If there is no redness, the ribs are done.

4. Turn off the heat, remove the pan from the oven, and let the spareribs cool for 10 minutes before cutting. Transfer the rack to a cutting board and, using a cleaver, cut between the ribs to separate. Serve immediately, with the basting sauce in the pan as an accompaniment.

BARBECUED PORK WITH LEEKS

|| MAKES 4 SERVINGS ||

大蒜炒义燒 In the past, I made this stir-fry with barbecued pork and garlic shoots, the sweet, mild green shoots that grow out of garlic bulbs. In recent years, these have become scarce, and I have used Chinese chive flowers and scallions in their place. But I now find that I prefer Western leeks, which look like oversized scallions, have a tender sweetness similar to that of garlic shoots, and are widely available. They are also far more tender than their Chinese counterparts, which have large bulbs and are quite tough. This recipe is a favorite of mine and an excellent illustration of barbecued pork as an ingredient.

INGREDIENTS

1½ pounds leeks

3 tablespoons peanut oil

1 tablespoon peeled and minced ginger

1¼ cups thinly sliced Barbecued Pork (page 103)

1½ tablespoons Shaoxing wine

3 tablespoons basting sauce from Barbecued Pork

1. Remove the tough outer leaves of the leeks and wash the leeks thoroughly to remove any sand and grit. Cut on the diagonal into ¼-inch-thick slices, using both the white and the tender green portions. You should have about 2 cups. Reserve.

2. Heat a wok over high heat for 45 seconds. Add the peanut oil and, using a spatula, coat the wok with the oil. When a wisp of white smoke appears, add the ginger and stir briefly. Add the pork and cook, stirring, for 1 minute, or until very hot. Drizzle in the wine, adding it along the edge of the wok, and mix well. Add the pork sauce and stir until well mixed. Add the reserved leeks and cook, stirring, for 2 minutes, or until the leeks are tender.

3. Turn off the heat, transfer to a heated dish, and serve.

LESSON 8
GOOD SOUPS

湯類

GOOD
SOUPS

In China, soups are nourishment and medicine, one-pot meals for a family and individual tonics. They can be—and are—made with almost anything available: chicken and bitter almonds; vegetables and meats, shrimp, fish, or snake meat; shark's fins; bean curd; noodles; duck feet and fungi; or the carefully assembled dried concoctions of herbalists. The Chinese believe that some soups cool in the summer and others give warmth in the winter.

In general, soups regularly perform different functions than they do in the West. A large tureen of soup is typically placed in the center of a family dinner table and eaten as an accompaniment to the other dishes that make up the meal, rather than as a separate course. Also, soup is never served at the beginning of a meal. Nor is it served at the beginning of a banquet or feast, as it might be in the West, because the host does not want to fill up her or his guests with liquid before a special meal. Rather, a soup is served at the midpoint of the banquet as a palate cleanser, quite like a sorbet.

Soups in China are always based on rich stocks. Even in the times before refrigeration, stocks were made in the morning from bones, innards, fats, and vegetable cuttings to flavor foods that night. These days, refrigeration permits stocks to be made in quantity and frozen for later use, a practice of which I am a disciple. Nothing makes a fine soup like a fine stock. I also borrow from the wisdom of herbalists and use boxthorn seeds, dried dates, and dates cooked in sugar in my stocks and soups.

A soup of fish heads cooked with not-quite-ripe papaya is said to increase the amount and quality of a nursing mother's milk. Soups made from the dried meat of litchi-like longans, also known as dragon eyes, are thought to adjust a person's internal balance. Seaweed in a soup cools the eater, and long-cooked black chicken soup warms. Bird's nest soup will keep your complexion flawless. Soups are even prescribed.

Singapore is home to a famous restaurant at which you stop by the desk of the resident physician for a soup prescription before you head to your table. Closer to my home, when my younger son has a cold, he will eat only chicken soup with a raft of beaten eggs floating on its surface. Hong Kong even has a restaurant called Ah Yee Lang Tong, or "Beautiful Soup from Number Two." The idea behind it is that if a man's wife is not providing fine soup at home, he has the right to go out for a better soup from a number two. I will leave for later discussion the question of looking elsewhere for better soups and move on to our collection here, beginning with hot and sour soup, perhaps the best known of all Chinese soups.

HOT AND SOUR SOUP

‖ MAKES 6 TO 8 SERVINGS ‖

  The roots of this soup probably rest in northern China, in the Beijing area, though it is claimed by Hunan and Sichuan equally. Traditionally, a congealed and cooked chicken-blood pudding was a prime ingredient, but over the years it has been replaced by pork. Although other variations of this classic exist, usually small whims of individual chefs, it remains essentially as it was.

INGREDIENTS

40 tiger lily buds

3 tablespoons cloud ears

5 cups Chicken Stock (page 54)

3 garlic cloves, lightly smashed

1-inch-thick slice fresh ginger, peeled and lightly smashed

½ cup julienned bamboo shoots

2 teaspoons pepper flakes from Hot Pepper Oil (page 55), more if needed

1 tablespoon Shaoxing wine

4 ounces pork loin, julienned

¼ cup red rice vinegar, more if needed

¼ cup cornstarch, mixed with ¼ cup water

3 extra-large eggs, lightly beaten

2 firm fresh bean curd cakes (8 ounces total), sliced into ¼-inch-thick strips

1½ tablespoons double dark soy sauce

1 tablespoon sesame oil

2 scallions, finely sliced

1. In a bowl, soak the tiger lily buds in hot water to cover for 30 minutes, or until soft. Drain, rinse well, discard the hard ends, and halve the buds crosswise.

2. In a bowl, soak the cloud ears in hot water to cover for 15 minutes, or until soft. Drain, rinse well, then break off and discard the hard ends and break the cloud ears into small pieces.

3. In a large pot, place the stock, garlic, and ginger and bring to a boil over high heat. Add the tiger lily buds, cloud ears, bamboo shoots, and pepper flakes and allow the stock to return to a boil. Add the wine, stir well, lower the heat to medium, and simmer for 10 minutes.

4. Raise the heat to high, add the pork, and stir to mix. Add the vinegar, mix well, and allow the liquid to return to a boil. Stir the cornstarch mixture, then, while stirring constantly, slowly add the mixture to the soup and continue to stir until the soup thickens. Next, slowly add the eggs while stirring constantly. Add the bean curd, stir to mix, and allow the soup to come to a boil. Add the soy sauce, stir to mix, and then stir in the sesame oil. Taste the soup for hotness and sourness and adjust it to taste with more pepper flakes and vinegar, if needed.

5. Turn off the heat and transfer to a heated tureen. Sprinkle with the scallions and serve.

SILK SQUASH AND WHITE MUSHROOM SOUP

|| MAKES 4 SERVINGS ||

 This is a perfect Cantonese summer soup. The oddly ridged gourd known as silk squash combines nicely with a wide range of vegetables, particularly in soups, where its sweetness can be appreciated. Here, it is combined only with fresh white mushrooms, which contribute their texture.

INGREDIENTS

1 silk squash, about 1¾ pounds

1¾ cups fresh white mushrooms, the size of a quarter

3 tablespoons Onion Oil (page 56)

1¼-inch-long piece ginger, peeled and lightly smashed

½ teaspoon salt

3 cups Vegetable Stock (page 53)

1½ cups water

1 tablespoon Shaoxing wine

1½ teaspoons sesame oil

1. Using a small knife, pare down the ridges along the silk squash's length, but do not remove all of the green. Then roll-cut the squash: Starting at one end, cut on the diagonal into ¾-inch-thick slices, rotating the squash one-quarter turn between each cut. The slices will resemble small ax blades. Reserve the slices.

2. Remove the stems from the mushrooms and cut the caps in half. Reserve.

3. Heat a wok over high heat for 30 seconds. Add the onion oil and, using a spatula, coat the wok with the oil. When a wisp of white smoke appears, add the ginger and salt and stir for 30 seconds. Add the squash and the mushrooms and stir-fry for 2 minutes, or until the squash softens. Turn off the heat.

4. Transfer the squash and mushrooms to a large pot, and add the stock and water. Cover and bring to a boil over high heat. Uncover, add the wine, and stir to mix. Lower the heat to medium and cook, uncovered, for 5 minutes, or until the squash is tender. Add the sesame oil and stir to mix.

5. Turn off the heat, transfer to a heated tureen, and serve.

TOMATO, BEAN CURD, AND CHICKEN LEG MUSHROOM SOUP

|| MAKES 6 SERVINGS ||

雞
脾
蕃
茄
湯

People are often surprised when I mention how plentiful tomatoes are in China, particularly in the south. This immigrant from the West to Guangdong—where it is called either *fon keh* (literally "foreign eggplant") or *jing jee jeh* (literally "gold corn tangerine")—was familiar to me when I was growing up. Our family regularly ate tomatoes in soups, braised with fish, stir-fried with beef, and in stews with pork. In Hong Kong, the tomato is ubiquitous. Meaty chicken leg mushrooms add a fine texture to this pleasantly tart soup.

INGREDIENTS

1 pound tomatoes	¾ teaspoon salt
4 cups boiling water	¼ cup ¼-inch-dice shallots
4 firm fresh bean curd cakes (1 pound total), frozen (see note)	4½ cups Chicken Stock (page 54)
1 fresh chicken leg mushroom (about 5 ounces)	2 tablespoons ⅛-inch-dice salted turnips
2 tablespoons Garlic Oil (page 56)	⅛ teaspoon white peppercorns
½-inch-thick piece ginger, peeled and lightly smashed	½ cup finely sliced scallions

1. Place the tomatoes in a large heatproof bowl and pour the boiling water over them. Let them rest for 1 to 2 minutes. Pour off the hot water and run cold water into the bowl. The tomato skins will loosen. Remove the tomatoes to a cutting board and discard the water in the bowl. Peel the tomatoes and cut them into ½-inch pieces. As you cut them, return any of their liquid to the bowl. Reserve the tomatoes and liquid separately.

2. Remove the bean curd from the freezer and allow it to thaw for 30 minutes. Cut each cake along its length into julienne ⅓ inch thick and wide. Reserve.

3. Cut the mushroom crosswise into ¼-inch-thick rounds, then cut each round into ¼-inch-wide strips.

4. Heat a large pot over high heat for 20 seconds. Add the garlic oil, ginger, and salt and stir for 20 seconds. Add the shallots, stir, and lower the heat to medium. Cook the shallots, stirring with a wooden spoon, for 2 to 3 minutes, or until they soften. Raise the heat to high, add the tomatoes, and mix well. Cook uncovered, stirring occasionally, for 5 minutes, or until the tomatoes begin to soften and break apart.

5. Add the stock and mix well. Then add the tomato liquid, mix well, and bring to a boil. Lower the heat to medium, and allow the tomatoes to cook for 5 minutes, or until they are very soft. Add the turnips, mix well, and cook for 1 minute. Raise the heat to high. Add the bean curd and peppercorns, stir, and bring to a boil. Add the mushroom strips, stir well, and allow the soup to return to a boil. Turn off the heat immediately.

6. Transfer to a heated tureen, sprinkle with the scallions, and serve.

NOTE: When you freeze bean curd and then thaw it, it develops a spongy, chewy consistency very different from the texture of fresh bean curd. This bit of clever artifice is a relatively new practice among chefs in Hong Kong, where the bean curd is a popular addition to hot pots. I like it in soups as well—not all soups, but certainly this one. To freeze the bean curd, drain, rinse, pat dry, place in a plastic bag, and freeze for 24 hours. Before using, allow it to thaw for 30 minutes, at which point it can be easily sliced.

FRESH BEAN CURD AND GREEN PEA SOUP

|| MAKES 4 TO 6 SERVINGS ||

I have nicknamed this delightful, light summer soup "red, green, and white soup" because of its green peas, white bean curd, and the carrots, which though orange, are called red turnips in China.

INGREDIENTS

¼ cup Scallion Oil (page 56)	2 tablespoons Shaoxing wine
1 tablespoon peeled and minced ginger	5 ½ cups Vegetable Stock (page 53)
1 teaspoon salt	4 fresh firm bean curd cakes (1 pound total), cut into ⅓-inch dice
2 carrots, cut into ⅓-inch dice (1 cup)	
1 ½ cups fresh or thawed frozen green peas	

1. Heat a large pot over high heat for 30 seconds. Add the scallion oil, ginger, and salt and stir briefly. Add the carrots and stir for 1 minute. Add the peas, mix, then add the wine and stir well. Add the stock, stir to blend all of the ingredients, and bring to a boil. Allow the soup to cook, uncovered, for 1 minute. Add the bean curd, stir to mix well, and bring back to a boil. Cook for 2 more minutes.

2. Turn off the heat, transfer to a heated tureen, and serve.

SHRIMP AND GINGER SOUP

|| MAKES 6 SERVINGS ||

I am proud of this simple but elegant soup. Several years ago in Singapore, I was entered in a cooking achievement competition, and I was asked to make soup for the 450 diners who would be attending the awards banquet. This is the soup I devised. It was, and is, an uncomplicated recipe, but with a fine mingling of the assertive flavor of a large amount of ginger with the shrimp. By the way, I won the competition, a lifetime achievement award. I think my soup helped.

INGREDIENTS

12 ounces extra-large shrimp, 18 shrimp (24 count)	1 cup water
5 tablespoons Shaoxing wine	2½-inch-long piece ginger, peeled and lightly smashed
⅛ teaspoon white pepper	2 scallions, cut on the diagonal into ¼-inch-thick pieces
6 cups Chicken Stock (page 54)	

1. Peel and devein the shrimp, leaving the tail segments intact, then clean them (see page 75). Transfer the shrimp to a bowl, add 2 tablespoons of the wine and the white pepper, and toss to coat the shrimp evenly. Allow the shrimp to marinate for 30 minutes.

2. While the shrimp are marinating, place the stock, water, and ginger in a large pot and bring to a boil over high heat. Lower the heat to medium, cover the pot, leaving the lid slightly cracked, and simmer for 30 minutes. Uncover, raise the heat to high, add the remaining 3 tablespoons wine, and allow the soup to return to a boil. Add the shrimp and their marinade and stir well, then stir in the scallions. When the shrimp turn pink and begin to curl, after 1 minute or less, the soup is ready.

3. Turn off the heat, transfer to a heated tureen, and serve.

LESSON 9
MAKING SENSE OF NOODLES

MAKING SENSE OF NOODLES

There is no place in China without its noodles—boiled, steamed, fried, or tossed. Historically, wheat-flour noodles were as important to Beijing and northern China as rice was to the south. But as the planting and consumption of rice spread northward, the importance of wheat moved to the south. Now, all of China loves noodles, both wheat and rice.

Many variations on the noodle, made from both wheat and rice flours, exist in China. Flour is *fen*, wheat flour is *mian fen,* and noodles made from wheat-flour doughs are known collectively as *mian* in Mandarin and *mein* in Cantonese. These noodles are either fresh or dried, of varied widths, and their doughs are made with water only or also with eggs. Dried shrimp eggs are added to the dough for some dried wheat noodles, and so-called milk noodles are made from wheat dough to which milk is added.

Noodles are also made from rice-flour doughs. Rice flour is known as *mifen* in Mandarin and *mai fun* in Cantonese, but noodles from rice-flour doughs are inexplicably called *fen* in Mandarin and *fun* in Cantonese. Rice noodles are also available fresh and dried and in varying widths. Very fine dried rice noodles are often called rice sticks.

Some noodles are fashioned from processed vegetables, such as mung beans and sweet potatoes, rather than from traditional doughs, though there is a debate over whether they ought to be considered noodles at all. In fact, they are often referred to as vegetable flours. However, in China, noodles are treated democratically. Packaged dried and resembling linguine, mung bean noodles need only be soaked in hot water before using. Noodles made from sweet potato starch must be boiled for about 5 minutes before using.

Italian pastas of particular sizes and widths can usually be substituted for Chinese wheat noodles, and I have provided examples in the descriptions that follow. But I have found that traditional Chinese noodles are widely available.

蛋麵 **EGG NOODLES.** These are made from wheat flour, eggs, water, and occasionally salt and are sold fresh, dried, parboiled, and prefried.

FRESH. Stocked in the refrigerated section of Chinese grocery stores, these pliable noodles are sold in 1-pound plastic sacks. They are pale yellow and come in various sizes that are equivalent to capellini no. 11, vermicelli no. 10, spaghetti no. 8, and linguine no. 17. They will keep in the refrigerator for 2 days or in the freezer for up to 3 months.

DRIED. These come in plastic or cellophane 1-pound packages and in boxes ranging from 2 to 5 pounds. Their sizes correspond to those of fresh noodles. Dried noodles will keep, well sealed, at room temperature for up to 6 months.

PARBOILED. Some people consider these fresh, but they have actually been boiled and are labeled "precooked." They are pliable, the size of spaghetti no. 8, have a thin oil sheen, and can be used right out of the package, with no preparation, usually for cold noodle dishes. There

are also thinner precooked noodles, the size of capellini no. 11, that are used in panfried dishes.

PREFRIED. These egg noodles, which come sized like spaghetti no. 6 and spaghetti no. 8, are sold in 6-ounce plastic packs, with two packs to each box. Although they appear dried, they have been fried briefly, then bent into circular bundles before they stiffen. They must be boiled to soften before use.

 EGGLESS NOODLES. These are made from wheat flour, water, and occasionally salt and are sold fresh and dried.

FRESH. Pliable and usually cream-colored, these noodles are sold in 1-pound plastic sacks and come in sizes similar to spaghetti no. 10 and linguine no. 17. They are stocked in the refrigerated section of Chinese groceries and are often labeled "Shanghai noodles." They can be refrigerated for 2 days or frozen for up to 3 months. As they cook, they develop a pleasing firmness and resist softening in sauce.

DRIED. Also creamy white and packed in 1-pound packages, these noodles come in sizes ranging from capellini no. 11 to linguine no. 17. They are usually labeled "creamy Chinese-style noodles" or "Shanghai Chinese-style noodles." They will keep, well sealed, at room temperature, for up to 6 months.

 RICE NOODLES. These noodles, made from rice flour and water, come both fresh and dried.

FRESH. This fresh rice noodle comes not in strands, but in rectangular sheets, about 18 by 2 inches and each weighing about 14 ounces. The sheets, which are pliable because they have been steamed, are usually sold only in Chinatown, in bean curd factories where they are made. They are rarely sold in grocery stores because their shelf life is short. When looking for them, ask for them by their Cantonese name, *sah hor fun,* or "sand river noodle," so-called for their slightly rough texture. The sheets are snowy white, have a shiny, glistening surface (they have been brushed with oil), and are folded when you buy them. You must cut them yourself to the size desired. Ideally, they are used the same day you purchase them. If necessary, they will keep in the refrigerator for about 3 days, but they will harden. To use them for wrapping foods, you must first steam them back to softness. If you will be stir-frying them or adding them to soups, they can be used as they are from the refrigerator, and brought to room temperature, though they will take a bit longer to cook. You can also freeze the fresh sheets for up to 2 months. Thaw them and allow them to return to room temperature before using.

You can also buy fresh rice noodles in strands in 1-pound packs similar to the size of spaghetti no. 8 and as hand-rolled tubular noodles, about 3½ inches long.

DRIED. These come in various sizes from roughly equivalent to capellini no. 11 (sometimes called rice sticks) and linguine no. 17 to wider noodles the size of fettuccine. To use, they are either soaked in hot water for about 20 minutes, or they are boiled for 45 seconds, or until they soften. They are also deep-fried.

THE WONDERFUL WONTON

|| MAKES 40 WONTONS, OR 10 SERVINGS ||

最佳美雲吞

There is no English equivalent to the noodle known as wonton. It translates literally as "swallow clouds," and when made properly, the description is apt. It is important to know that the wonton is a noodle, not a dumpling, as is often supposed. Years ago, wontons were served only in noodle shops, never in restaurants or dim sum parlors. Over time, the wonton, because of its form, mistakenly came to be regarded as a dumpling. It remains a filled noodle, and a very versatile one at that. When it is boiled, as in this recipe, it can be eaten as is or it can be added to soups, its most popular use. It is even combined in soups with other noodles. One such dish combines wontons and a historical noodle from Guangdong known as *jook sing mee,* or "bamboo stick noodles," in soup, which you will learn more about later.

When making wontons, the wrappers, or skins, should remain refrigerated until 1 hour before use. If the wrappers have been frozen, thaw them and let them come to room temperature before using.

INGREDIENTS

DIPPING SAUCE

2 tablespoons light soy sauce	2 teaspoons sugar
3 tablespoons Chicken Stock (page 54)	3 tablespoons finely sliced scallions
1½ teaspoons white rice vinegar	Pinch of white pepper

FILLING

12 ounces coarsely ground pork	1½ tablespoons oyster sauce
6 ounces shrimp, cleaned (see page 75), cut in half lengthwise and then into ½-inch pieces	1½ teaspoons light soy sauce
	1 teaspoon sesame oil
5 scallions, finely sliced	¼ cup cornstarch
1 tablespoon minced garlic	1½ teaspoons sugar
3 fresh water chestnuts, peeled and finely diced	1 teaspoon salt
	Pinch of white pepper
2 teaspoons white rice wine, mixed with 1 teaspoon ginger juice (page 70)	1 jumbo egg

2 tablespoons cornstarch for dusting	2 tablespoons salt
	1 tablespoon peanut oil
40 wonton wrappers	4 teaspoons sesame oil
3 quarts water	

1. To make the dipping sauce: In a small bowl, mix together all of the ingredients. Set aside to rest and allow the flavors to blend while you make and cook the wontons.

2. To make the filling: Place all of the filling ingredients in a large bowl. Using a wooden spoon or two pairs of wooden chopsticks, mix the ingredients together, stirring them in one direction. Stirring in this way ensures the mixture will become a cohesive filling. Cover and refrigerate for at least 6 hours or up to overnight. The longer the filling is refrigerated, the firmer it will become and the easier it will be to work with. Do not, however, refrigerate longer than overnight.

3. Dust a baking sheet with cornstarch. Have a small bowl of water at hand. Place the stack of wonton wrappers on the work surface and cover with a damp cloth. Work with only 1 wrapper at a time and keep the rest covered, or they will dry out and become brittle and unusable. Hold a wrapper in one hand and place 1 tablespoon of the filling in its center. Dip a blunt butter knife into the water and dampen the edges of the wrapper. Fold the wrapper in half, creating a rectangular envelope shape. Crimp the edges of the wrapper together with a forefinger and thumb. Dampen one corner of the folded bottom edge of the wrapper, and gently pull the side ends together, overlapping the wet corner slightly with its opposite dry one. Press them together to adhere creating a bowlike shape. The folded wontons will somewhat resemble a tortellino. Repeat until you have used all of the filling and wrappers. (The more you make, the simpler they will be to make.) As the wontons are finished, place them, not touching, on the prepared baking sheet.

4. In a large pot, bring the water, salt, and peanut oil to a boil over high heat. Add half of the wontons to the pot and allow the water to return to a boil. Cook for 5 to 7 minutes, or until the wontons float to the top and their skins become slightly translucent, with the shrimp of the filling showing

pink through them. Turn off the heat, remove the wontons with a Chinese strainer, and drain them over a bowl. Then transfer them to a bowl, add 2 teaspoons of the sesame oil, and mix well to coat evenly and prevent sticking.

5. As soon as the first batch of wontons is removed from the water, return the water to a boil and cook and drain the remaining wontons the same way, then mix with the remaining 2 teaspoons sesame oil.

6. Divide the dipping sauce among individual sauce dishes. Serve the wontons warm with the dipping sauce.

HOW TO STORE WONTONS

HOW TO STORE WONTONS

If you are making wontons to eat later in soup or to panfry or deep-fry, make them as directed, but cook each batch for only 4 minutes. When you remove the wontons from the pot, plunge them into a large bowl of ice water and leave for 5 minutes, to prevent further cooking. Then drain the wontons and place in a single layer on a baking sheet lined with waxed paper and allow to dry thoroughly. They will keep, tightly covered, in the refrigerator for up to 5 days or frozen for up to 2 months.

If the wontons have been refrigerated, allow them to come to room temperature before using. If they have been frozen, thaw them and allow them to come to room temperature before using. In both cases, they will finish cooking when you add them to a soup or when you panfry or deep-fry them.

WONTON AND WHOLE CHICKEN SOUP

‖ MAKES 8 SERVINGS ‖

 This is a simple name for a grand dish. It was created a few years ago as a fad by several chefs in Hong Kong and has become a new tradition. It calls for cooking a whole chicken in water, which creates a stock to which cooked wontons, sweet Tianjin bok choy, dates, mushrooms, and other vegetables are added, yielding a one-dish feast.

INGREDIENTS

1 whole chicken, 4½ pounds, with neck and giblets	6 celery stalks, cut crosswise into thirds
2 quarts plus ½ cup water	24 small dried black mushrooms, soaked in hot water to cover for 20 minutes, drained, rinsed, squeezed dry, and stems discarded
1½ tablespoons salt	
2-inch-long piece ginger, peeled and lightly smashed	
1 pound onions, quartered	18 dried red dates, soaked in hot water to cover for 20 minutes and drained
6 cups water	2 pounds Tianjin bok choy, stalks and leaves separated and cut crosswise into ½-inch-wide pieces
½-inch-thick slice ginger, peeled and lightly smashed	
1 teaspoon salt	
¾ teaspoon baking soda (optional)	
24 cooked wontons (page 116)	Salt

1. Clean the chicken as directed on page 54 and leave to drain for 10 minutes. Reserve the neck and giblets.

2. Pour the water into a large pot. Add the salt and stir. Add the ginger, onions, celery, mushrooms, and red dates. Place the chicken, breast side up, on top, add the neck and giblets, cover the pot, and bring to a boil over medium heat. Lower the heat to a gentle boil, just a bit higher than a simmer, and leave the lid slightly cracked. Allow to cook for 30 minutes. Then turn the chicken over and cook for 45 minutes longer, or until the chicken is cooked through and tender. To test for doneness, cut into the meat near the bone to check for redness. (The thickest part of the thigh is the best place to test.) If the chicken is not ready, cook it for 10 minutes more. Turn off the heat, cover the pot, turn the chicken, breast side up, and let rest for 20 minutes.

3. While the chicken rests, water-blanch the Tianjin bok choy. In a pot, bring the water to a boil over high heat. Add the ginger, salt, and baking soda (if using). When the water returns to a boil, add the bok choy stalks and cook for 45 seconds. Then add the bok choy leaves and cook for 30 seconds longer. Immediately turn off the heat. Run cold water into the pot, then drain off the water. Run cold water into the pot again, drain well, reserve the bok choy and discard the ginger. (It is necessary to water-blanch the bok choy, or the water it naturally contains will dilute the soup.)

4. Transfer the whole chicken from the pot to a heated platter. Remove the neck and giblets from the pot and reserve. Separate the chicken meat from its frame in 2-inch pieces and reserve. Remove the mushrooms from the pot and reserve. Drain the contents of the pot through a fine-mesh strainer and discard the solids. There should be about 7 cups liquid.

Continued . . .

. . . continued

5. Return the liquid to the pot, add the reserved mushrooms, and bring to a boil over high heat. Add the wontons, stir, and allow the soup to return to a boil. Add the bok choy, stir to mix, and allow the soup to return to a boil again. Taste the soup and adjust the seasoning with salt, if needed.

6. Turn off the heat, transfer the soup to a heated tureen, and serve in individual bowls. Place the platter of chicken, with the neck and giblets, in the center of the table. Invite diners to help themselves to the chicken, adding it to the bowls of soup and eating it together with the wontons, bok choy, and mushrooms.

WONTON AND JOOK SING MEE NOODLES IN SOUP

Wontons added to soups in combination with other noodles is a tradition in Guangzhou, and the *jook sing mee,* or "bamboo stick noodles" (described in the introduction to the wonton recipe), are among the most popular additions. They take their name from how they were once made. A dough fashioned from wheat flour and eggs was flattened into a wide mass, then converted into very fine noodles (like angel hair) by a skilled maker wielding a large bamboo stick. The process was highly physical. One end of the stick was permanently attached to the end of a work table, and the maker straddled the opposite end of the table. Holding the bamboo stick with both hands, the maker jumped up and down, back and forth, rhythmically smacking the flattened dough to create the noodles.

WONTONS

These noodles got their name not only because of how they were made, but also because of how they were sold. A noodle hawker would walk through the streets of Guangzhou, late in the evening, clacking two bamboo sticks together. When I visited relatives in Guangzhou as a girl, I would listen for the bamboo noise. Everyone knew that once they heard the ticktack, their after-dinner snack was on the way. People would call out from their windows their names, their floors, and their orders, and their bowls of soup, brimming with wontons and bamboo sticks, would be delivered piping hot. For many, sleep was not possible until they had eaten their evening bowls of soup. These noodles are no longer made the same way, but they are still called bamboo sticks and are sold in 3-ounce bundles, four to a package. Look for them in the market and try this Cantonese tradition.

WONTONS IN SICHUAN

The ubiquitous wonton is also enjoyed in Sichuan, where it is known as *chao shou,* and is served as *hong you chao shou,* or "red oil *chao shou.*" The wontons

of Sichuan are identical, in all respects, to Cantonese wontons, except for how they are served: tossed with a cayenne powder-laced Red Oil (page 149).

EGGLESS NOODLES WITH BARBECUED PORK

|| MAKES 4 TO 6 SERVINGS ||

 This noodle stir-fry uses the cream-colored fresh noodles typically labeled "Shanghai noodles," a courtesy to Shanghai, where noodles made without eggs are traditional. The barbecued pork meshes beautifully with its sister ingredients, and the noodles cook to a substantial bite.

INGREDIENTS

SAUCE

½ cup Chicken Stock (page 54)

2 tablespoons light soy sauce

2 tablespoons oyster sauce

1 tablespoon Shaoxing wine

2 teaspoons sesame oil

2½ teaspoons sugar

Pinch of white pepper

2 quarts water

2 teaspoons salt

1 pound fresh eggless noodles (similar in size to linguine no.17), cut into 5-inch lengths

4 tablespoons peanut oil

1 tablespoon peeled and minced ginger

½ cup julienned onions

3 scallions, cut into 2-inch lengths, the white portions julienned, and white and green portions separated

1 cup julienned Barbecued Pork (page 103)

1. To make the sauce: In a small bowl, mix together all of the ingredients and reserve.

2. In a large pot, bring the water and salt to a boil over high heat. Add the noodles, stir well with chopsticks, and cook for 1½ minutes, or until al dente. (Test by sampling a noodle.) Turn off the heat, run cold water into the pot, then drain the noodles with a mesh strainer. Return the noodles to the pot, run cold water into the pot, and drain again, allowing the noodles to drain for 10 minutes over a bowl. Loosen the noodles with chopsticks and reserve.

3. Heat a wok over high heat for 30 seconds. Add the peanut oil and, using a spatula, coat the wok with the oil. When a wisp of white smoke appears, add the ginger and stir briefly. Add the onions and julienned white portions of the scallions. Stir and cook for 1½ minutes, or until the onions soften. Add the pork and stir to mix. Add the green portions of the scallions, mix well, and stir and cook for 30 seconds. Make a well in the center of the mixture, stir the sauce, pour it into the well, and stir together with the pork. When the sauce comes to a boil, add the noodles, and stir-fry together for 2½ to 3 minutes, or until the sauce is absorbed by the noodles.

4. Turn off the heat, transfer to a heated dish, and serve.

PANFRIED EGG NOODLES WITH PORK

|| MAKES 4 SERVINGS ||

This is a classic noodle dish of Hong Kong and Guangzhou and it depends for its success on panfrying the noodles to a golden crispness on both sides. The Cantonese call this *liang mein wong,* which means "both sides fried golden yellow." The fried noodles become the base for a stir-fried topping; when properly cooked, their crispness resists softening, even under the topping and its sauce. This is an extraordinarily popular presentation, found in virtually every restaurant, from noodle shop to elegant dining room. Yellow chives, which are simply Chinese chives that have been deprived of the sun as they grow, are preferred for this dish, but if you cannot find them, use the white portions of scallions, finely julienned, in their place.

INGREDIENTS

2 quarts water	8 ounces fresh egg noodles (slightly thicker than vermicelli no. 10)
1 tablespoon salt	

SAUCE

½ cup Chicken Stock (page 54)	1 teaspoon Shaoxing wine
2 teaspoons double dark soy sauce	1½ teaspoons mung bean starch
1 teaspoon sesame oil	1 teaspoon sugar
1 teaspoon white rice vinegar	Pinch of white pepper

MARINADE

1½ teaspoons sesame oil	1 teaspoon mung bean starch
½ teaspoon light soy sauce	1 teaspoon sugar
½ teaspoon white rice vinegar	½ teaspoon salt
½ teaspoon Shaoxing wine	Pinch of white pepper

5 ounces pork loin, shredded (see Cleaver discussion, page 45)	3 fresh water chestnuts, peeled and julienned (about ¼ cup)
6 to 7 tablespoons peanut oil	¼ cup julienned bamboo shoots
2 teaspoons peeled and minced ginger	½ cup mung bean sprouts, ends removed
2 teaspoons minced garlic	⅓ cup cut-up yellow chives (2-inch lengths)
⅓ cup diagonally cut julienned snow peas	

1. In a large pot, bring the water and salt to a boil over high heat. Add the noodles, stir well with chopsticks, and cook for 1 minute, or until they are al dente. (Test by sampling a noodle.) Turn off the heat, then drain the noodles with a mesh strainer. Return the noodles to the pot, run cold water into the pot, and drain again. Repeat one more time, allowing the noodles to dry for 1½ hours in the strainer over a bowl, turning them occasionally so they dry completely.

2. To make the sauce: In a small bowl, mix together all of the ingredients and reserve.

3. To make the marinade: In a medium bowl, mix together all of the ingredients. Add the pork and turn to coat. Let rest at room temperature.

4. Heat a 10-inch cast-iron frying pan over high heat for 40 seconds. Add 3 tablespoons of the peanut oil and tip the pan to cover the bottom evenly with the oil. When a wisp of white smoke appears, place the noodles in an even layer in the pan, covering the entire bottom. Lower the heat to medium and fry for 2 minutes. Then, while moving the pan from side to side on the burner to ensure even browning, fry for 3 minutes longer, or until golden brown and crisp on the underside. Turn off the heat.

5. Slide the noodles from the pan onto a large, flat plate. Invert a second plate on top of the noodles and invert the plates together. Remove the top plate and slide the noodles, browned side up, back into the pan. Turn on the heat to medium, and add 1 tablespoon of the peanut oil to the pan. Cook the noodles on the second side for 2 minutes. Then, while moving the pan from side to side on the

burner, cook for 3 minutes longer, or until golden brown on the second side. If the noodles begin to stick, pour an additional tablespoon of oil into the pan, but only if necessary.

6. While the noodles are cooking on the second side, stir-fry the topping. Heat a wok over high heat for 40 seconds. Add 2 tablespoons of the peanut oil and, using a spatula, coat the wok with the oil. When a wisp of white smoke appears, add the ginger and garlic and stir briefly. Add the pork and its marinade and spread the pieces in a single layer. Cook for 2 minutes, or until the pieces turn white along the edges. Turn the pieces over and mix well.

7. Add the snow peas, water chestnuts, and bamboo shoots and stir-fry for 2 minutes, or until the vegetables soften slightly. Make a well in the center of the mixture, stir the sauce, and pour it into the well. Stir to mix well for 2 to 3 minutes, or until the sauce thickens and bubbles. Then add the bean sprouts and stir to mix. Turn off the heat and stir in the yellow chives.

8. Slide the browned noodles onto a heated serving plate and cut into 4 wedges. Pour the topping over the wedges and serve.

STIR-FRIED NOODLES
WITH STEAMED DRIED SCALLOPS

‖ **MAKES 4 SERVINGS** ‖

This preparation is a hallmark of many of Hong Kong's top restaurants. The dull-gold dried sea scallops are prized for their pungent taste and for the way they complement other ingredients, in this case, egg noodles. This now-classic dish was the creation of chef Chan Wing of Guangzhou, referred to by younger chefs as a master of masters. His dish illustrates Cantonese cooking at its simple, elegant best.

INGREDIENTS

4 dried scallops	2 tablespoons oyster sauce
6 cups water	1¼ teaspoons light soy sauce
1 teaspoon salt	
12 ounces fresh egg noodles (similar in size to capellini no.11)	1¼ teaspoons sugar
	½ cup 2½-inch-julienne white portion of scallions
3½ tablespoons Onion Oil (page 56)	3 ounces mung bean sprouts, ends removed
2½ tablespoons peeled and julienned ginger	

---

1. Steam the dried scallops as directed on page 83. Remove from the steamer and let cool. Shred into strands, removing any hard ends, and reserve.

2. In a large pot, bring the water and salt to a boil over high heat. Add the noodles, stir well with chopsticks, and cook for 10 seconds. Turn off the heat, run cold water into the pot, then drain the noodles with a mesh strainer. Return the noodles to the pot, run cold water into the pot, and drain again, allowing the noodles to dry for 1½ hours in the strainer over a bowl, turning them occasionally so they dry completely. With kitchen shears, cut the noodles into 1-inch lengths.

3. Heat a wok over high heat for 40 seconds. Add 2½ tablespoons of the onion oil and, using a spatula, coat the wok with the oil. When a wisp of white smoke appears, add the noodles and stir-fry for 1 minute. Lower the heat to medium and cook for 2 minutes more, or until very hot. Add the scallops, mix well, and stir and cook for 1 minute. Add the ginger, mix well, and stir and cook for 3 minutes, or until the mixture is very hot. Add the oyster sauce, soy sauce, and sugar and stir-fry for 1 minute. If the mixture is too dry and begins to stick to the wok, add the remaining 1 tablespoon oil and mix well. Add the scallions and stir to mix. Add the bean sprouts and stir-fry for 2 minutes, or until the mixture is well blended.

4. Turn off the heat, transfer to a heated dish, and serve.

SINGAPORE FRESH RICE NOODLES

‖ **MAKES 4 TO 6 SERVINGS** ‖

星洲炒河

This is a familiar way of serving fresh, elastic rice noodles, though it does not have the fame of its sister dish, Singapore noodles. The latter is a stir-fried medley of vegetables and pork, flavored with curry powder and mixed with dried rice noodles. This preparation calls for cutting a fresh rice noodle sheet (see page 115) into strips and mixing the strips with curry-flavored vegetables and pork. Both dishes made their way to China from Singapore.

INGREDIENTS

SAUCE

2½ tablespoons Chicken Stock (page 54)

1 tablespoon oyster sauce

1 tablespoon Shaoxing wine

2 teaspoons light soy sauce

1 teaspoon sugar

¼ teaspoon salt

2½ tablespoons curry powder

2⅓ tablespoons plus 1 teaspoon water

4 tablespoons peanut oil

4 teaspoons peeled and minced ginger

¼ teaspoon salt

⅓ cup peeled and julienned fresh water chestnuts

3 scallions, cut into 2-inch lengths and white portions julienned

¼ cup julienned bamboo shoots

2 teaspoons minced garlic

¾ cup julienned Barbecued Pork (page 103)

1 sheet fresh rice noodle, 14 ounces, cut into strips 6 inches long and ½ inch wide

4 ounces mung bean sprouts, ends removed

1. To make the sauce: In a small bowl, mix together all of the ingredients and reserve.

2. In another small bowl, mix together the curry powder and water to make a curry paste. Reserve.

3. Heat a wok over high heat for 30 seconds. Add 1½ tablespoons of the peanut oil and, using a spatula, coat the wok with the oil. When a wisp of white smoke appears, add 2 teaspoons of the ginger and the salt and stir briefly. Add the water chestnuts and stir briefly. Add the scallions and bamboo shoots, stir well, and cook for 2 minutes, or until the green portions of the scallions turn bright green. Turn off the heat, transfer to a dish, and reserve.

4. Wash and dry the wok and spatula. Heat the wok over high heat for 30 seconds. Add the remaining 2½ tablespoons peanut oil and, using the spatula, coat the wok with the oil. When a wisp of white smoke appears, add the remaining 2 teaspoons ginger and stir for 10 seconds. Add the garlic and stir for 10 seconds. Add the curry paste, stir to mix well, and cook for 15 seconds, or until the curry releases its aroma.

5. Stir the sauce, pour it into the wok, and mix well with the curry. Allow the mixture to come to a boil and cook for 15 seconds. Add the pork and stir to coat well. Add the rice noodle strips, stir to mix well, then lower the heat to medium. Cook, stirring, for 2 to 3 minutes, or until the rice noodles are evenly coated and uniformly yellow with the curry mixture. Add the reserved vegetables, raise the heat to high, and stir-fry for 2 minutes. Add the bean sprouts, mix well, and stir-fry for 1½ minutes, or until the whole mixture is evenly coated with the curry.

6. Turn off the heat, transfer to a heated dish, and serve.

SPINACH, SHRIMP, AND BEAN THREAD NOODLE SOUP

‖ **MAKES 4 TO 6 SERVINGS** ‖

菠
菜
蝦
粉
絲
湯

Spinach in China is called *bor chai,* or "waving vegetable," which describes its mature leaves ruffled by the wind. Here, it is combined with shrimp and bean thread noodles, which are fashioned from mung bean starch into long, hard strands that are appreciated for their smoothness after cooking.

INGREDIENTS

One 2-ounce package bean thread noodles	8 ounces (about 20) large shrimp (40 count per pound)
2 quarts water	½ teaspoon baking soda
1 tablespoon salt	1 pound spinach leaves
5 cups Chicken Stock (page 54)	3 garlic cloves, lightly smashed
1-inch-thick slice ginger, peeled and lightly smashed	1½ teaspoons salt
	¼ cup Garlic Oil (page 56)

1. In a bowl, soak the bean threads in hot water to cover for 10 minutes, or until they soften. Drain well, cut into 4-inch lengths, and reserve.

2. Clean the shrimp (see page 75) and drain well over a bowl. Reserve.

3. To water-blanch the spinach, in a pot, bring the water to a boil over high heat. Add the salt and baking soda. When the water returns to a boil, add the spinach and cook for 5 seconds, or until the leaves turn bright green. Immediately turn off the heat. Run cold water into the pot, then drain off the water. Run cold water into the pot again, drain well, and reserve the spinach.

4. In a large pot, place the stock, ginger, garlic, and salt and bring to a boil over high heat. Add the reserved spinach, stir well, and allow the stock to return to a boil. Add the garlic oil and stir to mix well. Add the reserved shrimp, stir in, and allow the soup to return to a boil. Add the bean threads, stir to mix well, and allow the soup to return to a boil once again. At this point, the shrimp will have curled and turned pink, indicating they are cooked.

5. Turn off the heat, transfer the soup to a heated tureen, and serve.

第二集

PART
2

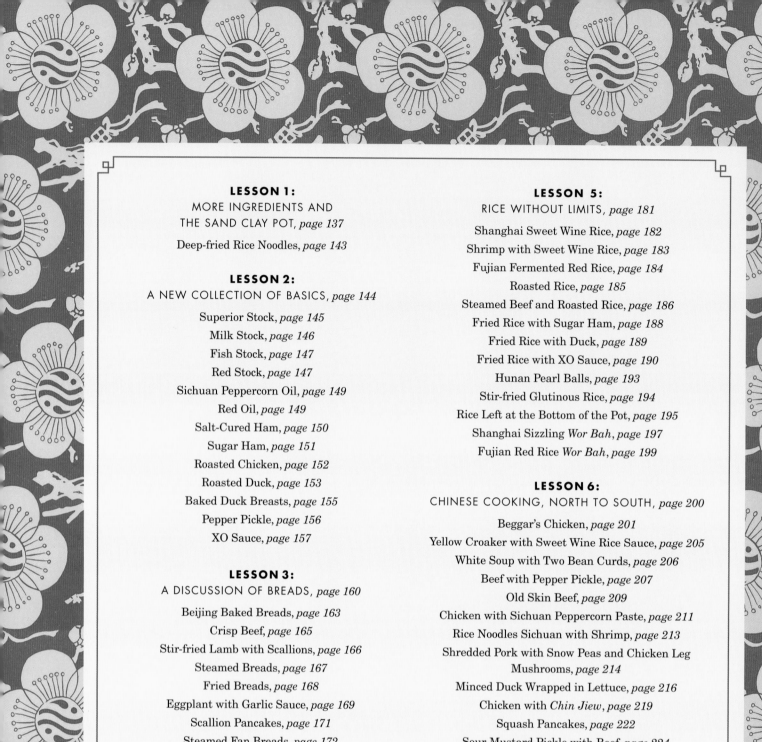

PART 2
THE MARKET BECOMES REGIONAL

Our lessons now become more advanced, more nuanced. First, we again set off to the Chinatown markets, not only to add to our storehouse of ingredients, but also to begin to learn about further subtleties in Chinese cooking. We walk the streets and the shops again, visiting, touching, and tasting, and I begin to tell my students about certain aspects of Chinese cooking that are unfamiliar to most of them. Yes, indeed, there are bread flours, and the Chinese do bake breads. They cure bacon, too, and preserve ducks in fat; use a type of bean curd that is formed into hard, brittle sticks; make sweet rice wines with yeast pills; and brine countless varieties of pickles. These traditions and many, many others are found in China's culinary regions, I explain as our studies deepen. At this point, I typically introduce the concept of regionalism within the great breadth of Chinese cooking, suggesting, in a paraphrase of Chairman Mao, that from many regions comes one cuisine. Cooking methods are essentially the same throughout China, but variations mark a dish from Sichuan, from Shanghai, from Fujian. Some of these differences are major and others are minor, but all are sufficiently significant to make the cooking of one province, one area, one city different from the others. My goal is for my students to have a thorough knowledge of Chinese cooking, of its traditions, of what makes it authentic.

Each new group of students is a recurring pleasure for me. Only a few of them come to me with prior cooking experience. With rare exceptions—very rare—I find them receptive, and my eagerness to teach is renewed. Of all of the experiences I have had, including writing, cooking on television, and consulting, teaching remains my first love. My students are varied. I have taught professors and teachers, food stylists and writers, teenagers and children, and hundreds of Chinese immigrants unfamiliar with the intricacies of their native cuisine. I recall teaching the executive of a brokerage firm in his sixties who told me that he loved Chinese

food and wanted to learn how to prepare it so he could cook for friends on his butler's day off. After just two classes, he called me one weekend morning to report with pride that, after shooing his wife from the kitchen, he prepared a multicourse Chinese banquet for eight guests.

Other students have come to my classes not knowing how to separate an egg or how to steam vegetables over boiling water. One woman confided that she never cooked, that she ate a great deal of peanut butter and jelly on toast, and could not think about looking at a live fish. Two days after her first class, she called to say that she had bought a live fish in a Chinatown market and steamed it at home. Another fellow, after a few classes, pronounced himself sufficiently confident to buy a varied collection of woks, convinced he could "cook anything." I have taught aspects of my cuisine to many well-known professional chefs and have taken my wok abroad,

teaching everywhere from England and Italy to Singapore and New Zealand.

It is insufficient, I preach, to buy yourself a wok and a bottle of soy sauce and declare yourself ready to cook in the Chinese manner. My students must learn proper techniques, respect for tradition, and some culinary history before they begin cooking. And there will be no shortcuts. Salt-baked chicken will be baked, not thrust into salted boiling water, as some restaurants do. Beggar's chicken will be made with a whole stuffed chicken, not with chicken breasts hidden in a Crock-Pot, as some restaurants do. Peking duck will be taught as tradition, not by flooding a purchased roasted duck with hoisin sauce, as some restaurants do. In other words, I teach truth, not shameful practices.

When teaching Chinese cooking in general, and the regional cooking of the country in particular, I have found that it is important to erase the prejudices and misinformation that exist about the foods of China. At this point in my classes, after marketing and cooking together, conversations are less constrained, questions are more numerous, and opinions are freer. There is curiosity without embarrassment. As my students and I walk and talk, opportunities arise to correct the many erroneous beliefs about the cooking of China that people have come to regard as true after reading them in generally respected journals, in glossy books, or on the Internet; seeing them on television; or hearing them on the radio.

Why is Sichuan cooking always so hot? It isn't. Why is everything cooked with chiles? It isn't. Many of the finest varieties of chiles in China are grown in Sichuan, and the Sichuanese are justly proud of them. It is also true that chiles are often used to mask the flavor of foods preserved by drying or salting, hallmarks of Sichuan cooking. But equally true is that a thoughtful, elegant banquet of ten courses in Sichuan, perhaps in Chengdu, may not include a single course flavored with chiles. A student comments that he read somewhere that melon balls in ginger ale is a special dish at a Chinese wedding. I respond that I have read the same account and that it is nonsense. I have seen the cooking of the cities of Suzhou and Fuzhou spoken of interchangeably, when the former is near Shanghai in east-central China, and the latter is in Fujian, perhaps a thousand miles south. I have read that in Melbourne, Australia, dim sum is cutely called *yum cha*, when that phrase is simply Cantonese for "drink tea," and not at all Australian slang. I have read that the Chinese sausages known as *lop cheong* are made in different flavors and should therefore be tasted before buying. These sausages are made from raw pork and are sold uncooked.

"Where do egg rolls come from?" I am asked. "The United States," I respond. They do not exist in China, though delicate, fingerlike spring rolls do. A well-known food writer opined that black tea is difficult to find in the United States, when all she had to do was look on any shelf, in any grocery, market, or tea shop. I have seen Chinese cookbooks, which

purport to be authentic, suggest that celery and bell peppers are substitutes for bamboo shoots; that salt can be used in place of fermented black beans; that thick, dry tortillas can replace the crepelike pancakes served with Peking duck; that a bouillon cube will make you forget your need for soy sauce; that smoked ham can be swapped for duck liver; that Italian prosciutto will stand in for the cured hams of Jinhua or Yunnan. Of course, all of these notions are pure nonsense. Yet they have been, and are, in print.

Isn't Cantonese cooking the blandest of all the regional cuisines, except when it is sweet and sour? No, it isn't. In fact, the cooking of Guangzhou—also known as Canton, its old English name—is regarded in China as the country's finest cuisine, and the most sought-after restaurants in nearly every Chinese city are Cantonese. Isn't Chiu Chow a region of Guangdong? No, the Chiu Chow, as they are known in Guangdong, are a people, not a region, with their own specialized cuisine. Why is everything swimming in oil in Shanghai? It isn't. Aren't taro cakes made with white turnips? No, they are made from taro roots. And so on.

Nor are such questions uncommon. They are posed by every class, by students who have been conditioned by restaurant reviewers and food writers to respect, and therefore like, one aspect of Chinese cooking and to dislike another. They have read that Beijing is known for its Peking duck and little else. This is wrong. They have also read that two Shanghai classics, soup buns and the oversized pork meatballs called Lions' Heads, are almost three-quarters pork fat by custom. Again, this is incorrect—indeed, it is so wrong as to destroy the tradition these two celebrated Shanghai dishes have long enjoyed.

Yet another food writer has suggested that anything north of Guangzhou should be judged northern cooking. This foolish statement is the ideal prelude to my own thoughts on how China's regional cuisines should be regarded: four different schools of a greater Chinese cooking, with each influenced primarily by local ingredients, geography, and climate.

Traditionally, northern China was, and is, rich in wheat and other grains, from which it produces breads and noodles; mutton-filled, thick-skinned dumplings; and tasty gruels as part of a warming diet for the north's often severe winters in and around Beijing and Hopei Province. The meats of the north, centered in Beijing, are lamb and mutton and, to a lesser extent, beef, the consequence of a long and traditional Muslim influence. Muslim restaurants abound in Beijing, as do others serving the specialized foods of Xianjiang, which includes roasted mutton and whole roasted goats. China's population includes a significant number of Muslims—conservatively twenty million—who live in parts of the north, but more densely in Xianjiang, Gansu, and Ningxia and to a lesser degree in Yunnan and Henan. Their gastronomic influence cannot be underestimated.

Beijing's most famous dish is Peking duck, the name by which its famed roasted duck is best known and which includes the old Western name for China's capital city. In some parts of China it is called *Beijing op.* In Beijing it is properly *Beijing kao ya,* simply translated as Beijing roasted duck, and the number of restaurants serving it is countless. Its crisp skin is served in thin pancakes or with a Beijing steamed bread, its flesh is eaten usually as a stir-fried second course, and from its bones is made a broth. This is its classic preparation.

South of Beijing and to the east, along China's lengthy seacoast, fish of many kinds are plentiful, as are crabs and all manner of seaweed, all of which find their way into the cookery of Shanghai and eastern China. The area's temperate growing season favors vegetables. Add the profound influence of the West on Shanghai and its environs during the days when foreign concessions governed much of the city, and you find the cooking of Shanghai, Suzhou, and Hangzhou is rich, eclectic, and often sweet and is distinguished by the use of the region's many wines and vinegars.

To the west, in the largely landlocked regions of Hunan and Sichuan, the land yields root vegetables, cabbages, beans, and mile after mile of soybeans. Much of the food of the west—including its meats and river fish—was, and is, preserved by smoking, drying, or salting. Chiles abound in western China, along with such other intense foodstuffs as garlic and ginger—all of which are used not only for flavor and piquancy but also to mask preservation. From Yunnan, just south of Sichuan, comes China's greatest ham, which bears its name. In Yunnan, bacon, sausages, and pork are also cured and exported elsewhere within the country.

To the south lie Guangdong and Fujian. Guangdong, best recognized for its chief city, Guangzhou, is the center of southern cooking. Its tropical weather gives it two, often three, growing seasons, and it was, and is, the center of China's massive rice production. The south is home to citrus, gourds, dates, and melons and to leafy green vegetables of all sorts. Its primary meat is pork, and poultry and eggs are plentiful. Freshness of ingredients is central to Guangdong cuisine, and the brisk stir-fry, which helps preserve that freshness, is the preferred cooking method. Longer cooking, with deeper flavors, is the hallmark of Fujian, where stews and soups are popular, where rice is cooked into a sweet puree, and where great tea plantations exist.

Spices entered China in the north along the desert routes and arrived in the south with mercantile traders in the South China Sea. This means that there is little in the way of seasonings that is not available to local Chinese cooks.

China's regional cooking has changed little over the centuries. Basically, traditions have held, despite small, occasional assaults on them from invaders waving fusion banners. But there have been changes. Today, regional boundaries and limits are not as sharp. For example, nowadays rice is as plentiful and is as widely consumed in Beijing as it is in

Guangzhou. Roasts and barbecues exist both north and south. The roasted duck of Beijing is common in the south, and roasted pork and pigs are plentiful in the north. The Cantonese dim sum parlor, once a southern institution, is dotted throughout China today. The dishes of the Hakka and Chiu Chow people of the south are now found in the north and west, and the foods of Sichuan and Hunan have spread eastward.

This shifting and broadening has increased over the years. I know the wider availability of foods, once deemed rare, has helped me to grow as a cook and a teacher. And as we walk the Chinatown streets and explore the many markets, I try to instill in my students the sense of discovery I feel when I find a new crock of fermented bean curd from Zhejiang, south of Shanghai, a bottled flavoring that according to its label comes from the Chenging Valley, near Shaoxing, just next to "The First North Bridge." Then, as we inch our way down aisles stacked with vegetables, I note that water chestnuts once came from Guilin, that Tianjin bok choy used to be grown only in the area around that northern city, that China's first potatoes sprouted in Sichuan, and that in the past the best winter melons came from Hunan. Then I tell them that all of these are now grown everywhere in China.

All of the country's once local foods are now at our fingertips: vinegars traditional to Shanxi and Shantou; German-style lagers from Qingdao, labeled Tsingtao, originally made by brewers during the foreign-concession era; fish balls that are the specialty of the Chiu Chow; loaves of coagulated blood from Fujian; a choice of peanut oils from Hong Kong or the mainland; brined snow cabbage from Shanghai; and custard tarts that originated with the Cantonese, who learned to make them in Macau. We see that China's cuisine is vast and that all of its regional parts contribute to the whole. Individual culinary regions express themselves, move restlessly into other parts of China, and readily welcome the regional cooking of others. Traditional ways of cooking the classics remain constant, however. This is what I believe, and it is what I teach.

LESSON 1
MORE INGREDIENTS AND THE SAND CLAY POT

砂煲

SAND CLAY POT

The foods we acquire at this point in our study of Chinese cooking increase the depth of the basic pantry we built in our earlier lessons, and add new, different aspects to the universal Chinese table.

BACON. Two provinces are known for their cured bacon. In Yunnan, which also produces fine salt-cured hams, bacon is known as *wu hua rou.* In Guangdong, it is called *ng far yuk.* In both, it is essentially a slab of fresh pork belly that is rubbed with an extra-thick, dark, rich pearl soy sauce and air dried to cure. It must be cooked before using and can be used as you would any bacon. It is most often added to stir-fries or cooked together with rice in such dishes as a glutinous rice stir-fry or a loaf of glutinous rice. It is also an ingredient in turnip and taro root cakes.

BEAN CURD STICKS. These "sticks" are fashioned from the sheets of bean curd milk that form on the curd as it is cooking. The pliable sheets are removed, rolled up, and allowed to dry. They are beige and do indeed look like sticks. Packaged in clear plastic, they are correctly labeled "bean curd sticks." However, they are also sometimes mislabeled "bean thread" or "dried bean thread," and their ingredients are listed as soy beans and water. This label makes them easily confused with bean thread noodles (page 29), which is yet another example of why it is best to shop with a photocopy of the proper Chinese characters.

SWEET BEAN SAUCES. This pureed sauce of soybeans typically includes sugar, maltose, garlic, sesame oil, and such ingredients as brown rice and wheat flour, depending on the manufacturer. It is similar to hoisin sauce and other thick brown sauces based on soybeans that are sweetened to varying degrees. Despite the name, sweet bean sauce is not actually all that sweet, and even has a touch of saltiness. In Cantonese it is called *tin min jeong,* and in Mandarin, *tian mian jiang,* or "sweet noodle sauce," because it is often eaten with noodles in Beijing, Shanghai, and western China. It comes in jars and cans labeled "sweet bean sauce," often with "Sichuan" added to indicate its origin. In Beijing, it is the sauce that arrives with the pancakes for Peking duck.

Another thick sauce, in terms of sweetness, is *chee hou* sauce, which originated in Guangdong. It has the same chocolate-brown color as sweet bean sauce, but is sweeter and milder and is used in steamed and braised dishes. Once opened, both this sauce and the sweet bean sauce will keep in the refrigerator for up to 6 months.

Hoisin sauce, which is discussed on page 32, accompanies Peking duck in the United States. It is sweeter than *chee hou* sauce and has vinegar and chiles added. It is used widely in Hong Kong and Shanghai to cook meats and to barbecue.

Finally, there is bean sauce (page 29), which, like hoisin sauce, was covered in our earlier ingredients list. I refer to it here because it has the same dark, thick consistency that these bean sauces have. This quartet of sauces illustrates how careful and specific you must be when shopping.

FISH SAUCE. This thin, brownish liquid—made from fish essence or extract, salt, and water—is widely used in Asia. In southern China, it is called *yue lo,* or "fish mist," and it is favored by the Chiu Chow. Essentially, it is the same as the *nam pla* of Thailand and the *nuoc mam* of Vietnam. It is widely available and comes in many brands made in China, Southeast Asia, and Taiwan. It is labeled either "fish sauce" or "fish gravy." It will keep at room temperature indefinitely.

FLOURS. Wheat flours have existed for centuries in many countries, and China is no exception. How flours perform varies according to country, climate, heat and cold, and moisture and dryness. Because flour usually does not travel well, you will not find Chinese flours in U.S. markets. What you may see are commercial Chinese flours meant mainly for restaurants. Chinese markets do stock many American brands, however. I have carefully tested all of these brands, and have come up with a selection that adapts well to Chinese doughs, steaming, and baking. Their labels read "Pillsbury Best Bread Flour, Enriched," which was once "Pillsbury Best Bread Flour, enriched, bromide, naturally white, high protein, high gluten" (the manufacturer assures me the newly labeled flour is identical to the old); "Pillsbury Best All-Purpose Flour, enriched, bleached"; and "Gold Medal All-Purpose Flour, enriched bleached."

HAM, SALT-CURED. In China, there are two salt-cured hams of note: Yunnan ham from the western province of that name, close to Sichuan and Hunan, and Jinhua ham, from the Shanghai region. Both are usually whole legs, often with the foot attached, that have been hand rubbed with salt and ground pepper, are uncooked, and are

quite hard after extensive air-drying. They are enjoyed throughout China, but neither can be imported into the United States, so the salt-cured hams of Smithfield, Virginia, are recommended in their place and are readily available in Chinatown markets. They are cloth-wrapped whole legs, minus the feet, that have been salt cured, aged, and smoked, but are uncooked. They weigh from 12 to 15 pounds, and the butt end of the leg is coated with a pepper paste. Usually they are sold whole, but trimmed slabs are sometimes available in butcher shops. If you buy a whole ham, you can ask the butcher to cut it into sections you specify. The pepper crust must be removed and the ham washed thoroughly before any primary preparation (see Salt-Cured Ham, page 150).

 LOTUS LEAVES. These large, fragrant leaves of the lotus plant are often used to wrap foods for steaming or other cooking processes and impart a faintly sweet taste to the foods they enclose. Once available only to restaurants, they can now be found in plastic packages in Chinese markets. They will keep in a cool, dry place for up to 1 year. Before using, soak them in warm water to cover until they are sufficiently pliable for wrapping.

NG GA PEI. This exceptionally strong spirit is drunk in China but is equally popular as a cooking ingredient. Made primarily in Tianjin, but also bottled elsewhere in China and in Taiwan, the sorghum-based amber spirit contains sugars and various herbs. Also known as *wu chia pi chiew,* it is typically sold in gourd-shaped crocks. It is also sometimes labeled *nga pei* or *nh ka pay.*

RED RICE. This distinctive deep red rice is used primarily as a coloring agent rather than eaten as a grain, usually in a fermented preparation called red rice that is favored by the people of Fujian and by the Chiu Chow and Hakka people of southern China and Southeast Asia. It is sold in packages labeled "red yeast rice," "yeast," or, inexplicably, "dried pearl barley." Ask for red rice.

 ROASTED RICE POWDER. This coarse powder is made from short-grain rice and Sichuan peppercorns that are dry-roasted, then ground to the consistency of breadcrumbs. It is available in boxes in Chinese and other Asian markets labeled in Chinese, except for the words "steam powder," which refers to its use. Not all markets carry it, so it is easier to make it yourself (see page 185).

 ROCK SUGAR. There are two kinds of rock sugar in China. The first, which is amber, is a compound of raw brown sugar, white sugar, and honey. The second omits the brown sugar and is crystalline white. Both are called rock sugar and are commonly used in sweet soups and in teas. They impart a more gentle sweetness than brown sugar or sugarcane sugar. I prefer the amber sugar for its subtlety. The white sugar is used in pale preparations. Both types resemble a collection of small stones and come in packages, usually weighing 14 ounces. Rock sugar should be kept in a glass jar in a cool, dry place; it will keep for at least 1 year.

 SHRIMP, DRIED. These are orange-pink shrimp that have been cooked and then salted and allowed to dry until hard. They are sold in clear plastic packages and sometimes loose by weight, and they must be soaked in warm water to cover for at least 20 minutes before using. They will keep in a tightly closed container in a cool, dry place for up to 3 months or frozen for up to 1 year. If they are tinged with gray, they have begun to lose their strength.

 SHRIMP ROE. These are the pungent, dried eggs of shrimp. They come in jars in the form of a reddish powder, and the calligraphy that identifies them translates as "babies that will become shrimp." In China, the eggs are only sun-dried before using. But the eggs exported from China are cooked first and then dried. A popular brand sold in 3-ounce jars is somewhat humorously labeled "prawn spawn." They are also sold loose by weight.

 SICHUAN MUSTARD PICKLE. Also called mustard pickle, this cured vegetable is made from *zhacai,* or "swollen stem mustard," a plant grown in Sichuan. The bulbous stem is cooked and cured with salt and powdered dried chiles and then used in stir-fries and in soups. It is sold loose by weight, but it is more often found in cans, both in its bulb form and shredded, labeled "Sichuan preserved vegetable" or "Sichuan mustard pickle"—yet another example of the need to shop with Chinese characters in hand. I prefer the pickle sold in cans. Once opened, store the unused portion in a tightly closed plastic container in the refrigerator for up to 6 months.

SOUR MUSTARD PICKLE. This traditional pickled vegetable is leafy and cabbage-like, with large, round, green-tinged bulbous stalks. The fresh vegetable, which is called leaf mustard cabbage and is strong tasting, is occasionally used in soups or in stir-fries, though it is more commonly used in its preserved form. To preserve it, the cabbage is water-blanched (see page 63), then cured with salt, sugar, and vinegar. Its heart is used as a garnish. The pickle can be bought loose by weight in packages or in cans labeled "sour mustard pickle," "sour mustard greens," or "mustard greens." If you buy the cured greens loose, they will keep in a tightly closed plastic container in the refrigerator for up to 3 months. Once a can or package is opened, you can store the unused portion the same way for the same amount of time.

WINE PILL. This is yeast in the shape of a round, hard-crusted ball, the size of a large marble. It is used in the fermentation of wine rice and red rice recipes. The balls come two to the package and are not labeled in English. Ask for Shanghai *jao ban yeun* (Shanghai wine cake pill), then show the clerk your calligraphy.

WINE RICE. This is white glutinous rice, steamed, then fermented with a wine pill. A favorite of Shanghai, it can be eaten much like a rice pudding, or it can be used to cook other dishes. It comes in jars, often labeled "wine rice sweetened," but it is best to make it yourself (page 182).

WINTER MELON. This large melon is nearly identical to a watermelon in shape, exterior color, and size. It is native to Hunan, and it is the centerpiece of a highly regarded banquet preparation throughout China. Its dark-green, mottled white rind is often ornately carved, and the soft white flesh at its center and all of its seeds are scooped out to create a tureen for steaming an elaborate soup. As the soup steams in the melon, the flesh of the melon becomes soft and translucent. The winter melon has no taste of its own, but absorbs the flavors of the foods that are cooked in it. It should be used immediately following purchase, for it tends to dry quickly, particularly when pieces are cut from the whole. It is best to buy a whole melon, but you can buy pieces by weight.

On our first marketing foray, we bought almost all of the basic cooking utensils you need to cook Chinese food traditionally and properly. The only item missing was a vessel with a pedigree that approaches that of the wok: the sand clay pot. It is not a *necessary* utensil, but it is a cook pot of tradition and history, made today as it was centuries ago, so I suggest you use it on occasion to experience the Chinese kitchen of the past.

Sand clay pots were, and are, made from coarse sandy clay. Once baked, the exterior of the pot acquires a rough beige color and the interior, because of an applied glaze, becomes a glossy deep brown. The pots have fitted lids, usually glazed, and either one or two handles, and the exterior of the bowl is banded with a steel-wire "cage" that delivers extra strength. Despite its appearance, the pot is used directly on the stove top, which is how it has been used since the time when ovens were largely non-existent in China and all foods were cooked over wood fires, in either a wok or a clay pot.

Soups, congees, stews, rice, and other long-cooked dishes were cooked in clay pots, which was the preferred vessel for the hot pot as well. The Chinese believed that foods cooked in these pots retained more flavor and fragrance than they would if they were cooked in an iron or bronze pot.

The pots came in various sizes to accommodate a variety of uses. Some of them were shaped like modern pots. Some were narrow, others bulbous; their capacities ranged from 1 quart to 3 gallons. These days, the most common—and useful—pots are about 10 inches in diameter, have a 2-quart capacity, and are outfitted with a single handle. If you wish a larger size, pots about 12 inches in diameter, with a 5-quart capacity and two handles, are also available. Both sizes have deep-brown, glazed tops and are handsome enough to go directly from the stove top to the table for serving. In fact, it is not uncommon to cook a dish in a common metal pot, then transfer the food to a sand clay pot for serving. I use the pots for some braised dishes, stews, and special rices, and I believe that certain dishes do have rounder flavors when cooked in them.

Sand clay pots can crack, as can any bowl or pot of ceramic or earthenware, which is one reason for the wire cage. Strength can also be added by tempering the pots. Before its first use, submerge the clay pot in cold water to cover for 24 hours. Remove it from the water, allow it to dry thoroughly, then fill it to the brim with cold water and bring it to a boil over medium heat. Boil the water for 30 minutes. Turn off the heat and let the water cool to room temperature. The pot is now "cured" and ready to use, and the curing process does not need to be repeated. However, if you use the pot only rarely, it is a good idea to soak it for about 1 hour before use.

A final word of caution: Never put an empty clay pot over a flame. Put whatever you are going to cook into the pot before placing it over fire.

SAND CLAY
POT

EXPANDING YOUR TECHNIQUES

At this point in my classes, in addition to clay-pot cookery, I usually introduce three more cooking techniques that we will use in the coming lessons.

STOCK-BLANCHING. Like water-blanching (see page 63), this process is designed to augment flavor and prepare foods for cooking. Briefly blanching foods in stock imparts taste to them and in some cases can reduce the amount of oil needed to cook them. The stock is placed in a wok or pot, with the amount determined by the amount of food being blanched, and brought to a boil. The food is lowered into the stock and left for the time specified in the recipe, generally less time for thinly sliced poultry or meat or for shrimp, and more time for hard vegetables, such as broccoli, cauliflower, and asparagus. The blanched food is removed, drained well, and then ready to use. The stock can be reserved for other uses, such as soups.

OIL-BLANCHING. This relatively simple technique seals in the flavor and juices of meats and retains—and enhances—the color in vegetables. Oil is poured into a wok and heated to a specific temperature, depending on the recipe. The food is lowered into the oil and left for the time indicated, usually no longer than 30 seconds for vegetables and 1 to 2 minutes for meats. It is then removed from the oil and drained well. The oil is usually, though not always, strained though a fine-mesh strainer for later use. The presence or absence of residue determines whether you need to strain or not. If any residue is visible, you must strain the oil. If no residue is visible, simply pour off the oil and reserve what you need for later use. My recipe for Shrimp with Salted Egg Yolks (page 225) is a good example of the need for straining when oil-blanching. The oil contains a good amount of residue after cooking the shrimp, and I double strain it through a fine-mesh strainer lined with a white paper towel. I also often recommend double straining oil that has been used for meats.

DEEP-FRYING. Properly deep-fried foods are cooked through and tender on the inside and lightly crusted and nicely colored on the outside. Most foods for deep-frying are first seasoned, marinated, or dipped into a batter. The temperature of the oil and its constant monitoring ensure that the taste of the deep-fried food, rather than the taste of the oil, is dominant.

When I use my wok as a deep fryer, I heat it briefly, then I pour in the amount of oil called for in the recipe, typically 4 to 6 cups. Next, I heat the oil, usually to 325°F to 375°F, depending on the recipe. The oil is heated to a temperature slightly higher than what is called for in the recipe because when food is placed in it, the temperature will immediately drop. The temperature will quickly rise again, so I use a deep-frying thermometer, which I leave in the oil, to monitor the temperature,

炸米粉 DEEP-FRIED RICE NOODLES

making sure it remains steady at the level indicated in the recipe. When you add the food to the hot oil, always slide it in along the edge of the wok to prevent splashing.

The best utensil for removing foods from hot oil is a Chinese mesh strainer. Its large capacity and strong bamboo handle are ideal for both lifting the foods from the oil and draining them. I prefer this strainer over a slotted spoon.

The following deep-fried preparation provides a perfect example of the deep-frying technique and is dramatic as well. As thin rice noodles are lowered into the oil, they expand to about four times their volume in less than 10 seconds. I demonstrate this to my classes, to what is always a chorus of oohs. It illustrates the transformative power of deep-frying better than any written explanation.

INGREDIENTS	
6 cups peanut oil	2 ounces dried thin rice noodles (rice sticks; similar in size to capellini no. 11)

1. Place the oil in a wok and heat to 350ºF on a deep-frying thermometer. When the oil is ready, carefully place the noodles in it. They will expand to four times their volume in about 8 seconds. Using a Chinese strainer, remove them from the oil and drain over a bowl.

2. This mass of fried rice noodles makes a fine garnish for various dishes, especially stir-fries. You can use the same method, delivering the same result, with bean thread noodles. The noodles can be deep-fried up to 2 days in advance of their use. Make sure they are well drained and completely cooled, then store in an airtight container at room temperature. They will remain crisp.

{ PART 2 }

LESSON 2
A NEW COLLECTION OF BASICS

加多基本實習

**A NEW
COLLECTION
OF BASICS**

Our brief drama over, it is now time to begin cooking again. Here, as in Part 1, I will start with some basics—more stocks, infused oils, condiments—that will enhance our second, and more advanced, selection of recipes. I am also including several basic preparations—two ham and three poultry recipes—that can, like the steamed and braised mushrooms (pages 81 and 98, respectively), be prepared earlier, be eaten and enjoyed as they are, or be used as harmonious ingredients in a variety of other recipes.

SUPERIOR STOCK

‖ MAKES ABOUT 4½ QUARTS ‖

上湯 The name of this stock is not simply a description of its character. No doubt you have seen on restaurant menus the phrases "cooked in superior stock" or "made with superior stock." The use of this special stock indicates that great care has been given to raising the level of flavor in a dish. The better chefs frequently use superior stock and make it in large amounts. It is so special that it is often called *seung tong,* or "best soup," in Guangzhou, where it was developed (or *shangtang* in Mandarin). It is the soup from which other soups proceed.

INGREDIENTS

8 quarts water	1 whole chicken, 5 pounds, cleaned (page 54) and quartered
4 pounds pork neck bones	
3 pounds fresh ham, with skin intact, cut into 3 equal pieces	
3½ pounds shank bone from Smithfield ham, pepper and salt coating brushed off, rinsed, and cut into 4 pieces	5 scallions, cut in half crosswise
	½ cup fried scallions from Scallion Oil (page 56)
8 ounces ginger, unpeeled, lightly smashed	4 teaspoons salt
9 quarts water	

1. To water-blanch the fresh meats, put the 8 quarts water, pork neck bones, fresh ham, and chicken in a large stockpot and bring to a boil over high heat. Allow to boil for 3 minutes, then turn off the heat. Pour off the water, run cold water into the pot to rinse off any residue on the meats, and pour off the water again. Remove the meats from the pot, wash and dry the pot, and return it to the stove top.

2. Place the blanched meats back in the pot. Add the Smithfield ham, ginger, and the 9 quarts water, cover, and bring to a boil over high heat. Reduce the heat to a gentle boil and cook for 30 minutes, checking from time to time and skimming off any residue that appears on the surface. Add the halved scallions, the fried scallions, and the salt and stir well to mix. Cover the pot, leaving the lid slightly cracked, and cook at a low boil for 5 hours, stirring occasionally to avoid sticking.

3. Turn off the heat, cover the pot, and let rest for 30 minutes. Then pour through a fine-mesh strainer into clean containers to store for later use. (See page 148 for tips on using the leftover meats.) Cover the containers and refrigerate for up to 4 days, or freeze for up to 3 months. A thin layer of fat will form on the surface of the refrigerated or frozen stock. Leave it in place until you are ready to use the stock, then skim it off with a large spoon just before using.

MILK STOCK

‖ **MAKES ABOUT 4¼ QUARTS** ‖

 Favored in Shanghai, this stock, despite its name, does not resemble white milk. Instead, it is an almond-white color. What makes it a favorite in Shanghai and elsewhere is its extraordinary richness, which makes it ideal for sauces and soups. It is also a good basic stock for anyone who prefers not to eat chicken.

INGREDIENTS

5 pounds pork feet, quartered by your butcher

3 pounds fresh ham, with skin intact, halved

13 quarts water

20 whole garlic cloves, peeled

16 scallions, white portions only (8 ounces)

1 pound onions, halved

½ teaspoon white peppercorns

2 tablespoons salt

⅓ cup Mei Kuei Lu Chiew (see Wines, page 41)

---

1. To water-blanch the meats, first, using a paring knife, scrape any impurities from the feet until they are almost white. Put the feet, ham, and 5 quarts of the water into a large stockpot and bring to a boil over high heat. Allow to boil for 2 minutes, then turn off the heat. Pour off the water, run cold water into the pot to rinse off any residue on the meats, then pour off the water again. Remove the meats from the pot, wash and dry the pot, and return it to the stove top.

2. Place the blanched meats back in the pot. Add the garlic, scallions, onions, and the remaining 8 quarts of water, stir to mix well, and bring to a boil over high heat. Reduce the heat to a gentle boil and cook for 15 minutes, checking from time to time and skimming off any residue that appears on the surface. Raise the heat to high, add the peppercorns and salt, stir to mix, and allow the liquid to return to a boil. Add the *chiew*, stir well, and again allow the liquid to return to a boil. Reduce the heat to a gentle boil, cover, leaving the lid slightly cracked, and cook for about 4½ hours, or until the skin falls off the bones of the pork feet.

3. Turn off the heat, cover the pot, and let rest for 30 minutes. Strain the stock through a fine-mesh strainer into clean containers to store for later use. (See page 148 for tips on using the leftover meats.) Cover the containers and refrigerate for up to 4 days, or freeze for up to 3 months. A thin layer of fat will form on the surface of the refrigerated or frozen stock. Leave it in place until you are ready to use the stock, then skim it off with a large spoon just before using.

FISH STOCK

‖ MAKES ABOUT 3 QUARTS ‖

 This stock was initially devised to pre-pare recipes for people who ate fish but no meats. In an effort to increase its flavor, lobster and shrimp shells and heads were added to fish parts. These gave the stock a more intense flavor, to be sure, but they also obscured the delicacy of a fish-only stock, so this recipe returns to the original.

INGREDIENTS

10 pounds fish heads and bones, washed well under cold running water

2 pounds onions, quartered

8 ounces ginger, unpeeled and lightly smashed

5 quarts cold water

6 scallions, cut in half crosswise

4 ounces fresh coriander sprigs, cut crosswise into thirds

¾ cup fried scallions from Scallion Oil (page 56)

¼ cup fried garlic from Garlic Oil (page 56)

2 teaspoons fried pepper-corns from Sichuan Peppercorn Oil (page 149)

2 tablespoons salt

½ cup white rice wine

1. In a large stockpot, place the fish heads and bones, onions, ginger, and water and bring to a boil over high heat. Reduce the heat to a gentle boil and cook for 15 minutes, checking often and skimming off any residue that appears on the surface. Add the halved scallions, cori-ander, fried scallions, fried garlic, fried peppercorns, and salt, raise the heat to high, stir to mix well, and return to a boil. Add the wine, stir well, and again allow to return to a boil. Reduce the heat to a gentle boil, cover the pot, leaving the lid slightly cracked, and cook for 3½ hours.

2. Turn off the heat, cover the pot, and let rest for 20 min-utes. Strain the stock through a fine-mesh strainer into clean containers for later use. Cover the containers and refrigerate for 2 or 3 days, or freeze for up to 3 months.

RED STOCK

‖ MAKES ABOUT 5 QUARTS ‖

 This dark, rich stock is from Hunan, where it is used widely in sauces and soups that require a deep reddish color. I also use it for recipes that do not originate in Hunan for the taste and the color it imparts.

INGREDIENTS

17 quarts water

3 pounds pork neck bones

2½ pounds fresh ham, with skin intact, halved

1 whole chicken, 5 pounds, cleaned (page 54) and quartered

1 whole duck, 4 pounds, cleaned as for chicken (page 54) and quartered

3 pounds onions, quartered

8 ounces ginger, unpeeled and lightly smashed

4 teaspoons salt

¾ cup double dark soy sauce

¾ cup Shaoxing wine

2 teaspoons fried peppercorns from Sichuan Peppercorn Oil (page 149)

1. To water-blanch the fresh meats, put 8 quarts of the water, the pork neck bones, the fresh ham, the chicken, and the duck in a large stockpot and bring to a boil over high heat. Allow to boil for 2 minutes, then turn off the heat. Pour off the water, run cold water into the pot to rinse off any residue on the meats, then pour off the water again. Remove the meats from the pot, wash and dry the pot, and return it to the stove top.

2. Place the blanched meats back in the pot. Add the remaining 9 quarts of water, onions, ginger, and salt and bring to a boil over high heat. Reduce the heat to a gentle boil and cook for 30 minutes, checking from time to time and skimming off any residue that appears on the sur-face. Raise the heat to high and allow the mixture to come to a rolling boil. Add the soy sauce, stir well, and allow to return to a boil. Add the wine, stir well, and allow to return

Continued . . .

. . . continued

to a boil again. Add the fried peppercorns and stir well to mix. Reduce the heat to a gentle boil, cover, leaving the lid slightly cracked, and cook for 4 hours, stirring occasionally to avoid sticking.

3. Turn off the heat, cover the pot, and let rest for 30 minutes. Strain the stock through a fine-mesh strainer into clean containers to store for later use. Cover the containers and refrigerate for up to 4 days, or freeze for up to 3 months. A thin layer of fat will form on the surface of the refrigerated or frozen stock. Leave it in place until you are ready to use the stock, then skim it off with a large spoon just before using.

MEATS LEFT OVER FROM MAKING STOCKS

MEATS LEFT OVER FROM MAKING STOCK

The preceding four stocks, combined with the stocks from Part 1, complete your library of stocks. In the stocks based on meats and poultry, there is a fair amount of meat left over once the stocks are made. What to do? Most of the flavor has gone from the meats to the stock. However, should you want to nibble, I suggest sprinkling a bit of salt on the meats before you begin.

Or, you can create a basic dip for the meats. In a small bowl, mix together

3 tablespoons light soy sauce

1 tablespoon sesame oil

2 teaspoons white rice vinegar

2 teaspoons sugar

3 tablespoons of the stock you have just made

Divide among 4 small sauce dishes and serve with the meats.

TWO MORE INFUSED OILS

Following are two additions to our collection of infused oils. I am sure you have noted how often I use flavored oils, and I trust that you are making, and using, them as well. Both of these come from western China, from the provinces of Sichuan and Hunan. One is mild and the other is hot.

SICHUAN PEPPERCORN OIL

‖ MAKES 1 SCANT CUP OIL AND
¼ CUP FRIED PEPPERCORNS ‖

INGREDIENTS

¼ cup Sichuan peppercorns	1 cup peanut oil

1. Heat a dry wok over high heat for 30 seconds. Add the Sichuan peppercorns and stir briefly to introduce the peppercorns to the heat. Reduce the heat to low and stir for 1½ minutes, or until the peppercorns release their fragrance. Add the peanut oil, raise the heat to medium, and bring the oil to a boil. Lower the heat until the oil is at a simmer and cook, stirring, for 4 to 5 minutes, or until the peppercorns turn black and their fragrance becomes more pronounced. (Don't worry about the peppercorns darkening. They won't burn.)

2. Turn off the heat. Strain the oil through a fine-mesh strainer into a heatproof bowl and allow to cool to room temperature. Set the fried peppercorns aside to cool. Pour the cooled oil into a sterilized glass jar and close tightly. The oil will keep at room temperature for up to 1 week, or refrigerated for up to 3 months. Transfer the fried peppercorns to a tightly capped jar and store in the refrigerator for up to 6 months.

RED OIL

‖ MAKES ABOUT ⅔ CUP ‖

INGREDIENTS

1 cup peanut oil	¼ cup ground fresh cayenne peppers

1. Heat a wok over high heat for 30 seconds. Add the peanut oil and reduce the heat to low. Add the cayenne and stir continuously so it does not stick to the wok bottom, clot, or burn. When smoke rises from the wok, after 1½ to 2 minutes, immediately turn off the heat.

2. Pour the oil into a heatproof bowl and allow to cool to room temperature. Pour the cooled oil into a sterilized glass jar and close tightly. The oil will keep at room temperature for up to 4 days, or refrigerated for up to 3 months. As the oil ages, it will become deeper red and hotter.

SALT-CURED HAM

|| YIELD DEPENDS ON THE SIZE OF THE SHANK ||

 In China, ham is a salted pork leg and is known as *huo tui,* or "fire leg," to indicate it has been treated and cured. Regional hams exist, but none has the prestige of either the Jinhua hams from the Shanghai region or the Yunnan hams from the far western province of the same name. To taste these hard, salty hams where they are made is a treat. They are not at all like the highly regarded prosciutti of Italy or *serrano* hams of Spain, though both are often wrongly suggested as substitutes.

But they are, in fact, quite close in texture and taste to the salt-cured bone-in leg hams of Smithfield, Virginia. Since Chinese hams cannot be exported to the United States, the Smithfield ham, with its partial crust of black pepper paste, is a creditable substitute. Some Chinatown butcher shops even display hams from Smithfield with the Chinese characters for Jinhua on wall signs next to them.

Preparing these cured hams for any of the recipes in which they are used is not difficult, though it is time-consuming. But again I caution, do not be tempted to use Italian prosciutti or any of the water-added hams found in supermarkets. They cannot replace a hard, salt-cured Smithfield ham.

The shank portion of a Smithfield, with its bone and skin, weighs about 3½ pounds and is used for making Superior Stock (page 145). You must buy a whole ham, which weighs about 15 pounds, to secure the shank because a butcher will not cut off that end and sell it on its own. The butcher will, however, cut the shank end into as many pieces as you need for the stock. You can also ask the butcher to cut the remaining ham into as many pieces as you like so you can use them as you need them. The pieces can be frozen for up to 1 year.

Smaller Smithfield shoulder hams weigh only 5 to 7 pounds, which you may find more practical. You can use the shank portion for stock and the meaty portions for other uses. Finally, you can buy small slabs of Smithfield ham, weighing about 1 pound each. I usually buy the whole 15-pound leg because I use the shank in stocks and the remainder for a variety of other recipes. But for my students, I suggest the 5- to 7-pound shoulder because it includes the shank end for stock and there is still plenty left over for other uses. Whatever size you buy, the ham must be prepared before you can use it in recipes.

INGREDIENTS

1 Smithfield ham shank, 3 to 5 pounds, cross-cut to include bone and with skin intact	9 quarts cold water Ice water to cover

---

1. Soak the ham slab in hot water to cover for 10 minutes to soften it. With a stiff brush, remove the pepper coating from the slab and rinse the slab clean. Soak the slab in 5 quarts of the cold water for 8 hours, replacing the 5 quarts of water twice.

2. In a large pot, place the remaining 4 quarts cold water and the ham and bring to a boil over high heat. Reduce the heat to low, cover, leaving the lid slightly cracked, and simmer for 2½ hours.

SUGAR HAM

‖ ABOUT 2 POUNDS ‖

3. Turn off the heat. Cut off a small piece of the ham to taste for saltiness. If it is too salty, cook it for another 30 minutes, then turn off the heat again. Pour off the water from the pot, and add the ice water to the pot to cover the ham. This will reduce shrinkage. Allow the ham to cool in the ice water for 30 minutes.

4. The ham is now ready to use in any recipe that calls for cured ham, such as soups, rice dishes, and stir-fries, or it can be used to make the Sugar Ham recipe that follows, another basic. The prepped ham can also be stored in a tightly closed container in the refrigerator for up to 1 month, or in the freezer for up to 6 months.

NOTE: If you trim the skin and fat from the prepared ham and remove the central bone, the original 3½-pound slab will yield about 1½ pounds meat. If you are making the Sugar Ham that follows, leave the skin, fat, and bone intact and steam the prepared slab with the rock sugar. After steaming, you can trim the ham and remove the bone. The yield will be about the same.

If you buy a 1-pound ham slab, it will be already trimmed and its salt and pepper coating and skin will have been removed. All you will need to do is bring it to a boil in 2½ quarts water, then simmer it for 2 hours to remove the salt.

This sweetened ham is created by steaming salt-cured ham with rock sugar. I use rock sugar instead of sugarcane sugar or brown sugar because it imparts a light, delicate sweetness—what the Chinese call a "clean sweetness." This ham is a favorite in Hunan, where it is served with its sweet, syrupy sauce and accompanied by small steamed breads.

INGREDIENTS	
1 prepared ham slab, 3½ pounds (see Salt-Cured Ham, facing page 150)	10 ounces rock sugar (about two-thirds of a 1-pound bag) ½ cup water

1. Place the ham, rock sugar, and water in a 9-inch cake pan, with the sugar pieces under, on top of, and around the ham. Place the pan in a steamer, cover, and steam for 2½ hours, turning the ham over every 30 minutes and basting it with its liquid 4 or 5 times. Make certain to replace any boiling water as it evaporates.

2. Turn off the heat. Remove the cake pan from the steamer and allow the ham to cool. The ham is now ready to use. It can be stored with its syrup in a closed container in the refrigerator for up to 1 month, or in the freezer for up to 6 months.

ROASTED CHICKEN

∥ MAKES 6 TO 8 SERVINGS ∥

 This recipe was inspired by a childhood memory. When I was growing up in China, I loved the taste of roasted chicken. But our family kitchen did not have an oven, so most of the chickens we purchased in the market were raw, and we used their meat in stir-fried dishes and in soups. Already-prepared roasted chickens were special treats. What I do now is purposely roast a very large chicken, first to enjoy it after roasting, and later to use its meat in different ways. I prefer the meat of a whole chicken to chicken parts, because the flavor is superior.

INGREDIENTS

1 whole roasting chicken, 7½ pounds	3 slices ginger, ½ inch thick, peeled
¼ cup Mei Kuei Lu Chiew (see Wines, page 41)	6 garlic cloves, cut into ¼-inch-thick slices
1 tablespoon sesame oil	⅓ cup cold water
1 tablespoon salt	½ cup boiling water, if needed
½ teaspoon white pepper	

---

1. If the neck and giblets are included with the chicken, freeze them for another use. Clean the chicken as directed on page 54 and leave to drain for 20 minutes. While the chicken drains, preheat the oven to 400°F.

2. Place the chicken in a roasting pan and rub the bird inside and out with the *chiew*. Coat the outside with the sesame oil and sprinkle inside and out with the salt and then with the white pepper. Place 1 ginger slice in the body cavity and slide each of the remaining slices under the skin on the chicken legs. Place 1 garlic slice in the cavity and slide the remaining slices under the skin on the breasts and legs, distributing them evenly. Secure the neck and tail openings closed with poultry skewers. Truss the legs with kitchen string.

3. Place a rack under the chicken in the roasting pan, positioning the chicken breast side up. Add the cold water to the pan, place in the oven, and roast the chicken for 15 minutes. Lower the oven temperature to 350°F and roast for 30 minutes. Turn the chicken over and roast for another 30 minutes. Turn the chicken over again and pierce the skin on the breasts and thighs with a cooking fork to allow the fat to run off. Lower the oven temperature to 325°F and roast for 1 hour more, adding the boiling water to the pan if it begins to dry out. The chicken should be done at this point (roasted at 20 minutes per pound).

4. Turn off the heat. Remove the pan from the oven and let the chicken rest for 15 minutes. If the chicken is to be eaten immediately, transfer it to a heated platter, carve it in the Western manner, and serve. There should be about 1 cup sauce in the pan to serve with the chicken. Or, the whole chicken can be reserved for future use. Cover the whole chicken or the leftovers well and store in the refrigerator for up to 3 days or in the freezer for up to 6 weeks. Before using, thaw the chicken and allow to come to room temperature.

ROASTED DUCK

|| MAKES 6 TO 8 SERVINGS ||

Ducks are roasted throughout China; some, as in Beijing, in elaborate fashion, and others in simpler ways. This is a classic roasted duck, which is glazed with its own fat. It is the type of duck you see hanging from racks in the windows of markets and restaurants in China and in Chinatowns in other countries. You can, of course, buy one of these cooked, glazed ducks, but preparing one yourself is gratifying. The roasted duck can be eaten as prepared or cold as the first course of a large meal, or it can be refrigerated or frozen for use in other recipes.

INGREDIENTS	
1 duck, 6 pounds, preferably freshly killed, head on and its feet and wing tips removed	3 tablespoons white rice wine
	1 tablespoon salt
MARINADE	
2 tablespoons bean sauce	¼ teaspoon white pepper
2 tablespoons light soy sauce	2 tablespoons minced fresh coriander
3 tablespoons dark brown sugar	
1-inch-thick slice ginger, unpeeled, lightly smashed	3 eight-star anise
2 scallions, cut in half crosswise	1 cinnamon stick, 2 inches long

1. Clean the duck as directed for chicken on page 54. Dry the duck, inside and out, with paper towels. Rub the body and cavity of the duck with the rice wine, then sprinkle the salt on the skin and rub it in.

2. Preheat the oven to 400°F for 20 minutes.

3. To make the marinade: In a small bowl, mix together all of the ingredients. Pour the marinade into the duck cavity and rub it in well. Place the ginger, scallions, anise, and cinnamon in the cavity, then secure it closed with a poultry skewer.

4. Line a roasting pan with heavy-duty aluminum foil. Place a rack in the pan and place the duck, breast side up, on the rack. Roast the duck for 15 minutes. Turn the duck over and roast for another 15 minutes. Turn the duck again, breast side up. Using a cooking fork, pierce the skin all over to allow the fat to run out from under the skin. This will help form a glaze. Roast the duck for 20 minutes longer, or until it is cooked and glazed. To test, insert an instant-read thermometer into the thickest part of a thigh without touching bone. It should register 190°F.

5. Remove the pan from the oven and allow the duck to cool for 10 minutes.

6. Remove the skewer, then remove the ginger, scallions, anise, and cinnamon from the cavity and discard them. Transfer the juices from the cavity to a sauce boat.

7. Traditionally, the duck is cut into bite-size pieces to serve. It may also be carved into larger pieces. Accompany the duck with the juices.

NOTE: If the duck has been cooked in order to use its meat in other preparations, it can be covered and stored in the refrigerator for up to 2 days. Or, to store longer, split the duck in half lengthwise, and freeze the halves for up to 6 months. Before using, thaw the halves and allow to come to room temperature.

HOW TO CUT UP FOWL

1. BIRD BEING CUT, BACK FACING YOU

2. PULLING BIRD OPEN

3. CUTTING BIRD IN HALF

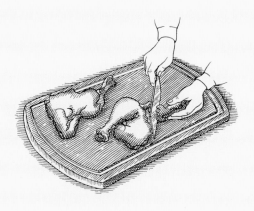

4. CUTTING WINGS FROM BIRD

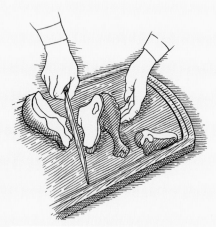

5. CUTTING THIGHS FROM BIRD

6. CUTTING BREAST INTO PIECES

BAKED DUCK BREASTS

‖ MAKES 4 SERVINGS ‖

 This is an alternative to roasting a whole duck. The technique is simple and quick. Once cooked, the breasts can be eaten as they are or saved for future use. They have a pleasantly faint sweetness, which makes the meat a good addition to stir-fries and other recipes. I recommend accompanying them with Stir-fried Shanghai Bok Choy (page 62).

INGREDIENTS

MARINADE	
2 tablespoons oyster sauce	2 teaspoons light soy sauce
1½ tablespoons Shaoxing wine	1½ teaspoons peeled and minced ginger
1 tablespoon sesame oil	1 tablespoon sugar
4 teaspoons bean sauce	¾ teaspoon five-spice powder (page 103)
2 teaspoons double dark soy sauce	½ teaspoon salt
	Pinch of white pepper

2 boneless, skin-on whole duck breasts, 1½ pounds total

1. To make the marinade: In a small bowl, mix together all of the ingredients and reserve.

2. Rinse the duck breasts under cold running water and dry well with paper towels. Cut each breast in half lengthwise to create 4 pieces total. Using a sharp knife, score the skin, without piercing the meat, in a crisscross pattern. Place the breast pieces, skin side up, in a small roasting pan lined with heavy-duty aluminum foil. Pour the marinade over the breasts and rub in well. Refrigerate the breasts for 2 hours, turning them over after 1 hour.

3. About 20 minutes before the breasts have finished marinating, preheat the oven to 450°F.

4. Remove the breasts from the refrigerator. Turn the breasts meat side up and baste them with the marinade. Place the pan in the oven and bake for 10 minutes. Turn the breasts over, raise the oven temperature to 550°F, and bake for 10 minutes more, or until the breasts are done. The fat will have run off, and the skin will be brown and crisp at the edges.

5. Turn off the heat. Remove the pan from the oven and let the duck breasts rest for 10 minutes. Remove them to a platter and serve them with the sauce remaining in the pan. There should be 4 to 5 tablespoons.

NOTE: If the duck breasts have been cooked in order to use their meat in other preparations, they can be covered and stored with their sauce in the refrigerator for up to 1 week. Or, they can be frozen with their sauce for up to 6 weeks. Before using, thaw the breasts and allow to come to room temperature.

TWO NEW CONDIMENTS

Here I add, as I did in our earlier lessons, some condiments we will use as we move along through the recipes. One is a straight-forward spicy pickle. The other is my personal unraveling of a condiment that has acquired a certain cachet among Hong Kong's chefs, most of whom suggest—while smiling slyly—that only they know how to make it.

PEPPER PICKLE

‖ MAKES ABOUT 2 CUPS ‖

This pickle is from western China, the home of a wide variety of hot peppers, and it appears in many dishes in Hunan and Sichuan. I use red jalapeño chiles—green jalapeños become red, and hotter, as they ripen—which are similar to the peppers used in China for this recipe.

INGREDIENTS

1 pound red jalapeño chiles	1½ tablespoons salt
4½ cups cold water	3 tablespoons sugar
2-inch-long piece ginger, unpeeled, lightly smashed	½ cup white rice vinegar
1 teaspoon Sichuan peppercorns	¼ cup white rice wine

1. Wash and dry the chiles thoroughly. Then, using a thin metal skewer, pierce 6 holes evenly around the base of the stem of each chile.

2. In a large pot, place the water, ginger, peppercorns, salt, sugar, and vinegar and bring to a boil over high heat. Lower the heat to medium, cover the pot, and simmer for 5 minutes. Raise the heat to high, add the wine, stir to mix well, and then turn off the heat. Let the mixture cool to room temperature.

3. Using a slotted spoon, transfer the chiles to a steril-ized jar, pour in the liquid to cover, cap tightly, and refrig-erate for at least 48 hours. At this point, they are ready to use. The chiles will keep in the refrigerator for up to 6 months. As they age, they will soften and the liquid will become hotter.

XO SAUCE

‖ MAKES 5½ CUPS (THE RECIPE MAY BE HALVED) ‖

Chinese restaurant chefs occasionally delight in mystery. You need only look in some restaurants at the wall posters full of Chinese writing, detailing dishes that chefs believe no Westerner would be interested in eating. One of the most recent exercises in restaurant mystery surfaced in Hong Kong less than a decade ago, when small dishes of a spicy, pungent, oily paste that had been placed on restaurant tables for years began to attain culinary status and to attract attention. It was called XO sauce, its name presumably borrowed from the expensive XO-grade cognac popular in Hong Kong. I first tried this textured hot condiment years ago when a tiny dish of it was served at the beginning of a restaurant meal. It was delicious: salty, hot, and tasting of chiles, dried seafood, and cured ham. When I asked the captain what it was, he said simply, "XO." And from what is it made? "That," he replied, "is the chef's secret."

I moved the small shards of food around with my chopsticks and kept tasting. In addition to the hotness of chiles, I detected peanut oil, dried scallops and shrimp, garlic and shallots, Yunnan ham, and shrimp roe. I noted these to the captain, who congratulated me, but smiled and said, "Ah, but you do not know how it is made." It made me determined to uncover the mystery of XO sauce. This first taste was followed by many others, as the fad swept through the kitchens of Hong Kong's Chinese restaurants. Soon, restaurants were putting the sauce into decorated jars and boxing them as gifts for sale. And always when I asked how the sauce was made, the answer remained the same: "It is a secret."

My first gift jar was not a mystery, for the ingredients were listed in both English and Chinese on the label, and they confirmed what I had detected in my first tasting. Jars from other restaurants contained the same ingredients and sometimes also included such flavorings as sugar, salted fish, soy sauce, and sesame oil. But the basics were the same, so how the sauce was cooked became the mystery. I resolved to decipher the secret, and over the next several months I made batch after batch of XO sauce. My refrigerator shelves were lined with bottles labeled "XO 1," "XO 2," and so on, and my grocery bills went skyward with the recurring purchase of the very expensive dried scallops, dried shrimp, and shrimp roe, not to mention bags and bags of chiles.

Eventually, I solved the mystery. This recipe produces an XO sauce that is as good as you will get anywhere, I promise. This fine, versatile concoction can be eaten alone, served as an introduction to a meal, eaten with other foods, or used as an ingredient in cooking. Enjoy the mystery.

Continued . . .

. . . continued

INGREDIENTS

3 cups peanut oil

⅔ cup ¼-inch-dice shallots

3 tablespoons minced garlic

16 Steamed Sea Scallops (see page 83), shredded to yield 2 cups (see note)

¾ cup ⅛-inch-dice Salt-Cured Ham (page 150)

1 cup dried shrimp, soaked in hot water to cover for 20 minutes, drained, and minced, to yield 1½ cups

85 small dried chiles, preferably Thai

1 teaspoon salt

6 tablespoons shrimp roe

1. Heat a wok over high heat for 45 seconds. Add ½ cup of the peanut oil and, using a spatula, coat the wok with the oil. When a wisp of white smoke appears, add the shallots and garlic and cook, stirring, for 2 minutes, or until the garlic browns. Add the remaining 2½ cups peanut oil along with the scallops, ham, dried shrimp, chiles, and salt, stir to mix well, and bring the mixture to a boil. Lower the heat to medium and cook for 7 minutes, making certain the oil continues to bubble and stirring continuously so no ingredients burn. Add the shrimp roe, allow the oil to return to a bubble, and cook for 3 minutes more, stirring to avoid burning or sticking.

2. Turn off the heat, transfer the contents to a bowl, and let cool to room temperature. Cover the bowl and refrigerate overnight. The sauce is now ready to use. It will keep in a tightly closed sterilized jar in the refrigerator for up to 3 months. The longer it sits, the more the flavors will blend, and the spicier it will become. To serve it as a condiment, allow it to come to room temperature.

NOTE: Make the recipe for Steamed Sea Scallops as directed, but quadruple all of the ingredient amounts.

CHILES FOR XO SAUCE

CHILES

My XO Sauce is quite hot. The use of dried Thai chiles is preferred because they can be depended on for their heat. The number of chiles I specify is not arbitrary. Exactly 85 chiles test perfectly, and though that sounds like a lot, these dried chiles are very small and very lightweight. Do not use more than 85 chiles, or the balance of the recipe will be upset and the sauce will be too hot. In Chinese and Asian markets, plastic packages of dried chiles are clearly marked with Thailand as the country of origin. Use them.

LESSON 3
A DISCUSSION OF BREADS

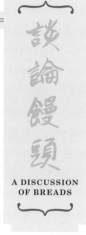

談論饅頭

A DISCUSSION OF BREADS

Our new ingredients are stored in the pantry. We have talked about three new cooking techniques and our latest kitchen tradition, the sand clay pot, and we have added to our storehouse of basic recipes. Once again, we move on to cooking—actually, to bread making. Most people do not associate bread with Chinese cooking. Yet there is a long history of breads—baked, steamed, and fried—in China that extends back more than two thousand years. Just as rice was the staple in the south, other grains such as wheat, millet, and barley were plentiful in the north, which made wheat-based breads especially dominant.

Food scholars believe that China's first breads, which were pitalike flat breads, came from Tibet. In Shandong and around Beijing, they were followed by oven-baked and steamed breads, developments made possible after flour-milling filtered in with the Silk Road traders. Other early breads resembled the puffy *naan* of India, cooked by slapping them against the wall of a clay oven, where they then baked. During the Ming court in Beijing, breads were varied and sought after. There were rolled and fried breads, steamed rolls filled with mutton, sweet biscuits, oven-baked breads, sugar-filled steamed breads, flaky breads and pastries, sesame-filled steamed breads and sesame-topped baked breads, and breads filled with animal fats.

The more recognizable breads of Beijing, and later of the west and northwest, were loaves and rolls, baked or steamed. Many of them had their origins with the Muslims of the area around Urumqi, in the northern Chinese region of Xinjiang. There they were eaten with mutton and lamb, never pork. Elsewhere in the north, in Shanxi Province, a tradition of intricate, sculpted baked breads sprang up. So fine were these sculptures that they became traditional wedding gifts. For example, the groom's family would receive a sculpture of two tigers, symbolizing strength, and the bride's family would be presented with a swimming carp and bouquets of lotus flowers, both symbolic of long life and fertility. These breads were usually not eaten.

In Beijing, people commonly ate small baked breads as accompaniments to strongly flavored beef and lamb dishes. Even today, in this home of the Peking duck, the duck and its meat are eaten as often with steamed breads as they are with pancakes. In Sichuan, steamed breads regularly leavened the spicy tastes of chiles, and in Hunan, a favorite and felicitous combination was salt-cured ham, sweetened with sugar syrup, and small steamed breads. These steamed breads were adopted much later by other parts of China. In Shanghai, they are often eaten with tea-smoked duck and long-cooked pork shoulder. Even in Hong Kong, that bastion of Cantonese cooking, steamed breads are served alongside roasted suckling pig skin and with dishes from other Chinese provinces.

Historically, the shortening for breads, whether baked or steamed, was lard. It is still the best. I use lard in my recipes for two reasons: authenticity and taste. You can use the same amount of peanut oil and the results will be fine. But I suggest you use lard, for the taste and the texture it imparts to the breads.

BEIJING BAKED BREADS

|| MAKES 16 BREADS ||

北京焗麵色

In Beijing and northern China, these small breads are restaurant staples. They are eaten with the intensely flavored stir-fries, braised dishes, and stews and the roasted meats of the north. As I just mentioned, I prefer lard over peanut oil for the shortening, but you can opt to use oil.

I also specify Scallion Oil instead of peanut oil for the final brushing, for the added flavor of the scallions, a Beijing favorite. Following this recipe are two Beijing classics that are typically served with the breads, Crisp Beef (page 165) and Stir-fried Lamb with Scallions (page 166).

INGREDIENTS

DOUGH

1 package (¼ ounce) active dry yeast	½ teaspoon baking powder
⅓ cup sugar	1 jumbo egg, lightly beaten (¼ cup)
½ cup warm water (110°F)	7 tablespoons lard, at room temperature, or peanut oil
2½ cups Pillsbury Best Bread Flour	

1 large egg beaten with 1 tablespoon water for an egg wash	3 tablespoons Scallion Oil (page 56)
¼ cup white sesame seeds	

---

1. To make the dough: In a large bowl, mix the yeast and sugar in the warm water, dissolving them. Set the bowl in a warm place for 30 minutes to 1 hour, or until the mixture rises and a brownish foam appears on the surface. (Because weather and temperature can affect the progress, the timing cannot be more precise.) The cooler the outdoor temperature, the longer the time.

2. Add the flour, baking powder, egg, and lard to the yeast mixture. Continuously stir the mixture with your hand until well mixed, then knead in the bowl for about 5 minutes, or until a cohesive, elastic dough forms. Cover the bowl with plastic wrap, set it in a warm place, and allow the dough to rise for 2 to 4 hours, or until tripled in size. (Again, the cooler the outdoor temperature, the longer the time.)

3. To form the breads, cut sixteen 3-inch squares of waxed paper and place the squares in a single layer on a baking sheet. Remove the dough from the bowl to a work surface, sprinkle it lightly with flour, and knead it for about 10 minutes. This increases the elasticity. Using your palms, roll the dough into a log 16 inches long. Cut the log into 1-inch pieces. Form each piece into a ball, and place each ball on a waxed-paper square. Let the balls rise, uncovered, in a warm place for about 1 hour. They will increase in size by about one-third. About 20 minutes before the balls are ready, preheat the oven to 350°F.

4. Spray each ball with a fine mist of warm water, then brush with the egg wash and sprinkle evenly with the sesame seeds. Place in the oven and bake for 15 minutes, or until the breads are browned. About halfway through the baking time, rotate the baking sheet front to back to ensure even browning.

5. Remove from the oven. The breads tend to cool quickly and their crusts harden. To keep them soft and to add some faint flavor, brush them with the scallion oil. Serve warm.

CRISP BEEF

‖ MAKES 4 SERVINGS ‖

乾炒牛肉絲 The name of this extremely popular dish translates as "two deep-fry, one stir-fry," which describes the cooking method. It is eaten widely in Beijing, though, as with many historical dishes from China's capital city, it has been adopted by other parts of the country. This version, which I ate in Beijing just a few years ago, even makes use of a paste made from Sichuan peppercorns, a tasty example of ingredient interchange.

INGREDIENTS

12 ounces flank steak

COATING

¾ teaspoon sugar	¼ teaspoon salt
½ teaspoon baking soda	

1 tablespoon lightly beaten egg white	⅔ cup julienned white portion scallions
2 tablespoons cornstarch	1 tablespoon hot bean sauce
3½ cups peanut oil	1 tablespoon sweet bean sauce
2 teaspoons minced peeled ginger	
2 teaspoons minced garlic	2 teaspoons sugar
1½ tablespoons Sichuan Peppercorn Paste (page 211)	½ teaspoon Hot Pepper Oil (page 55)
	2 tablespoons finely sliced green portion of scallions
½ cup shredded carrots (see Cleaver discussion, page 45)	Beijing Baked Breads (page 163)

1. Slice the flank steak across the grain into precise strips each 3 inches long by ¼ inch wide and ¼ inch thick. Place the beef in a bowl, add all of the coating ingredients, and toss together to coat evenly. Cover and allow to rest in the refrigerator for 2 hours.

2. Add the egg white and cornstarch to the beef mixture, mix well, and let rest for 10 minutes more.

3. Heat a wok over high heat for 1 minute. Add the peanut oil and heat to 375°F on a deep-frying thermometer. Add the coated beef and deep-fry, loosening the strips of meat with chopsticks to keep them separate, for 3 minutes, or until medium brown. Turn off the heat. Remove the beef with a Chinese strainer and drain well.

4. Heat the oil again to 375°F. Place the beef back into the wok and deep-fry again for 3 minutes, or until crisp. Turn off the heat, remove the beef with the strainer, and drain well.

5. Pour off all but 1 tablespoon of the peanut oil from the wok and heat over high heat for 15 seconds. When a wisp of white smoke appears, add the ginger, garlic, and peppercorn paste and stir for about 1 minute, or until the paste releases its fragrance. Add the carrots and stir for 30 seconds. Add the white portion of scallions and stir for 30 seconds. Add the beef, mix well, and stir-fry for 1 minute. Add the hot bean sauce, sweet bean sauce, sugar, and hot pepper oil, mix well, and stir-fry for 1½ minutes, or until well combined and all of the ingredients are hot.

6. Turn off the heat. Transfer to a heated platter, sprinkle with the green portions of scallions, and serve with the breads.

STIR-FRIED LAMB WITH SCALLIONS

‖ **MAKES 4 SERVINGS** ‖

In Beijing, this classic would be made with strong-tasting mutton. I use a fillet from a lamb leg. Ask your butcher to trim 8 ounces of lamb in a single piece. Scallions in Beijing are large and meaty and at their best are about the size of leeks. Do not use leeks in their stead, however, because leeks tend to have a garlic taste, while scallions taste like onions.

INGREDIENTS

1 lamb fillet, 8 ounces

MARINADE

4 teaspoons double dark soy sauce	¾ teaspoon white rice vinegar
2 teaspoons sesame oil	1¾ teaspoons cornstarch
2 teaspoons peanut oil	1½ teaspoons sugar
1 teaspoon Shaoxing wine	Pinch of white pepper

SAUCE

3 tablespoons Chicken Stock (page 54)	1 teaspoon Shaoxing wine
	1¼ teaspoons cornstarch
1½ teaspoons double dark soy sauce	1 teaspoon sugar
	¼ teaspoon salt
1 teaspoon white rice vinegar	Pinch of white pepper

2½ tablespoons peanut oil	4 teaspoons minced ginger
8 ounces scallions, cut into 1½-inch lengths, white portions quartered lengthwise	2 teaspoons Shaoxing wine
	1 teaspoon sesame oil
1½ teaspoons minced garlic	Beijing Baked Breads (page 163)

1. Cut the lamb across the grain into precise slices 2 inches long by 1½ inches wide and ⅛ inch thick. Place the slices in a bowl, add all of the marinade ingredients, and toss to coat well. Let the lamb rest in the refrigerator for 1 hour.

2. To make the sauce: In a small bowl, mix together all of the ingredients and reserve.

3. Heat a wok over high heat for 1 minute. Add 1 tablespoon of the peanut oil and, using a spatula, coat the wok with the oil. When a wisp of white smoke appears, add the scallions and stir-fry for 30 seconds, or until they wilt. Turn off the heat, remove the scallions to a dish, and set aside.

4. Wipe the wok and spatula with paper towels. Heat the wok over high heat for 1 minute. Add the remaining 1½ tablespoons peanut oil and, using the spatula, coat the wok with the oil. When a wisp of white smoke appears, add the garlic and ginger and stir for about 40 seconds, or until the garlic browns. Add the lamb and its marinade and spread the slices in a single layer. Cook for 1 minute, or until the edges lose their redness. Turn the slices over.

5. Drizzle in the wine, adding it along the edge of the wok, and mix well. Add the reserved scallions and mix thoroughly. Make a well in the center of the mixture, stir the sauce, and pour it into the well. Stir to mix for about 1½ minutes, or until the sauce thickens and turns dark brown. Add the sesame oil and mix well.

6. Turn off the heat. Transfer to a heated platter and serve with the baked breads.

‖ A STIR-FRY RULE ‖

This is a good point at which to talk about an important stir-fry rule. In the recipes for Crisp Beef and Stir-fried Lamb with Scallions, or any other stir-fry, do not double the recipe if you want to make twice the amount. Instead, cook two batches. The reason is simple: You will be unable to create the best amount of heat, the principle of *wok qi* (page 60), to cook twice the volume of ingredients. The same heat affects larger or smaller amounts of food differently, which means cooking times will vary. If you try to compensate by doubling the cooking time, too, the food will cook unevenly and will usually be overcooked. So, for the best results, cook separate batches. If you prep your ingredients and are organized as I have suggested, the cooking will go quickly.

STEAMED BREADS

‖ MAKES 6 SMALL LOAVES, OR 6 SERVINGS ‖

Consumption of this traditional bread of Beijing is no longer limited to its place of birth. It is eaten widely in Hunan and Sichuan, as well as in Shanghai. It serves as a mild counterpoint to dishes hot and spicy, oily and sweet.

INGREDIENTS	
½ cup Pillsbury Best Bread Flour	½ cup lukewarm milk
2 cups Pillsbury Best All-Purpose Flour	¼ cup lukewarm water, plus more as needed
⅓ cup sugar	3 tablespoons lard, at room temperature, or peanut oil
4 teaspoons baking powder	

1. On a work surface, mix together the flours, sugar, and baking powder and make a well in the center. Gradually add the milk to the well and use your fingers to combine it with the flour until it is absorbed. Then add the water and work it into the flour mixture with your fingers until it is absorbed. Add the lard and continue to work the dough until it is well blended.

2. Using a dough scraper, lift the dough from the surface with one hand and begin kneading it with the other hand. Knead for 12 to 15 minutes, or until smooth and elastic. If the dough is dry and shows traces of flour, add 1 teaspoon lukewarm water at a time and continue to knead. If the dough is too wet, sprinkle a bit of flour on the work surface and on your hands and continue to knead. When the dough is smooth and elastic, cover it with a damp cloth and let rest for 1 hour.

Continued . . .

. . . continued

3. To shape the breads, cut six 3-by-5-inch rectangles of parchment paper or waxed paper and set aside. Divide the dough in half. Roll each half into a log 12 inches long. Cut each log crosswise into thirds. Work with 1 piece at a time and keep the others covered with a damp cloth. With wet hands, shape the first piece into a small loaf about 3½ inches long, pressing and rounding the ends. Place the loaf on a parchment rectangle. Repeat with the remaining dough pieces and parchment rectangles.

4. Divide the 6 loaves, on their parchment, between two bamboo steamers, placing three loaves in each steamer. Stack the steamers, cover, and steam the loaves for 20 to 25 minutes (see Steaming, page 79), or until they are soft and spongelike. Because of flour and climate variations, a loaf will occasionally split on top during steaming. This is a natural occurrence.

5. Turn off the heat, remove the breads from the steamer, and serve.

NOTE: You can freeze these loaves for future use. Let them cool to room temperature, wrap them well in plastic wrap, then in heavy-duty aluminum foil, and freeze for up to 2 months. To use, thaw them and let them come to room temperature, then steam them for 3 to 4 minutes, or until hot.

FRIED BREADS

|| **MAKES 6 SMALL LOAVES, OR 6 SERVINGS** ||

 This pleasing variation on plain steamed breads calls for deep-frying the loaves until they turn golden and develop a thin, crisp exterior. The fried breads are as popular as the plain steamed breads, and with good reason.

INGREDIENTS

Steamed Breads (page 167)   6 cups peanut oil

---

1. Steam the loaves as directed and remove them from the steamer.

2. Heat a wok over high heat for 40 seconds. Add the peanut oil and heat to 350°F on a deep-frying thermometer. Peel away the paper from the bottom of each loaf. Place 2 loaves on a Chinese strainer, lower the loaves into the oil, and then remove the strainer. Allow the breads to brown, turning frequently, for 3 to 4 minutes, or until they are pale gold. Lift the loaves out of the oil with the strainer, allow the excess oil to drain, and place on paper towels to drain. Repeat with the remaining loaves. The breads will have a sheen, a thin crust, and a pleasant taste from the peanut oil. Slice the loaves and serve warm.

EGGPLANT WITH GARLIC SAUCE

‖ MAKES 4 SERVINGS ‖

 This eggplant dish, which is equally at home in Beijing and in western China, is complemented by steamed or fried bread.

INGREDIENTS

SAUCE

1 tablespoon double dark soy sauce

2 teaspoons oyster sauce

1 teaspoon white rice vinegar

½ teaspoon Shaoxing wine

½ teaspoon pepper flakes from Hot Pepper Oil (page 55)

2 teaspoons sugar

½ teaspoon cornstarch mixed with 2 teaspoons Chicken Stock (page 54)

¼ teaspoon salt

4 cups peanut oil

1 pound eggplants, peeled and sliced lengthwise into ½-inch-wide strips

2 teaspoons minced garlic

Steamed Breads (page 167) or Fried Breads (page 168)

1. To make the sauce: In a small bowl, mix together all of the ingredients and reserve.

2. Heat a wok over high heat for 45 seconds. Add the peanut oil and heat to 350°F on a deep-frying thermometer. Place the eggplant strips in a Chinese strainer and lower them into the oil. Cook the strips for 2 to 3 minutes, or until they soften. Using the strainer, lift out the strips and allow the eggplant to drain over a bowl.

3. Pour off all but 1½ tablespoons of the peanut oil from the wok and heat over high heat for 30 seconds. When a wisp of white smoke appears, add the garlic and stir for 35 seconds, or until it releases its fragrance. Return the eggplant to the wok and stir-fry for 1½ minutes, or until it is well mixed with the garlic. Make a well in the center of the mixture, stir the sauce, and pour it into the well. Stir to mix well for about 2 minutes, or until the sauce thickens.

4. Turn off the heat, transfer to a heated dish and serve with the breads.

‖ EGGPLANTS ‖

EGGPLANT

Both Western and Chinese eggplants are available. Western ones are large, egg-shaped, and dark purple and have a thick skin that is usually peeled before the flesh is used. Chinese eggplants are bright purple to pale purple and are often mottled with white. They are smaller and more slender than their Western cousins, usually no more than 2 inches in diameter at their thickest. The taste is similar, but Chinese eggplants are more tender and do not need to be peeled before use.

SCALLION PANCAKES

‖ MAKES 4 PANCAKES, 4 TO 8 SERVINGS ‖

 The scallion pancake is often thought of as a bread, and it is, in fact, reminiscent of the Indian naan: thin, browned, and crisp, yet textured in the center. It is eaten as a snack or a course in a large meal and is a Shanghai tradition. Indeed, some insist that no one but a chef from Shanghai should even attempt to cook these pancakes. Despite this, the scallion pancake, in various forms, is known and enjoyed throughout China. Most scallion pancakes are made from a basic dough and call for fresh scallions, though some are made from a batter. Some are thin and flat, and others thick. None is baked. Instead, they are all fried. The secrets to making the best scallion pancake are to fry the scallions before you add them to the dough and to use the traditional shortening, lard.

INGREDIENTS

⅓ cup melted lard	½ cup warm water (110°F)
¼ cup finely sliced scallions	Peanut oil for work surface
1 ½ cups Pillsbury Best All-Purpose Flour	7 tablespoons Scallion Oil (page 56), or peanut oil, or more if needed
¼ teaspoon salt	

1. Heat a wok over medium heat for 20 seconds. Add the lard, then immediately add the scallions. Cook for 4 to 5 minutes, stirring continuously to avoid burning. Turn off the heat. Pour the contents of the wok into a small bowl and let cool for 10 minutes.

2. Mix together the flour and salt and make a well in the center. Gradually add the warm water to the well and use your fingers to combine it with the flour until it is absorbed. Add the lard and scallions and continue to mix with your fingers until the lard is absorbed and the scallions are evenly distributed.

3. Using a dough scraper, lift the dough from the surface with one hand and begin kneading it with the other hand. Knead the dough for 10 minutes, or until smooth and elastic. Cover it with a damp cloth and let rest for 30 minutes.

4. Lightly rub a work surface with peanut oil. Transfer the dough to the oiled surface and roll out to 6 inches long. Fold the long sides toward the center, overlapping them slightly. Roll out again to a 6-inch length and then fold as before. Repeat this one more time, then shape the dough into a log 4 inches long and cut crosswise into 4 equal pieces. Place the pieces in a warm place, preferably on a warm stove, and cover with plastic wrap. Let rest for 30 minutes, or until the pieces are very soft.

5. Work with 1 piece at a time and keep the others covered with the damp cloth. Again, rub the work surface with peanut oil and transfer the dough to the oiled surface. Roll out into a circle about 8 inches in diameter. Cover the circle with a piece of waxed paper. Repeat with the remaining 3 pieces.

6. Heat a cast-iron frying pan over high heat for 30 seconds. Add the scallion oil to the pan; it should be ¼ inch deep. When a wisp of white smoke appears, turn off the heat. Gently place a pancake into the pan and shallow-fry for 20 seconds. Then turn the heat to medium and shallow-fry the pancake for 50 seconds more, or until it begins to brown. Using a spatula, turn the pancake over and fry for 1 minute, or until it browns. Remove the pancake to a plate lined with a paper towel. Repeat with the remaining 3 pancakes. The oil should always be ¼ inch deep, so add more if needed.

7. You can cut each pancake into 4 wedges as it is removed from the pan and serve it immediately. Or, you can cook all 4 pancakes, stacking them separated by paper towels, and then cut and serve them all at the same time.

STEAMED FAN BREADS

|| MAKES 30 STEAMED FANS ||

In Beijing, but particularly in Hunan, there is a long tradition of small, decorative steamed breads, usually served to accompany meats and poultry. They are often formed with open sides so they can be used for making small sandwiches with cooked meats or poultry. Some are round, some are shaped like lotus leaves, and some, like these, are fashioned into fans or scallop shells without open sides.

INGREDIENTS

1 cup Pillsbury Best All-Purpose Flour	¼ cup lukewarm milk
¼ cup Pillsbury Best Bread Flour	2 tablespoons lukewarm water, plus more as needed
¼ cup sugar	1½ tablespoons lard, at room temperature, or peanut oil
2 teaspoons baking powder	

---

1. On a work surface, mix together the flours, sugar, and baking powder and make a well in the center. Gradually add the milk to the well and use your fingers to combine it with the flour until it is absorbed. Then add the water and work it into the flour mixture with your fingers until it is absorbed. Add the lard and continue to work the dough until it is well blended.

2. Using a dough scraper, lift the dough from the surface with one hand and begin kneading it with the other hand. Knead for 12 to 15 minutes, or until elastic. If the dough is dry and shows traces of flour, add 1 teaspoon lukewarm water at a time and continue to knead. If the dough is too wet, sprinkle a bit of flour on the work surface and on your hands and continue to knead. When the dough is smooth and elastic, cover it with a damp cloth and let rest for 1 hour.

3. Cut thirty 2½-inch squares of parchment paper or waxed paper and set aside. Divide the dough in half. Roll each half into a log 15 inches long. Cut each log crosswise into 15 equal pieces. Work with 1 piece at a time and keep the others covered with the damp cloth.

4. Roll 1 piece into a ball, then press it down on a floured work surface to flatten it. Shape the flattened piece into a triangle, rounding the top slightly. Using a dinner fork, press on the rounded top to create fanlike lines and ridges. It should resemble a small, open fan. Place the fan on a parchment square. Repeat with the remaining dough pieces and parchment squares.

5. Divide the thirty fans, on their parchment, among three bamboo steamers, placing ten fans in each steamer. Stack the steamers, cover, and steam the fans for 10 to 12 minutes, or until they are opaque white.

6. Turn off the heat, remove the fan breads from the steamer, and serve. These breads are the classic accompaniment to Sugar Ham (page 151). To serve, slice the heated ham into pieces 2 inches square and ⅛ inch thick and place in a serving dish. Pour the syrup from the ham over the squares and serve one piece of ham with each steamed fan bread.

LESSON 4
COOKING IN THE SAND CLAY POT

SAND CLAY POT

As I mentioned earlier, the sand clay pot was a necessity in our family kitchen when I was growing up. The pots of rough, grainy clay with glazed insides and tops were used in many ways. We cooked congees, made stocks, brewed soups, and simmered stews and braises. We also used them to cook rice with different soy sauces, various meats, taro root, sausages, and bacon.

One of my favorite childhood clay-pot dishes was rice cooked with *lop cheong* (sausage), Chinese bacon, and pieces of roasted duck, which we called *lop mei fan,* or "cured-meats rice." We children also knew that when we were ill, *bo chai fan* would be prepared for us in a sand clay pot. It combined pork liver and rice and was believed to be a restorative.

Today that tradition still exists, but it has also given birth to a new concept. In Chinese cities, you now see variously sized clay pots displayed in front of restaurants, with signs advertising *bo chai fan* for two, four, or more. They are promoted not only as health foods, but also as satisfying one-pot dinners.

The pot, because it was clay, was simultaneously strong and fragile, and once it was cured, it could stand long, intense heat. But if it was allowed to dry out during cooking, it could easily crack. So it had to be watched carefully, which remains the case today.

Following are recipes that are cooked in a clay pot. All of them call for some braising, which is a strength of the clay pot. And all of them are served at the table in the clay pot because it is such an impressive piece of culinary sculpture. If you have just acquired a sand clay pot, be sure to cure it before you use it the first time (page 141).

WUXI BRAISED PORK RIBS

|| MAKES 4 SERVINGS ||

This famous dish is named for the city where it originated. Wuxi, which lies northwest of Shanghai, was once known for the production of pewter, a reputation that died when the tin mines were exhausted. That prompted locals to call the town Wuxi, or "no more tin." Nowadays, the city is more famous for ribs than for its past metal industry. In this dish, I blanch the ribs in a wok or pot before I braise them in a sand clay pot because I find using a wok for that step is easier.

INGREDIENTS

1 rack pork spareribs, 4½ pounds	8 tablespoons ketchup (page 75)
9½ cups water	6 tablespoons red rice vinegar
1½ teaspoons salt	3 tablespoons Shaoxing wine
7 tablespoons bean curd juice	6 tablespoons sugar

---

1. To prepare the ribs, trim off the flap from the rack and cut off the cartilage at the top of each rib. Cut the rack into individual ribs to yield 10 large and 2 smaller ribs. You should have about 3½ pounds trimmed.

2. To water-blanch the ribs, place 5 cups of the water in a pot and bring to a boil over high heat. Add the ribs and stir to immerse. Let the water return to a boil and boil the ribs for 2 minutes. Turn off the heat, run cold water into the pot, and pour off the water. Run water into the pot again, rinse off any remaining residue from the pork, and pour off the water again. Remove the ribs from the pot and reserve.

3. In a sand clay pot, place the remaining 4½ cups of water and the salt and mix together. Add the ribs. Turn on the heat to medium and bring the water to a boil. Lower the heat to a gentle boil, cover, and braise for 1¾ hours. Turn off the heat, remove the ribs, and reserve.

4. There should be 2½ cups liquid remaining in the clay pot. Remove 1 cup and reserve for another use. (It is a good pork stock.) Add the bean curd juice, ketchup, vinegar, wine, and sugar to the clay pot and stir to mix well. Return the ribs to the clay pot, turn the heat to medium, cover, and bring the contents to a boil. Lower the heat to a gentle boil and braise for 45 minutes, gently moving the ribs in the liquid occasionally to prevent sticking and being careful not to loosen the meat from the bones. The ribs are done when they are very tender, the meat is beginning to fall from the bones, and the sauce is syrupy and glistening. If they do not test done, cook for an additional 15 minutes, or until tender.

5. Turn off the heat. Serve the ribs in the sand clay pot.

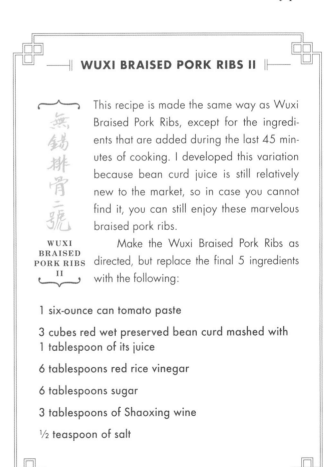

|| WUXI BRAISED PORK RIBS II ||

WUXI BRAISED PORK RIBS II

This recipe is made the same way as Wuxi Braised Pork Ribs, except for the ingredients that are added during the last 45 minutes of cooking. I developed this variation because bean curd juice is still relatively new to the market, so in case you cannot find it, you can still enjoy these marvelous braised pork ribs.

Make the Wuxi Braised Pork Ribs as directed, but replace the final 5 ingredients with the following:

1 six-ounce can tomato paste

3 cubes red wet preserved bean curd mashed with 1 tablespoon of its juice

6 tablespoons red rice vinegar

6 tablespoons sugar

3 tablespoons of Shaoxing wine

½ teaspoon of salt

FUZHOU DRUNKEN PORK RIBS

|| MAKES 4 SERVINGS ||

 This dish comes from the city of Fuzhou, in the southeastern province of Fujian. In general, people from Fujian value richness and sweetness in their foods, and this preparation of small-cut pork ribs cooked in fermented red rice and its liquid, which the Fujianese regard as a *chiew*, or wine, meets that standard of richness and accounts for its name. In Fuzhou, the ribs are deep-fried before braising. I sear them, which I have found makes them tender and better able to absorb the strength of the "wine."

INGREDIENTS

1¼ pounds pork spareribs	1 teaspoon baking soda

COATING

1 tablespoon liquid form Fujian Fermented Red Rice (page 184)	1½ tablespoons cornstarch
	1 teaspoon sesame oil

SAUCE

2 tablespoons oyster sauce	3 tablespoons dark brown sugar
1½ tablespoons Fujian Fermented Red Rice (page 184)	¼ teaspoon salt
	Pinch of white pepper
1 teaspoon light soy sauce	

2 tablespoons peanut oil	1½ teaspoons liquid from Fujian Fermented Red Rice (page 184)
1 tablespoon peeled minced ginger	
1 tablespoon minced garlic	¾ cup Red Stock (page 147)

1. Most pork spareribs come in racks weighing 3½ to 4½ pounds. You may have to purchase a whole rack to get the ribs you need for this recipe. If you buy the ribs in a Chinatown butcher shop, you will find them already cut into strips, and you will be able to buy the 1¼ pounds you need. There will be 3 or 4 strips, each 1 inch wide, made by cutting across the rib bones along the length of the rack. If you must buy the whole rack, ask the butcher to remove the flap from the rack and to cut the rack lengthwise into 1-inch-wide strips. Once you have the strips, cut the meat between the ribs to arrive at a batch of meat-bordered rib pieces, each about 1 inch square.

2. In a large bowl, place the ribs and baking soda and toss to coat the ribs thoroughly. Cover and refrigerate for at least 8 hours or up to overnight.

3. Remove the bowl from the refrigerator, fill the bowl with cold water, and then pour off the water. Repeat twice to rinse off all of the baking soda from the ribs, then drain well. Spread the ribs in a single layer and allow to dry for about 1 hour.

4. To make the coating: In a bowl, mix together all of the ingredients. Add the dry ribs and toss well, coating them evenly. Let them rest for 30 to 40 minutes.

5. To make the sauce: In a small bowl, mix together all of the ingredients and reserve.

6. Heat a wok over high heat for 40 seconds. Add the peanut oil and, using a spatula, coat the wok with the oil. When a wisp of white smoke appears, add the ginger and stir briefly. Add the garlic and stir briefly. Add the ribs and spread them in a single layer. Cook for 1 minute, or until they are browned. Turn the ribs over, mix well, and stir and cook for 1 minute. Add the red rice liquid and stir to mix well. Stir the sauce, pour it into the wok, and mix well to coat the ribs thoroughly. Turn off the heat.

7. Transfer the contents of the wok to a sand clay pot. Add ¼ cup of the red stock to the wok over high heat to loosen and dissolve any remains from the ribs, and pour over the ribs in the clay pot. Add the remaining stock to the clay pot and mix well. Cover, turn the heat to medium, and bring the contents to a boil. Stir the pot, lower the heat to a gentle boil, and braise, stirring often to prevent sticking, for 50 minutes, or until the meat is tender. Cut off a small piece to test if it is ready. If the meat is not tender, cook for an additional 15 minutes, or until tender.

8. Turn off the heat. Serve the ribs in the clay pot.

HAKKA STUFFED BEAN CURD

‖ **MAKES 6 SERVINGS** ‖

Stuffed bean curd dishes abound in China, in countless varieties. The fillings range from minced fresh or dried shrimp to minced fish to ground pork. Once stuffed, the bean curd can be panfried, deep-fried, steamed, or simmered in a soup. The nomadic Hakka people (see page 218), who centuries ago migrated from northern to southern China, make perhaps more versions of this ubiquitous dish than any other group. They panfry the stuffed bean curd cakes and then braise them in a sand clay pot. Make certain you use firm bean curd cakes for this recipe.

INGREDIENTS

FILLING

6 ounces shrimp

1 tablespoon lightly beaten egg white

2 teaspoons oyster sauce

1 teaspoon sesame oil

½ teaspoon ginger juice (page 70) mixed with 1½ teaspoons white rice wine

½ teaspoon light soy sauce

¾ teaspoon sugar

¼ teaspoon salt

Pinch of white pepper

1½ tablespoons mung bean starch

3 scallions, finely sliced

---

6 firm fresh bean curd cakes (about 1½ pounds total)

1 tablespoon mung bean starch for dusting

3 to 5 tablespoons peanut oil

3 cups Fish Stock (page 147)

1-inch-thick slice ginger, peeled and lightly smashed

2½ cups cut-up iceberg lettuce leaves (2-by-3-inch pieces)

---

1. To make the filling: First clean the shrimp (see page 75). Pat them dry with paper towels, place them on a chopping board, and chop with a cleaver to a paste. Transfer to a bowl, add all of the remaining filling ingredients, and mix thoroughly. Refrigerate, uncovered, for 3 to 4 hours, or until the filling is firm.

2. While the filling is firming up, prepare the bean curd cakes. Remove them from their water, place them in a strainer over a bowl, and refrigerate, uncovered, until dry, about 2 hours.

3. When the bean curd is ready, remove it from the refrigerator and pat dry with paper towels. Place the cakes on a cutting board and cut each cake in half on the diagonal. With a small, sharp knife, cut a horizontal pocket in the long side of each triangular cake, making a cut about 1½ inches long and 1 inch deep. Dust all of the pockets with the mung bean starch. Remove the shrimp filling from the refrigerator and place 1 tablespoon of the filling in a pocket. Then, using a blunt butter knife, press the filling firmly into the pocket and smooth the surface. Repeat until all of the cakes are stuffed.

4. Heat a large cast-iron frying pan over high heat for 1 minute. Add 3 tablespoons of the peanut oil. When a

Continued . . .

FILLING THE POCKET OF BEAN CURD CAKE

. . . continued

wisp of white smoke appears, turn off the heat and place six of the bean curd triangles, stuffed end down, into the pan. Turn on the heat to medium and fry the stuffed cakes for 2 minutes. Using chopsticks or a spatula, turn the cakes and cook on a flat side for 2 minutes. Turn the cakes again and cook on the opposite flat side for 2 minutes, for a total of 6 minutes, or until browned on all sides. Transfer the six fried triangles to a sand clay pot. Fry the remaining bean curd triangles the same way, adding the remaining 2 tablespoons peanut oil to the pan if needed to prevent sticking. Transfer the cakes to the clay pot.

5. Add the fish stock and the ginger to the clay pot, cover, and bring to a boil over medium heat. Reduce the heat to low and braise for 5 minutes. Raise the heat to medium, add the lettuce, stir gently to mix, and return to a boil. Cook for 2 minutes, or until the lettuce softens.

6. Turn off the heat. Serve the stuffed bean curd cakes, the lettuce, and the soup from the clay pot, ladling them into individual bowls.

‖ CHOOSING SHRIMP ‖
FOR FILLINGS

揀
蝦

**CHOOSING
SHRIMP**

When purchasing shrimp that will be used for making a shrimp filling or paste, choose raw shrimp that are pale gray. They have body and will form a firm mixture when combined with other filling ingredients. Do not use raw reddish shrimp, as they will not firm up or combine well with other ingredients.

LESSON 5
RICE WITHOUT LIMITS

白飯

RICE
WITHOUT
LIMITS

We will revisit the sand clay pot and how rice is cooked in it later, as we move into our second excursion into the world of rice in China. In Part 1, we cooked plain rice and one simple fried rice, and we fried rice noodles and simmered congees. Rice is also made into pudding-like sweets; spongy, elastic steamed cakes; and fruit-laden molds. It is the basis of noodles of various kinds and shapes, and its flours go into the brightly colored layered cakes of Southeast Asia. It is stuffed into poultry and enclosed in fragrant leaves and cooked to absorb the flavor of its wrapping. Its uses are limitless. Its adaptability is celebrated.

I have talked about rice in general, of its life-sustaining importance throughout China. Now we will explore this staple more deeply, frying it, roasting it, steaming it, and more. First, however, we begin with two preparations that call for fermented rice.

SHANGHAI SWEET WINE RICE

|| MAKES ENOUGH FOR THREE 20-OUNCE JARS ||

上海
甜酒
釀

This sweet rice, a favorite of Shanghai, is versatile. Not only is it the basis for other dishes, including a sweet soup, but it is also eaten as Westerners might eat a rice pudding. Its sweetness is created by mixing glutinous rice with a crushed white ball of yeast, or wine pill, which causes the rice to ferment. In Shanghai, this rice is usually made in the hot summer, when fermentation is better, so it yields a more intense flavor. It is sold in jars often labeled "fermented sweet rice sauce (rice pudding–style)." But just as often, the jars are not labeled in English, so you will need to refer to the Chinese calligraphy. The best idea is to make your own. You will need three Mason jars, preferably Atlas brand, each with a capacity of 20 ounces.

INGREDIENTS

2 cups glutinous rice	2¼ cups room-temperature water
2 cups cold water	1 wine pill, crushed

---

1. Place the rice in a large bowl and fill the bowl with water. Wash the rice by rubbing it between your palms, then discard the water. Do this two more times, then drain the washed rice well. Place the rice in an 8-inch cake pan and add the 2 cups cold water. Place the cake pan in a steamer, cover, and steam for 30 to 40 minutes. The cooked rice will have a glaze and be translucent.

2. Sterilize three 20-ounce Mason jars. Remove the cake pan from the steamer, transfer the rice to a large bowl and let cool to lukewarm. Add the 2¼ cups room-temperature water and the crushed wine pill to the bowl and mix the contents of the bowl thoroughly with your hand. Divide the rice evenly among the three prepared jars. With a pair of wooden chopsticks, push down through the rice to the bottom of each jar to create holes for the air and the yeast to interact. Make about five holes in each jar of rice.

3. Cover each jar tightly with plastic wrap. Place the jars in a warm part of the kitchen to allow the fermentation to begin, which should take 24 to 30 hours. When you can see liquid seeping into the holes in the rice, the fermentation has begun. The mass of rice will rise from the bottom of each jar, while liquid will be visible on the bottom. In summer, fermentation will be complete about 24 hours after the rice rises. In winter, it will take about 3 days.

4. When the fermentation is complete, there will be a distinct sweet aroma, and the rice itself will taste quite sweet. The rice is now ready to use. Remove the plastic wrap from the jars, replace with screw tops, and refrigerate the jars. The rice will keep for up to 1 year.

SHRIMP WITH SWEET WINE RICE

|| MAKES 4 TO 6 SERVINGS ||

Shanghai residents dote on sweet flavors, so this classic Shanghai stir-fry, which contrasts the sweetness of the wine rice with the spice and heat of the chili sauce and the tartness of the rice vinegar, is a favorite in the city.

INGREDIENTS

SAUCE

3 tablespoons Shanghai Sweet Wine Rice (page 182)

¼ cup ketchup (page 75)

¼ cup Chicken Stock (page 54)

1 tablespoon white rice vinegar

2 teaspoons light soy sauce

1½ teaspoons Homemade Chili Sauce (page 58)

1 teaspoon sesame oil

1½ tablespoons cornstarch

1 tablespoon sugar

¾ teaspoon salt

---

1 pound large shrimp (40 count per pound)

3 cups Chicken Stock (page 54)

2 tablespoons peanut oil

1 tablespoon peeled and minced ginger

2 teaspoons minced garlic

1½ tablespoons Shaoxing wine

3 tablespoons shredded white portion of scallions (see Cleaver discussion, page 45)

---

1. To make the sauce: In a small bowl, mix together all of the ingredients and reserve.

2. Peel the shrimp, leaving the tail segments intact, then devein and clean them (see page 75). In a large pot, bring the stock to a boil over high heat. Add the shrimp, immersing them in the stock, and blanch them for 40 seconds. Turn off the heat, remove the shrimp with a Chinese strainer, and drain them well over a bowl. Pat them dry with paper towels and reserve.

3. Heat a wok over high heat for 40 seconds. Add the peanut oil and, using a spatula, coat the wok with the oil. When a wisp of white smoke appears, add the ginger and garlic and stir for 45 seconds, or until the garlic releases its aroma. Add the shrimp and stir-fry for 1 minute, or until they are well coated with the seasonings. Drizzle in the wine, adding it along the edge of the wok, and mix well. Stir-fry for 1 minute more. Make a well in the center of the mixture, stir the sauce, and pour it into the well. Stir-fry for 1 to 1½ minutes, or until the sauce thickens and bubbles.

4. Turn off the heat. Transfer to a heated dish, sprinkle with the scallions, and serve.

FUJIAN FERMENTED RED RICE

‖ MAKES ABOUT 4 CUPS RICE AND 3 CUPS LIQUID ‖

 Although this fermented rice is made from glutinous rice and a wine pill just as Shanghai Sweet Wine Rice (page 182) is, it is not sweet. That's because red rice is added to the mix, which also accounts for the final color. Nor is this rice ever eaten as cooked. It is always an ingredient and, in Fujian, a treasure. It is usually made in winter—it requires coolness to ferment—in quantities sufficient for a year's use.

INGREDIENTS

2 cups glutinous rice	5 cups cold water
5 tablespoons plus ⅓ cup red rice	¼ wine pill, crushed

---

1. Place the glutinous rice in a large bowl and fill the bowl with water. Wash the rice by rubbing it between your palms, then discard the water. Do this two more times, then drain the washed rice and return it to the bowl. Add water to cover by 2 inches and allow it to soak overnight at room temperature.

2. The next day, drain off the water and place the rice in an 8-inch cake pan. Place the cake pan in a steamer, cover, and steam for 30 to 40 minutes, or until the rice is translucent and is tender but not soft. Turn off the heat, and remove the pan from the steamer. Spread the rice in a thin layer on a baking sheet and allow it to cool.

3. Place the 5 tablespoons red rice in a spice grinder and grind to a powder.

4. In a large plastic container, mix together the 5 cups cold water, the powdered red rice, the ⅓ cup red rice, and the crushed wine pill. Add the cooked glutinous rice to the container and mix it in with your hand. Cover and let rest in a cool place or in the refrigerator for 1 week. Uncover, stir the contents well, re-cover, and let rest for another week in a cool place or in the refrigerator. Uncover, stir again, re-cover, return to the refrigerator, and let rest for 1 month. The rice is now ready to use.

5. Strain the rice through a fine-mesh strainer and reserve the rice and its liquid in separate sterilized jars. Both the rice and the liquid are used in recipes, such as Fuzhou Drunken Pork Ribs (page 176) and Fujian Red Rice *Wor Bah* (page 199). Store the rice and the liquid in the refrigerator. They will keep for up to 1 year.

ROASTED RICE

|| MAKES 1 CUP ||

 A classic ingredient from Sichuan, this ground mixture of cooked short-grain rice and Sichuan peppercorns is used to coat meats before steaming. Its name in Chinese translates as "steamed rice powder," and you will find boxes labeled that way in Chinese markets. But read carefully because the packaged ground rice usually contains rice only and not the traditional combination of rice with Sichuan peppercorns. As with other such ingredients, this one is simple to make, and its flavor will be more intense if homemade.

INGREDIENTS

1 cup short-grain rice	1 tablespoon Sichuan peppercorns

1. Place the rice in a large bowl and fill the bowl with water. Wash the rice by rubbing it between your palms, then discard the water. Do this 2 more times, then drain the washed rice and return it to the bowl. Add water to cover and allow it to soak for 2 hours.

2. Drain the rice thoroughly, preferably overnight. (This may seem like a good deal of effort for a mixture that is going to be dry-roasted, then ground, but it is necessary. Unsoaked ground raw rice will dry out any meat it coats because it will draw out the moisture.)

3. Heat a wok over high heat for 40 seconds. Add the dried rice and the peppercorns and stir to mix well. Stir and cook the mix for 7 minutes, or until the rice turns a sandy color and the peppercorns release their fragrance. If the rice begins to brown too quickly, or if it smells like it is burning, lower the heat to medium. Turn off the heat, transfer the mix to a shallow bowl, and let cool to room temperature.

4. Place the rice mixture in a blender and blend to the consistency of coarse breadcrumbs. Immediately transfer the ground mixture to a glass jar and cover tightly to prevent any loss of fragrance. It will keep at room temperature for up to 2 months.

STEAMED BEEF AND ROASTED RICE

‖ **MAKES 4 TO 6 SERVINGS** ‖

The popularity of this preparation, once unique to Sichuan, has spread to Beijing and to other parts of China over the years. In Beijing, where the dish is cooked in virtually the same way as it is in Sichuan, the Sichuan peppercorns have been replaced by cinnamon sticks. Rice-based coatings are also used in Hunan and Fujian, to cite just two more examples.

INGREDIENTS	
MARINADE	
3 tablespoons hoisin sauce	¾ teaspoon Red Oil (page 149)
2½ tablespoons Sichuan Peppercorn Oil (page 149)	4 teaspoons double dark soy sauce
2 tablespoons Shaoxing wine	1½ tablespoons peeled and minced ginger
1½ tablespoons oyster sauce	1½ tablespoons minced garlic
1 tablespoon white rice vinegar	1 tablespoon sugar
	Pinch of white pepper
1 pound lean beef brisket	8 to 10 scallions, white portions only, cut on the diagonal into ¼-inch-thick pieces
¼ cup Roasted Rice (page 185)	
⅔ cup Superior Stock (page 145)	⅓ cup finely sliced green portion of scallions

1. To make the marinade: In a small bowl, mix together all of the ingredients and reserve.

2. Cut the brisket across the grain into pieces 2½ inches long by 1 inch wide and 1 inch thick. Place the slices in a steamproof dish, pour the marinade over them, and mix well to coat the beef. Add the roasted rice and mix thoroughly. Add the stock and mix well. Add the white portions of scallions and mix well. Marinate the mixture, uncovered, in the refrigerator for 2 hours.

3. Place the dish of beef in a steamer, cover, and steam for 50 minutes, or until the beef is tender.

4. Turn off the heat. Remove the dish from the steamer, sprinkle the beef with the green portions of scallions and serve.

中國調煮實習菜譜

MASTERING THE ART OF CHINESE COOKING

FRIED RICE

炒飯

Stir-frying rice is an adaptable, accommodating cooking method. Almost any food can be cut into small pieces and added to cooked rice, but the combination of foods must be compatible. The tradition of fried rice exists throughout China, and most banquets of any consequence will include one. A notable exception is a birthday banquet, where noodles usually replace rice because they symbolize longevity, though often both noodles and rice are served on those occasions.

The method for making fried rice is essentially the same throughout China, but ingredients and flavorings differ from place to place. In my childhood home in Sun Tak Yuen, a district near Guangzhou, fried rice made with salted fish was, and is, a tradition. In Yangzhou, a famous fried rice named for the city must always contain barbecued pork, baby river shrimp, eggs, and scallions. In Shanghai, Jinhua ham is added to fried rice, and in Yunnan, that province's ham appears.

All fried rice begins with cooked rice. If the rice is cooked between one and three days before it is fried, the result will be markedly better, especially if fine long-grain jasmine rice is used.

In an earlier lesson, I introduced fried rice with an easy recipe that called for only a few ingredients (see page 78). The recipes that follow are not more difficult; they simply have more ingredients. As I have stressed before, it is necessary to have all of your ingredients cut, measured, and at hand before you begin cooking, and these recipes are no exception. The best fried rice is one that is stirred continuously, as its ingredients are seamlessly slipped into the wok.

The first recipe is Shanghai style, with Jinhua ham. The second, made with duck meat, would be a suitable final course for a festive banquet, and the third is flavored with Hong Kong's celebrated XO sauce.

FRIED RICE WITH SUGAR HAM

‖ **MAKES 6 TO 8 SERVINGS** ‖

INGREDIENTS

8 ounces (about 20) large shrimp (40 count per pound)

MARINADE

2 teaspoons oyster sauce

1½ teaspoons sesame oil

1 teaspoon light soy sauce

¾ teaspoon ginger juice (page 70) mixed with 2 teaspoons white rice wine

¾ teaspoon sugar

Pinch of white pepper

SAUCE

2 tablespoons oyster sauce

1½ tablespoons light soy sauce

1½ tablespoons white rice wine

1 tablespoon sesame oil

2 teaspoons sugar

Pinch of white pepper

6 cups cooked rice (page 50), at room temperature

4 to 5 tablespoons peanut oil

5 extra-large eggs beaten with ¼ teaspoon salt

1 cup ¼-inch-dice Sugar Ham (page 151)

5 scallions, finely sliced

1. Clean the shrimp (see page 75), then leave to drain over a bowl for 20 minutes. Pat dry thoroughly with paper towels. Cut the shrimp in half lengthwise, then in half crosswise. Reserve.

2. To make the marinade: In a bowl, mix together all of the ingredients. Add the shrimp and toss to coat evenly. Reserve.

3. To make the sauce: Mix together all of the ingredients in a small bowl and reserve.

4. Place the cooked rice in a bowl. Using your hands, break up any lumps and reserve.

5. Heat a wok over high heat for 30 seconds. Add 1½ tablespoons of the peanut oil and, using a spatula, coat the wok with the oil. When a wisp of white smoke appears, add the beaten eggs and scramble with the spatula for about 1½ minutes, or until medium firm. Turn off the heat and transfer to a plate. Cut into coarse small pieces and reserve.

6. Wash and dry the wok and spatula. Heat the wok over high heat for 30 seconds. Add 2½ tablespoons of the peanut oil and, using the spatula, coat the wok with the oil. When a wisp of white smoke appears, add the shrimp and their marinade and spread the pieces in a single layer. Cook for 1 minute, or until they begin to turn pink. Turn the pieces over, mix well, and cook for about 1 minute, or until they turn pink. Add the ham, stir to mix well, and stir-fry for 1 minute. Then add the reserved rice and stir together until well mixed. Lower the heat to medium and stir-fry continuously for 4 to 5 minutes, or until very hot. If the rice seems dry and begins to stick to the surface of the wok, add the remaining 1 tablespoon peanut oil and mix well.

7. Raise the heat to high, stir the sauce, and drizzle it over the rice. Stir to mix for 1 minute. Lower the heat to medium and stir constantly for 2 minutes, or until the rice is coated with the sauce. Add the eggs and stir to mix for about 2 minutes, or until all of the ingredients are well blended. Add the scallions and stir-fry for 1 minute, or until well mixed.

8. Turn off the heat, transfer to a heated dish, and serve.

FRIED RICE WITH DUCK

‖ MAKES 4 TO 6 SERVINGS ‖

INGREDIENTS

SAUCE

3 tablespoons sauce from Baked Duck Breasts (page 155)	1 tablespoon light soy sauce
2 tablespoons Shaoxing wine	1 teaspoon sesame oil
1½ tablespoons oyster sauce	1½ teaspoons sugar
	¼ teaspoon salt
	Pinch of white pepper

5 cups cooked rice (page 50), at room temperature	1 tablespoon minced garlic
5 tablespoons Scallion Oil (page 56)	½ cup ½-inch-dice shallots
5 extra-large eggs beaten with ¼ teaspoon salt and pinch of white pepper	½ cup ¼-inch-dice peeled fresh water chestnuts
	1 cup ½-inch-dice skinned Baked Duck Breast meat (page 155)
1 tablespoon peeled and minced ginger	3 tablespoons finely sliced fresh coriander leaves

1. To make the sauce: In a small bowl, mix together all of the ingredients and reserve.

2. Place the cooked rice in a bowl. Using your hands, break up any lumps and reserve.

3. Heat a wok over high heat for 30 seconds. Add 2 tablespoons of the scallion oil and, using a spatula, coat the wok with the oil. When a wisp of white smoke appears, add the beaten eggs and scramble with the spatula for about 1½ minutes, or until medium firm. Turn off the heat and transfer to a plate. Cut into coarse small pieces and reserve.

4. Wash and dry the wok and spatula. Heat the wok over high heat for 30 seconds. Add the remaining 3 tablespoons oil and, using the spatula, coat the wok with the oil. When a wisp of white smoke appears, add the ginger and stir for 45 seconds. Add the garlic and stir briefly. Add the shallots, lower the heat to medium, and stir to mix for 2 minutes, or until the shallots are translucent. Raise the heat to high, add the water chestnuts, and stir to mix for 1 minute. Add the duck meat and stir-fry for 2 minutes, or until very hot. Then add the reserved rice and stir together until well mixed. Lower the heat to medium and stir-fry continuously for 3 to 4 minutes, or until the rice is very hot.

5. Raise the heat to high, stir the sauce, and drizzle it over the rice. Stir to mix for 1 minute. Lower the heat to medium and stir constantly for about 2 minutes, or until the rice is coated with the sauce. Add the eggs and stir to mix for about 2 minutes, or until all of the ingredients are blended. Add the coriander and stir to mix.

6. Turn off the heat, transfer to a heated dish, and serve.

FRIED RICE WITH XO SAUCE

|| **MAKES 4 TO 6 SERVINGS** ||

メ口醬炒飯

INGREDIENTS

6 cups cooked rice
(page 50), at room
temperature

SAUCE

3 tablespoons oyster sauce	1 teaspoon sesame oil
1½ tablespoons Shaoxing wine	¼ teaspoon salt
	Pinch of white pepper
1 tablespoon light soy sauce	

3½ tablespoons peanut oil	6 tablespoons XO Sauce (page 157)
6 extra-large eggs beaten with ½ teaspoon salt	1 cup finely sliced scallions
1½ tablespoons peeled and minced ginger	2 tablespoons finely sliced fresh coriander leaves
1 tablespoon minced garlic	

1. Place the cooked rice in a bowl. Using your hands, break up any lumps and reserve.

2. To make the sauce: In a small bowl, mix together all of the ingredients and reserve.

3. Heat a wok over high heat for 30 seconds. Add 2 table-spoons of the peanut oil and, using a spatula, coat the wok with the oil. When a wisp of white smoke appears, add the beaten eggs and scramble with the spatula for about 1½ minutes, or until medium firm. Turn off the heat and transfer to a plate. Cut into coarse, small pieces and reserve.

4. Wash and dry the wok and spatula. Heat the wok over high heat for 30 seconds. Add the remaining 1½ table-spoons oil and, using the spatula, coat the wok with the oil. When a wisp of white smoke appears, add the ginger and stir for 10 seconds. Add the garlic and stir briefly. Add the XO sauce, mix well, and then add the rice.

5. Lower the heat to medium and stir-fry continuously for about 4 minutes, or until the rice is very hot.

6. Raise the heat to high, stir the sauce, and drizzle it over the rice. Stir to mix for 1 minute. Lower the heat to medium and stir constantly for 3 to 4 minutes, or until the rice is coated with the sauce. Add the eggs and stir to mix for about 2 minutes, or until well mixed. Add the scallions and stir and cook for 1 minute more, or until mixed well. Add the coriander and mix well.

7. Turn off the heat, transfer to a heated dish, and serve.

HUNAN PEARL BALLS

‖ MAKES 20 PEARL BALLS, OR 5 TO 10 SERVINGS ‖

 This unusual dish from Hunan is both flavorful and beautiful and is customarily eaten as the first course at a banquet or sometimes as a course for a family meal. The balls are made from ground pork studded with other ingredients, predominantly the salt-cured Yunnan ham from Hunan's neighboring province. The "pearls" are grains of glutinous rice that become glossy and almost translucent when steamed.

INGREDIENTS

12 ounces ground pork

¾ cup ⅛-inch-dice Salt-Cured Ham (page 150)

⅓ cup ¼-inch-dice Steamed Black Mushrooms (page 81)

4 fresh water chestnuts, peeled and cut into ⅛-inch dice

2 tablespoons dried shrimp, soaked in hot water to cover for 20 minutes, drained, and cut into ⅛-inch pieces

2 scallions, finely sliced

1½ teaspoons peeled and minced ginger

1 large egg, lightly beaten

1½ tablespoons cornstarch mixed with 2 tablespoons cold water

2 tablespoons peanut oil

2 teaspoons light soy sauce

1½ teaspoons Shaoxing wine

1 teaspoon sesame oil

2½ teaspoons sugar

1 teaspoon salt

Pinch of white pepper

1½ cups glutinous rice

3 or 4 large iceberg lettuce leaves for lining steamer

1. In a large bowl, combine all of the ingredients except the rice and lettuce. Using a wooden spoon or two pairs of wooden chopsticks, mix the ingredients together, stirring them in one direction, until the mixture is soft and the ingredients are evenly distributed and stick together. Stirring in this way ensures the mixture will be cohesive. Cover and refrigerate for at least 8 hours or up to overnight.

2. Begin making the rice coating for the balls about 3 hours before you will be using it. First, place the rice in a large bowl and fill the bowl with water. Wash the rice by rubbing it between your palms, then discard the water. Do this two more times, then drain the washed rice and return it to the bowl. Add water to cover by 1 inch and allow it to soak for 1 hour. Then pour off the water and drain the rice in a strainer placed over a bowl for 2 hours. At this point it will be dry but there will still be some moisture. Line a baking sheet with waxed paper and spread the rice in a thin layer on the prepared baking sheet. Let sit while you shape the meatballs.

3. Remove the mixture from the refrigerator. Line a second baking sheet with waxed paper. Pick up a handful of the mixture, move it around in your hand gently, then squeeze. The amount that oozes through the top of your hand will be a ball about 1 inch in diameter. Place the ball on the prepared baking sheet. Repeat until all of the mixture is used. There should be 20 balls. Roll 1 ball through the rice, coating it evenly with the grains. Repeat until all of the balls are coated.

4. Line a bamboo steamer with the lettuce leaves. Place the balls on the leaves, cover the steamer, and steam for 15 to 20 minutes, or until the rice is translucent and the pork is thoroughly cooked.

5. Serve at once from the steamer.

STIR-FRIED GLUTINOUS RICE

|| MAKES 4 TO 6 SERVINGS ||

生炒糯米飯

This unusual stir-fried rice dish, created as part of the dim sum repertoire, is a tradition in Guangzhou. In its most familiar form, it is served as a molded dome of rice, but that is a simplified version of this classic. These days the rice is steamed, rather than stir-fried. What follows is the classic version of this dish as it was, and is, prepared in the home. This is the recipe of my number 5 aunt, Ng Ku Cheh, in Hong Kong. There are many steps, but they result in a dish of elegance and extraordinary taste.

The Cantonese consider this a winter dish because they believe it warms the body. My aunt always used lard, and I do so as well, but you can substitute peanut oil, though the taste will not be as good. The traditional cooking method is faintly reminiscent of how Italians cook risotto. Perhaps Marco Polo brought the recipe back to Venice.

INGREDIENTS

2 cups glutinous rice

2 quarts boiling water, to scald rice

3 tablespoons lard or peanut oil

1¼ cups Chicken Stock (page 54)

1 cup ¼-inch-dice Chinese bacon

½ cup ¼-inch-dice Chinese sausage (*lop cheong*)

¼ cup dried shrimp, soaked in hot water to cover for 20 minutes, drained, and cut into ¼-inch dice

½ teaspoon salt

2 tablespoons double dark soy sauce

⅓ cup finely sliced scallions

¼ cup finely chopped coriander

1. Place the rice in a large bowl. Ladle the boiling water over it until all of the water has been added. Drain the rice in a strainer, then spread it in a thin layer around the bowl of the strainer, leaving a small hole uncovered at the bottom to allow any water to run off. Place the strainer over a bowl and let the rice drain for 30 to 45 minutes.

2. Heat a wok over high heat for 45 seconds. Add the lard, allow to melt, and then, using a spatula, coat the wok with the lard. When a wisp of white smoke appears, add the rice, mix well, and stir and cook for 1 minute. Add ½ cup of the stock and stir to mix well. Reduce the heat to low, cover the wok, and allow the rice to cook for 1 minute, or until the stock is absorbed. Remove the cover and stir-fry the rice for 45 seconds. Add ¼ cup of the stock, stir to mix, cover the wok again, and cook the rice for 1 minute, or until the stock is absorbed. Watch carefully and adjust the heat as necessary to prevent burning.

3. Uncover the wok, add the remaining ½ cup stock, and stir to mix well for 1 minute. Cover the wok again and cook for 1 minute more. Remove the cover and stir to mix the rice thoroughly. The rice will be moist, but there will be no liquid. Add the bacon, sausage, and shrimp and stir-fry vigorously to mix all of the ingredients. Raise the heat to medium and continue to stir the rice. Add the salt, mix well, reduce the heat to low, and stir-fry for 7 minutes, or until the bacon and sausage are cooked and their fat is translucent. Add the soy sauce and stir-fry for 3 to 4 minutes, or until well blended. Add the scallions and cook, stirring for 1½ minutes, or until all of the ingredients are well blended. Add the coriander, mix it in well, and stir for 1 minute more.

4. Turn off the heat, transfer to a heated dish, and serve.

RICE LEFT AT THE BOTTOM OF THE POT

‖ MAKES 1 *FAN JIU,* OR 4 SERVINGS ‖

 This rice preparation exists throughout China. It is known by several names, including *guor bah,* its name from its beginnings in Shanghai; *wor bah,* a Western corruption of the Shanghainese term; and the Cantonese *fan jiu.* It is, in simplest terms, the overcooked, crisp layer of rice that is sometimes found on the bottom of the pot in which rice has been cooked. Often this is accidental, and just as often it is deliberate. Either way, it has evolved into a classic.

Perhaps the phrase "sizzling *wor bah*" will spark some recognition. It is seen on English-language menus, and it describes what happens when a piece of this hardened rice is deep-fried, placed still piping hot in a bowl, and hot soup is ladled over it, producing a hiss, a sizzle, and a cloud of steam.

Although the dish began in Shanghai, it did not remain there, instead spreading westward to Hunan and southward to Fujian, with many stops between and beyond, particularly in Guangzhou and Taiwan. Traditionally, it was made by leaving a layer of cooked rice on the bottom of the pot and then turning the heat on to allow the layer to overcook but not burn. Ideally, it will brown slightly. The rice is removed, often in a single piece, and reserved. Then a soup is cooked, and when the hot soup is ready to eat, the rice layer is deep-fried and combined with the soup. The rice softens slightly, but retains its bite and is eaten as an ingredient of the soup.

The layer of crisp rice on the bottom of the pot is called *fan jiu.* It does not become *guor bah* or *wor bah* until it is combined with the soup.

INGREDIENTS

½ cup extra-long-grain rice   ½ cup water

---

1. Place the rice in a bowl and fill the bowl with water. Wash the rice by rubbing it between your palms, then discard the water. Do this 2 more times, then drain the washed rice and place it in a 10-inch nonstick frying pan. Add the water and spread the rice in a thin, even layer. Let the rice rest for 1½ hours. All of the water will be absorbed during this resting period.

2. Place the frying pan over medium heat, cover, and cook the rice for 5 minutes. Reduce the heat to low and cook for 3 minutes more. The rice will become translucent. Remove the cover and cook for 2 to 3 minutes more, moving the pan from side to side on the burner to loosen the rice. Once the rice is loose and moves freely, it is done. Turn off the heat and let the rice cool to room temperature in the pan.

3. Invert a large plate over the frying pan and invert the plate and pan together so the rice layer falls out onto the plate in a single piece. It should be cooked and hardened and be free of moisture. If it is not completely dry, let sit until it is. Use immediately or store in an airtight container in a cool, dry place for up to 6 months.

HOW TO SIZZLE A *WOR BAH*

To make a sizzling *wor bah*, heat 3 cups peanut oil in a wok to 375°F on a deep-frying thermometer and deep-fry the crisp rice layer for 1½ to 2 minutes, or until the rice layer expands to about double its size and browns. Using a Chinese strainer, remove from the oil, draining well, and use piping hot. For *wor bah* dishes, timing is important. Ideally, both the soup and the *wor bah* are as hot as possible, so that when they are combined, they will sizzle and steam. The recipes detail how to time the two elements.

锅巴

WOR BAH

BUYING *WOR BAH*

Cooking the rice for a *wor bah* is a satisfying exercise, and I recommend it, as I do other techniques, for understanding a process of Chinese cooking. But if you want to shorten your cooking time, you can buy these crisp rice layers in Chinese markets. They are sold in squares, cooked but not fried, in plastic packages. Made in Taiwan, they are fashioned from glutinous rice, water, and salt and are labeled "instant sizzling rice." They need only be deep-fried for 3 to 4 seconds on each side, or until light brown. They are then ready to be topped with the soup. I have tried these prepared rice squares several times and have found them to be quite good. But, in the interest of learning, I strongly suggest that you make your own.

SHANGHAI SIZZLING *WOR BAH*

上海鍋巴湯

‖ **MAKES 4 SERVINGS** ‖

INGREDIENTS

3½ cups Milk Stock (page 146)

1-inch-thick slice ginger, peeled and lightly smashed

¼ teaspoon salt

⅛ teaspoon white pepper

2 cups ½-inch-dice Roasted Chicken meat (page 152)

1½ tablespoons Scallion Oil (page 56)

3 cups peanut oil

3 ounces snow peas, ends and strings removed and cut into ½-inch pieces

4 ounces fresh-cooked crabmeat

1 *fan jiu* (page 195)

1 scallion, finely sliced

---

1. Place the stock, ginger, salt, and white pepper in a sand clay pot cover, and bring to a boil over medium heat. Add the chicken and scallion oil, stir to mix, and allow the soup to return to a boil. Lower the heat to simmer.

2. Heat the peanut oil as directed in How to Sizzle a *Wor Bah* (see facing page). It will take 5 to 7 minutes.

3. While the oil is heating, raise the heat under the soup to medium, add the snow peas and crabmeat, stir to mix well, re-cover, and allow to return to a boil. Uncover the clay pot and lower the heat to a bare simmer to keep the soup at the boiling point.

4. When the oil is ready, deep-fry the *fan jiu* as directed, until it expands and browns. Turn off the heat, remove the rice from the oil with a mesh strainer, drain well, and immediately transfer to a heated platter. Turn off the heat under the soup and immediately bring both the clay pot and the platter to the table.

5. To serve, and for dramatic effect, quickly immerse the *fan jiu bah* in the soup so it sizzles and steams and becomes *guor bah*, or *wor bah*. Sprinkle the soup with the scallions, and serve in individual bowls, ladling it over pieces of the *wor bah*.

NOTE: If you are cooking the soup in a regular pot instead of a clay pot, place the deep-fried *wor bah* at the bottom of a heated tureen and pour the hot soup over it. The sizzle and the steam will be the same.

榅州紅糟鍋巴湯

FUJIAN RED RICE
WOR BAH

|| MAKES 4 SERVINGS ||

INGREDIENTS

12 ounces (18 to 22) extra-large shrimp (26 to 30 count per pound)

3 tablespoons Garlic Oil (page 56)

1-inch-thick slice ginger, peeled and lightly smashed

½ cup ¼-inch-dice onions

½ cup ¼-inch-dice celery

½ cup Fujian Fermented Red Rice (page 184)

¼ cup liquid from Fujian Fermented Red Rice (page 184)

4 cups Fish Stock (page 147)

½ teaspoon salt

3 cups peanut oil

1 *fan jiu* (page 195)

---

1. Peel the shrimp, leaving the tail segments intact, then devein and clean them (see page 75). Reserve.

2. Heat a wok over high heat for 30 seconds. Add the garlic oil and, using a spatula, coat the wok with the oil. When a wisp of white smoke appears, add the ginger and stir for 30 seconds. Add the onions and stir for 30 seconds, then lower the heat to medium and cook for 2 minutes more, or until the onions soften. Raise the heat to high, add the celery, and stir-fry for 1 minute. Turn off the heat and transfer the contents of the wok to a sand clay pot.

3. Add the red rice, red rice liquid, fish stock, and salt to the clay pot and stir to mix well. Cover and bring to a boil over medium heat. Lower the heat to a simmer.

4. Heat the peanut oil as directed in How to Sizzle a *Wor Bah* (see page 196). It will take 5 to 7 minutes. When the oil is ready, deep-fry the *fan jiu* as directed, until it expands and browns. Turn off the heat, remove the rice from the oil, drain well with a mesh strainer, and transfer to a heated platter.

5. While the rice is draining, raise the heat under the soup to medium. Add the reserved shrimp and stir to mix. Allow the soup to return to a boil, then turn off the heat. Immediately bring both the clay pot and the platter to the table.

6. To serve, and for dramatic effect, quickly immerse the *fan jiu* in the soup so it sizzles and steams and becomes *wor bah*. Serve in individual bowls, ladling the soup over pieces of the *wor bah*.

NOTE: If you are cooking the soup in a regular pot, instead of a clay pot, place the deep-fried *wor bah* at the bottom of a heated tureen and pour the hot soup over it. The sizzle and the steam will be the same.

{ PART 2 }

LESSON 6
CHINESE COOKING, NORTH TO SOUTH

It is at this point in my intermediate cooking classes that I turn my attention to some of the regional characteristics of Chinese cooking. I have been doing this all along to some degree, but here I reinforce the idea of one vast Chinese cuisine with regional distinctions dictated by usage, folklore, tradition, and small

中國南北菜

CHINESE COOKING, NORTH TO SOUTH

changes in techniques and cooking methods. To do this, we embark on a culinary tour of China, beginning in the north in Beijing, then moving south to the east and the west, and finally to the far south, to explore all of China's recognized cooking regions. We start our journey in the capital, with one of its classics.

BEGGAR'S CHICKEN

‖ MAKES 6 TO 8 SERVINGS ‖

叫化鶏 The story of this dish of many flavors is rooted in a northern folktale. It is said that a beggar, without a home, money, or food, stole a chicken from a farm and ran away until he was satisfied that he was sufficiently far from the farm to cook it. But because he had no home, he had no stove. To cook his stolen chicken, he dug a hole in the ground, filled it with twigs and sticks, ignited them, covered the chicken with pond mud, put it on the fire, and baked it. When it was cooked, he cracked the dried mud and plucked the feathers from the chicken before eating it. That simple repast evolved into a court preparation that was often called *fu guai ji,* or "rich and noble chicken."

This dish requires care to prepare, but it is worth the effort. Unfortunately, what some restaurants call beggar's chicken is not. Pieces of chicken breast are cooked with spices and flavorings, put into a crock covered with imitation ceramic clay, and presented with great fanfare. It is enough to make any self-respecting beggar cringe.

What follows is the traditional way to make this dish, including the use of potent *ng ga pei,* the brandylike spirit distilled in Tianjin, not far from Beijing. In Beijing today, the chicken is prepared classically, with the beggar's mud replaced by pure, clean clay from Shaoxing, a practice also followed in Hong Kong. Such clay is rarely available outside of China, so I have replaced it with a flour-and-water dough and heavy-duty aluminum foil wrap.

INGREDIENTS

1 whole chicken, 3½ pounds

MARINADE

3 tablespoons *ng ga pei* or brandy

1 cinnamon stick, 3 inches long, broken into 4 pieces

2 eight-star anise

2½ teaspoons sugar

1¼ teaspoons salt

Pinch of white pepper

STUFFING

1½ tablespoons peanut oil

1½ cups ¼-inch-dice onions

½ cup ⅛-inch-dice pork fat

6 dried black mushrooms, 1½ inches in diameter, soaked in hot water to cover for 30 minutes, drained, rinsed, squeezed dry, stems discarded, and caps cut into ½-inch dice

½ cup preserved mustard, stalks separated, leaves opened and rinsed 4 times to remove any sand and the preserving salt, squeezed dry, and finely sliced

2 teaspoons *ng ga pei*

1 teaspoon sesame oil

2 teaspoons sugar

1 teaspoon five-spice powder (page 103)

½ teaspoon salt

Pinch of white pepper

DOUGH

5 cups Pillsbury Best All-Purpose Flour

2 cups hot water

2 tablespoons peanut oil

2 lotus leaves, soaked in hot water to cover for 20 minutes until pliable, drained, rinsed, and damp-dried

Continued . . .

. . . continued

1. If the neck and giblets are included with the chicken, freeze them for another use. Clean the chicken as directed on page 54 and leave to drain for 15 minutes. Pat the chicken dry inside and out with paper towels.

2. To make the marinade: Combine all of the ingredients in a small bowl and let rest for 15 minutes.

3. When both the chicken and the marinade are ready, rub the chicken thoroughly, inside and out, with the marinade, then set the chicken aside.

4. To make the stuffing: Heat a wok over high heat for 30 seconds. Add the peanut oil and, using a spatula, coat the wok with the oil. When a wisp of white smoke appears, add the onions and stir-fry for about 2½ minutes, or until light brown. Lower the heat to medium, add the pork fat, and stir-fry for about 2 minutes, or until the fat becomes translucent. Add the mushrooms and preserved mustard and stir to mix. Raise the heat to high, add the *ng ga pei,* and stir. Add the sesame oil, sugar, five-spice powder, salt, and white pepper and stir to mix for 1 minute, or until blended. Turn off the heat, transfer the stuffing to a large plate, and spread it to cool.

5. To make the dough: Mound the flour on a work surface and make a well in the center. Slowly add the hot water to the well with one hand while mixing the water and flour together with the fingers of the other hand. When all of the water has been absorbed, knead for about 2 minutes, or until a dough forms. If the dough feels a bit dry, add a little more hot water, as it needs to be slightly moist. Coat your hands with the peanut oil and rub the dough, applying some pressure, to coat it evenly. Then rub your hands over the work surface, lightly oiling it. Using your hands, flatten the dough until it is large enough to enclose the chicken completely.

6. Fill the body cavity of the chicken loosely with the stuffing, then secure the neck and tail openings closed with poultry skewers. Preheat the oven to 350°F for 15 minutes.

Continued . . .

. . . continued

7. While the oven is heating, wrap the chicken. On a clean work surface, place the lotus leaves, smooth side up. Because the leaves are ribbed like an umbrella, each one must be pleated in the center so it will lie flat. Once you have pleated them, stack them so they are overlapping slightly. Then, place the chicken, breast side up, in the center of the leaves, and fold the leaves up and over the chicken, overlapping the edges and covering the bird completely. The leaves are damp and soft, so they will stay in place without tying.

8. Place the leaf-wrapped chicken in the center of the flattened dough and wrap it, folding the dough up and around the bird and pressing the edges to seal. Lay a 2-foot-long sheet of heavy-duty aluminum foil on a clean work surface and place the dough-wrapped chicken, breast side up, on the foil. Fold the foil around the bird to cover completely and seal closed.

9. Place the wrapped chicken in a roasting pan and bake for 1 hour. Lower the oven temperature to 300°F and continue to bake for 3 hours longer.

10. Turn off the heat, remove the chicken from the oven, and place it on a large platter. Unwrap the foil from around the chicken and roll the edges so it forms a frame around the dough-wrapped chicken. The dough will be browned and quite hard. Using kitchen shears, cut a large oval in the top of the dough and remove the cut-out so the lotus-leaf wrap can be seen. Then cut open the lotus leaves in the same manner. Discard both cutouts. The aromas of the *ng ga pei* and the spices, particularly the five-spice powder, will rise the moment the chicken is exposed. The chicken itself will be falling off the bone, so there is no need to cut it.

11. Serve the chicken with chopsticks or a fork, and spoon the stuffing over the meat.

NOTE: The chicken can be cooked in advance. After removing the chicken from the oven, leave the foil intact. The chicken will remain hot for an hour.

YELLOW CROAKER WITH SWEET WINE RICE SAUCE

‖ MAKES 4 SERVINGS ‖

This fried fish is a favorite in Shanghai. The yellow croaker, which is called *huang hua yu,* or "yellow flower fish," is a saltwater fish found in large schools around ocean reefs. The Shanghainese like the delicate, inherently sweet taste of this small fish. It takes its English name from the croaking sound it makes; Chinese fishermen locate croakers by running long bamboo poles into the waters to cause them to croak.

The secret to deep-frying this fish is to keep it moist and not overcook it. It is often served upright, as if swimming, a traditional symbol of good fortune.

1. To make the sauce: In a small bowl, combine all of the ingredients and reserve.

2. Rinse the fish well under cold running water, remove any errant membranes, and pat dry, inside and out, with paper towels. Lay the fish on a cutting board and make 3 diagonal slits in the flesh, each about 2¼ inches long and spaced about 2 inches apart, and cutting to, but not into, the bone. Turn the fish over and repeat on the second side. Sprinkle the fish, inside and out, with the vinegar. Then sprinkle the fish, inside and out, with the wine, salt, and white pepper. Spread the cornstarch on a sheet of waxed paper and coat the fish thoroughly on both sides, including inside the slits.

3. Heat a wok over high heat for 40 seconds. Pour the peanut oil into the wok and heat to 375°F on a deep-frying thermometer. Shake off the excess cornstarch from the fish, place it in a Chinese strainer, and lower it into the hot oil. (If the oil will not cover the whole fish, tip the strainer so the oil covers one side of the fish and ladle the oil over the other side.) Fry the fish for 5 to 6 minutes. It is done when it is lightly browned and still moist.

4. Turn off the heat. Using the strainer, remove the fish from the oil, draining it well, and place on a heated

INGREDIENTS

SAUCE

2 tablespoons Shanghai Sweet Wine Rice (page 182)

⅓ cup Fish Stock (page 147)

2 tablespoons white rice vinegar

2 tablespoons Shaoxing wine

1 tablespoon double dark soy sauce

1 teaspoon Hot Pepper Oil (page 55)

2 tablespoons sugar

1½ teaspoons cornstarch

½ teaspoon salt

Pinch of white pepper

---

1 whole yellow croaker, 1¼ pounds, purchased live, then cleaned by the fishmonger

1½ teaspoons white rice vinegar

2 tablespoons Shaoxing wine

1 teaspoon salt

Pinch of white pepper

½ cup cornstarch for coating

6 cups peanut oil

⅓ cup ¼-inch-dice shallots

1 tablespoon peeled and minced ginger

3 tablespoons ⅛-inch-dice carrots

3 tablespoons ⅛-inch-dice bamboo shoots

2 tablespoons finely sliced scallions

1 tablespoon finely sliced fresh coriander leaves

platter. Cover your hands with a cloth and position the croaker upright, stomach side down, then press down gently so it is firmly set.

5. Pour off all but 1½ tablespoons of the oil from the wok. Heat the wok over high heat for 20 seconds. When a wisp of white smoke appears, add the shallots and stir-fry for about 2 minutes, or until translucent. Add the ginger and stir briefly. Add the carrots and bamboo shoots and stir-fry for about 1½ minutes, or until very hot. Stir the sauce, pour it into the wok, and stir-fry for about 2 minutes, or until the sauce thickens and bubbles.

6. Turn off the heat. Pour the sauce over the fish, sprinkle it with the scallions and coriander, and serve.

WHITE SOUP WITH TWO BEAN CURDS

|| **MAKES 6 TO 8 SERVINGS** ||

Shanghai restaurant chefs often cook white foods in combination. They will variously steam white crabmeat, scramble egg whites, mince white fish for soups, and cook with a pearly white milk stock, a Shanghai favorite. Occasionally, they even use a white soy sauce known as *yin bai jiang,* which is rarely found outside of China. This tribute to bean curd and the soybean is a familiar white soup in Shanghai restaurants. It melds two opposite textures, soft silken bean curd and hard dried bean curd sticks, and it includes white soybean sprouts as well. The addition of the area's salt-cured Jinhua ham provides the soup with a flavorful and artistic contrast.

INGREDIENTS

8 pieces bean curd sticks (4 ounces total)	1½-inch-long piece ginger, peeled and lightly smashed
1 package (19 ounces) silken bean curd	¾ cup ⅓-inch-dice Salt-Cured Ham (page 150)
6 cups Milk Stock (page 146)	6 ounces soybean sprouts

---

1. Soak the bean curd sticks in hot water to cover for 30 minutes, or until elastic and pliable. Drain and cut crosswise into ½-inch pieces. Reserve.

2. Cut the silken bean curd into ½-inch cubes and reserve.

3. In a large pot, place the stock and ginger and bring to a boil over high heat. Add the ham and allow the stock to return to a boil. Lower the heat to medium and cook for 5 minutes. Raise the heat to high, add the bean curd sticks, and stir to mix. Lower the heat to medium and cook for 10 minutes. Raise the heat to high, add the bean sprouts, and mix well. Cook the soup for 2 to 3 minutes, or until the beans at the ends of the sprouts are tender. Add the silken bean curd, stir to mix well, and allow the soup to return to a boil. Boil for 1 minute, then turn off the heat.

4. Transfer the soup to a heated tureen and serve.

BEEF WITH PEPPER PICKLE

‖ **MAKES 4 SERVINGS** ‖

泡椒炒牛肉

This is a classic preparation of Hunan, but because of the constant exchange of cooking between Hunan and neighboring Sichuan, it has become familiar in Sichuan as well. Yet it is essentially a Hunan dish, with its heat complementing its sourness and slight touch of sweetness. For this recipe, I use filet mignon because of its taste and tenderness. Serve with rice or Steamed Breads (page 167).

INGREDIENTS

12 ounces filet mignon

MARINADE

1½ tablespoons oyster sauce	2 teaspoons sugar
1½ teaspoons double dark soy sauce	2¼ teaspoons mung bean starch
1 tablespoon Shaoxing wine	¼ teaspoon salt
1 tablespoon sesame oil	⅛ teaspoon ground Sichuan peppercorns (page 37)
1½ teaspoons white rice vinegar	

3½ tablespoons peanut oil	4 scallions, white portions only, lightly smashed and cut into ½-inch pieces, to yield ¼ cup
1 tablespoon peeled and minced ginger	
⅛ teaspoon salt	½ cup 2-inch-julienne celery
½ cup 2-inch-julienne carrots	1 tablespoon minced garlic
2 Pepper Pickles (page 156), cut into ¼-inch dice, to yield 3 tablespoons	1 tablespoon Sichuan Peppercorn Paste (page 211)

1. Cut the beef across the grain into precise strips 2 inches long by ¼ inch wide and ¼ inch thick. Reserve.

2. To make the marinade: In a bowl, mix together all of the ingredients. Add the beef and turn to coat well. Let rest for 20 minutes.

3. Heat a wok over high heat for 45 seconds. Add 1½ tablespoons of the peanut oil and, using a spatula, coat the wok with the oil. When a wisp of white smoke appears, add the ginger and salt and stir briefly. Add the carrots, pickles, and scallions and stir to mix well. Add the celery and stir-fry for 1½ minutes, or until all of the ingredients are well mixed. Turn off the heat, transfer to a bowl, and reserve.

4. Wipe the wok and spatula with paper towels. Heat the wok over high heat for 20 seconds. Add the remaining 2 tablespoons peanut oil and, using the spatula, coat the wok with the oil. When a wisp of white smoke appears, add the garlic and the peppercorn paste and stir to mix for about 1½ minutes, or until the garlic releases its aroma.

5. Turn off the heat, add the beef and its marinade, and spread the strips in a single layer. Turn on the heat to high and cook for 1 minute, or until the edges of the strips turn color. Then turn the strips and stir-fry for about 1½ minutes, or until they lose their redness. Add the reserved vegetables and stir-fry for 1½ to 2 minutes, or until the mixture is well-blended and very hot.

6. Turn off the heat, transfer to a heated dish, and serve.

OLD SKIN BEEF

‖ MAKES 4 SERVINGS ‖

陳皮牛肉

I have chosen another beef preparation from Hunan for two reasons. First, it reflects an ancient tradition, and second, it demonstrates a different way of cooking beef in Hunan, crisply fried. The "old skin" of this recipe is dried tangerine skin, or peel, and the ingredient's literal translation from the Chinese implies that the peel is so old that it is covered with dust. Such skin, carefully dried in the sun, is kept for many years, even for many generations, by both professional chefs and households. It never disintegrates, but remains dry and hard, and is extraordinarily costly. I knew a Hong Kong chef who would never use tangerine skin unless he was assured it was at least thirty years old.

The tradition of cooking with old tangerine skin originated in Hunan, but the practice has spread throughout China, with differing results. This dish is often referred to as orange beef, especially in the West, because it is made with fresh or recently dried orange peel instead of dried tangerine skin, which is not available in sufficient quantities. Traditionally, old skin was never made with orange peel, only tangerine peel. To make your own old skin, dry tangerine peels in the sun until they are quite hard and then store them in a tightly capped jar in a cool, dry, dark cupboard. Let them sit for as long as possible before using, as the older they are, the better they are. While the peels are aging, you can buy old skin in some Chinese markets and in herbal shops. But be prepared to spend a good deal of money, for the older the skin, the dearer it is.

INGREDIENTS

8 ounces flank steak	2 tablespoons old tangerine skin, broken into 6 pieces
¾ teaspoon baking soda	

MARINADE

2 tablespoons lightly beaten egg whites	Pinch of white pepper
2 teaspoons Shaoxing wine	2 tablespoons peanut oil
	¼ cup cornstarch

SAUCE

2 tablespoons Red Stock (page 147)	1 teaspoon sesame oil
1 tablespoon double dark soy sauce	½ teaspoon Red Oil (page 149)
1 tablespoon Shaoxing wine	1½ tablespoons sugar
1 tablespoon white rice vinegar	1 teaspoon cornstarch
	⅛ teaspoon salt
	Pinch of white pepper

3 cups peanut oil	1 tablespoon minced garlic
5 dried Thai chiles	2 scallions, cut on the diagonal into ½-inch-thick slices
1 tablespoon peeled and minced ginger	

1. Cut the beef across the grain into precise strips 3 inches long by ⅛ inch wide and ⅛ inch thick. Place the beef in a bowl, add the baking soda, and toss to coat evenly. Cover and place in the refrigerator to rest for 8 hours, or overnight.

2. Remove beef from the refrigerator, rinse off the baking soda, drain, dry, and set aside.

3. While the beef rests, prepare the old tangerine skin. In a small bowl, soak the pieces in hot water to cover for 20 minutes, or until they soften. Drain and finely slice to yield about 2 tablespoons. Reserve.

Continued . . .

. . . continued

4. To make the marinade: Add all of the ingredients, one by one, in the order listed, tossing each one with the beef to mix well before you add the next one. Re-cover the bowl and return to the refrigerator to rest for 30 minutes.

5. To make the sauce: In a small bowl, mix together all of the sauce ingredients and reserve.

6. When the beef is ready, heat a wok over high heat for 1 minute. Add the peanut oil and heat to 300°F on a deep-frying thermometer. When the oil is hot, add the beef and its marinade and immediately turn off the heat. Using chopsticks, separate the strands of beef. Turn on the heat to high and deep-fry the beef for 10 to 12 minutes, or until it is crisp. Turn off the heat, remove the beef from the oil with a Chinese strainer, and drain over a bowl.

7. Pour off all but 2 tablespoons of the oil from the wok. Turn on the heat to high, and when a wisp of white smoke appears, add the chiles. Stir to mix them until they turn black. Add the reserved tangerine skin and stir to mix. Add the ginger and garlic and stir to mix. Add the scallions and stir to mix. If the scallions begin to scorch, lower the heat to medium-high. Add the beef and stir-fry for 1 minute, or until well mixed. Make a well in the center of the mixture, stir the sauce, and pour it into the well. Stir-fry for about 1½ minutes, or until the beef is evenly coated and the sauce is absorbed.

8. Turn off the heat, transfer to a heated dish, and serve.

CHICKEN WITH SICHUAN PEPPERCORN PASTE

‖ MAKES 4 SERVINGS ‖

 This snack, an example of Sichuan street food, is made with cooked chicken and eaten cold. It calls for a marvelously pungent seasoning mixture made by mashing together Sichuan peppercorns, ginger, and scallions, a paste known for its "strange taste" in Chengdu and elsewhere in Sichuan.

INGREDIENTS

½ Roasted Chicken (page 152)

SAUCE

3 tablespoons Chicken Stock (page 54)

2½ tablespoons double dark soy sauce

2 tablespoons Chinkiang vinegar

2 tablespoons Sichuan Peppercorn Paste (see sidebar)

2 tablespoons sesame seed paste

1 tablespoon Shaoxing wine

2 teaspoons sesame oil

1 teaspoon Hot Pepper Oil (page 55)

¼ cup finely sliced scallions

2 teaspoons peeled and minced ginger

2 teaspoons minced garlic

2 tablespoons sugar

¼ teaspoon salt

2 cups finely julienned iceberg lettuce

1. Remove the meat from the chicken half, discarding the skin and bones. Place the meat on a cutting board and pound it with the side of a cleaver blade to break its fiber, then shred it by hand. You should have 2 cups.

2. To make the sauce: In a large bowl, mix together all of the ingredients. Add the shredded chicken and mix together, making sure the chicken shreds are evenly coated.

3. Arrange the lettuce around the rim of a platter. Mound the chicken with its sauce in the center and serve.

NOTE: The chicken can be served at room temperature or cold. To serve it cold, refrigerate the shredded chicken, mixed with the sauce, for 2 hours before plating. Refrigerate the lettuce separately.

‖ SICHUAN PEPPERCORN PASTE ‖
MAKES ABOUT ½ CUP

SICHUAN PEPPER-CORN PASTE

Created in Sichuan, this simple paste is often referred to as a "secret ingredient." It is not at all secret, but it is definitely a fine addition to recipes, blending with and enhancing other ingredients. Consequently its fame and use have spread beyond Sichuan.

1 tablespoon Sichuan peppercorns

3 tablespoons peeled and minced fresh ginger

⅔ cup finely sliced scallions

In a small bowl, preferably stainless steel, place all of the ingredients and crush to a coarse paste with the handle of a cleaver. Or, use a mortar and pestle. Store in a tightly covered container in the refrigerator for up to 3 days.

RICE NOODLES SICHUAN WITH SHRIMP

‖ MAKES 2 SERVINGS FOR LUNCH, OR UP TO 8 SERVINGS AS PART OF A LARGE MEAL ‖

Traditionally, this Sichuan classic was made with dried shrimp, a circumstance of Sichuan's once-isolated inland location. Because fresh fish and shellfish were rare in this landlocked province, they were often imported preserved in salt or dried. Made with dried shrimp, this simple preparation was customarily a one-dish meal, usually served at lunch with tea. No longer isolated, Sichuan has access to fresh fish and seafood today, so I have made it with fresh shrimp.

INGREDIENTS

12 ounces dried thin rice noodles (rice sticks; similar in size to capellini no. 11)	12 ounces (about 30) large shrimp (40 count per pound)

MARINADE

2 tablespoons oyster sauce	1 teaspoon sesame oil
2 teaspoons white rice wine	2 teaspoons cornstarch
2 teaspoons light soy sauce	1½ teaspoons sugar
1 teaspoon ginger juice (page 70)	1 teaspoon salt
	Pinch of white pepper

4½ to 5½ tablespoons Scallion Oil (page 56)	2 Pepper Pickles (page 156), cut into a fine julienne (2 tablespoons)
2 slices ginger, ¼ inch thick, peeled and lightly smashed	¾ cup finely julienned red bell peppers
4 ounces snow peas, ends and strings removed and cut on the diagonal into fine julienne	4 scallions, cut into 2-inch lengths and white portions quartered lengthwise
3 tablespoons Sichuan mustard pickle	2 garlic cloves, lightly smashed
	½ teaspoon salt

1. In a bowl, soak the noodles in hot water to cover for 15 to 20 minutes, or until they soften. Drain them in a strainer placed over a bowl for 1 hour, loosening them with chopsticks 3 times as they dry. Cut the noodles into 5-inch lengths and reserve.

2. While the noodles are drying, clean the shrimp as directed on page 75. Cut each shrimp in half lengthwise.

3. To make the marinade: In a bowl, mix together all of the ingredients. Add the shrimp, turn to coat well, and let rest for 20 minutes.

4. Heat a wok over high heat for 30 seconds. Add 1 tablespoon of the scallion oil and, using a spatula, coat the wok with the oil. When a wisp of white smoke appears, add 1 ginger slice and stir for 45 seconds. Add the snow peas and stir-fry for 30 seconds, or until they begin to turn bright green. Add the mustard pickle and the pepper pickles and stir-fry for 1 minute. Add the bell peppers and scallions, mix well, and stir-fry for 1½ minutes, or until very hot. If the mixture seems too dry, sprinkle some water into the wok to create steam. Turn off the heat, and remove to a bowl.

5. Wipe the wok and spatula with paper towels. Heat the wok over high heat for 20 seconds. Add 1½ tablespoons of the scallion oil and, using the spatula, coat the wok with the oil. When a wisp of white smoke appears, add the remaining ginger slice and the garlic and stir for 45 seconds, or until the garlic releases its fragrance. Add the shrimp and their marinade and spread in a thin single layer. Cook for 1 minute, or until they begin to turn pink. Turn the shrimp over, mix well, and stir-fry for 1 minute longer, or until they turn pink. Turn off the heat, and remove the shrimp to a bowl.

Continued . . .

. . . continued

6. Wash and dry the wok and spatula. Heat the wok over high heat for 45 seconds. Add 2 tablespoons of the scallion oil and the salt and, using the spatula, coat the wok with the oil. When a wisp of white smoke appears, add the rice noodles by slowly and gently dropping them off the spatula into the wok, to avoid spattering. Stir-fry the noodles for 1 minute, lower the heat to medium, and then stir-fry them for 6 minutes more, or until very hot. If the wok becomes dry, add the remaining 1 tablespoon oil and adjust the heat as needed to ensure even cooking.

7. Raise the heat to high, add the shrimp and their liquid to the noodles, and stir-fry for 2 minutes. Add the vegetables and stir-fry together for 2 minutes longer, or until well mixed. Again, adjust the heat as needed to ensure the noodles do not burn.

8. Turn off the heat, transfer to a heated platter, and serve.

SHREDDED PORK WITH SNOW PEAS AND CHICKEN LEG MUSHROOMS

‖ **MAKES 4 TO 6 SERVINGS** ‖

雪
荳
肉
絲
炒
鷄
肶

Once again, meaty chicken leg mushrooms appear in a stir-fry, this time in a classic Cantonese preparation with snow peas and shredded pork that demonstrates the mix of textures and tastes so characteristic of the cooking of Guangdong. The mushrooms are meaty, slightly chewy; the snow peas deliver crunch; and the pork provides bite.

INGREDIENTS

MARINADE

4 teaspoons oyster sauce	1½ teaspoons sugar
2 teaspoons light soy sauce	2 teaspoons cornstarch
2 teaspoons Shaoxing wine	¼ teaspoon salt
1½ teaspoons sesame oil	Pinch of white pepper
1 teaspoon white rice vinegar	

12 ounces pork loin, shredded (see Cleaver discussion, page 45)

SAUCE

⅓ cup Superior Stock (page 145)	1 teaspoon white rice vinegar
1 tablespoon Shaoxing wine	4 teaspoons cornstarch
1 tablespoon oyster sauce	1 teaspoon sugar
2 teaspoons sesame oil	¼ teaspoon salt
1½ teaspoons light soy sauce	Pinch of white pepper

中國調煮實習菜譜

MASTERING THE ART OF CHINESE COOKING

8 ounces snow peas	2 teaspoons salt
5 cups water	¾ teaspoon baking soda (optional)
½-inch-thick slice ginger, peeled and lightly smashed	

3 tablespoons peanut oil	1 tablespoon Superior Stock (page 145), if needed
1 tablespoon peeled and minced ginger	
1 tablespoon minced garlic	1 fresh chicken leg mushroom (about 5 ounces), cut crosswise into ¼-inch-thick rounds, then cut into ¼-inch-wide strips
1 tablespoon plus 1 teaspoon Shaoxing wine	

1. To make the marinade: In a bowl, mix together all of the ingredients. Add the pork, turn to coat evenly, and reserve.

2. To make the sauce: In a small bowl, mix together all of the ingredients and reserve.

3. To water-blanch (see page 63) the snow peas, first trim the ends and strings from the peas, then cut each pea into thirds on a sharp diagonal.

4. In a pot, bring the water to a boil over high heat. Add the ginger, salt, and baking soda (if using). When the water returns to a boil, add the snow peas and blanch and stir for 30 seconds. Turn off the heat, run cold water into the pot, then drain off the water. Run cold water into the pot again, drain well, discard the ginger, and drain the snow peas in a strainer for at least 10 minutes.

5. Heat a wok over high heat for 30 seconds. Add the peanut oil and, using a spatula, coat the wok with the oil. When a wisp of white smoke appears, add the ginger and stir briefly. Add the garlic and stir briefly. Add the pork and its marinade and spread the pieces in a single layer. Cook for 1 minute, or until the pieces turn white along the edges. Turn the pork over and mix well.

6. Drizzle in the wine, adding it along the edge of the wok, and stir-fry for 2 to 3 minutes, or until the pork turns white. If the pork begins to stick to the wok, add the stock and mix well.

7. Add the snow peas and stir-fry for 1½ minutes, or until well mixed. Make a well in the center of the mixture, stir the sauce, and pour it into the well. Stir to mix well. Add the mushroom strips and stir-fry for 2 minutes, or until the sauce thickens and bubbles.

8. Turn off the heat, transfer to a heated dish, and serve.

MINCED DUCK WRAPPED IN LETTUCE

|| MAKES 4 SERVINGS ||

This is my adaptation of a Cantonese classic. It is widely believed that the practice of wrapping foods in lettuce leaves in China originated in the province of Guangdong, home to a special lettuce quite like iceberg, called *bor lei sang choi* in Cantonese. The first two words translate as "glass," to indicate that light is visible through the leaves. Lettuce itself, or *sang choy* in Cantonese, is a recurring symbol of new life and growth, and it is hung over the entry door of houses in Guangdong on the Lunar New Year.

Over the years, this method of wrapping foods in lettuce has spread beyond the borders of Guangdong, and today, cooks elsewhere in China serve baby clams, minced squab, shrimp and diced mushrooms, and other foods this way. The traditional Cantonese recipe calls for minced squab. Here, I have used minced duck in its place.

INGREDIENTS

Deep-fried Rice Noodles (page 143)

SAUCE

3 tablespoons Chicken Stock (page 54)	1 teaspoon sesame oil
1½ tablespoons oyster sauce	1 teaspoon white rice wine
1 tablespoon Shaoxing wine	1½ teaspoons mung bean starch
1½ teaspoons light soy sauce	1½ teaspoons sugar
	Pinch of white pepper

2½ tablespoons peanut oil	6 dried black mushrooms, 1½ inches in diameter, soaked in hot water to cover for 30 minutes, drained, rinsed, squeezed dry, stems discarded, and caps cut into ¼-inch dice
1 tablespoon peeled and minced ginger	
2 tablespoons minced garlic	
4 fresh water chestnuts, peeled and cut into ¼-inch dice	
⅓ cup ¼-inch-dice celery	1 Baked Duck Breast (page 155), skinned and cut into ¼-inch dice
⅓ cup ¼-inch-dice bamboo shoots	8 leaves iceberg lettuce, cut into 5-inch rounds
¼ cup ¼-inch-dice shallots	

1. Deep-fry the noodles as directed, drain them well over a bowl, and then spread them in an even layer on a platter. Reserve.

2. To make the sauce: Combine all of the ingredients in a small bowl and reserve.

3. Heat a wok over high heat for 30 seconds. Add the peanut oil and, using a spatula, coat the wok with the oil. When a wisp of white smoke appears, add the ginger and stir briefly. Add the garlic and stir briefly. Add the water chestnuts, celery, bamboo shoots, shallots, and mushrooms and stir-fry for 3 minutes, or until very hot. Add the duck meat, stir to mix well, and cook for 2 more minutes, or until well mixed. Make a well in the center of the mixture, stir the sauce, and pour it into the well. Stir and mix well for about 1½ minutes, or until the sauce thickens and the ingredients have a glistening coat.

4. Turn off the heat and ladle the filling atop the noodles. Place the lettuce rounds on a separate platter. Invite diners to serve themselves by scooping a heaping tablespoon of the duck filling onto a lettuce round, topping it with some of the fried rice noodles, and then folding the lettuce around the filling.

THE CUISINES OF THE CHIU CHOW AND THE HAKKA

朝州和客家

Two special cuisines of southern China, often lumped together with the Cantonese kitchen, deserve particular mention. They are the Chiu Chow and the Hakka, one native, one a cuisine of immigrants. The Chiu Chow people are indigenous to the region around the old port city of Swatow, now known as Shantou, in northeastern Guangdong. They were seafarers who sailed to Taiwan and to ports in Southeast Asia, often settling in their destinations, and they are variously known as Chiu Chow or Chiu Chao by the Cantonese, as Chaozhou elsewhere in China, and as Teochiu or Teochew in Taiwan, Singapore, and as far away as Thailand and Vietnam.

Chiu Chow cooking, once thought to be part of the Cantonese table, is unique, direct, and pungent. Diners relish shark's fin and bird's nest soups, and they dote on all manner of seafood soup. Cooks flavor their foods with a salty fermented fish sauce, a cousin to Thai *nam pla* and Vietnamese *nuoc mam,* and make sweet marmalades and preserves. They pickle and preserve cabbage, mustard greens, shallots, and ginger; bottle their own vinegar and tangerine oil; and make a sweet soy sauce by cooking it with sugar.

The Hakka, unlike the Chiu Chow, are immigrants to the south. The history of the Hakka continues to be debated, but the most common theory puts their origins in northern China, from which they first fled to the south many centuries ago. That initial flight was followed by others during the Jin, Northern Song, T'ang, and Qing Dynasties. Today, the Hakka are found primarily in Guangdong, Fujian, and Jiangxi provinces and in Hong Kong's New Territories. They are regarded as insular and hardworking and highly protective of their ancestral and cultural customs and are often successful in their professional lives. In Hong Kong, for example, many of the descendants of early immigrants are both wealthy and politically influential.

Because the Hakka were nomadic, they developed a cooking style on the move. They preserved foods so they could carry them; they boiled vegetables and ate them with cold sauces. The soybean has long been important: the boiled beans are eaten, the milk made from ground beans is drunk, and the curd is prepared in imaginative ways. The Hakka use wild leafy vegetables, and one of their famous dishes, salt-baked chicken, was once cooked in a hole in the ground.

CHICKEN WITH *CHIN JIEW*

‖ **MAKES 6 SERVINGS** ‖

川椒鷄

In this traditional Chiu Chow dish, two ingredients particular to Chiu Chow cooks in southern China are used. The first is Sichuan peppercorns, which they call *chin jiew,* and which, until recently, were not used by other cooks in Guangdong. The second is what the Chiu Chow call *jun jiu choi,* or "pearl vegetable," which are wild green leaves that are shaped like tiny maple leaves. They are deep-fried and used as a garnish for many different dishes, especially chicken dishes. They are unavailable anywhere else, but large-leaf basil is a good substitute.

INGREDIENTS

1 pound boneless, skinless
chicken breasts

MARINADE

1 tablespoon oyster sauce	½ teaspoon ginger juice (page 70)
2 teaspoons Shaoxing wine	
1½ teaspoons fish sauce	1 large egg white, lightly beaten
1½ teaspoons sesame oil	3 tablespoons cornstarch
1 tablespoon double dark soy sauce	1 teaspoon sugar

SAUCE

3 tablespoons Superior Stock (page 145)	1¼ teaspoons cornstarch
	½ teaspoon sugar
1 tablespoon oyster sauce	

1 teaspoon Sichuan peppercorns	3 scallions, finely sliced
	1 tablespoon Shaoxing wine
3 cups peanut oil	
1 cup large basil leaves, washed and well dried	

---

1. Cut the chicken into 1-inch cubes and reserve.

2. To make the marinade: In a bowl, combine all of the ingredients. Add the chicken and turn to coat evenly. Let rest for 30 minutes.

3. To make the sauce: In a small bowl, combine all of the ingredients and reserve.

4. To dry-roast the peppercorns, heat a wok over high heat for 30 seconds. Add the peppercorns and stir for 20 seconds. Lower the heat to medium and stir for 1½ minutes, or until the peppercorns release their fragrance. Turn off the heat and transfer to a bowl. Let the peppercorns cool completely, then crush or grind them coarsely with the handle of a cleaver. Or, use a mortar and pestle. Reserve.

5. To deep-fry the basil leaves, heat the wok over high heat for 30 seconds. Add the peanut oil and heat to 300°F on a deep-frying thermometer. Add half of the basil leaves to the hot oil and deep-fry, turning them once, for 1½ minutes, or until they are crisp and bright green. Using a Chinese strainer, remove them to a plate lined with paper towels and let them drain. Repeat with the remaining leaves. Reserve.

6. Heat the oil in the wok to 350°F. Add the chicken and its marinade, spreading the cubes to prevent them from sticking together. Deep-fry the cubes, turning them constantly, until they are golden brown, about 3 minutes. Turn off the heat. Using the strainer, lift out the chicken, draining well, and reserve.

Continued . . .

. . . continued

7. Pour off all but 2 tablespoons of the oil from the wok. Place the wok over high heat for 20 seconds. When a wisp of white smoke appears, add two-thirds of the scallions and all of the reserved peppercorns and cook, stirring for 45 seconds. Add the reserved chicken and stir-fry for 1 minute. Add the wine and stir to mix, turning the chicken to coat it evenly. Make a well in the center of the mixture, stir the sauce, and pour it into the well. Stir-fry for about 2 minutes, or until the sauce is absorbed and the chicken is well coated.

8. Turn off the heat and transfer the chicken to a platter. Arrange the fried basil leaves around the chicken, sprinkle with the remaining scallions, and serve.

SQUASH PANCAKES

|| MAKES 4 TO 6 SERVINGS ||

This dish, a specialty of the Chiu Chow, calls for a vegetable native to southern China, the water squash, or *soi guah* in Cantonese. It gets its name from the fact that it is customarily planted along riverbanks, lakeshores, and the edges of fish ponds, so that its vines can draw nourishing water. It is a summer vegetable and only occasionally is it available in Chinatown markets, but zucchini can be used in its place. The two squashes have a similar texture and both are green and long, though the water squash is larger. It can grow to 18 inches in length and have a diameter of more than 3 inches. Smaller zucchini, which the Chiu Chow call phonetically *ee dai lei guah,* or "Italian squash," are the best choice. Look for zucchini about 7 inches long and weighing about 12 ounces each.

INGREDIENTS

2 tablespoons raw peanuts

1½ cups ½-inch-thick peeled zucchini slices, cut into ¼-inch-wide strips

3 tablespoons ¼-inch-thick scallion slices

1 large egg, lightly beaten

1 tablespoon light soy sauce

1½ teaspoons Shaoxing wine

4½ tablespoons Pillsbury Best All-Purpose Flour

½ teaspoon sugar

Pinch of white pepper

3½ to 5 tablespoons peanut oil

1. First, dry-roast the peanuts. Heat a wok over high heat for 30 seconds. Add the peanuts, spread them in a single layer, lower the heat to medium, and allow to roast for 30 seconds. Turn the peanuts over and stir continuously for about 5 minutes, or until they are light brown. Turn off the heat and transfer the peanuts to a dish. Allow them to cool completely, then place them on a sheet of waxed paper and crush them with a rolling pin.

2. In a large bowl, combine the peanuts, zucchini, scallions, egg, soy sauce, wine, flour, sugar, and pepper and stir until a smooth batter forms.

3. Heat the wok over high heat for 1 minute. Add 2½ tablespoons of the peanut oil and, using the spatula, coat the wok with the oil. Pour in the batter and spread in a thin layer. Using both handles of the wok, move the wok over the burner in a circular motion so the pancake moves around as well and does not stick. Cook for about 2½ minutes, or until the bottom browns.

4. Slide the pancake from the wok onto a large, flat plate. Invert a second plate of the same size over the top and invert the plates together. Lift off the top plate. Slide the pancake, browned side up, back into the wok and lower the heat to medium. Cook, occasionally patting the pancake down with the spatula, for about 3 minutes. Adjust the heat as needed so that the pancake is neither undercooked nor burned and add the remaining 1½ tablespoons oil only if the pan becomes too dry and the pancake begins to stick. The pancake is done when the zucchini has softened and tiny brown spots appear on the second side.

5. Turn off the heat. Slide the pancake onto a heated platter, cut it into wedges, and serve.

NOTE: If you want to serve individual pancakes, proceed as directed, but separate the batter into 4 equal portions. Then, cook each smaller pancake separately according to the directions for cooking a single large one.

SOUR MUSTARD PICKLE WITH BEEF

|| MAKES 4 TO 6 SERVINGS ||

酸菜炒牛肉 A classic of the nomadic Hakka, this dish is based on a pickled leafy mustard, one of the many vegetables the Hakka preserved so it could be easily transported as they moved about. Called *seun choi* in Cantonese, sour mustard pickle is no longer found only in the Hakka kitchen and nowadays can be purchased in most Chinatown markets. This dish is made with either pork or beef. Among the Hakka, beef is preferred because they find its flavor sufficiently strong to complement the equally strong taste of the sour mustard pickle. Chinese Buddhists, who oppose the consumption of beef, will eat this dish made with pork.

You need a tender cut of beef for this dish. I have found filet mignon to be the best choice.

INGREDIENTS

SAUCE

½ cup Chicken Stock (page 54)

3 tablespoons oyster sauce

1½ tablespoons Shaoxing wine

1 tablespoon double dark soy sauce

1½ teaspoons sesame oil

5 teaspoons cornstarch

1 tablespoon sugar

Pinch of white pepper

¾ cup plus 2 tablespoons Chicken Stock (page 54)

12 ounces filet mignon, cut across the grain into slices 2 inches long by 1 inch wide and ¼ inch thick

2½ tablespoons peanut oil

2 tablespoons peeled and minced ginger

1 tablespoon minced garlic

2 celery stalks, cut into julienne (¾ cup)

9 ounces sour mustard pickle, thinly sliced crosswise (1½ cups)

⅓ cup julienned red bell peppers

1½ tablespoons Shaoxing wine

---

1. To make the sauce: In a bowl, mix together all of the ingredients and reserve.

2. To stock-blanch the beef, place the ¾ cup stock in a wok and bring to a boil over high heat. Add the beef and stir once with a spatula. Turn off the heat and continue to stir for about 1 minute, or until the beef turns color. Remove the beef with a Chinese strainer and drain well over a bowl. Reserve.

3. Wash and dry the wok and spatula. Heat the wok over high heat for 30 seconds. Add the peanut oil and, using the spatula, coat the wok with the oil. When a wisp of white smoke appears, add the ginger and stir briefly. Add the garlic and stir for about 45 seconds, or until it releases its aroma. Add the celery and sour mustard pickle and stir-fry for 2 minutes, or until well mixed. Add the 2 tablespoons stock and stir to mix well. Add the reserved beef and the bell peppers and stir-fry for 1 minute. Add the wine and stir to mix. Make a well in the center of the mixture, stir the sauce, and pour it into the well. Stir and mix for about 2½ minutes, or until the sauce thickens and bubbles.

4. Turn off the heat, transfer to a heated dish, and serve.

RESTAURANT COOKING, HONG KONG STYLE

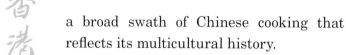

These next four dishes are from the inventive and accommodating restaurant chefs of Hong Kong. Most of the restaurants are Cantonese, which reflects the territory's geographic location bordering Guangdong Province. But over the years, Hong Kong has been a British colony and a refuge for White Russians fleeing the Bolshevik Revolution, Chinese fleeing troubles on the mainland, and others. These newcomers brought their culinary traditions, and Hong Kong chefs embraced them all, so today its restaurants provide a broad swath of Chinese cooking that reflects its multicultural history.

But Hong Kong is also a place where traditional dishes can be left as they are or can be changed, sometimes with just a tuck here and there and just as often with a contemporary overhaul. Reverence for the classics is strong, but the local chefs also readily welcome new vegetables, fruits, and meats. To eat in Hong Kong is not only a constant joy, but also a culinary adventure.

SHRIMP WITH SALTED EGG YOLKS

‖ MAKES 4 SERVINGS ‖

This dish is a fine example of the inventiveness of Hong Kong's chefs: basic ingredients combined in an unusual manner to create a perfect blend. Salted eggs are a Cantonese tradition, and cooking with their grated yolks is a Fujianese custom. In other parts of China, salted egg yolks are used in different ways, perhaps most notably set in the center of Autumn Festival moon cakes, which nowadays are found not only in Beijing, but elsewhere as well. Hong Kong has taken these salted egg yolks and created a new classic.

In Hong Kong and in China, this preparation is usually made with perfectly salted duck egg yolks. You can find cooked salted duck eggs imported from China in Chinatown markets, but as I pointed out earlier, these should be avoided because there is no way to determine their freshness. I have also said that I find the domestically produced salted duck eggs excessively salty and recommend against them as well (see discussion of salted eggs with congees, page 93).

Duck eggs are difficult to obtain, so if you cannot find them, you can use salted chicken egg yolks in this recipe with good results.

Continued . . .

. . . *continued*

Do not be tempted to use unsalted hard-boiled egg yolks for this dish, however. They will not provide the proper taste or texture. This lovely dish of shrimp blended with salted egg yolks is usually served as a first course in a larger meal.

INGREDIENTS

8 ounces (13 to 15) extra-large shrimp (26 to 30 count per pound)	2 salted duck or chicken egg yolks (page 93)

COATING

⅛ teaspoon salt	2½ teaspoons cornstarch
1 teaspoon sesame oil	

3 cups peanut oil

1. To prepare the shrimp, peel and devein them, leaving the tail segments intact, then clean them (see page 75). Leave them to drain in the strainer placed over a bowl for about 1 hour.

2. While the shrimp are drying, hard-boil the eggs as directed, then cool and peel. Remove the egg whites (to snack on). Using the back of a spoon, press the egg yolks through a fine-mesh strainer placed over a bowl. The sieved yolks should resemble sand. Scrape any residue clinging to the bottom of the strainer into the bowl. Reserve.

3. To oil-blanch the shrimp, remove them from the strainer and pat them thoroughly dry with paper towels, particularly the tails.

4. To make the coating: Place the shrimp in a bowl, add all of the coating ingredients, and toss to coat evenly.

5. Heat a wok over high heat for 20 seconds. Add the peanut oil and heat to 325°F on a deep-frying thermometer. Add the shrimp and their coating and immediately turn off the heat. Using chopsticks, loosen the shrimp to separate them. Turn on the heat to high, stir the shrimp, and cook for about 1 minute, or until they turn pink. Turn off the heat, remove the shrimp with a Chinese strainer, and drain them over a bowl.

6. Double strain the oil as directed in oil-blanching, then return 1½ tablespoons of the strained oil to the wok. Turn the heat to low, add the sieved egg yolks, and cook, stirring, for about 1 minute, or until the yolks and the oil combine into a puree. Turn off the heat. Add the shrimp and toss gently with the yolk puree until the shrimp are evenly coated with the puree.

7. Transfer to a heated serving platter and serve.

VEAL IN BLACK PEPPER SAUCE

|| MAKES 4 SERVINGS ||

黑椒牛仔肉 Veal is not widely known in China except in larger cities such as Shanghai, Beijing, Guangzhou, and Hong Kong, where it is known as "meat of the suckling cow." In Hong Kong, it is commonplace. Black pepper is also rare in Chinese cooking.

This preparation is a fine example of what Hong Kong does well: taking Western foodstuffs and making them Chinese.

INGREDIENTS

12 ounces veal loin, cut across the grain into 4 equal slices	3 tablespoons Onion Oil (page 56)
	¼ teaspoon salt

SAUCE	
¾ cup Chicken Stock (page 54)	1½ teaspoons light soy sauce
3 tablespoons oyster sauce	1½ tablespoons cornstarch
1½ tablespoons Shaoxing wine	2 teaspoons sugar

3 cups water	1½ teaspoons peeled and minced ginger
1½-inch-long piece ginger, peeled and lightly smashed	1½ teaspoons minced garlic
1½ teaspoons salt	1 teaspoon sesame oil
½ teaspoon baking soda (optional)	2 tablespoons finely sliced scallions
1¼ teaspoons crushed black peppercorns	4 ounces snow peas, ends and strings removed
3 tablespoons minced onions	

1. In a bowl, place the veal, add 1½ tablespoons of the onion oil and the salt, and toss to coat the veal evenly. Cover and let rest in the refrigerator, for 1 hour.

2. To make the sauce: In a small bowl, mix together all of the ingredients and reserve.

3. When the veal is ready, remove it from the refrigerator. Heat a cast-iron frying pan over high heat for 1 minute, or until it is very hot. Place the 4 veal slices in the hot pan and sear on each side for 1 minute. Turn off the heat, transfer the veal to a dish, and reserve.

4. To water-blanch the snow peas, in a pot, bring the water to a boil over medium heat. Have the ginger, salt, and baking soda ready.

5. While the water is heating, heat a wok over high heat for 30 seconds. Add the remaining 1½ tablespoons onion oil and, using a spatula, coat the wok with the oil. When a wisp of white smoke appears, add the peppercorns and stir for 20 seconds. Add the onions, ginger, and garlic, stir to mix well, and stir-fry for 1 minute, or until the onions are translucent. Stir the sauce, pour it into the wok, and stir until it comes to a boil. Add the seared veal slices, cover with the sauce, and allow the sauce to return to a boil. Turn the veal slices over and cook for 1 minute, or until they are well coated. Turn off the heat, add the sesame oil, and mix well. Transfer the veal to a heated platter and sprinkle with the scallions.

6. At this point, the water in the pot should be boiling. Raise the heat to high and add the ginger, salt, and baking soda (if using). When the water returns to a boil, add the snow peas and blanch for 1 minute, or until bright green and crisp. Turn off the heat and remove the peas with a Chinese strainer, draining well.

7. Place the snow peas around the edge of the platter, surrounding the veal, and serve.

XO SHRIMP

‖ MAKES 4 SERVINGS ‖

XO醬炒蝦 This is one of the many ways in which Hong Kong chefs use XO sauce as the dominant flavoring ingredient in a recipe. The dish is made with what local chefs often call a "dry" sauce because the recipe contains no stock and the XO sauce and all of the other ingredients are absorbed by the shrimp as the dish cooks. A small amount of water in the sauce keeps the mixture moist, but it evaporates in the cooking. The shrimp are first blanched in stock to seal them, which does not affect their "dryness."

INGREDIENTS

SAUCE

1 tablespoon oyster sauce	1 teaspoon white rice vinegar
1 tablespoon Shaoxing wine	
1½ teaspoons light soy sauce	1 teaspoon sugar
	¼ teaspoon salt
1 teaspoon sesame oil	

1 pound large shrimp (40 count per pound)	3 tablespoons ¼-inch-dice shallots
2½ cups Chicken Stock (page 54)	3 tablespoons XO Sauce (page 157)
½-inch-thick slice ginger, peeled and lightly smashed	1½ teaspoons mung bean starch mixed with 1½ teaspoons water
1 tablespoon peanut oil	
1½ tablespoons peeled and minced ginger	

1. To make the sauce: In a small bowl, mix together all of the ingredients and reserve.

2. Peel and devein the shrimp, leaving the tail segments intact, then clean them (see page 75).

3. To stock-blanch the shrimp, place the stock and ginger slice in a wok and bring to a boil over high heat. Add the shrimp and blanch for 30 to 40 seconds, or just until they begin to turn pink. Turn off the heat, remove the shrimp with a Chinese strainer, and drain well over a bowl. Reserve. Empty the stock into a bowl, remove and discard the ginger, and reserve the stock for another use.

4. Dry the wok with paper towels, then heat it over high heat for 30 seconds. Add the peanut oil and, using a spatula, coat the wok with the oil. When a wisp of white smoke appears, add the minced ginger and stir briefly. Add the shallots and stir-fry for 1 minute, or until they soften. Add the XO sauce and stir-fry for 2 minutes, or until well blended. Add the shrimp and stir-fry for 1 minute, or until they are well-coated with the XO sauce. Stir the reserved sauce and drizzle it over the shrimp. Stir to mix until the shrimp are well-coated. Stir the starch-water mixture, pour it into the wok, and stir just until any liquid thickens. The shrimp should be well-coated, and there should be no moisture in the wok.

5. Turn off the heat, transfer to a heated dish, and serve.

STEAMED EIGHT-TREASURE WINTER MELON SOUP

|| **MAKES 10 TO 12 SERVINGS** ||

It is fitting that we conclude this culinary tour of China with a banquet preparation, one that recurs in many parts of the country on many festive occasions. A whole winter melon is used. It is the pot in which an eight-treasure soup is cooked and from which it is served, and its presentation almost always produces joyful awe. The soup's provenance is not known. It seems to exist everywhere. There is a version of this dish in Changsha and in Suzhou, in Shanghai and in Guangzhou, in Hangzhou, with its tradition for intricate vegetable carving, and in Hong Kong. Fujian has a recipe, so does Beijing, and there is a Buddhist vegetarian version.

These versions differ from place to place only in what the eight treasures are and what cooking stock is used. The winter melon, though historically grown in southern China, is now found throughout the country, particularly from early summer on. It is about the size of an oval, medium-size watermelon and looks like that melon on the outside: mottled green and white, often with a powdery dusting.

The melon is hollowed out and carved to become both the cook pot and the tureen. Its special property is its lack of taste. It has essentially none, yet it has the capacity to absorb the tastes of the foods that are cooked in it. At the table its flesh, now flavored, is shaved off and served with its steamed soup.

This dish is not difficult to make, but assembling the ingredients will take time. As you can see, its eight treasures come mostly from the basic preparations we have mastered. A wide, two-piece steamer, such as a clam steamer, is the best utensil for steaming the winter melon.

INGREDIENTS

1 winter melon, 9 to 10 pounds

½ cup ⅓-inch-dice Roasted Duck meat (page 153)

½ cup ⅓-inch-dice Roasted Chicken meat (page 152)

½ cup ⅓-inch-dice Barbecued Pork (page 103)

½ cup ⅓-inch-dice Salt-Cured Ham (page 150)

⅓ cup fresh-cooked crabmeat

½ cup dried black mushrooms, soaked in hot water for 30 minutes, drained, rinsed, squeezed dry, stems discarded, and caps cut into ⅓-inch dice

½ cup fresh or thawed frozen green peas

⅓ cup ¼-inch-dice peeled fresh water chestnuts

1 tablespoon peeled and minced ginger

3 tablespoons Onion Oil (page 56)

2½ quarts boiling water

5½ cups Superior Stock (page 145)

1. First place the winter melon in a two-piece steamer (see Headnote) for measuring purposes. Put a cake rack on the bottom of the top tier of the steamer and set the melon on the rack. With a pencil, make a line around the circumference of the melon about 1 inch below the rim of the steamer pan. Remove the melon and the rack. Cut the melon crosswise at the pencil line and discard the top.

2. Using a small, sharp knife, such as a grapefruit knife, cut away and remove the seeds and soft center pulp from the melon. Then, with the same knife, cut a saw-toothed edge around its top. Place all of the meats, the crabmeat, mushrooms, peas, water chestnuts, ginger, and onion oil into the hollowed-out melon.

Continued . . .

. . . continued

HOW TO PREPARE THE WINTER MELON
See steps **2–3.**

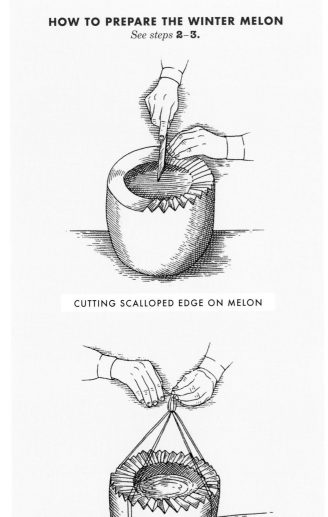

CUTTING SCALLOPED EDGE ON MELON

SECURING MELON TO RACK WITH STRING

3. Tie four lengths of string, each about 2 feet long, to the cake rack, spacing them evenly around the rack. Place the melon on the rack, bring the strings up and over the top of the melon, pulling them tight so the melon is secure, and tie the strings together in a single knot.

4. Pour the boiling water into the bottom pot of the steamer and place it on the stove top. Lower the melon into the top tier of the steamer, making certain it sits firmly, then set the top tier in the bottom pot. Pour the superior stock into the melon and stir the ingredients gently. Turn the heat to high, cover the steamer, and steam the winter melon for 1 to 1½ hours. Every 20 minutes, replenish any boiling water that has evaporated.

5. After the first hour, check every 8 to 10 minutes to see if the melon is tender. Younger melons usually steam more quickly than older ones. Do not overcook the melon or it will sag. The melon and the soup are done when the flesh on the sides of the melon is tender.

6. Turn off the heat, lift the melon and the rack by the knotted strings, and remove them to a plate in the center of the dining table for presentation. Cut and remove the strings. Ladle the soup into individual bowls, then carefully shave pieces of the flesh from the sides of the melon, adding 2 pieces to each bowl.

第三集

PART 3

PART 3
THE MARKET PARTICULAR

特
别
食
品

When I am in the Chinatown markets with a class, I cannot resist telling this true story. Years ago, federal agents of the Bureau of Alcohol, Tobacco, Firearms, and Explosives, following a lengthy period of surveillance, raided a restaurant one afternoon in the center of New York's Chinatown.

The raiders swooped into the establishment and systematically went through its kitchen and food stores in search of illegal substances. As reported in Chinatown's many Chinese-language newspapers, what they found was quite a few packages of odd, unfamiliar dried substances that, after being opened, sniffed, tasted, and tested, were found to be strange but not illegal and were promptly thrown into the rear compartment of a waiting sanitation truck for disposal.

This final action delighted the Chinatown onlookers, who watched impatiently as the items were tossed, then raced as one to the sanitation truck and grabbed up every package of shark's fin, bird's nest, abalone, sea cucumber, and other dried delicacies the agents had pitched. Chinatown knew what the raiders did not: These dried foods were quite valuable. As high in value as the illegal substances that were being sought? Perhaps not, but of significant value indeed. The Chinese newspapers reported the episode with glee, under similar headlines that more or less read, "These people did not know anything." None of New York's major English-language dailies reported the incident. The raided restaurant is no longer in business, but at the time, it was regarded as one of Chinatown's best.

This story elicits amusement each time I tell it, and I make a point of repeating it, not only for its irony, but also to illustrate the special nature of some of the odd and exotic foods that are so highly regarded in Chinese cooking. These foods are typically quite expensive, regularly grace banquet tables, honor guests and reflect well on the person or family who serves them to guests,

usually require extensive preparation, and are traditionally valued parts of wedding dowries.

It is said often, and rarely contested, that the Chinese and the French will cook and eat any food grown in the ground or picked from a tree and any living thing that wriggles, crawls, hops, walks, or flies. The Chinese prize those fat sea worms, known as slugs, or euphemistically as sea cucumbers, that live on the ocean bottom. They steam the dried roe of scallops and shrimp, fry goose intestines and duck tongues, stew fish stomachs and dried preserved crocodile, roast the hind paws of bears, and make soup from snakes. Relating this sort of thing invariably draws gasps and remarks such as "Not me!" from my students.

I reserve consideration of these foods—the fins of sharks, the nests of swifts, the abalones that live only in the waters off the Japanese island of Honshu—for my advanced classes to bring to them another aspect

of a cuisine that throughout its long history wasted nothing and ate practically everything.

Historically, the Chinese have eaten camel humps and cranes, donkeys and civet cats, and suckling dogs raised for food. They have dined on land crabs and field rodents, snails and worms from their rice paddies, the ovaries of snow frogs, and the testicles of roosters. They have consumed coagulated pork blood and goat blood, monkey brains and bear paws, and sea horses and sea turtles, including a jellied turtle essence that is regarded as a restorative. Many of these exotics first appeared on the banquet tables of Chinese emperors and some are banned nowadays. But others are still found on the menus of restaurants that attempt to imitate such feasts, though they are not recurring elements of the everyday Chinese diet.

I have discussed many traditional dried foods in earlier lessons, and here I will add to them by exploring in depth four dried exotics that many of my students have either eaten or were aware of. All of them have been popular through the centuries because the Chinese believe they are highly nutritious or possess other beneficial properties.

For example, shark's fins, the most desirable of which can cost up to $600 a pound and are best braised or cooked in stock-rich soups, convey honor on guests and heighten the appetite for the banquet dishes that will follow. Perfect egg-shaped bird's nests, costing $3,000 a pound, are ideally served in sweet soups and are said to clean the blood and prolong a woman's youthful skin. Dried abalones, at $800 a pound, symbolize wealth when they are served. Dried sea cucumbers, the finest of them priced at about $70 a pound, contain no cholesterol and are thought to aid both digestion and male virility. All of these claims, which are believed to greater or lesser degree in China, account for the continued popularity of these culinary oddities.

But these pricey dried foods aren't the only culinary curiosities. As I lead my class through a vegetable market that makes a point of stocking out-of-the-ordinary items, I gesture toward a pyramid of oblong taro roots, the top one sliced in half to reveal its creamy white interior marked with the purple threads that indicate quality. Nearby are sausagelike links of lotus root, and next to them is a pile of small, sweet *mi gua* (*mut guah* in Cantonese), or "honey melons," no bigger than pears, that are steamed in summer. Over there are matching piles of litchis and longans, small, shell-covered fruits from Chinese evergreens. We buy some to take to our class, where we will refrigerate them so they will be cold and sweet when we eat them. Stacked packages of the jet-black, frizzy seaweed the Cantonese call *fat choy,* or "hair seaweed," because of its looks, stand not far from bitter melons, long, rough-skinned gourds that are bitter indeed, but are delicious paired with seasoned meats and steamed. I tell my classes again and again to roam the Chinatown markets because there will always be one that has some food that another one doesn't.

At this point in our shopping excursion, I make sure we visit a dim sum restaurant, where we can immerse ourselves in an important and unique subculture of China's culinary heritage. This has become easier in recent years, as dim sum has become more familiar. I can recall days when most Westerners thought wontons were dumplings, rather than noodles; when they wondered if a dim sum meal included a pupu platter; when they believed egg rolls were Chinese; when dispensers filled with sugar accompanied pots of oolong and jasmine teas; and when lakes of soy sauce were poured over everything before it was eaten. Most such misinformation is nearly nonexistent nowadays, though misconceptions still exist.

Today, many people have been to dim sum restaurants, once referred to as parlors, and they know that *yum cha* means "to drink tea" and the difference between *har gau* and *siu mai.* We taste the various dim sum, and I have them pick apart some of the dumplings so that they can see and feel the differences in the doughs, which are variously made from rice or wheat flour and are often identified indiscriminately by food writers. I want them to remember these doughs, their thicknesses and consistencies, as we begin preparing them. I want them to taste the teas we order and remember these tastes as we discuss Chinese teas and their relationship to food.

In this group of lessons we will also discuss a special offshoot of Chinese cooking—the vegetarian traditions of Buddhism and Taoism—in which foods are cooked to fool the eye and please the palate. We will continue our tour of the regions of China as well, cooking traditional preparations, large and small, some requiring extra effort, some not, but all of them foods that I like to call dishes of occasion.

LESSON 1
A FINAL COLLECTION OF BASICS

Now we will complete our basic Chinese pantry with a final collection of necessary ingredients. As you gather them, begin thinking about two overriding concepts that describe the eight lessons in our final series of classes: tradition and art.

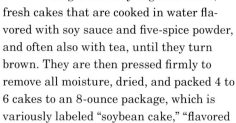

加多基本實習

A FINAL
COLLECTION
OF BASICS

ABALONE. The best specimens of these highly prized mollusks come from Japan, where they are harvested and dried for export. Although abalones exist in waters throughout Asia, particularly off Taiwan, none satisfies the Chinese desire for perfection like those from Japan, and the Chinese will cheerfully pay whatever is asked for a tender whole abalone, or *bao yu,* perfectly braised in rich stock. The smooth meat rests on a lustrous mother-of-pearl bed inside of a shell with a rough exterior, and is customarily eaten only after a long soaking and braising process. Abalones are rarely eaten fresh, except for those small abalone called nine holes, because of the nine small pinholes in its shell. In the United States abalones are harvested along the California coast. They are pounded thin, breaded, and fried and are quite good. But in China they would never be eaten that way. Store dried abalones in a tightly covered container in a cool, dry place until using.

BEAN CURD, SEASONED. These processed cakes of bean curd are available domestically made or imported from China, mainly from Hangzhou. They begin as small, fresh cakes that are cooked in water flavored with soy sauce and five-spice powder, and often also with tea, until they turn brown. They are then pressed firmly to remove all moisture, dried, and packed 4 to 6 cakes to an 8-ounce package, which is variously labeled "soybean cake," "flavored tofu," "dried tofu," or "spiced thick dry tofu." The cakes have a faint but distinct taste of anise from the seasoning in the five-spice powder. An unflavored white pressed bean curd is also available. Once plentiful and now rare are pressed cakes flavored with chiles. They have a brown exterior and a creamy white center and are quite spicy. Once you have opened a package of seasoned bean curd, store the unused cakes in a sealed plastic bag in the refrigerator. They will keep for up to 2 weeks.

BEAN CURD SKIN. This thin film, a fresh by-product of the making of soybean milk, forms on top of the milk as it boils. The skin, which is pliable, is removed from the surface of the cooked milk in thin sheets measuring about 24 inches in diameter. The sheets are folded, packed 8 to a package, and frozen. On delivery to a market, the retailer allows the sheets to thaw, repacks them 2 sheets to a plastic package, and puts them in the store's refrigerated section. The thawed skins remain pliable, perfect for immediate use. Once purchased, they will keep in the refrigerator in a closed plastic bag for up to 2 weeks.

 BIRD'S NEST. This delicacy is the nest of a swallow-like cave swift, a small bird of Southeast Asia. The nests are actually the dried spittle of the birds. The most prized specimens are almost pure white because the twigs, bits of leaves, grasses, and feathers they once contained have been removed. Darker nests are still flecked with some of these materials. Others that are even darker, almost red, are called blood nests, the color the result of iron in the spittle. Like other exotic dried foods, such as shark's fin, abalone, and sea cucumber, bird's nests require a good deal of preparation before cooking. They are sold loose and in boxes and should be stored in a cool, dry cupboard until using.

CHO GUOR. These hard, nutlike ingredients are used in pungent sauces. They look like a nutmeg, though they taste slightly different, and unlike the nutmeg, which is usually grated, the *cho guor* is used whole. After cooking, the *cho guor* displays a spongy interior and has a sweetened, medicinal taste. It wrinkles with age, though its taste is affected only slightly. It has no English name and is rarely known by its Mandarin name, *cao guo,* so in markets you need to ask for *cho guor*, its Cantonese name. It is sometimes found in packages marked *tsao ko,* which is a good example of the confusion that occurs in a Chinese market. If you ask most shopkeepers for *tsao ko,* they wouldn't know what you want. But if you ask for *cho guor,* they will. So, again, I suggest bringing a photocopy of the name in Chinese characters to make sure you get the correct item. *Cho guor* can be stored indefinitely in a closed jar in a cool, dry place.

 GLUTEN. The Chinese call this elastic protein "tendon flour" because of its tensile nature. It is a component of wheat flour and is made by combining wheat flour and water and kneading it into a dough. The dough is then washed thoroughly to remove its starch, thus concentrating the gluten. Sometimes used as a substitute for meat in vegetarian recipes, gluten has no taste of its own, but readily absorbs the flavors of the foods with which it is combined. To give it texture and make it more digestible, gluten is usually fried first until hard and then braised with other foods that give it taste and a chewy, sponge-like consistency. This rough-surfaced gluten, called *mian jin,* is the one I prefer. You will also find gluten with a moist, doughy texture, which is known as *kaofu.* The latter expands when thawed. Both types are sold in plastic packages and are usually found in the refrigerated sections of markets and sometimes in the freezer section. Domestically made gluten and imported gluten from China, mainly Hangzhou and Taiwan, are available. The packages are often labeled "dried gluten cake" or "wheat dough" and hold squares, cubes, or irregular shapes. Once a package is opened, the unused portion should be stored in a sealed plastic bag in the refrigerator, where it will keep for up to 2 weeks.

 HAIRY MELON. This gourd-shaped, green melon is about the size of a large cucumber and is covered with a fine fuzz, thus its name. It is related to the winter melon, and, like that larger melon, it is essentially tasteless but takes on the flavors of the foods with which it is cooked.

 LOTUS ROOT. This odd-looking root of the lotus resembles a string of fat sausages, with each root 4 to 5 inches long and 3 inches in diameter. When cut crosswise, it reveals a pattern of holes not unlike those in Swiss cheese, and its texture is light, slightly dry, and crisp. It is a highly symbolic food, often eaten for New Year. Its Cantonese name, *lin ngau,* translates as "every year there will be plenty," and the holes represent paths through which knowledge passes. Store lotus roots in a brown paper bag in the refrigerator. Use them as soon as possible after purchase, as they tend to lose both flavor and texture quickly.

蓮子 **LOTUS SEED.** Regarded as a delicacy, the dried, olive-shaped seeds of the lotus pod are cooked and mashed and used as fillings in teahouse sweets. They are sold by weight in Chinese markets, and will keep for at least a month at room temperature in a tightly sealed jar. However, their flavor fades and their texture toughens as they age.

蓮蓉 **LOTUS SEED PASTE.** This deep red-brown paste is made by cooking lotus seeds with sugar. It comes in cans, with many brands of equal quality available. Once the can is opened, transfer the unused portion to a tightly closed container and refrigerate. It will keep for about 1 week.

麥芽糖 **MALTOSE.** A thick syrup made by malting grain starches, mostly barley, maltose is pleasant and sweet, though not as sweet as raw sugar, and it provides the essential flavoring for Peking duck. Mixed with vinegar and boiling water, it is used to coat the skin of the duck before roasting. Once

sold in small ceramic pots, maltose now comes in plastic containers and will keep in its closed container at room temperature for up to 3 months.

紅荳 **RED BEANS.** These small, deep-red beans are a favorite ingredient in Chinese sweets, particularly a sweet soup, though they are often found in savory, long-cooked dishes as well. They are sold dried in plastic sacks, by weight, and will keep indefinitely in a cool, dry place.

紅荳沙 **RED BEAN PASTE.** This paste is the most common way red beans are used in China. The beans are soaked, boiled, mashed, and cooked with sugar and lard into a red, sweet paste, which is used as a filling for dumplings, pastries, and buns. It comes in cans, and like lotus seed paste, several brands of equal quality are available. Once the can is opened, refrigerate the unused paste in a tightly covered container for up to 6 weeks.

SAND GINGER. This cousin to ginger is called "galangal" throughout Southeast Asia, where it is used widely. It is used in southern China, where the Cantonese call it *sah geung,* or "sand ginger," because of its texture when grated. It is a small, tender root that looks like young ginger, is either sandy white or yellow, and has an aroma slightly reminiscent of fresh coriander. It is sold both fresh and dried. The fresh root is used in the same manner as fresh ginger, and powdered sand ginger is used in sauces. The roots are sold loose or are packaged and labeled "sand ginger." The ground dried root is packaged and labeled "sand ginger powder." I use both whole fresh roots and powder and prefer the white root over the yellow because of its intensity.

 SEA CUCUMBER. A wormlike creature, this grayish-brown sea slug lives on the sea bottom. It is fingerlike and gelatinous and can be as small as your pinkie or quite large, more than 6 inches long and 2 inches in diameter. Highly prized, sea cucumbers have been harvested for more than a millennium by the Chinese, who regard them as warming and beneficial to health. They are either gathered wild or raised on farms along China's eastern seacoast. When they are pulled from the water, they are slit, cleaned, and dried and then sold loose, by weight, with the larger specimens more expensive. Even though they have been cleaned, their insides must be thoroughly cleaned again before use. Stored in a sealed jar, they will keep at room temperature for up to 6 months. Recently, frozen cleaned sea cucumbers have appeared in markets, but like their dried counterparts, they still require additional cleaning.

 SHARK'S FIN. This is arguably the most highly regarded exotic foodstuff in China. The fins, which are laboriously cleaned, processed, soaked, and then cooked, have been a Chinese tradition for almost five hundred years. They are said to benefit the heart, lungs, and kidneys and to enhance the complexion. The most highly regarded fin is the top, or dorsal, fin. But the fin itself is almost never eaten. Rather it is the thin, gelatinous strands of cartilage that make up the fin that are consumed, usually in soups or braises. Whole dried fins can be bought, but their prices are prohibitive. The strands, processed and dried, are sold in markets and herbal shops for use in soups. While their quality does not match that of whole fins, they will give diners the shark's fin soup experience, if treated with care. Check fin strands closely when purchasing to make sure they are well cleaned. Sometimes they have been poorly processed and have bits of fin meat adhering to them. Store the strands in a tightly covered container in a cool, dry cupboard until using.

 WATER CHESTNUT POWDER. Here is another of the starches, or powders, used as a basis for steamed cakes or to thicken sauces. Like mung bean starch, it imparts a shiny, glazed finish to the foods with which it is used. It will keep in a tightly sealed container in a cool, dry place for up to 1 year.

 WHEAT STARCH. This is what remains of wheat flour after its protein has been removed to make gluten (see page 241). It is the basis for some dumpling wrappers, and it will keep in a tightly sealed container in a cool, dry place for up to 1 year.

LESSON 2
TAMING THE WILD EXOTICS

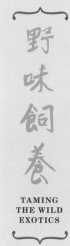

野味飼養

**TAMING
THE WILD
EXOTICS**

Given the propensity of the Chinese for adventurous eating, it is not at all strange that some of the world's oddest, most inaccessible foods are prized, and sought, by the Chinese, with little attention paid to expense or risk. Their sea hunters will sail the oceans, or subsidize others to do so, hunting for sharks, particular sharks with particularly desirable dorsal fins, destined for an extraordinary banquet, or simply a bowl of expensive soup. They will employ agile young men to scale steep cliffs in Malaysia and other lands of Southeast Asia to collect the small nests of tiny swifts. They will scour the sea bottoms for fat, gelatinous slugs that they believe enhance male virility. They will spend untold amounts of money for special abalone, which grow only in northern Japan, abalone the Chinese equate with "eating gold."

All of this to grace banquet tables, to give face to honored guests, and to enjoy foods that to the Chinese are not only symbolic of good fortune, but which happen to be quite healthful as well. Common to all these foods as well is the fact that they must be processed, in some cases laboriously, to bring them to the table. This, too, is eminently satisfactory to the Chinese as well, for to them, the enjoyment of exceptional foods such as these is heightened by efforts to prepare them.

SHARK'S FINS

魚翅

The Chinese are most particular about the sharks that carry their favorite fins. They give them names depending on their sizes, body colors, sizes of fins, and the waters in which they are found. The South China Sea, once the richest shark hunting area, is essentially barren today, the result of over-hunting. The sharks in the Indian Ocean and Middle-Eastern waters are deemed too salty and must be processed longer than those from Mexican and Floridian waters, which are considered prime. Why? Because, a fin trader in Hong Kong told me, the tuna off the coast of Mexico eat shrimp, the sharks eat the tuna and thus are big, with considerable fat. The waters off the coast of Costa Rica yield smaller sharks, such as the gummys, with softer, smaller fins, which are like eating egg white. The fins from waters far north or far south are usually considered too small.

The best sharks, with the best fins, are the dusky and the Galapagos, with names such as manila yellow, blue, blacktip, ocean white, dogfish, nurse, weasel, goblin, crucible, sea tiger, gold mountain hook, tooth root, five coats, sky nine, and sandbar. These names, while essentially descriptive, are not random. To the more than a thousand dealers in sharks' fins in both Hong Kong and Singapore, for example, they determine price. They are also codes for the size and quality of the dorsal fins, most prized, and most expensive, though all five fins are cut from the shark when it is pulled from the ocean.

After they are cut from the shark, the fins are dried, and when hardened, the black outer skin of the fin is scraped off with a curved knife. The fin is then split open, and its structural cartilage is removed. The fin is boiled and soaked to remove all vestiges of skin and cartilage, then boiled again, until it becomes yellowish-white, clear, and odorless. It is thoroughly dried for storage until ready to use.

As with virtually all dried foods, the fin must be prepared before cooking. The amount you spend for dried sharks' fins depends on whether an entire fin or loose strands of the fin are to be used. The bigger the fin, the more expensive; the thicker the strands, the more expensive. Whole fins can cost as much as $600 a pound, with the cheapest, a piece of fin cartilage with some strands attached, as little as $28 per pound. The whole fin can be braised or cooked in stock, so that it looks like a floating fan. When cooked this way, the Chinese call it a "comb" because it resembles a traditional Chinese wooden comb. The comb can be broken into pieces and cooked. The strands, in addition to being cooked in soup, are also used as dim sum fillings or served stuffed into the hollows of pieces of bamboo pith or scrambled with eggs.

The way most people are introduced to sharks' fins is usually in an elegant soup made from the richest of stocks.

SHARK'S FIN SOUP

‖ MAKES 8 SERVINGS ‖

 No occasion of importance in China—no festival, no major holiday, no reunion, no family celebration—is considered complete without a banquet. And no banquet of any consequence is complete without shark's fin soup, prepared and served in the classic manner. The soup is always accompanied with crisp mung bean sprouts, shredded Yunnan or Jinhua ham, and red vinegar.

INGREDIENTS

4 ounces dried shark's fin strands

2½ cups water

2 teaspoons white rice vinegar

2 tablespoons white rice wine

3 scallions, cut in half crosswise

1-inch-thick slice ginger, peeled and lightly smashed

3 ounces pork fat, cut into 8 equal cubes

8 cups Superior Stock (page 145)

1 cup finely shredded Salt-Cured Ham (page 150; see Cleaver discussion, page 45)

1¼ cups mung bean sprouts, ends removed

¼ cup red rice vinegar

¼ cup mung bean starch mixed with ¼ cup water

1½ teaspoons sesame oil

1. In a bowl, soak the shark's fin strands in warm water to cover for about 2 hours, or until they soften. Drain the strands in a fine-mesh strainer, rinse well under cold running water, and then drain well. Return the strands to the bowl, add the 2½ cups water and the white rice vinegar, and let soak overnight at room temperature.

2. The next day, drain the strands again and then place them in a steamproof dish. Add the wine, scallions, ginger, pork fat, and 1 cup of the stock. Place the dish in a steamer, cover, and steam for 30 minutes. Turn off the heat, remove the dish from the steamer, and discard all of the ingredients except the fin strands. There should be about 1 cup of strands. Reserve.

3. In a large pot, place the remaining 7 cups stock, add the fin strands, and bring to a boil over high heat. Reduce the heat to low, cover the pot, leaving the lid slightly cracked, and simmer for 25 minutes.

4. As the soup simmers, place the shredded ham, mung bean sprouts, and red rice vinegar in small serving bowls and place them in the middle of the table.

5. After 25 minutes, raise the heat under the soup to medium, stir the starch-water mixture, and then slowly add the starch mixture to the soup while stirring continuously until the soup thickens. Turn off the heat, add the sesame oil, and stir well.

6. Transfer the soup to a heated tureen and serve in the Chinese manner. At the table, ladle the soup into individual bowls, then invite your guests to sprinkle their servings with the ham and bean sprouts and to spoon in red vinegar to taste.

BIRD'S NESTS

燕富

The Chinese prize these small, cup-shaped bird's nests, which are used to make sweet and savory soups, as highly as they do shark's fins. The homes of tiny swifts that migrate annually to the islands and cliffs of Southeast Asia, the nests are the dried spittle the birds use to weave their abodes from twigs, leaves, and feathers. For more than half a millennium, the Chinese have treasured these rare nests, believing they extend life, strengthen the immune system, encourage growth, and preserve youthful complexions.

Since the time of the Ming Dynasty, Chinese traders have crossed the waters to Southeast Asia to what are now the Maylaysian states of Sarawak and Sabah, to Borneo, to Thailand, and to Indonesia to trade silks, porcelains, gold, and iron for these nests. Today, nests from these same Southeast Asian areas are exported to China, with the caves in Niah on Sarawak regarded as the source of the finest nests. Those who collect them are a brave lot. They scale cliffs and climb beams in rotting houses to gather the small nests, each weighing about an ounce.

The swifts build their nests high up, often on nearly vertical cliffs or in shallow caves. During their breeding season, the birds secrete their gelatinous spittle, which becomes the basis for their nests. Some of these nests, of almost pure spittle, are called white, and they are the most desirable and thus most expensive. As noted earlier, whole white nests, always labeled "wild," can cost thousands of dollars a pound. Pieces of these white nests are called dragon teeth, and even they command steep prices. Among the most expensive nests are the so-called wild gold nests from Vietnam and the Thai blood nests, which describes their color, the result of iron in the bird's diet. So-called black nests, which contain bits of other materials the birds use to build their nests, are the least expensive.

Almost all bird's nests must be soaked and rinsed twice to remove impurities. Expensive white nests need minimal preparation, and black nests require a good deal more. Bird's nests are usually sold loose by weight and sometimes in packages. Packaged nests typically have many impurities mixed with the dried strands of saliva, necessitating considerable cleaning.

Throughout China, bird's nest soup is prepared as a health and beauty tonic. Tea shops serve sweet soups, and restaurants offer savory soups midmeal or sweet soups to end a meal. In Fujian, children are sent to bed, but after they have slept for a while, they are awakened and fed sweet bird's nest soup because the Fujianese believe the soup is more beneficial if it is consumed while the body is at rest.

STEAMED SWEET BIRD'S NEST SOUP

‖ **MAKES 4 TO 6 SERVINGS** ‖

Bird's nest soup is as highly regarded as shark's fin soup as a component of a grand and festive banquet. When the Chinese hear it will be served, most of them automatically think of the sweet soup, in which the nests, their strands silky smooth after soaking and steaming, are cooked with white or rock sugar. In a variation on that classic, nests are steamed with sugar and rice into a kind of pudding. And in some restaurants, chefs add strands of the nests to sweet custard tarts.

The Chinese consider a steamed sweet bird's nest soup a true gastronomic experience, a dish that marries simplicity and refinement. The silkier the strands of the nest, the more honor is conferred on the guest to whom it is served. Sweetening the soup with white sugar is also a mark of respect, for the whiter the nest, the purer the message, and the more face is given to guests.

INGREDIENTS

2 bird's nests (2 ounces total)	½ cup sugar
3 cups hot water, about 150°F, or hot to the touch	¾ cup coconut "milk" (see sidebar)
	3 cups boiling water

1. Combine the nests and hot water in a bowl and allow to soak for 4 to 4½ hours, or until they soften, loosen, and separate into strands. Rinse them well, drain them in a fine-mesh strainer, and then repeat the rinsing again, to remove any remaining impurities. Drain the strands well.

2. Place the strands in a steamproof dish. Add the sugar and coconut "milk." Then pour in the boiling water and stir to mix the ingredients well and to dissolve the sugar. Place the dish in a steamer, cover, and steam for 20 minutes. At this point, all of the ingredients will be well blended.

3. Turn off the heat. Remove the dish from the steamer, transfer the soup to a heated tureen, and serve.

‖ **COCONUT "MILK"** ‖

COCONUT "MILK"

What I call coconut "milk" is the clear liquid found in unripe coconuts in the warm summer months. (Do not confuse it with the canned white coconut milk extracted from the grated flesh of mature coconuts.) Buy an immature coconut, cut off its top with a cleaver, and pour out the liquid. You should have about 1 cup. This coconut liquid, or water, has a natural sweetness. In fact, unripe coconuts, their tops cut off and straws inserted, are sold as refreshments by street vendors in Thailand and elsewhere in Southeast and South Asia. You can also buy this liquid, sweetened and unsweetened, in cans usually labeled "coconut juice," "young coconut juice," or "coconut water." If you use fresh coconut liquid, use the amount of sugar specified in the recipe. If you use canned coconut liquid, reduce the amount of sugar to 2 tablespoons. Be sure to taste the liquid before adding any sugar.

BIRD'S NEST SOUP WITH MINCED CHICKEN

|| **MAKES 4 TO 6 SERVINGS** ||

This savory bird's nest soup is typically eaten at the midpoint of a meal or banquet. The texture of the chicken and cured ham complements the smoothness of the nest strands.

INGREDIENTS

2 bird's nests (2 ounces total)

3 cups hot water, about 150°F, or hot to the touch

4 cups Chicken Stock (page 54)

1 tablespoon Shaoxing wine

1 teaspoon salt

Pinch of white pepper

4 ounces chicken breast meat, minced

1 extra-large egg white, lightly beaten

2 tablespoons cornstarch mixed with ¼ cup of Chicken Stock (page 54)

⅓ cup minced Salt-Cured Ham (page 150)

1. Combine the nests and hot water in a bowl and allow to soak for 4 to 4½ hours, or until they soften, loosen, and separate into strands. Rinse them well, drain them in a fine-mesh strainer, and then repeat the rinsing again, to remove any remaining impurities. Drain the strands well.

2. In a large pot, place the stock and bring to a boil over high heat. Add the wine, salt, and white pepper, stir well, and allow to return to a boil. Add the strands, stir well to mix, and allow to return to a boil. Reduce the heat to low and simmer for 10 minutes.

3. Raise the heat to high, add the chicken, stir to mix and loosen, and allow the soup to return to a boil. Slowly add the egg white, stirring constantly, until well blended. The egg white will form into strands. Stir the cornstarch-stock mixture, then slowly add it while stirring constantly. Continue stirring until the soup thickens and bubbles. Add the ham and stir to mix well.

4. Turn off the heat, transfer to a heated tureen, and serve.

SEA CUCUMBERS

海参

The Chinese name for this creature of the sea is rather grand for something that is essentially a sea slug. It is called *hai shen,* or "ginseng of the sea," to describe what are considered its healthful properties. They are indeed a healthful, if not attractive, food, with more protein than an equal amount of beef and no cholesterol. The sea cucumber is liked by the elderly, who can digest its softness easily, and I have already noted that males regard it highly as a restorative. Because of its strength-giving properties, it is sometimes referred to in recipes as the black dragon.

The sea cucumber, a scavenger, lives on the ocean floor and is usually harvested from the beds of coral reefs. The waters off the North China Sea, off Japan, and along the coasts of Southeast Asia yield them, and the Chinese have gone as far as Australia in search of them. Once collected, they are plunged into boiling water, slit open to remove their entrails, then dried in the sun until quite hard. It is these sea cucumbers, hard and dried, that sit in large glass jars in Chinese markets and that range in price, depending on their provenance, from $100 to $300 a pound. The most expensive come from the waters off Japan.

Before they can be eaten, these dried sea cucumbers must be soaked, cleaned, and rinsed, usually over a 2-day period. First, place them in a bowl, add hot water to cover, and allow to soak for 1 day, changing the hot water three times. Drain and rinse the sea cucumbers. Slit them lengthwise, open them flat, and scrape away any residue of the entrails clinging to the flesh. Place them back in the bowl, cover them with hot water again, and allow to soak for another day, again changing the hot water three times. Drain and rinse again and place in a pot. Add water, ginger, and scallions in amounts indicated in individual recipes and simmer until tender. The sea cucumbers are now ready to use. Sea cucumbers also come presoaked and ready to use (see page 243), and they are also sold frozen. The latter do not need extensive cleaning or soaking. Just thaw them, clean any residue from their insides with your hands, and rinse well, and they are ready to use.

Sea cucumbers can be added to soups, braises, or stir-fries. Like many other dried foods, they have little or no taste of their own, absorbing the tastes of what they are paired with. What follows is a traditional sea cucumber preparation.

SEA CUCUMBERS BRAISED WITH STEAMED BLACK MUSHROOMS

|| MAKES 8 SERVINGS ||

INGREDIENTS

8 ounces dried sea cucumbers (4 pieces)

3 cups cold water

1-inch-thick slice ginger, peeled and lightly smashed

3 scallions, cut in half crosswise

SAUCE

1 cup Chicken Stock (page 54)

2 tablespoons Shaoxing wine

1½ tablespoons double dark soy sauce

1 teaspoon sesame oil

2 teaspoons sugar

¼ teaspoon salt

Pinch of white pepper

3 tablespoons peanut oil

1-inch-thick slice ginger, peeled and lightly smashed

3 scallions, cut into 3-inch lengths and white portions smashed

½ cup sliced bamboo shoots (⅓ inch thick)

24 Steamed Black Mushrooms (page 81)

1 tablespoon cornstarch mixed with 1½ tablespoons water

1. Soak, clean, and rinse the sea cucumbers for 2 days as directed on page 251.

2. In a large pot, combine the soaked sea cucumbers, water, ginger, and scallions and bring to a boil over high heat. Reduce the heat to low, cover, leaving the lid slightly cracked, and simmer for 1½ hours, or until tender. Turn off the heat and let the sea cucumbers cool to room temperature in the liquid.

3. When cool, pour off the liquid and discard the ginger and scallions. Place the sea cucumbers on a chopping board, and cut them in half lengthwise. Then cut each half into 1-inch-thick pieces on the diagonal and reserve.

4. To make the sauce: In a small bowl, mix together all of the ingredients and reserve.

5. Heat a wok over high heat for 40 seconds. Add the peanut oil and, using a spatula, coat the wok with the oil. When a wisp of white smoke appears, add the ginger and stir for 30 seconds. Add the scallions and cook for 45 seconds, or until the scallions release their fragrance. Stir the sauce, pour it into the wok, stir together with the ginger and scallions, and bring to a boil. Add the sea cucumbers, bamboo shoots, and mushrooms, stir to mix well, and allow the sauce to return to a boil. Reduce the heat to low, cover the wok, and braise the mixture for 15 minutes.

6. Raise the heat to high, stir the cornstarch-water mixture, make a well in the center of the wok mixture, and pour in the starch mixture. Stir and mix thoroughly for about 2 minutes, or until the sauce thickens and bubbles.

7. Turn off the heat, transfer to a heated dish, and serve.

|| **BUYING PRESOAKED** ||
SEA CUCUMBERS

PRESOAKED SEA CUCUMBERS

Sea cucumbers can be found already soaked and cleaned in some markets, usually sitting in large containers of water. They are ready for cooking with ginger and scallions as directed in the accompanying recipe. Presoaked sea cucumbers, like dried sea cucumbers, are sold by weight. To use them in recipes calling for dried sea cucumbers, you will need to buy about double the weight.

ABALONE

The Chinese phrase for this highly regarded mollusk is *bao yu,* a homonym that sounds like "assured wealth." Indeed, the Chinese say that eating abalone is like "eating gold." Given the Chinese desire to eat both symbols and foods, the name for abalone alone is sufficient reason to seek out this seafood and eat it, whatever the cost. Even its shell's glittering mother-of-pearl lining is desirable, ground into a fine powder for medicine that is said to improve eyesight and lower blood pressure.

Abalones are to be found in the Pacific off the coast of Mexico and the Americas, in the waters off Australia and Japan, and in the Persian Gulf. The finest abalones, without question, are the Oma, which are harvested in northern Japan near the village of the same name, in the strait separating the islands of Honshu and Hokkaido. These swiftly moving waters, with the Sea of Japan to the west and the Pacific to the east, are consistently pure and thus contribute to the innate fragrance of the abalones. The mollusks, which are small and rare, are dried to tiny, beige disks, and can cost as much as $3,000 per pound, or about $300 each. They are hoarded by collectors. The slightly larger Yoshihama abalones, which grow in the small straits at the northeastern tip of Honshu and dry to a

meaty red, are almost as highly regarded. A third Japanese variety, the Amidori, grows along the coast of Honshu facing the Sea of Japan and dries to a lovely gold. The Amidori, though less aromatic than the others, is favored for banquets because its size and color allow the host to best demonstrate wealth: the guests are truly "eating gold."

When abalones are harvested, their shells are opened and the small disks of meat are removed, bathed in salt water, boiled, and air-dried. For the Chinese, these are not dry enough, and a repetitive process of exposing the abalone meats to the sun for several hours, then storing them, while still warm, in glass jars, continues until they are completely dry and hard. These are the abalones you see for sale in large glass jars in Chinese markets.

Time and effort is needed to prepare these dried mollusks for eating, an effort that does not irk the Chinese because the result is worth the trouble. Inexpensive abalones of good quality are available. What follows is the traditional way of preparing abalones. You can use your sand clay pot—the Chinese believe that abalone tastes better when cooked in a clay pot—or a nonstick pot for this recipe.

BRAISED ABALONE

|| **MAKES 10 SERVINGS** ||

INGREDIENTS

10 whole dried abalones

4 cups water

1½ pounds pork spareribs, in one piece

1 pound chicken wings, cut in half at joint

1 pound whole chicken legs, cut at joint of thigh and drumstick

2 teaspoons salt

2 tablespoons melted lard or peanut oil

1 tablespoon Shaoxing wine

3 tablespoons oyster sauce

1½ cups Superior Stock (page 145)

2½ tablespoons tapioca starch mixed with 2½ tablespoons water

---

1. In a sand clay pot or nonstick pot, place the abalones and water, cover, and bring to a boil over medium heat. Reduce the heat to low and simmer for 30 minutes. Turn off the heat and let the abalones soak overnight at room temperature.

2. The next day, drain the abalones and rinse them under cold running water. Wash and dry the pot.

3. Place the pork ribs at the bottom of the pot. Arrange the abalones in a layer on top of the ribs. Place the chicken wings on top of the abalones and the chicken legs on top of the wings. Add water to cover the contents, sprinkle with the salt, and bring to a boil over low heat. Cover and simmer for 4½ hours. Turn off the heat, remove the abalones from the pot, and reserve.

4. At this point, the abalones are initially flavored and ready to use as an ingredient in other dishes. Or, they can be covered and refrigerated for 2 to 3 days before using. The ribs and the chicken may be snacked on. Only about 1 cup liquid will remain in the pot. Remove it to a container and reserve for another use.

5. Wash and dry the sand clay pot and heat it over low heat for 20 seconds. Add the lard, wine, oyster sauce, abalones, and stock. Cover the pot, raise the heat to medium, and bring to a boil. Reduce the heat to low and simmer for 20 minutes. Raise the heat to medium. Stir the tapioca starch–water mixture and slowly pour it into the pot while stirring continuously until the liquid thickens.

6. Turn off the heat. Place an abalone in each of 10 heated individual dishes. Divide the sauce from the pot evenly among the dishes and serve. Eat the abalone as the Chinese do traditionally, with knife and fork. Cut tiny slices from around the edges of the abalone, saving its center, *tang xin,* or "sugar heart," for last.

|| **ABALONES IN XO SAUCE** ||

ABALONES IN XO SAUCE

Abalones are used in a variety of ways in Chinese cooking, including in the festive banquet dish called Buddha Jumps over the Wall (page 323). They can also be used in a variation on my recipe for XO Sauce (page 157), after their initial long braising with the chicken and pork.

Some of the secretive chefs in Hong Kong quietly boast that their XO sauces are different and better because they add expensive abalone rather than shrimp roe. I have made the sauce both ways and have found that one version is no better than the other. However, should you wish to join those Hong Kong chefs, do the following:

Use 3 or 4 cooked abalones, cut into ⅛-inch dice (¾ cup) in place of the shrimp roe in the original recipe. After you have cooked the shallots and ginger in the oil, add the diced abalones with the scallops, ham, dried shrimp, and other ingredients and cook in the bubbling oil for 10 minutes.

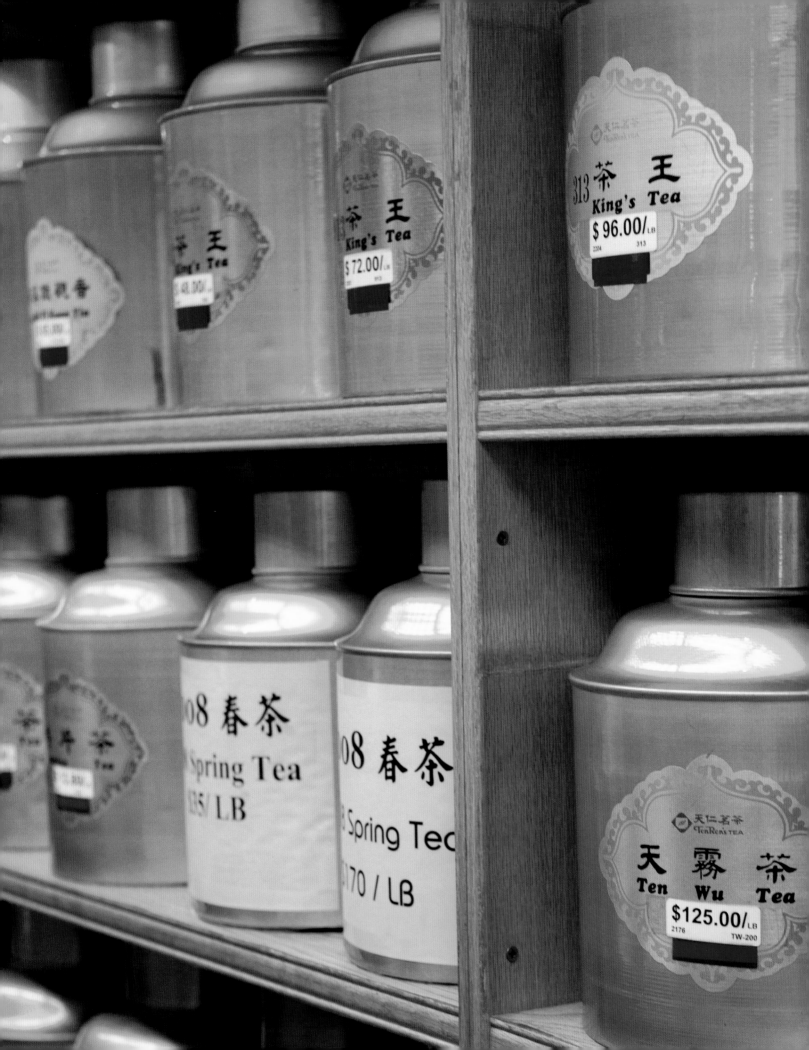

LESSON 3
A TASTE OF TEA

試茶

A TASTE
OF TEA

The history of tea in China spans thousands of years. It has been suggested that the tea bush came to China from India in the second century A.D., yet even if that was so, according to Chinese scholars, tea was first cultivated as a crop in China—specifically as a cousin to the camellia bush—in Hunan and later in Sichuan. Historians have written that tea, rare and dear, was drunk either as a stimulant or to induce serenity by China's rulers and the upper classes perhaps as early as the Han Dynasty, two thousand years before the birth of Christ, but certainly by the time of the Zhou Dynasty, in the eleventh century B.C. Tea became a more widely enjoyed drink, even among among the less privileged, by the Tang Dynasty days, in the eighth century A.D.

Not only does tea have a long history, but it has also brewed many myths, tales, and folklore to add to its flavor. Among them is that the pleasurable enjoyment of tea was the happy accidental discovery of Emperor Shennong, a fastidious man who insisted that all of his drinking water be boiled. One day, as his water was bubbling, a camellia leaf fell into the pot. The fragrance so captivated the emperor that he drank what has been suggested was the first pot of brewed tea. Not surprisingly, the story is often disputed. Shennong—one of China's divine emperors and considered the father of Chinese medicine—reigned about 2700 B.C., and the story of his "discovery" of tea appears in *The Divine Farmer's Herb-Root Classic*, a collection of his observations on the medicinal value of hundred of herbs compiled by others in about 300 B.C.

To this day, the Chinese add camellias, jasmine, rose, and orange blossoms and the flowers of litchi and orange leaves to their teas. Another recurring, if less gentle, myth suggests that tea was instead discovered by a Buddhist monk who, to ensure that he would not fall asleep and thus fail to do his duty to keep watch, cut off and tossed away his eyelids. These became China's first tea plants.

Whatever the belief, lore, or fancy, it is a fact that the brewing of camellia leaves, and those of its relative, the tea bush, to make "t'u," later "ch'a," and still later "tei," was written about as early as the twelfth century B.C. and widely practiced by the time of Confucius, 500 years before the birth of Christ. And it was around A.D. 760 that Lu Yu, China's first master of tea, wrote his *Classic of Tea*, now considered by many not only the first, but also the finest compendium ever written for the care and preparation of tea. Tea, he wrote, was a drink for both body and soul, a stimulant for the mind, and its study was perhaps one path to immortality. He dictated how tea should be grown and cultivated; how tea leaves should be processed; how tea should be stored, brewed, steeped, and served; and even how to create a tea caddy.

Lu Yu's tea ceremony was never as rigidly formal as the highly stylized tea ceremony of Japan, known as *Chanoyu*, but he did dictate what could be termed "the proper way." He ordered that an earthenware pot should be placed atop burned, but smokeless, charcoal made from olive pits. Water, which had to be taken from a slow-moving stream, was put into the pot and boiled. Rushing water was thought to be harmful to the throat, and still water should not even be considered. Once boiled, the water was to be poured into and over cups of underglaze blue porcelain. The water was promptly poured off. Similarly, the pot was emptied and tea leaves placed in it, and freshly boiled water poured over them. Only then would a tea be drinkable, and to further its enjoyment, it should be drunk in the company of beautiful women, in a pavilion.

Unfortunately, not many of us have pavilions or water-lily ponds, but we can and should follow Lu Yu's precepts on the making of tea. To brew a fine cup, the water should be drawn from a slowly streaming tap, then boiled until the first bubbles appear. An earthenware teapot is best. It should be preheated with some of the boiling water, then the water poured off. The leaves, one teaspoon per person and one for the pot, should be put into the teapot.

Pour in 3 ounces of the boiling water for each teaspoon of leaves and let steep for 3 to 6 minutes—the longer, the stronger. Serve the tea in porcelain cups. Lu Yu would approve.

Tea in China is a beverage, a health aid, and a ceremonial presentation. It is offered to ancestors at temple altars. It is tea that binds betrothals and weddings. It is drunk with meals as a beverage and after meals as a digestive. Because its leaves grow on old bushes, it is regarded as a symbol of longevity and fidelity, and cups of tea are always presented by the young to elders as signs of respect.

Initially, tea leaves were ground into a fine powder. Later, the art of roasting and processing leaves arose. Still later the nuances of fermenting, semifermenting, and curing leaves to dryness without fermentation were mastered. Hundreds of teas of various designations, from both China and Taiwan, many with fanciful names, are available in Chinatown tea shops. To be simple, all teas can be divided into three broad categories: unfermented, semifermented, and fully fermented. In general, all green teas are unfermented, oolongs are semi-fermented, and black teas are fermented. No matter the process, the smaller the tea leaf, the better.

Though rare, some teas, mostly black, are pressed into bricks, many of which are often embossed with scenery. With these teas, the older the better. In fact, some bricks of Bo Lei black tea, aged for 60 years, will sell for $2,500.

Tea is grown throughout China, but for particular kinds, specific regions are important. In general the southeastern region of Fujian is said to produce not only most of the teas in China, but also the finest, with two provinces in the west, Hunan and Yunnan, not far behind. But for green tea, there is no better growing region than Hangzhou, near Shanghai.

Even tea leaves have their lore, as this story about the green teas of Hangzhou illustrates. Centuries ago, hordes of monkeys descended upon the monasteries of Buddhist monks in the region and hungrily stripped the fruits, vegetables, and tea leaves from branches and stems and ate them.

Rather than try to rid the monastery grounds of the monkeys, the monks decided to befriend them, and they began leaving food for them. One morning, the monks arose to find all of their tea plants carefully picked of their leaves, the leaves packed in sacks. Since then, the best and smallest green tea leaves are said to have been "monkey picked," and are quite expensive indeed. It is a profitable tale.

Other names persist: Iron Goddess, Water Fairy, Cloud Mist, Silver Needles, White Peony, Noble Beauty, Bird's Tongue, Black Dragon, and Gunpowder, to name only a handful. But all of them fall into one of the three basic categories already mentioned.

Following are some of the best teas in each category.

UNFERMENTED. Dragon Well, Soh Mei, Pi Lo Chun, and Gunpowder. These are all similarly processed green teas. The leaves are picked, spread out in shallow bamboo trays, dried briefly in the sun, and then heated briefly for a short time to prevent natural fermentation. As the leaves dry, they curl into tiny balls and acquire the dull green of the best green teas. The finest is Dragon Well—known through a variety of spellings as Long Jing, Lung Ching, or Loong Tsing—which is the tea of choice for most Chinese state banquets. It has a fine aroma, a sweet taste, and is best drunk young. It is the tea I use for Tea-Smoked Duck. Soh Mei is wind-dried and is pleasantly bitter. Pi Lo Chun, which was the tea of the Ching Dynasty court, is faintly sweet. Pungent, slightly smoky Gunpowder is grayish green, and its rolled balls resemble pellets, thus its name.

SEMIFERMENTED. Iron Goddess, Soi Sin (or Shui Hsien), and Pouchong. These are all oolong teas semi-fermented, and must be picked at a prescribed time and processed immediately. The leaves are wilted in the sun, shaken, then spread out so that the leaves fade from green to yellow. They are heated and regarded as cured. Iron Goddess, or "Teh Kuan Yin," for the Iron Goddess of Mercy is the most notable of the oolongs. It has a strong, direct, metallic taste that is favored by the Chiu Chow people (page 218) for settling the stomach after dinner. It is typically brewed to what is called a "gongfu" method, steeped twice to make it exceptionally strong. Mild Siu Sin is from Fujian and is a favorite morning wake-up tea in China. Pouchong tea leaves are wrapped in tissue to ferment. The process as they ferment and dry yields a mildly sweet, amber-colored afternoon tea.

FULLY FERMENTED. Bo Lei, Luk On, Ch'i-Men, and Lapsang Souchong. These blackened tea leaves, all fermented, are also referred to as Black by Westerners and Red by the Chinese. These tea leaves are spread out and allowed to wither in the shade, not the sun. When they are limp, they are rolled to break up their structure and then spread again to oxidize to a coppery red color. Finally, the leaves are heated and turn black. The Chinese believe that strong, double-fermented Bo Lei is good for digestion and gets better with age. It is usually Bo Lei teas that are pressed into bricks. Luk On, which smells strong but is mild, is a black tea that is favored by the elderly. Ch'i-Men is another "gongfu" tea; it is processed into tiny strips and steeped twice to yield a deep brown, faintly sweet tea. Lapsang Souchong is made from special black tea from Fujian that calls for fermenting the withered leaves in cloth. After withering, they are placed in barrels and covered with cloth to ferment. Finally they are smoked over burning pine, which accounts for the tea's distinctive, refined, smoky taste.

FLAVORED TEAS. Finally, we have flavored and scented teas. In China, teas are often combined with dried flower blossoms, buds, or petals to create aromatic brews. Among the most common are jasmine, chrysanthemum, orange blossom, and rose. For example, dried jasmine blossoms are added to green tea to make the fragrant, popular jasmine tea, or chrysanthemum blossoms are added to a fully fermented black tea to make a scented tea the Cantonese call *guk bo*.

THE TEAHOUSE AND DIM SUM

茶
樓
點
心

The drinking of tea met the eating of dumplings early in the twelfth century. Not only were meat-filled pouches of dough part of the cuisine of the palace in Kaifeng, China's capital during those years of the Southern Song Dynasty, but dumpling houses were commonplace in the city. According to Meng Yuan Lao, a scholar of the period who wrote extensively about food consumption in the capital, these and other small food-and-drink rest stops for travelers—what we would call modest restaurants—were plentiful.

The invasion of the Mongols in the thirteenth century forced the emperor and his court, as well as many of his subjects, southward to what is now Guangdong Province. They brought with them the custom of drinking tea and the culture of eating wheat, concepts eagerly seized on by the people of Guangdong in general and the city of Guangzhou in particular. This is how today's southerners, now known familiarly as the Cantonese, believe the gift of dim sum came to them. Yet they were quick to make it uniquely their own. Dim sum, with its literally hundreds of creative variations, exists nowhere else in China.

To be sure, dumplings, as both street and restaurant foods, are eaten throughout China, and dim sum restaurants, the lineal descendants of the early tea parlors of Kaifeng, are found in every Chinese city, but they tend to be Cantonese exports. For the concept of *yum cha,* drinking specific teas and eating dumplings unhurriedly in the morning, is a Cantonese

creation—a creation that over the centuries has developed its own unique set of characteristics, modes, and manners.

The earliest dim sum restaurants were noisy social and business centers that catered to men only. The customers, who were of a certain social standing—not farmers, for example—would arrive early to read their newspapers, visit with their friends, and discuss and do business. Some of them would bring their rare pet birds in cages to show them off. And they would sit, talk, read, and listen to their chirping charges for hours, all the while drinking tea and eating baskets of steamed dumplings.

In the Cantonese strongholds of Guangzhou and Hong Kong, dim sum restaurants have remained much the same through the centuries, though now, of course, everyone—men, women, families of every social standing—frequents them. And wherever the Cantonese have migrated, they have taken dim sum and tea with them. Many dim sum restaurants continue the custom of wheeling carts carrying small bamboo steamers lined with dumplings and small dishes holding countless other items around the room, with the waitpeople announcing in a singsong refrain the Cantonese names of the foods: *"Har gau, siu mai. Har gau, siu mai. Char siu bau, pai guat, siu mai. Char siu bau, pai guat, siu mai."* I first heard these chants in the dim sum house of my village of Siu Lo Chun, near Guangzhou, when I was a little girl and my brother Ching Moh took me there on his shoulders. I remember them still.

Nor have the dim sum rituals been discarded. When your teapot is empty, you don't need to call for a refill. You simply ease the lid of the teapot open, and the pot will be replenished. Nor do you ever pour your own tea. It is poured for you, and you pour for others. And you thank another for pouring by tapping your right forefinger on the table, an economical way of saying thank you without interrupting a conversation.

Within the world of Chinese cooking, dim sum occupies an uncharacteristic niche. Dim sum foods are rarely prepared at home. They are eaten in restaurants, where family generations come together around big, round tables to catch up. Occasionally, such as on New Year, a family might make dumplings and sweets as gifts for guests. But the traditional steamed, baked, and fried dim sum are eaten in restaurants.

The filled crescents, buns, balls, and cakes are assembled by skillful Chinese chefs, masters of many years. That is their only work, and a recurring art in which the only medium is dough. They are dedicated men who have fashioned a particular culinary form. They have created different doughs, though from similar ingredients, for particular dim sum. For these chefs, special dim sum demand special doughs.

I want my students to come away from my classes understanding the basics of my native cuisine, and there is no better path to comprehending dim sum than to make buns and dumplings. Those who like working with doughs will enjoy themselves as they make and use these doughs. Of course, there are already-formed dumpling wrappers, too, and there is great pleasure in working with them as well.

DUMPLINGS, BUNS, AND THEIR DOUGHS

In the markets of every Chinatown, all manner of dim sum dumpling wrappers, or skins—*pei* in Cantonese, *pi* in Mandarin—are sold. They are fresh and frozen, large and small, square and round, and their labeling can often be confusing. Following are the wrappers that are used for most dim sum that do not require special doughs. As has been the case with all of your shopping, take along the names in Chinese characters to make sure you are buying the correct product. When you can choose between prepared wrappers and homemade doughs, I have mentioned both in the recipes.

 WONTON WRAPPERS. These wrappers are discussed at length in Part 1, in Creating a Chinese Pantry. When the wrappers are left square, they are formed into wontons (see page 116) or certain dim sum. For other dumplings, they are cut into circles 2 to 3 inches in diameter. Wontons are considered noodles, even though the wrappers are used for dim sum, a point I discussed at length in The Wonderful Wonton (page 116).

 DUMPLING WRAPPERS. These pliable wrappers are similar to wonton wrappers except that they are round, usually 3¼ to 3½ inches in diameter, and labeled "dumpling wrappers" or "dumpling skins." Like wonton wrappers, they come 60 to 80 per package; are made from wheat flour, water, and eggs; and are dusted with cornstarch. They are also made without eggs. Dumpling wrappers made with eggs are yellow, and those without are cream-colored and labeled "Shanghai." Well wrapped, they will keep in the refrigerator for 3 to 4 days and in the freezer for up to 3 months. Thaw and allow to come to room temperature before using.

 SPRING ROLL WRAPPERS. These large, usually round wrappers, made from wheat flour and water, are soft and sufficiently pliant to roll. They are cooked on a griddle, packaged in plastic, and sold by weight. Usually they come 15 to 25 to the package, and are 6 to 6½ inches in diameter. Like other wrappers, they are found in the refrigerated section of the market. Square spring roll wrappers, 8 inches square, are also sold and, like the round wrappers, are in the refrigerated section. Sometimes spring roll wrappers, both round and square, are erroneously labeled "egg roll skins." If the wrappers are white, which you should be able to see through the plastic packaging, they can be used to make spring rolls. Both square and round wrappers are also available frozen. Thaw and allow to come to room temperature before using. The storage rules for dumpling wrappers apply here as well.

╫ EGG ROLL SKINS ╫

These large, uncooked, wrappers, about 7½ inches square, come in packages weighing about 2 pounds. Their texture is the same as that of thick wonton skins, and they are usually sold wrapped in waxed paper and identified as "egg roll wrappers" or "egg rolls skins" on a brown paper label. That said, I don't recommend that you use these wrappers. Contrary to what most people believe, the egg roll is not Chinese. It is a bastardized concoction that was created for serving in Chinese-American restaurants, and I mention the wrappers here only in an effort at clarity.

SHRIMP DUMPLINGS

|| MAKES 50 DUMPLINGS, OR 10 SERVINGS ||

蝦餃 This classic is surely the most popular of the many filled dumplings in the dim sum repertoire. These small, pleated, rounded crescents, called *har gau,* are found in every teahouse. They are made in only one way, with a particular dough, and cannot be made with ready-made wrappers. They always contain shrimp—sometimes chopped, sometimes finely minced, sometimes coarsely cut, with such variations usually the whim of the maker. Yet, these dumplings have been essentially the same for centuries—classics not to be tampered with.

INGREDIENTS

FILLING

1½ cups water	1½ teaspoons oyster sauce
2 ounces pork fat	¼ teaspoon sesame oil
8 ounces shrimp, cleaned (see page 75) and finely diced	Pinch of white pepper
¼ teaspoon salt	½ cup peeled and finely diced fresh water chestnuts
1 teaspoon sugar	¼ cup finely sliced white portion of scallions
1 medium egg white, lightly beaten	2 tablespoons finely diced bamboo shoots
1½ tablespoons tapioca starch	

HAR GAU DOUGH

1½ cups wheat starch	1 cup plus 3 tablespoons boiling water
⅔ cup tapioca starch	3 tablespoons melted lard or peanut oil
¼ teaspoon salt	

Mustard condiment or chili-mustard condiment (see Dumpling Sauces, page 268)

1. To make the filling: In a small pot, bring the water to a boil over high heat. Add the pork fat, cover, leaving the lid slightly cracked, and keep the water at a boil. Cook the pork fat for 30 minutes. Turn off the heat, remove the fat to a bowl, run cold water over it, and let stand for several minutes until cool. Remove the fat, pat dry, and cut into ⅛-inch dice.

2. Place the shrimp in the bowl of a stand mixer fitted with the paddle attachment. Turn on the mixer to low speed and add the following ingredients, one at a time, in order, mixing well after each addition: salt, sugar, egg white, tapioca starch, oyster sauce, sesame oil, and white pepper. Then add the diced pork fat, water chestnuts, scallions, and bamboo shoots and continue mixing until the ingredients are thoroughly blended. Stop the mixer, transfer the shrimp mixture to a shallow dish, cover, and refrigerate for at least 4 hours or up to overnight.

3. To make the dough: Rinse and dry the bowl of the mixer and return it to the stand. Place the wheat starch, tapioca starch, and salt in the bowl. Fit the mixer with the dough hook and turn to medium speed and slowly add the boiling water. Then add the lard and continue to beat until the mixture comes together as a dough and forms a ball. If the dough is too dry, add 1 additional teaspoon boiling water. Stop the mixer, remove the dough from the bowl, and knead it several times on a clean work surface until it forms a cohesive dough. Divide into 4 equal pieces, and cover with plastic wrap so its moisture is retained.

4. Oil the work surface. Then soak a paper towel with peanut oil and run a cleaver blade across it a few times to oil the blade well. Remove 1 piece of dough from the plastic and place it on the oiled work surface. Using your palms, roll it into a log 8 inches long and 1 inch in diameter. Cut the log crosswise into ½-inch pieces. Work with 1 piece at a time and keep the others covered with plastic wrap. Roll the piece into a small ball, then press down with your palm to flatten it. Using a flat side of the oiled cleaver blade, press down on the dough to the right, then reverse back left to create a thin round 2½ inches in diameter. Repeat with the remaining ½-inch pieces and

then with the remaining dough in the bags, reoiling the cleaver blade as needed to prevent sticking. Make 4 rounds at a time, then form 4 dumplings, keeping remaining dough pieces covered with plastic wrap to prevent them from drying out.

5. Place 1 round on the palm of one hand, place 1½ teaspoons of the filling in the center of each round, pressing slightly to flatten, and then fold the wrapper in half to create a half-moon. Holding the filled dumpling securely in one hand, form about 5 small pleats along one side of the open edge with the fingers of the other hand, pressing the pleats against the other edge to seal the dumpling closed. Then tap the rounded, folded edge lightly with a knuckle to give the dumpling its final shape. Repeat until all of the filling is used (see note).

6. Oil 3 bamboo steamers. As you make the dumplings, place the first one-third of them in a prepared bamboo steamer, making certain they do not touch one another, or they will stick together. Cover the steamer and steam for 7 minutes, or until the dough is translucent and the filling is visible through it. As the first batch steams,

Continued . . .

. . . continued

prepare the second one-third of the dumplings, place in another steamer, and then steam that batch when the first one is done. Repeat with the third and final batch.

7. Turn off the heat and serve. The dumplings are best served hot, so serve them the moment they are cooked, directly from the bamboo steamer. Accompany with the mustard condiment.

NOTE: This recipe will yield about 60 skins. The filling is sufficient for 50 dumplings. I prefer that you have extra skins to allow for any mistakes in forming the dumplings.

These dumplings can also be frozen for future use. Steam them for 4 minutes, instead of 7 minutes, and then let them cool completely. Stack them neatly, separated by sheets of waxed paper. Wrap the stack in a double layer of plastic wrap and then again in heavy-duty aluminum foil. Freeze for up to 2 months. To reheat them, allow them to thaw and come to room temperature, then steam for 3 to 5 minutes.

HOW TO FORM THE DUMPLINGS *See steps* **4–5.**

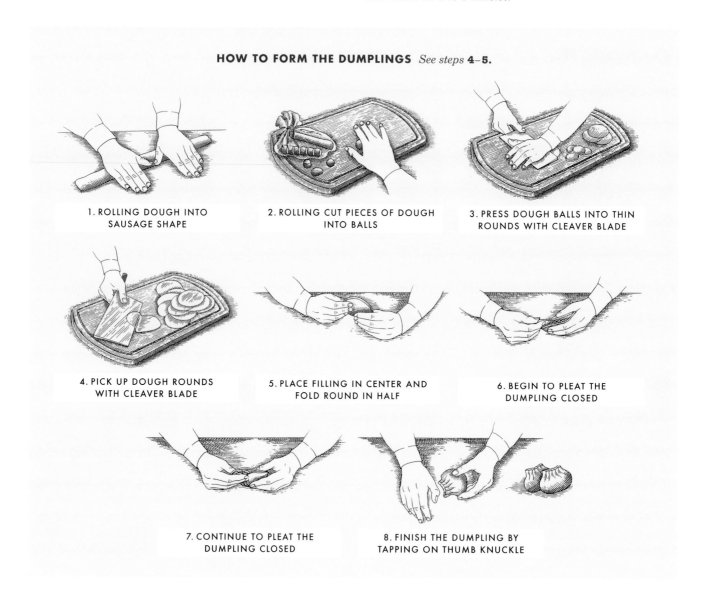

1. ROLLING DOUGH INTO SAUSAGE SHAPE

2. ROLLING CUT PIECES OF DOUGH INTO BALLS

3. PRESS DOUGH BALLS INTO THIN ROUNDS WITH CLEAVER BLADE

4. PICK UP DOUGH ROUNDS WITH CLEAVER BLADE

5. PLACE FILLING IN CENTER AND FOLD ROUND IN HALF

6. BEGIN TO PLEAT THE DUMPLING CLOSED

7. CONTINUE TO PLEAT THE DUMPLING CLOSED

8. FINISH THE DUMPLING BY TAPPING ON THUMB KNUCKLE

VEGETABLE DUMPLINGS

‖ **MAKES 50 DUMPLINGS, OR 10 SERVINGS** ‖

Here is a variation on the preceding recipe for Shrimp Dumplings. Called *jai gau* in Cantonese, these dumplings contain no shrimp or pork fat and are rooted in the vegetarian traditions of China's Buddhists and Taoists. In the past, they were eaten primarily by monks, but nowadays they are enjoyed by a wider audience of vegetarians.

INGREDIENTS

12 dried black mushrooms,
1 inch in diameter

SAUCE

3½ tablespoons water	2½ tablespoons tapioca starch
2 tablespoons oyster sauce	2 teaspoons sugar
1½ teaspoons double dark soy sauce	1½ teaspoons salt
1½ teaspoons sesame oil	Pinch of white pepper

3 cups peanut oil	4 fresh water chestnuts, peeled and finely shredded
1 cup finely shredded snow peas (1½ inches long)	
1 cup finely shredded carrots (1½ inches long)	*Har Gau* Dough (page 264)
1 cup finely shredded celery (1½ inches long)	Mustard condiment or chili-mustard condiment (see Dumpling Sauces, page 268)
¾ cup finely shredded bamboo shoots (1½ inches long)	

1. In a bowl, soak the mushrooms in hot water to cover for 30 minutes. Drain, rinse the mushrooms thoroughly, and then squeeze out the excess water. Remove and discard the stems and finely shred the caps (see Cleaver discussion, page 45). Reserve.

2. To make the sauce: In a small bowl, mix together all of the ingredients and reserve.

3. Heat a wok over high heat for 30 seconds. Add the 3 cups peanut oil and heat to 350°F on a deep-frying thermometer. Add the reserved mushrooms and all of the vegetables and oil-blanch for 40 seconds. Turn off the heat. Using a Chinese strainer, remove the vegetables from the wok and drain well over a bowl. Pour off the oil from the wok and strain if needed to remove residue. Set aside 1½ teaspoons. Reserve the remaining oil for another use.

4. Wipe the wok with a paper towel. Add the reserved 1½ teaspoons of peanut oil and place over high heat. When a wisp of white smoke appears, stir the sauce, pour it into the wok, and cook for about 2 minutes, or until it thickens and turns dark brown. Turn off the heat.

5. Place the vegetables in the bowl of a stand mixer fitted with the paddle attachment. Turn on the mixer to low speed, add the sauce from the wok, and mix thoroughly for 2 minutes, or until all of the ingredients are well blended. Turn off the mixer, remove the mixture to a shallow dish, cover, and refrigerate for at least 4 hours or up to overnight.

6. Prepare the dough and shape into 2½-inch rounds as directed.

Continued . . .

. . . continued

7. Place one round on the palm of one hand, place 1 to 1½ teaspoons of the filling on the center, and press down lightly on the filling. Fold the round into a half-moon and, using the thumb and forefinger of the other hand, press around the edge to seal. Repeat to form more dumplings until all of the filling is used (see note).

8. Oil three bamboo steamers. As you make the dumplings, place the first one-third of them in a prepared bamboo steamer, making certain they do not touch one another, or they will stick together. Cover the steamer and steam for 6 minutes, or until the dough is translucent and the filling is visible through it. As the first batch steams, prepare the second one-third of the dumplings, place in another steamer, and then steam that batch when the first one is done. Repeat with the third and final batch.

9. Turn off the heat and serve. The dumplings are best served hot, so serve them the moment they are cooked, directly from the bamboo steamer. Accompany with the mustard condiment.

NOTE: This recipe will yield about 60 skins. The filling is sufficient for 50 dumplings. I prefer that you have extra skins to allow for any mistakes in forming the dumplings.

These vegetable dumplings cannot be frozen for future use, but they can be steamed and stored in the refrigerator for up to 3 days. Steam as directed, let cool completely, cover, and refrigerate. To reheat, allow the dumplings to come to room temperature and then steam for 2 minutes.

DUMPLING SAUCES

I recommend a spicy condiment for serving with the Shrimp Dumplings and the Vegetable Dumplings. When I was a child, my family bought our mustard in the village market. We would mix it with water and spread the hot paste on freshly made sour mustard pickle (see page 140). A similar use of hot mustard perfectly complements these steamed dumplings. The powdered mustard that is closest to what I remember from my childhood is an English brand, Coleman's Mustard, Double Superfine Compound. (Do not use Coleman's prepared mustard.) To make a simple mustard condiment, mix 3 tablespoons each mustard powder and water until smooth. Or, you can duplicate the condiment found in many dim sum restaurants: Mix the mustard powder and water as directed, then add an equal amount of Homemade Chili Sauce (page 58) and blend together. Both the mustard condiment and the chili-mustard condiment heighten the flavor of the dumplings.

POT STICKERS

|| MAKES 36 DUMPLINGS, OR 8 TO 10 SERVINGS ||

 上海鍋貼 These small dumplings come with both a story and a significant history. According to legend, they were born in the imperial kitchen when a cook, making dumplings for the emperor, forgot a batch that was slowly cooking. They were singed brown, slightly burned. With no time to spare, and an impatient, hungry emperor waiting, the cook, a nimble and adaptive fellow, arranged the dumplings on a platter, burned sides up, and presented them to the emperor as a new dish that he called *quotie,* which means "stuck bottom." The emperor was delighted. Legend or not, it is a fact that these browned half-moons filled with pork and vegetables were eventually sold daily by the thousands from small streetside stands to satisfy the morning habits of people in Beijing and Tianjin, who called them *jiaozi,* or "little dumplings." It is a tradition that exists to this day.

As popular foods do, these *jiaozi* migrated to Shanghai, where they became known by their imperial name of *quotie,* to describe their cooking process. The habit of morning pot stickers swept Shanghai, and to this day they are sold, as in Beijing, from small streetside stands. Over the years, they migrated south to Guangzhou and Hong Kong, carried by Shanghainese fleeing the Japanese invasion of their city, and sold first by refugees on the streets as a way of making a living.

They have become part of the accommodating dim sum repertoire, and are referred to in Cantonese as *wor tip,* or "pot stickers." Serve them with a ginger-vinegar sauce (see note).

INGREDIENTS

FILLING

4 cups water	2 teaspoons peeled and grated ginger
1 tablespoon salt plus 1 teaspoon	2 teaspoons white rice wine
½ teaspoon baking soda (optional)	1 medium egg, lightly beaten
¾ cup sliced bok choy stalks (¼-inch-wide pieces)	1½ teaspoons light soy sauce
	2 teaspoons sesame oil
1½ cups firmly packed sliced bok choy leaves (¼-inch-wide pieces)	2 teaspoons sugar
	Pinch of white pepper
14 ounces ground pork	2 tablespoons cornstarch
⅓ cup finely sliced scallions	

DOUGH

2 cups Pillsbury Best All-Purpose Flour	¾ cup plus 2 tablespoons water
6 tablespoons peanut oil	1 cup water

1. To make the filling: First water-blanch the bok choy. In a pot, bring the water to a boil over high heat. Add the 1 tablespoon salt and the baking soda (if using). When the water returns to a boil, add the bok choy stalks and allow the water to return to a boil. Add the bok choy leaves and blanch for 1 minute, or until the leaves turn bright green. Immediately turn off the heat. Run cold water into the pot, then drain off the water. Repeat.

2. In a large bowl, place the bok choy, the 1 teaspoon salt, and all of the remaining filling ingredients. Using a wooden spoon or 2 pairs of wooden chopsticks, mix the ingredients together, stirring them in one direction. Stirring in this way ensures the mixture will become a cohesive filling. Cover and refrigerate for at least 6 hours or up to overnight. The longer it rests, the easier it will be to work with.

Continued . . .

. . . continued

3. To make the dough: In a large bowl, place the flour and make a well in the center. Gradually add water to the well and use your fingers to combine with the flour until it is absorbed and a firm dough forms. If the dough is too dry, add a little more water. Knead the dough in the bowl for about 15 minutes, or until smooth and elastic. Cover the dough with a damp cloth and allow to rest for 1½ hours.

4. Dust a work surface with flour. Divide the dough into 3 equal pieces. Work with 1 piece at a time and keep the others covered with the damp cloth. Using your palms, roll into a log 12 inches long. Cut crosswise into 12 equal pieces. Using a small rolling pin, roll out each piece into a 3-inch round. Keep the work surface well dusted with flour as you work.

5. Place 1 round on the palm of one hand, place 1 tablespoon of the filling on the center, and fold the round into a half-moon. Using the thumb and forefinger of the other hand, pleat the seam closed, making from 5 to 7 pleats. Repeat to form more dumplings until all of the rounds are used. Cover the dumplings with plastic wrap to prevent them from drying out, then repeat with the remaining two pieces of dough in two batches to make a total of 36 dumplings.

6. In a cast-iron frying pan, heat 3 tablespoons of the peanut oil over high heat. When a wisp of white smoke appears, turn off the heat and place 18 of the dumplings in the pan. Turn on the heat to medium and allow

the dumplings to cook for 3 minutes. Pour ½ cup of the water into the pan and allow the dumplings to cook for 7 to 10 minutes, or until the water evaporates. Reduce the heat to low and allow the dumplings to cook for about 2 minutes, or until they are golden brown on the bottom and the skins are translucent on top. To ensure the dumplings cook evenly, move the pan back and forth on the burner to distribute the heat evenly and prevent sticking.

7. Remove to a heated dish and serve. Because these dumplings are best eaten hot, serve in batches.

NOTES: These dumplings can be frozen uncooked for up to 6 weeks. Dust them liberally with flour to prevent sticking, then stack them neatly, separating the layers with sheets of waxed paper. Next, wrap them in a double layer of plastic wrap, and then wrap again in heavy-duty aluminum foil and slip into the freezer. To cook them, thaw and allow to come to room temperature, then cook as directed.

These dumplings are eaten with a ginger-vinegar dipping sauce that is as traditional as they are. In a bowl, mix together ⅓ cup red rice wine vinegar, and ¼ cup peeled and finely shredded ginger (see Cleaver discussion, page 45). Let stand for 30 minutes before use. Then serve the sauce in a common bowl, from which each diner can spoon the sauce over a dumpling. Makes 8 to 10 servings.

WHEAT FLOUR DOUGH

|| MAKES ENOUGH FOR ABOUT 40 DUMPLING WRAPPERS ||

 The two classic dim sum dumplings that follow, Cook and Sell Dumplings (facing page) and Water Dumplings (page 276), are traditionally made with this dough. But you can make them with purchased wonton wrappers or dumpling wrappers (page 263) as well. As I noted earlier, I include such recipes as teaching tools and for cooks who enjoy working with doughs. The advantage of using the commercial skins is that they are rolled to a thinness that is usually quite difficult for the home cook to achieve.

INGREDIENTS

1½ cups Pillsbury Best All-Purpose Flour	2 extra-large eggs
½ teaspoon baking soda	2 tablespoons water
½ teaspoon salt	⅓ cup cornstarch

1. On a work surface, mix together the flour, baking soda, and salt. Make a well in the center and add the eggs to the well. Using the fingers of one hand, work the eggs into the flour mixture until all of the eggs are absorbed. Slowly dribble in the water, mixing with your fingers as you pour, until the water is thoroughly absorbed and the ingredients begin to adhere to one another. Using a dough scraper, pick up the mixture from the work surface and then knead it on the work surface for about 10 minutes, or until it becomes an elastic dough. Cover the dough with a damp cloth and allow to rest for 3 hours.

2. When the dough is ready, lightly dust the work surface with a little of the cornstarch. With a rolling pin, roll out the dough into a sheet ¼ inch thick. Pick up the sheet, dust the work surface again with cornstarch, and continue rolling the dough until it is ⅛ inch thick. Roll the dough around a wooden dowel about 1 inch in diameter or a length of broom handle. Dust the work surface again with cornstarch and unroll the dough sheet onto it. Roll the dough again with the rolling pin until it is about ¹⁄₁₆ inch thick, then roll it around the dowel again. (The only way you can pick up the dough is by rolling it around the dowel; otherwise, it will tear.) The dough should be quite thin at this point.

3. Dust the work surface again with cornstarch and unroll the dough sheet on it. Roll the sheet with the rolling pin until it is about 22 by 20 inches. It should be thin enough that, if you lift a corner, you will be able to see light through it. Roll the dough sheet around the dowel again and then dust the work surface again. Then, using the edge of the dough scraper and a ruler, cut out 3-inch squares. Stack the squares, dusting between the layers with cornstarch. To ensure the squares remain pliable, wrap them well in plastic wrap, then refrigerate them overnight. Even though you use rounds for making the dumplings, it is best to cut squares now because you will get a better yield from the sheet. You will also have more control when you trim squares into rounds than if you cut rounds from the sheet.

4. These homemade skins are now ready for use. You should have about 40 wrappers. Each of the dumpling recipes makes 36 dumplings, so you will have a few extra wrappers as insurance against mistakes when forming the dumplings. As you fill the wrappers, work with 1 wrapper at a time and keep the others covered with a damp cloth to prevent them from drying out. If you decide to use commercial wrappers, treat them the same way.

COOK AND SELL DUMPLINGS

|| MAKES 36 DUMPLINGS, OR 8 TO 10 SERVINGS ||

  These traditional basket-shaped dumplings are called *siu mai,* which translates as "cook and sell," to indicate that they are so good that the moment they are cooked and out of the pot they are bought and eaten. The tops are open and are often decorated before steaming with such foods as dried fish roe, green peas, and grated hard-boiled egg yolks. They are typically served with a cooked sauce of oil and soy (see note).

INGREDIENTS

FILLING

10 dried black mushrooms, 1½ inches in diameter, soaked in hot water to cover for 30 minutes, drained, rinsed, squeezed dry, stems discarded, and caps cut into ¼-inch dice

12 ounces coarsely ground pork

8 ounces shrimp, cleaned (see page 75) and cut into ⅓-inch dice

1½ tablespoons oyster sauce

1 tablespoon peanut oil

2 teaspoons sesame oil

2 tablespoons cornstarch

2 teaspoons sugar

¾ teaspoon salt

Pinch of white pepper

Wheat Flour Dough (facing page) or 40 commercial wonton or dumpling wrappers

---

1. To make the filling: In a large bowl, combine all of the filling ingredients. Using a wooden spoon or two pairs of wooden chopsticks, mix the ingredients together, stirring them in one direction, until the mixture is smooth and has an even consistency. Stirring in this way ensures the filling will be cohesive. Remove the mixture to a shallow dish and cover and refrigerate for at least 4 hours or up to overnight.

2. Prepare the dough and cut out squares as directed. Cut the homemade squares or the commercial wrappers into rounds 2¼ inches in diameter.

3. Work with 1 wrapper at a time and keep the others covered with a damp cloth. Place 1 round on the palm of one hand and place 4 teaspoons of the filling on the center. Holding a round-bladed knife in the other hand, gently flatten the filling in a circular motion while using your fingers to lift the sides of the wrapper, creating a stubby, cylindrical basket shape with pleats around the top edge. Pack down the filling and smooth the open top of the dumpling. Squeeze the dumpling gently in the middle to create a slight indentation. This will ensure that the dumpling and the filling will remain intact during steaming. Tap the bottom of the dumpling lightly on a work surface to flatten it, which will ensure it will sit upright in the steamer. Repeat until you have made 18 dumplings.

Continued . . .

. . . continued

HOW TO FORM THE DUMPLINGS *See step* **3.**

PLACE FILLING IN CENTER
OF DUMPLING SKIN

SQUEEZE THE DUMPLINGS TO CREATE
PLEATED BASKET SHAPE

4. Oil two bamboo steamers. Place the first 18 dumplings in a prepared bamboo steamer, making certain they do not touch one another, or they will stick together. Cover the steamer and steam for 7 minutes, or until the dough is translucent and the filling is visible through it. Remove the bamboo steamer from the wok and keep it covered. As the first batch steams, form the remaining dumplings, place in the second prepared steamer, and then steam them when the first batch is done.

5. When the second batch is ready, resteam the first batch for 2 minutes so they are piping hot, then serve both batches at the same time directly from the bamboo steamers.

NOTE: These lovely little open dumplings taste best when accompanied with a simple cooked sauce. Heat a wok over high heat for 30 seconds. Add ¼ cup Scallion Oil (page 56), ½ cup dark soy sauce, 3½ tablespoons sugar, and 3 tablespoons water and stir clockwise until the ingredients are thoroughly mixed and begin to boil. Turn off the heat. Pour the sauce into a bowl, let cool to room temperature, and divide among small sauce dishes for serving. Or, pour into a glass jar, cover tightly, and refrigerate. It will keep for up to 3 weeks. Makes 8 to 10 servings.

WATER DUMPLINGS

|| MAKES 36 DUMPLINGS, OR 8 TO 10 SERVINGS ||

 These crescent-shaped dumplings are called *soi gau*, or "water dumplings," because they are cooked in boiling water. They are simple yet versatile, served in different ways in dim sum restaurants: Eaten directly out of the pot, with a dipping sauce (see note), or sitting in bowls of chicken stock flavored with sliced Chinese chives.

INGREDIENTS

FILLING

8 ounces ground pork	1 tablespoon oyster sauce
4 ounces shrimp, cleaned (page 75) and cut into ¼-inch dice	1½ teaspoons sesame oil
	2 tablespoons tapioca starch
¼ cup finely sliced white portions of scallions	2 teaspoons sugar
3 tablespoons ⅛-inch-dice bamboo shoots	1¼ teaspoons salt
	Pinch of white pepper
3 tablespoons ⅛-inch-dice peeled fresh water chestnuts	

Wheat Flour Dough (page 272) or 40 commercial wonton or dumpling wrappers	2 quarts water
	1 tablespoon salt
	1 tablespoon peanut oil
1 large egg, lightly beaten	

1. To make the filling: In a large bowl, combine all of the filling ingredients. Using a wooden spoon or two pairs of wooden chopsticks, mix the ingredients together, stirring them in one direction, until the mixture is smooth and has an even consistency. Stirring in this way ensures the filling will be cohesive. Remove the mixture to a shallow dish and cover and refrigerate for at least 4 hours or up to overnight.

2. Prepare the dough and cut out squares as directed. Cut the homemade squares or the commercial wrappers into rounds 2¾ inches in diameter.

3. Work with 1 wrapper at a time and keep the others covered with a damp cloth. Place 1 round on the palm of one hand and place 1 heaping tablespoon of the filling on the center. With a round-bladed butter knife, press the filling down gently, then dip the knife into the beaten egg and brush along the edges of the wrapper. Fold over into a half-moon shape and press along the curved edge with your thumb and forefinger to seal securely. Repeat to form more dumplings until all of the filling is used.

4. Place the water, salt, and peanut oil in a large pot and bring to a boil over high heat. Place the dumplings in the pot and allow the water to return to a boil. Cook for 5 minutes, or until the skins are translucent and the filling can be seen through the skin.

5. Turn off the heat, remove the dumplings with a Chinese strainer to a heated dish and serve.

NOTE: A mixture of soy sauce and ginger is a traditional sauce for these dumplings. In a small bowl, combine 1 teaspoon sugar, 1 tablespoon each dark soy sauce and light soy sauce, 1 teaspoon Scallion Oil (page 56), 3 tablespoons Chicken Stock (page 54), ½ teaspoon sesame oil, 1½ tablespoons peeled and finely shredded ginger (see Cleaver discussion, page 45), 1½ tablespoons shredded white portion of scallions (½-inch lengths), and a pinch of white pepper. Let rest for 30 minutes, then divide among individual sauce dishes. Makes 8 to 10 servings.

STEAMED PORK BUNS

|| MAKES 16 BUNS, OR 8 SERVINGS ||

These are the first dim sum items I remember eating during my childhood, when my brother took me to our village teahouse. Called *jing char siu bau* in Cantonese, their history dates to when ovens were rare in China and most foods, including these buns, were cooked in steamers over a fire. It is one of the recipes that has never changed, and I expect never will. The filled buns soften and open like flowers as they steam.

INGREDIENTS

FILLING

5 tablespoons Chicken Stock (page 54)	Pinch of white pepper
1 tablespoon oyster sauce	1 tablespoon peanut oil
1 tablespoon ketchup (page 75)	½ cup ¼-inch-dice onions
1½ teaspoons double dark soy sauce	¾ cup thin, ½-inch-square Barbecued Pork slices (page 103)
2½ teaspoons sugar	1½ teaspoons white rice wine
2¼ teaspoons cornstarch	½ teaspoon sesame oil

DOUGH

2¼ cups Gold Medal All-Purpose Flour	6 tablespoons milk
½ cup sugar	3 tablespoons water
3½ teaspoons baking powder	2½ tablespoons melted lard or peanut oil

---

1. To make the filling: In a small bowl, mix together the stock, oyster sauce, ketchup, soy sauce, sugar, cornstarch, and white pepper. Reserve to use as a sauce.

2. Heat a wok over high heat for 40 seconds. Add the peanut oil and, using a spatula, coat the wok with the oil. When a wisp of white smoke appears, add the onions, lower the heat to medium, and stir for about 2 minutes, or until they turn light brown. Add the pork, raise the heat to high, and stir-fry for about 2 minutes, or until well mixed.

3. Drizzle in the wine, adding it along the edge of the wok, and mix well. Stir the sauce, pour it into the wok, and stir for about 2 minutes longer, or until the mixture thickens and turns brown. Add the sesame oil and mix well.

4. Turn off the heat, remove the filling to a shallow dish, and let cool to room temperature. Refrigerate, uncovered, overnight until firm, then leave refrigerated until ready to use.

5. To make the dough: On a work surface, mix together the flour, sugar, and baking powder and make a well in the center. Gradually add the milk to the well and use your fingers to combine it with the flour mixture until it is absorbed. Then add the water and work it into the flour mixture with your fingers until it is absorbed. Add the lard and continue to work the dough until it is well blended.

6. Using a dough scraper, gather the dough with one hand and then begin kneading it. Knead for 12 to 15 minutes, or until smooth and elastic. If the dough is dry and shows traces of flour, add 1 teaspoon lukewarm water at a time and continue to knead. If the dough is too wet, sprinkle a bit of flour on the work surface and on your hands and

Continued . . .

. . . continued

continue to knead. When the dough is smooth and elastic, cover it with a damp cloth and allow it to rest for at least 1 hour but not more than 2 hours.

7. Cut sixteen 2½-inch squares of waxed paper and reserve. On a floured work surface, roll the dough with your palms into a log 16 inches long. Cut the log cross-wise into 1-inch pieces. Roll each piece into a ball. Work with 1 ball at a time and keep the others covered with the damp cloth. Press down lightly on the ball of dough with your palm, then use your fingers to shape it into a dome with an indentation at the center.

8. Hold the dough in one hand and place 1½ tablespoons of the filling in the center of the indentation with the other hand. Gather the edges of the dough and pull them up and over the filling, using your fingers to pleat the top until the filling is completely enclosed. Then twist the top to seal and pinch off any excess dough. Place the bun, peak side up, on a waxed-paper square. When you feel confident shaping the buns, you can increase the amount of filling to 2 tablespoons. Repeat to make 16 buns in all.

9. Divide the buns, on their waxed paper, between two bamboo steamers, spacing them at least 2 inches apart. Stack the steamers, cover, and steam for 15 to 20 minutes, or until the buns are snowy white and the pleats have opened like a flower.

10. Turn off the heat and serve the buns directly from the steamers.

NOTE: These buns can be frozen after steaming. Allow to cool to room temperature, then place in plastic freezer bags, seal closed, and freeze. They will keep for up to 2 months. To reheat the buns, thaw and allow to come to room temperature, then steam for about 5 minutes, or until they are very hot.

HOW TO FORM THE BUNS *See steps* **7–8.**

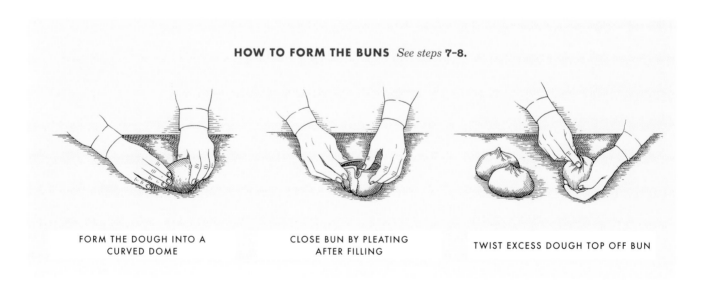

FORM THE DOUGH INTO A
CURVED DOME

CLOSE BUN BY PLEATING
AFTER FILLING

TWIST EXCESS DOUGH TOP OFF BUN

BAKED PORK BUNS

|| MAKES 16 BUNS, OR 8 SERVINGS ||

焗
叉
燒
飽

Called *guk char siu bau,* these baked variations on the steamed buns on page 277 are perhaps the most popular dim sum outside of China. The dough and the cooking methods differ for the two buns, but the filling is the same. Some people believe this baked version originated in Hong Kong, and others suggest that it first appeared in that outpost of Western-style baking, Shanghai. No matter which provenance is correct, today these buns are enjoyed around the world. Even people who are not familiar with dim sum often know of pork buns, and a visit to every Chinatown finds locals eating them at Sunday-morning family dim sum get-togethers or for weekday lunchtime "sandwiches."

INGREDIENTS

Filling for Steamed Pork
Buns (page 277)

DOUGH

1 package (¼ ounce) active dry yeast	2 cups Pillsbury's Best Bread Flour
⅓ cup sugar	½ large egg, lightly beaten
½ cup warm water (110°F)	5 tablespoons melted lard or peanut oil

1 extra-large egg, lightly beaten	2 tablespoons Scallion Oil (page 56)

1. Prepare the filling as directed and refrigerate overnight. Leave refrigerated until ready to use.

2. To make the dough: In a large bowl, mix the yeast and sugar in the warm water, dissolving them. Set in a warm place for 30 minutes to 1 hour, or until the mixture rises and a brownish foam appears on the surface. (Because weather and temperature can affect the progress, the timing cannot be more precise. The cooler the outdoor temperature, the longer the time.)

3. Add the flour, egg, and lard to the yeast mixture. Continuously stir the mixture with your hand until well mixed, then begin kneading the dough in the bowl. When the dough is cohesive, sprinkle a work surface lightly with flour. Place the dough on the prepared work surface and continue to knead, picking up the dough with a dough scraper and sprinkling flour on the work surface as needed to prevent sticking, for about 15 minutes, or until smooth and elastic.

4. Place the dough in a large bowl, cover the bowl with a damp cloth, set in a warm place, and let the dough rise for 2 to 4 hours, or until tripled in size. (Again, the cooler the outdoor temperature, the longer the time.)

5. Cut sixteen 3½-inch squares of waxed paper and place the squares in a single layer on a baking sheet. Remove the dough from the bowl to a floured work surface, and knead it several times until it becomes elastic. Using your palms, roll the dough into a log 16 inches long. Cut the log into 1-inch pieces. Roll each piece into a ball. Work with 1 ball at a time and keep the others covered with the damp cloth. Press down lightly on the ball with your palm, then use your fingers to shape it into a dome with an indentation at the center.

6. Hold the dough in one hand and place 1 tablespoon of the filling in the indentation with the other hand. Gather the edges of the dough over the filling and pinch the top closed, pressing firmly to seal. If there is excess dough, pinch it off. Turn the bun over and place, sealed side down, on a waxed-paper square. The top will be smooth. Repeat to make 16 buns in all. The buns should be 2 inches apart on the baking sheet to allow for expansion. Place the buns in a warm place for 1 hour, or until they rise to half again their size. About 20 minutes before the buns are ready, preheat the oven to 350°F.

7. Spray the buns with a fine mist of warm water, then brush with the beaten egg. Place in the oven and bake for 15 to 20 minutes, or until browned. About halfway through the baking time, rotate the baking sheet front to back to ensure even browning.

8. Remove from the oven. The buns tend to cool quickly and their crusts harden. To keep them soft and to add some faint flavor, brush them with the scallion oil. Serve warm.

NOTE: These buns can be frozen after baking. Cover them individually with plastic wrap, then with heavy-duty aluminum foil, and freeze for up to 2 months. To reheat them, thaw and allow to come to room temperature. Place on a baking sheet, cover with foil, and place in a preheated 350°F oven for about 15 minutes, or until hot.

SAUCES FOR BUNS

SAUCES FOR STEAMED AND BAKED BUNS

The buns on pages 277 and 280 are delicious without an accompanying sauce, or you can serve them with individual dishes of Homemade Chili Sauce (page 58) or with a condiment of hot mustard and chili sauce (see Dumpling Sauces, page 268).

SPRING ROLLS

‖ **MAKES 12 ROLLS, OR 6 SERVINGS** ‖

 It feels, on occasion, that we are about to be engulfed in an avalanche of spring rolls. These small, classic fried fingers of dough, a symbolic food of the Chinese Lunar New Year, have become a culinary obsession of nearly every Chinese chef, who readily packs them with his or her current fancy. There is no food, no flavoring, no garnish that doesn't find its way into a spring roll. Nor has this iconic food traveled well over the years. In its migration to and translation by the West, this petite, delicate food has become the thick, cumbersome log known as the egg roll.

It is time to rescue the Cantonese *chun geun* (or *chun juan,* as it is known elsewhere in China), "the roll of spring." This symbolic food—its shape, reminiscent of a gold bar, is a harbinger of good fortune—is synonymous with New Year's Day and is enjoyed throughout the ensuing half-month celebration of the beginning of spring. The wrappers are the product of a special dough, and you can make your own to continue your understanding of core Chinese cooking. Or, you can buy good ready-made spring roll wrappers (see page 263) in Chinatown markets. You will need 12 wrappers, each 6 inches in diameter. What follows is the spring roll of tradition.

INGREDIENTS

DOUGH

3 cups Pillsbury Best All-Purpose Flour	1 teaspoon salt
	1 ½ cups water

FILLING

4 ounces shrimp, cleaned (page 75) and finely shredded (see Cleaver discussion, page 45)	3 scallions, cut into 1 ½-inch lengths and white portions shredded
3 ounces pork butt, shredded (see Cleaver discussion, page 45)	1 ½ tablespoons peanut oil
	1 pound mung bean sprouts, ends removed
1 teaspoon salt	2 large eggs, lightly beaten
½ teaspoon light soy sauce	

6 cups peanut oil	Chili-mustard condiment (see Dumpling Sauces, page 268)

---

1. To make the dough: In a large bowl, mix together the flour and salt and make a well in the center. Gradually add the water to the well and use your fingers to combine it with the flour until it is absorbed and a loose dough forms. If the dough is too dry, add a little more water. Knead the dough in the bowl for about 20 minutes, or until it becomes elastic. Cover the dough with a damp cloth and let rest for 3 to 4 hours.

2. Wash and dry a griddle, making certain it is completely free of any vestiges of grease. Heat the griddle over low heat. When it is hot, grasp a large handful of dough from the bowl, hold it up, and rotate your wrist in a constant, slow motion. Keep the dough upward, working it with your fingers and palm. Then quickly press the dough onto the center of the hot griddle, using a circular motion, and then just as quickly pull back, leaving a thin, rough layer of dough about 6 inches in diameter on the griddle.

Continued . . .

. . . continued

3. The dough will begin to dry at its edges in 10 to 12 seconds, which means the wrapper is ready. Carefully peel the wrapper from the griddle and remove it to a large plate.

4. Repeat until you have made 6 wrappers, stacking them as they are made, then wrap them in a damp cloth to prevent them from drying out. Repeat to make 6 more wrappers, so you have 12 wrappers total, in two batches. Leave each batch wrapped in its damp cloth, slide the batches into separate plastic bags, seal, and refrigerate for at least overnight or up to 4 days. (They can also be frozen for up to 2 months.) Allow to come to room temperature before using. The wrappers must be made at least a day in advance of use because they are too dry and brittle to work with when freshly made. Storing them in the refrigerator makes them pliable.

5. To make the filling: Place the shrimp and pork in separate small bowls. Add ½ teaspoon salt and ¼ teaspoon soy sauce to each bowl, mix well, and allow to marinate for 30 minutes next to the work surface where you will be forming the rolls. Place the scallions in a small bowl nearby. Heat a wok over high heat for 30 seconds. Add the peanut oil and, using a spatula, coat the wok with the oil. When a wisp of white smoke appears, add the bean sprouts and stir-fry for 1½ minutes, or until they are wilted. Turn

off the heat, remove the bean sprouts with a Chinese strainer, and drain them well over a bowl. Pat dry with paper towels and place in a small bowl near the other filling ingredients. Wash and dry the wok and reserve.

6. Place the wrappers and beaten eggs near the filling ingredients. Lay a wrapper on a large, flat plate. Add together, one at a time, 1½ to 2 tablespoons bean sprouts, large pinches each of the marinated shrimp and pork, and some scallions, arranging the ingredients in a line 3 to 3¼ inches long and equal distance from the sides of the wrapper and about 2 inches from the edge nearest you. Dip your fingers into the beaten egg, rub the egg all along the edge of the wrapper, and begin rolling from the edge nearest you. As you roll, fold in the sides of the wrapper. Keep lightly dampening the edges of the wrapper with the beaten egg as you roll and fold to ensure a secure closing. Once the roll is done, dampen the seam with more beaten egg and press to seal. The spring roll should be packed, rolled, and folded tightly and should be about 4 inches long. Repeat with the remaining filling and wrappers. (If you are using store-bought square wrappers, position the wrapper so a corner is facing you, position the line of filling ingredients across the wrapper about 2½ inches from the corner nearest you, and then roll the same way.)

HOW TO MAKE THE WRAPPER *See step* **2.**

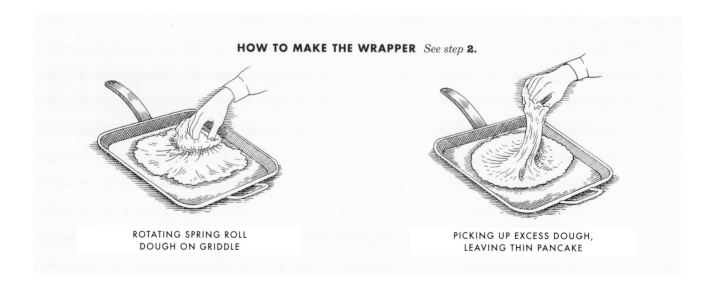

ROTATING SPRING ROLL
DOUGH ON GRIDDLE

PICKING UP EXCESS DOUGH,
LEAVING THIN PANCAKE

7. Heat the wok over high heat for 1 minute. Add the peanut oil and heat to 350°F on a deep-frying thermometer. Cook 4 rolls at a time, quickly sliding them into the oil one at a time. Deep-fry for 1 minute, then turn the rolls over and continue to cook, moving the rolls back and forth and turning them, for about 3 minutes longer, or until they are an even light brown. Adjust the heat as needed to prevent burning. Using the Chinese strainer, remove the rolls from the oil and drain them well over a bowl. Repeat with the remaining 8 rolls in 2 batches. When the last batch is the same light brown as the first 2 batches, return the first 8 rolls to the wok and deep-fry, adjusting the heat as needed and moving the rolls about in the oil, for 1½ to 2 minutes, or until all of the rolls are golden brown.

8. Turn off the heat, remove the spring rolls with the strainer, and drain them briefly over a bowl. Then transfer them to a heated plate and serve. Accompany with the chili-mustard condiment.

⊣ NO WORCESTERSHIRE, PLEASE ⊢

WORCES-TERSHIRE

I saw it happen once and thought it an aberration. Then I saw it again, and I was aghast. What I saw repeatedly was waiters in dim sum restaurants pouring Worcestershire sauce into small condiment dishes for serving with spring rolls. Never, ever do that. Instead, do as I have suggested in the spring roll recipe and make a batch of the same hot mustard and chili sauce mixture (see Dumpling Sauces, page 268) that I serve as a sauce for some of my dumplings.

HOW TO FORM THE SPRING ROLLS *See step* **6.**

PLACE FILLING IN SPRING ROLL

FOLD EGG-BRUSHED SPRING ROLL

COMPLETE ROLLING

GLUTINOUS RICE LOAF

‖ MAKES 2 LOAVES, OR 10 SERVINGS ‖

Reminiscent of strudel, this flavorful loaf was once a popular steamed preparation in dim sum restaurants, but nowadays it is seldom seen. In China, this traditional dish, called *nor mai geun* by the Cantonese, is regarded as a winter dish because it warms the body. It was a personal favorite in the dim sum teahouses when I was growing up, a dish for sharing, and I continue to share it with my students in my dim sum classes.

INGREDIENTS

2 cups glutinous rice	2 cups cold water

FILLING

2½ tablespoons oyster sauce	½ cup ¼-inch-dice Chinese bacon
2 teaspoons light soy sauce	3 Chinese sausages (*lop cheong*), cut into ¼-inch dice
1½ teaspoons sugar	
1 teaspoon five-spice powder (page 103)	⅓ cup finely sliced scallions
1 teaspoon peanut oil	½ teaspoon salt, if needed
2 tablespoons dried shrimp, soaked in hot water to cover for 20 minutes, drained, and cut into ¼-inch pieces	

Dough for Steamed Pork Buns (page 277)

1. Place the rice in a large bowl and fill the bowl with water. Wash the rice by rubbing it between your palms, then discard the water. Do this two more times, then drain the washed rice well. Place the rice in an 8-inch round cake pan, add the cold water, place the cake pan in a steamer, cover, and steam for 30 to 40 minutes, or until the rice is soft and sticks together. Remove from the steamer and set aside.

2. Line the bottom of a 9-inch square cake pan with aluminum foil and set aside.

3. To prepare the filling: In a small bowl, mix together the oyster sauce, soy sauce, sugar, and five-spice powder and reserve. Heat a wok over medium heat for 30 seconds. Add the peanut oil and, using a spatula, coat the wok with the oil. Add the shrimp and stir-fry for 40 seconds. Add the bacon and sausage and stir-fry with the shrimp for about 5 minutes, or until the meats turn color. Add the reserved rice, raise the heat to high, and stir well to mix thoroughly. Lower the heat to medium low, stir the reserved sauce, and drizzle it over the rice mixture. Stir-fry until all of the ingredients are well mixed. Add the scallions and stir to mix well. Taste for seasoning, and add salt if needed.

4. Turn off the heat and transfer the rice mixture to the prepared cake pan. Press down on the mixture, then press it against one side of the pan to create a loaf shape 9 inches long, 4 inches wide, and 2 inches deep. Allow the rice mixture to cool to room temperature, then cover it loosely with aluminum foil and refrigerate for at least 6 hours or up to overnight.

5. Make the dough as directed and cut it in half. On a clean work surface, roll out half of the dough into a 9-inch square, ¼ inch thick. If the dough is sticky, dust the work surface and the rolling pin with flour. Cut the rice loaf in half lengthwise, and place half of it in the center of the sheet of dough. Fold one edge of the dough sheet up over the rice filling and press down lightly to secure. Fold the other edge up over the filling, overlapping the first edge

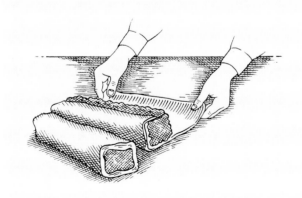

WRAP DOUGH AROUND GLUTINOUS RICE

and pressing down to seal. Repeat to make a second loaf with the remaining dough and rice.

6. Cut two 10-by-3-inch sheets of waxed paper. Place one loaf on each piece of waxed paper. Place each loaf on its waxed paper in a bamboo steamer, stack the steamers, cover, and steam for 20 to 25 minutes, or until the loaves are opaque.

7. Turn off the heat and remove the loaves to a heated dish. Slice and serve.

NOTE: These loaves cannot be frozen because the glutinous rice will lose its cohesiveness.

BAKED *LOP CHEONG* BUNS

|| MAKES 16 BUNS, OR 5 TO 8 SERVINGS ||

焗
腊
肠
卷

The final recipe in this lesson is a perfect illustration of the unending flexibility of Cantonese dim sum—its ability to adapt and create. Among dim sum chefs, there is an unspoken, but understood, goal to create one new dim sum every day. I have created this one, which I call *lop cheong geun,* with Chinese sausages and a traditional dough I particularly like. I made these buns once on a whim more than ten years ago, and they were received with pleasure, which is what the little dishes of dim sum ideally elicit.

INGREDIENTS

Dough for Beijing Baked Breads (page 163)

8 Chinese sausages (lop cheong)

3 tablespoons oyster sauce

3 tablespoons double dark soy sauce

1 teaspoon sesame oil

1 large egg lightly beaten with 3 tablespoons water

3 tablespoons Scallion Oil (page 56)

1. Make the dough and set aside to rise until tripled in size as directed.

2. Cut each sausage in half crosswise on the diagonal. Place the halves in a bowl. Add the oyster sauce, soy sauce, and sesame oil and mix thoroughly to combine and to coat the sausages evenly. Let the mixture rest for 20 minutes.

3. Cut sixteen 3½-by-2-inch rectangles of waxed paper and place them, well spaced, in a single layer on a baking sheet. Set them aside.

4. Place the dough from the bowl on a work surface, sprinkle it lightly with flour, and knead it for about 10 minutes,

or until elastic. Using your palms, roll the dough into a log 16 inches long. Cut the log into 1-inch pieces. Roll each piece into a thin, round pencil-like rope 12 inches long. Work with one piece of dough at a time and keep the others covered with the damp cloth. Holding a sausage half by the cut end, press one end of the dough strip onto the cut end. Then carefully wrap the strip around the sausage half until it is completely enclosed. It will resemble a croissant. Press the edges of the dough at both ends of the sausage half to seal. Place the bun on a waxed-paper rectangle. Repeat to make 16 buns in all. Let the buns rise, uncovered, in a warm place for about 1 hour. They will increase in size by about one-third. About 20 minutes before the buns are ready, preheat the oven to 350°F. Spray the buns with a fine mist of warm water.

5. Brush the buns with the egg wash, place the baking sheet in the oven, and bake for 20 to 25 minutes, or until the buns are golden brown. About halfway through the baking time, rotate the baking sheet front to back to ensure even browning.

6. Turn off the heat and remove the buns to a heated plate. Brush them with the scallion oil to keep them soft and moist and serve.

CONTINUE TO WRAP SAUSAGE WITH THE ROPE OF DOUGH

第三集 試茶

PART 3 || LESSON 3: A TASTE OF TEA

LESSON 4
VEGETABLES AS THE WAY

蔬菜是健康食品

**VEGETABLES
AS THE WAY**

In China, the tradition of eating only vegetables lies in the confluence of its soybean and rice culture with its religion and philosophies. Historically, the choice of foods has been influenced by the religious beliefs inspired by Buddha and the behavioral philosophies of Lao Tzu and his Taoism and of Confucius. Lao Tzu and Confucius were contemporaries, but while Confucius laid out precise principles of behavior and manners, Taoism rested on intuitive behavior, on a person seeking and hopefully finding an individual way. However, all of these belief systems were, and are, intrinsically linked with food.

In general, Buddhist monks and nuns in China are forbidden to eat meat, poultry, fish, eggs, or just about everything that once lived in the animal world. Oddly, they are permitted to eat oysters, clams, and mussels—defined as vegetables of the sea—to replace three strong-flavored forbidden vegetables, leeks, chives, and shallots. Observant Buddhists either refrain from eating foods that once lived or refrain only on specific days, such as the first fifteen days of the lunar year or the first and fifteenth day of each month. Strict Taoists can choose to eat or not to eat meat, though most do not. Confucius saw merit in vegetarianism because of its disciplines, yet devoted treatises to the precise preparation of all foods, giving as much importance to meat as to vegetables.

I saw all of these choices made by people around me as I was growing up in the village of Siu Lo Chun. A few ate vegetables, nuts, and fruits on specific days. A very few were strict vegetarians, one of whom I remember vividly. She was the mother of one of my playmates, and she became not only a Buddhist overnight, but a vegetarian as well, when her husband took a second wife. I am certain less traumatic choices were, and are, made. But most of the people around me ate everything.

Over the centuries, the presentation of vegetables—whether for observant Buddhists or not—became Chinese art, particularly in Hangzhou, south of Shanghai. This lovely city of many gardens is situated around the large, tranquil West Lake, a place of pleasure boats and pavilions, where the wealthy traditionally came to linger over banquets. Restaurants vied to present edible beauty, tasty art, with large, flat plates as the canvases. No banquet was complete without exquisite portrayals of peacocks and roosters, dragons and phoenixes, butterflies and fans, "drawn" with threads and slices of bean curd and vegetables.

There were, to be sure, the whole range of vegetables in China—stir-fried, deep-fried, braised, steamed, stewed, and cooked in soup—many examples of which you have already made in previous lessons. But the artistic materials of vegetable cooking are bean curd, or *doufu,* which can be cut, sculpted, and molded, and, to a lesser extent, wheat gluten. In the hands of Hangzhou's accomplished chefs, fresh bean curd, cut in particular ways, seasoned with particular ingredients, became "chicken" and "pork." Seasoned bean curd—cooked in soy sauce and spices, then dried and pressed—became "beef" for stir-frying with other vegetables. Mashed taro became "fish," and gluten became "scallops."

All of this culinary disguise began in the Buddhist temples with monks and nuns who sought substitutes for meat. Efforts to duplicate meat flavors were often made, but it was more important for the artistic creation to look like food that was forbidden. The intention was to fool the eye and thus surprise the palate. The artifice of this so-called temple food became art. The recipes that follow are just a handful of examples of that ingenuity.

"CHICKEN" WITH VEGETABLES

|| MAKES 4 TO 6 SERVINGS ||

The twice-cooked bean curd in this dish duplicates the texture of cooked chicken breast meat. This stir-fry, with the exception of the bean curd, is prepared exactly as it would be with chicken.

INGREDIENTS

SAUCE

5 tablespoons Vegetable Stock (page 53)

2 teaspoons Shaoxing wine

1½ teaspoons sesame oil

1 teaspoon light soy sauce

1 teaspoon double dark soy sauce

1 teaspoon white rice vinegar

2 teaspoons cornstarch

1½ teaspoons sugar

¼ teaspoon salt

Pinch of white pepper

---

4 cups water

2 firm fresh bean curd cakes (8 ounces total)

3 tablespoons Scallion Oil (page 56)

1½ teaspoons peeled and minced ginger

1 teaspoon minced garlic

5 dried black mushrooms, 1½ inches in diameter, soaked in hot water to cover for 30 minutes, drained, rinsed, squeezed dry, stems discarded, and caps thinly sliced (⅓ cup)

⅓ cup julienned bamboo shoots

2 scallions, julienned (½ cup)

2 to 3 fresh water chestnuts, peeled and julienned (¼ cup)

½ cup julienned carrots

2 tablespoons julienned Sichuan mustard pickle

1 tablespoon Vegetable Stock (page 53), if needed

---

1. To make the sauce: In a bowl, mix together all of the ingredients and reserve.

2. In a pot, bring the water to a boil over high heat. Add the bean curd cakes and cook for 5 minutes. Turn off the heat, run cold water into the pot, pour off the water, and allow the bean curd to cool. Cut the bean curd into slices 2 inches long by 1 inch wide and ⅓ inch thick. Dry well with paper towels.

3. Heat a wok over high heat for 30 seconds. Add 1½ tablespoons of the scallion oil and, using a spatula, coat the wok with the oil. When a wisp of white smoke appears, add the bean curd slices, spread them in a single layer, and fry for 1½ minutes. Turn the slices over and fry for another 1½ minutes. The bean curd should be light brown on both sides. Turn off the heat, remove the bean curd slices to a plate, and reserve.

4. Wipe the wok and spatula with paper towels. Heat the wok over high heat for 20 seconds. Add the remaining 1½ tablespoons scallion oil. When a wisp of white smoke appears, add the ginger and garlic and stir for about 30 seconds, or until the garlic turns light brown. Then add the mushrooms, bamboo shoots, scallions, water chestnuts, carrots, and mustard pickle and stir-fry for 2 minutes, or until very hot. If the vegetables are too dry, add the stock. Add the reserved bean curd and stir to mix well. Make a well in the center of the mixture, stir the sauce, and pour it into the well. Stir to mix well for about 2½ minutes, or until the sauce thickens and bubbles.

5. Turn off the heat, transfer to a heated dish, and serve.

MINCED "SQUAB" ROLLED IN LETTUCE

‖ **MAKES 8 LETTUCE ROLLS, OR 4 SERVINGS** ‖

 This is a vegetarian version of a classic. Traditionally squab, or pigeon, is eaten roasted, either cut into bite-size pieces or minced, and packed into lettuce leaves. Here, seasoned bean curd cakes, browned with soy, flavored with five-spice powder, and pressed dry, are minced to become the "squab."

INGREDIENTS

SAUCE

3 tablespoons hoisin sauce	1 teaspoon Shaoxing wine
1 teaspoon sesame oil	1 teaspoon sugar

2½ tablespoons peanut oil	8 dried black mushrooms, 1 inch in diameter, soaked in hot water to cover for 30 minutes, drained, rinsed, squeezed dry, stems discarded, and caps minced (½ cup)
1½ teaspoons minced garlic	
3 seasoned bean curd cakes, minced	
1¼ teaspoons peeled and minced ginger	
1 teaspoon sugar	1 tablespoon oyster sauce
½ teaspoon salt	1 tablespoon Shaoxing wine
½ cup minced carrots	¼ teaspoon light soy sauce
⅓ cup minced jicama	8 large lettuce leaves (crisp inner leaves)

---

1. To make the sauce: In a small bowl, mix together all of the ingredients and reserve.

2. Heat a wok over high heat for 30 seconds. Add 1 tablespoon of the peanut oil and, using a spatula, coat the wok with the oil. When a wisp of white smoke appears, add the garlic and stir briefly. Add the bean curd and stir-fry for 1½ minutes, or until the bean curd is hot. Turn off the heat, transfer to a small bowl, and set aside.

3. Turn on the heat to high under the wok. Add the remaining 1½ tablespoons peanut oil and, using the spatula, coat the wok with the oil. When a wisp of white smoke appears, add the ginger and stir briefly. Add the sugar and salt and stir briefly. Add the carrots, jicama, and mushrooms and stir-fry for 2 minutes. Add the reserved bean curd and stir to mix well. Add the oyster sauce and stir to mix well. Add the wine and stir to mix well. Add the soy sauce and stir-fry for about 3 minutes, or until all of the ingredients are very hot.

4. Turn off the heat, transfer to a heated dish, and serve. Arrange the lettuce on a dish and place the lettuce and sauce on the table. Invite each diner to brush a lettuce leaf with a little of the sauce, place 2 tablespoons of the minced "squab" in the center of the leaf, fold and roll to enclose, and then enjoy.

ROAST "GOOSE"

|| MAKES 16 PIECES, OR 4 TO 6 SERVINGS ||

 Just as roast goose and its crisp skin would be the centerpiece of a banquet, so would this representation of goose be the core of a vegetarian feast, which would also include mock fish and mock meat. The skin of the "goose" is fashioned from lengths of bean curd skin, which are fried to imitate both the color and texture of the skin.

INGREDIENTS

SAUCE

⅓ cup Vegetable Stock (page 53)

5 teaspoons sesame oil

5 teaspoons double dark soy sauce

4½ teaspoons sugar

⅛ teaspoon white pepper

FILLING

2 tablespoons peanut oil

10 dried black mushrooms, 1½ inches in diameter, soaked in hot water to cover for 30 minutes, drained, rinsed, squeezed dry, stems discarded, and caps julienned (⅔ cup)

⅔ cup julienned bamboo shoots

⅔ cup julienned carrots

1 sheet bean curd skin, about 24 inches in diameter

1½ cups shredded iceberg lettuce

6 tablespoons peanut oil

---

1. To make the sauce: In a small bowl, mix together all of the ingredients and reserve.

2. To make the filling: Heat a wok over high heat for 30 seconds. Add the peanut oil and, using a spatula, coat the wok with the oil. When a wisp of white smoke appears, add the mushrooms, bamboo shoots, and carrots and stir-fry briefly to mix well. Stir the sauce, pour it onto the vegetables, and stir-fry for about 4 minutes, or until the vegetables absorb all of the sauce. When there is no more moisture in the wok, turn off the heat, remove the vegetables to a plate, divide them into 4 equal portions, and reserve.

3. Spread the sheet of bean curd on a flat work surface. Have a small bowl of water nearby. With kitchen shears, cut out four pieces, each 6 by 4½ inches, from the sheet. Work with 1 piece at a time and keep the others covered with plastic wrap. Lay the piece on the work surface, with a long side facing you. Dip your fingers in the water and moisten the skin lightly. Arrange one portion of the filling in a ridge along the edge of the skin nearest you, positioning it about 1½ inches from the edge. Roll up the skin tightly around the filling and press the roll closed, leaving the ends of the roll open. Repeat with the remaining three skin pieces and filling portions.

4. Place the rolls in a steamproof dish, place in a steamer, cover, and steam for about 15 minutes, or until the surface of the roll shows small bubbles and wrinkles. Turn off the heat, and transfer the rolls to a dish to cool. While they are cooling, spread the shredded lettuce in a bed on a small platter.

5. Heat a cast-iron frying pan over high heat for 1 minute. Add the peanut oil. When a wisp of white smoke appears, add the rolls and lower the heat to medium. Cook the rolls for 5 to 6 minutes, turning them so they fry and brown evenly and adjusting the heat as needed to prevent burning. When they are golden brown, turn off the heat, and transfer the rolls to a heated plate. With the kitchen shears, cut each roll into 4 equal pieces.

6. Arrange the pieces on the bed of lettuce and serve.

STIR-FRIED "BEEF" WITH BROCCOLI

|| MAKES 4 TO 6 SERVINGS ||

西蘭花炒牛 Once again, as with the minced "squab" dish on page 293, seasoned bean curd is standing in for meat, this time beef. Many of these vegetarian versions of familiar dishes that use bean curd, both fresh and preserved, are found in the kitchens of the Taoist monastery of Ching Chung Koon, in Hong Kong's New Territories. It is where I first observed them being prepared and later cooked them.

INGREDIENTS

SAUCE

2 tablespoons oyster sauce	1 tablespoon cornstarch
2 teaspoons dark soy sauce	Pinch of white pepper
2 teaspoons Shaoxing wine	½ cup Vegetable Stock (page 53)
½ teaspoon sesame oil	
1¼ teaspoons sugar	

3 heads broccoli, 1 pound each	1 tablespoon salt
2 quarts water	1 teaspoon baking soda (optional)
½-inch-thick slice ginger, peeled and lightly smashed	

3 tablespoons peanut oil	¼ teaspoon salt
2 teaspoons minced garlic	2 tablespoons minced ginger
6 seasoned bean curd cakes (8 ounces), cut into ⅛-inch-thick slices	

---

1. To make the sauce: In a small bowl, mix together all of the ingredients and reserve.

2. To water-blanch the broccoli, first trim the broccoli heads into florets. You should have about 1 pound florets. In a pot, bring the water to a boil over high heat. Add the ginger, salt, and baking soda (if using). When the water returns to a boil, add the broccoli and blanch for 10 seconds, then turn off the heat. The broccoli will turn bright green immediately on being immersed in the water. The extra seconds will tenderize the florets. Run cold water into the pot, then drain off the water. Run cold water into the pot again, then drain the broccoli in a strainer over a bowl and reserve. Discard the ginger.

3. Heat a wok over high heat for 30 seconds. Add 1½ tablespoons of the peanut oil and, using a spatula, coat the wok with the oil. When a wisp of white smoke appears, add the garlic and stir briefly until the garlic turns light brown. Add the bean curd slices and stir-fry for 2 minutes, or until thoroughly mixed with the garlic. Turn off the heat, transfer to a small dish, and reserve.

4. Turn on the heat to high under the wok. Add the remaining 1½ tablespoons peanut oil, the salt, and ginger and stir for 45 seconds, or until very hot. Add the reserved broccoli and stir-fry for 2 minutes, or until the broccoli is well coated with the ginger and oil. Add the reserved bean curd and stir-fry for 1½ minutes, or until all of the ingredients are well mixed and very hot. Make a well in the center of the mixture, stir the sauce, and pour it into the well. Stir to mix for about 2 minutes, or until the sauce thickens and bubbles.

5. Turn off the heat, transfer to a heated plate, and serve.

BRAISED "PORK" WITH BLACK MUSHROOMS

‖ MAKES 6 SERVINGS ‖

Here, gluten in its role as a meat substitute is cut into rough-edged scallops. Use the rough-surfaced gluten that has been prefried for this recipe, rather than smooth gluten cakes. The slices are deep-fried until golden brown and then braised with stock and vegetables to enhance their texture and flavor.

INGREDIENTS

5 cups peanut oil

10 ounces gluten, cut into ½-inch-thick slices

½-inch-thick slice ginger, peeled and lightly smashed

4 scallions, cut crosswise into 1-inch pieces

1⅓ cups cut-up bamboo shoots (1 inch square by ½ inch thick)

2 carrots, peeled, halved lengthwise, and cut into ¼-inch-thick half-moons (1 cup)

30 Steamed Black Mushrooms (page 81)

2 tablespoons Shaoxing wine

2½ cups Vegetable Stock (page 53)

1 tablespoon double dark soy sauce

1½ teaspoons sugar

¼ teaspoon salt

1. Heat a wok over high heat for 1 minute. Add the peanut oil and heat to 350°F on a deep-frying thermometer. Add half of the gluten slices and deep-fry, turning them to prevent sticking, for 2 minutes, or until they are golden brown. Remove with a Chinese strainer and drain over a bowl. Repeat with the remaining gluten slices. Reserve.

2. Pour off all but 2 tablespoons of the peanut oil from the wok.

3. Heat the wok for 20 seconds over high heat. Add the ginger and stir for 30 seconds. Add the scallions and stir-fry for 45 seconds, or until the scallions release their fragrance. Add the reserved gluten slices and stir-fry for 30 seconds longer. Add the bamboo shoots, carrots, and mushrooms and stir to mix well. Add the wine and mix well. Add 2 cups of the stock and bring to a boil. Add the soy sauce, sugar, and salt and mix well. Cover the wok, reduce the heat to low, and braise at a simmer for 20 minutes. Stir the mix frequently as it simmers to prevent sticking. If the mixture begins to dry out, add the remaining stock, ¼ cup at a time. The mixture should absorb the liquid, but it should still be moist.

4. Turn off the heat, transfer to a heated dish, and serve.

LESSON 5
A SECOND COOKING TOUR, NORTH TO SOUTH

再談南北菜

COOKING FROM NORTH TO SOUTH

In this lesson, we return once again to the breadth of China and its regional preparations, with emphasis on dishes for feasts, and again we begin in Beijing. With its long history as the seat of imperial China, it is known for its feast dishes, elaborate preparations that were created to please emperors and empresses but have since filtered down the social ladder and are now regional hallmarks. Over the years, this palace cuisine, which demanded long hours and laborious work by the imperial chefs, acquired the name Mandarin cooking, an often misunderstood appellation that is typically described as a regional cuisine. It is not; it is merely a definition of style.

As we leave Beijing and head east to west to south, we encounter other dishes of distinction. Some are centuries-old recipes, some are more recent. Some are famous, with familiar names, and others are not. There are feasts from Shanghai and its region to the east, from Hunan and Sichuan to the west, from Fujian and Guangdong to the south, and from Hong Kong in the far south, where all of China's cooking melds these days.

Many of these dishes take time to prepare. But as I have said before, and as I repeat to all of my classes, the joy is in the making. Once you have actually prepared a Peking duck, you will have a greater appreciation for any Peking duck served to you. And the same experience awaits you when you tea-smoke a duck, long-cook a shoulder of pork, fry crabs like the so-called boat people do in Hong Kong's Causeway Bay Typhoon Shelter, bake a chicken in salt, or prepare General Tso's chicken.

The common denominator of all of these classic preparations is that they are dishes with histories. Together they comprise the vast, seamless world of Chinese cooking, and they can be mastered.

PEKING DUCK

‖ **MAKES 12 FILLED PANCAKES, OR 6 SERVINGS** ‖

北京鴨

Even in Beijing, this famed Chinese reparation is referred to as both Peking duck, after the old English name of the capital, and Beijing duck. Regardless of what the dish is called, it must be prepared in the classic manner, in three courses: The crisp skin, with a hoisin-based sauce; then the duck meat stir-fried with vegetables; and finally a soup made with the duck's bones.

In the West, it is customarily served as scallops of skin and meat together, wrapped in pancakes, which is wrong. The name Peking duck has also mistakenly been applied to any roasted duck bathed in hoisin sauce. Some even believe the glazed ducks hanging in the windows of Chinatown food shops and restaurants are Peking ducks. They are not.

The preparation of Peking duck has a long, honored history, first in the imperial palace and then, most notably, in the Quanjude restaurant, which had just recorded serving Peking duck number 115,081,852 on my last visit in 2008—enough ducks to encircle the world two and a half times. Believe it. Although many restaurants in Beijing offer Peking duck, Quanjude is perhaps the only one that still roasts the birds as it was historically done: The restaurant fills its stone-and-brick ovens with date wood—only date wood—cleans the ducks and plugs their openings, inserts a hook into their neck, hangs the other end of the hook from a long pole, and roasts the ducks over the oven fire.

When you eat duck at Quanjude, you will be told that the restaurant opened in the third year of the reign of Emperor Tongzhi of the Qing Dynasty. If, after you have enjoyed the duck's crisp skin, you let the staff know that your appreciation for duck is without bounds, they will happily serve you deep-fried duck gizzards, fried duck livers with

nuts, duck wings cooked with garlic, and duck feet cooked over balsam boughs.

What follows is the traditional way to prepare Peking duck in three courses, first the skin, then the stir-fried meat (page 306), and finally the soup (page 306). But some planning is required to ensure your guests eat the three courses in sequence, without interruption. Make your pancakes and prepare the vegetables for the stir-fry and the ingredients for the soup ahead of time. Then, as the duck roasts, you can steam the pancakes. As your guests eat the duck skin in the pancakes, you can easily cut up the duck meat and stir-fry it with the readied vegetables and boil the duck bones for the soup. Served in this manner, your Peking duck will be a complete dinner for 6 people.

INGREDIENTS

1 duck, 7 pounds, preferably freshly killed, with head, wings, and feet intact	⅓ cup salt
	4 cups boiling water

COATING

3 cups boiling water	¼ cup maltose
3 tablespoons white rice vinegar	

12 Pancakes (page 304)

SAUCE

½ cup hoisin sauce	2 teaspoons sesame oil
2 teaspoons sugar	2 teaspoons Shaoxing wine

6 scallions, white portions only, cut into 2-inch lengths

Continued . . .

. . . continued

1. Clean the duck as directed for chicken on page 54, using the ⅓ cup salt to rub on the duck because of its larger size. Allow the duck to drain thoroughly. Retain the heart and gizzard for the soup and reserve the liver for another use. When you buy the duck, sometime it will have already been cleaned once and sometimes not. If it has been cleaned, the stomach will have been cut open and will be clean, though the heart, liver, and gizzard will be in place. If the stomach has not been cleaned, you will have to cut into it to remove the innards. Then after thorough cleaning, using poultry skewers, secure the stomach opening tightly closed.

2. When the duck has finished draining, tie off its neck with kitchen string and insert the nozzle of the air pump into the neck opening, under the skin. Inflate with the pump until the skin separates from the meat.

3. Remove the pump nozzle. With a cleaver, remove the first two joints of the duck's wings and legs. Insert the chopstick under the wings, along the back, to lift them away from the body. (Do not cut the joints of the wings and legs before pumping air into the duck. If you do, the skin will not inflate and no air will be retained.) Take care not to nick the skin of the duck as you cut off the wings and legs. There should be no holes in the skin.

4. Insert one end of a large, sturdy S-hook through the string around the duck's neck. Working over the sink, hold the duck up by the S-hook with one hand and use the other hand to ladle the 4 cups boiling water over the skin, scalding the entire duck. If possible, suspend the duck by it S-hook as you scald to ensure more even coverage. Using the S-hook, hang the duck over a drip pan for 30 minutes to allow the skin to dry (on a humid day this may take longer).

5. To make the coating: Heat a wok over high heat and pour in the 3 cups boiling water. Add the vinegar and maltose and allow the water to return to a boil to make sure the maltose dissolves and mixes well with the vinegar. Remove the duck from where it is hanging and, holding it by the S-hook, suspend it over the wok. Ladle the coating mixture over the hanging duck, being careful to coat the skin completely and thoroughly. After coating, the skin will darken to a gray-beige. Return the duck to its hanging position over the drip pan and allow to dry thoroughly for 10 to 12 hours in a cool place with good air

HOW TO PREPARE THE DUCK *See steps* **2–3.**

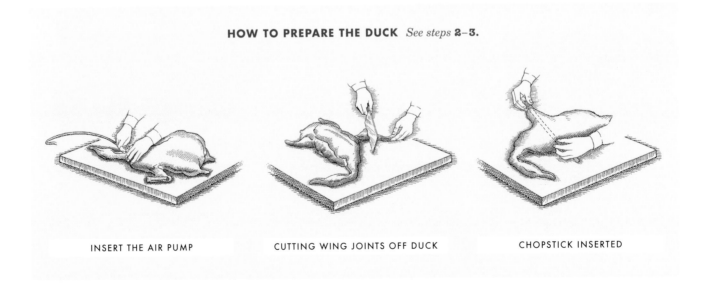

INSERT THE AIR PUMP   CUTTING WING JOINTS OFF DUCK   CHOPSTICK INSERTED

circulation. (You can use a fan to blow air onto the duck, which will reduce the drying time by half.)

6. While the duck is drying, make the pancakes.

7. Preheat the oven to 450°F for 30 minutes. Pour water to a depth of 1½ inches into a roasting pan and place on the bottom shelf of the oven. Place the duck, breast side down, on the oven rack directly above the roasting pan, not in the pan. The pan only catches the drippings as the duck roasts. Roast the duck for 10 minutes, then reduce the oven temperature to 425°F. Turn the duck over, breast side up, and roast for 10 minutes. If it begins to burn, reduce the temperature to 400°F. Allow the duck to roast evenly for another 35 to 45 minutes, turning frequently to ensure the head and tail do not burn. The duck is ready when the skin is a deep brown and crisp. Remove the duck from the oven, and let cool for 7 minutes.

8. To make the sauce: In a small bowl, mix together all of the ingredients and reserve.

9. Make a series of closely spaced ½-inch-long cuts in both ends of each scallion length to create "bristles." Place the scallion brushes in ice water so the bristles will open and stay crisp.

10. Make sure the pancakes are steamed and hot. Slice the duck skin carefully away from the meat in irregular scallops about 2½ inches long. To fill each pancake, lay out a pancake, use a scallion brush to brush it with 2 teaspoons of the sauce, and lay the brush on the sauce. Cover with 2 pieces of duck skin, wrap the pancake into a bundle by overlapping its edges, and serve. Or, bring the slices of duck skin, the steamer basket with the pancakes, the scallion brushes, and the sauce to the table and let the diners serve themselves.

NOTES: If you are using a convection oven, you won't need to keep turning the duck. But it should be checked for evenness in roasting. The roasting time will also probably be shorter by 5 to 10 minutes. Otherwise, all of the other directions apply.

You can use cucumber cut into julienne 1½ inches long in place of the scallion brushes. You will need about ½ cup.

Although the pancakes are traditional, you can opt to serve the duck skin with Steamed Fan Breads (page 172) or Beijing Baked Breads (page 163), as is occasionally done in Beijing.

HOW TO PREPARE THE DUCK *See step* **5.**

SCALDING THE DUCK

DRYING THE DUCK WITH FAN

PANCAKES

|| MAKES 12 PANCAKES ||

 These are the classic pancakes, or *baobing,* used for wrapping the crisp skin of Peking duck and for serving Mu Shu Pork (page 307). I have seen tortillas suggested as a substitute, but their taste is inadequate and they are too thick and chewy. You may also find ready-made fresh or frozen pancakes. I don't recommend them. They lack elasticity and tend to crumble when heated.

INGREDIENTS

1 ¼ cups Pillsbury Best All-Purpose Flour

¼ cup boiling water

½ cup flour for dusting

1 tablespoon sesame oil for brushing dough

1. Place the flour in a bowl. Slowly add the boiling water and mix with a wooden spoon or chopsticks in one direction. When the flour absorbs the water and cools, knead the dough into a ball in the bowl, then transfer it to a work surface dusted with some of the flour. Knead the dough for about 2 minutes, or until it is thoroughly blended. Place the dough in a bowl, cover with plastic wrap, and let rest at room temperature for 30 minutes.

2. Dust the work surface with some of the flour. Place the dough on the work surface and use your palms to roll it into a log 12 inches long. Cut the log crosswise into twelve equal pieces. Work with 2 pieces at a time and keep the others covered with plastic wrap. Roll each piece into a ball, then flatten it with your palm, dusting the dough with flour if it begins to stick to the surface. Brush the tops of the two flattened pieces with some of the sesame oil. Stack the two pieces, oiled sides in. With a rolling pin, roll out the double-layer pancake into a round 7 inches in diameter, lightly dusting with flour if necessary to prevent sticking.

3. Heat a wok over medium heat for 1 minute. Put the double pancake in the hot, dry wok and cook for 1 minute, or until the pancake begins to bubble up. Watch closely, as the heat must be controlled carefully. If it is too high, the pancakes will burn. Turn the pancake over and cook until

a few brown spots are visible on the underside. Remove the pancake from the wok and separate the layers. You will have two pancakes, each lightly browned on one side, white on the other. Repeat until all twelve pancakes are made (see note for directions on storing the pancakes until ready to steam).

4. To steam the pancakes for serving, invert a steamproof dish in a steamer and brush the upturned bottom with sesame oil. Stack the pancakes on the inverted dish, cover, and steam for 5 to 7 minutes, or until hot and pliable.

5. Serve as directed in individual recipes.

NOTES: These pancakes can be made up to 5 days in advance, cooled, stacked, wrapped in plastic wrap, and refrigerated. They may also be frozen, wrapped in plastic wrap, then in heavy-duty aluminum foil, for up to 2 months. Before using, thaw the pancakes, allow them to come to room temperature, then steam as directed until they are hot. They will retain their elasticity.

You can double this recipe and refrigerate or freeze half of the pancakes for future use.

HOW TO PREPARE AND COOK THE PANCAKES *See steps* **2–3.**

ROLLING PANCAKE DOUGH

MAKING PANCAKES IN A WOK

PEKING DUCK WITH MIXED VEGETABLES

|| MAKES 6 SERVINGS ||

PEKING DUCK BONES SOUP

|| MAKES 6 SERVINGS ||

INGREDIENTS

SAUCE

¼ cup Chicken Stock (page 54)

1 tablespoon Shaoxing wine

1 tablespoon oyster sauce

2 teaspoons light soy sauce

1 teaspoon white rice vinegar

1 teaspoon sesame oil

2 teaspoons cornstarch

1 teaspoon sugar

½ teaspoon salt

2 teaspoons peeled and minced ginger

---

3 tablespoons peanut oil

2 teaspoons peeled and minced ginger

½ teaspoon salt

¼ cup 2-inch-julienne carrots

¼ cup peeled and julienned fresh water chestnuts

¼ cup 2-inch-julienne celery

1 cup 2-inch-long green portion of scallions

1 cup mung bean sprouts, ends removed

1½ cups julienned Peking Duck meat (page 301)

---

1. To make the sauce: In a small bowl, mix together all of the ingredients and reserve.

2. Heat a wok over high heat for 30 seconds. Add 1½ tablespoons of the peanut oil and, using a spatula, coat the wok with the oil. When a wisp of white smoke appears, add the ginger and salt and stir briefly. Add the carrots, water chestnuts, and celery and stir-fry for 1½ minutes. Add the scallions and bean sprouts and stir for 15 seconds. Turn off the heat, transfer to a bowl, and reserve.

3. Wipe the wok clean. Heat the wok over high heat for 20 seconds. Add the remaining peanut oil and coat the wok with the oil. When a wisp of white smoke appears, add the meat and stir-fry for 1½ minutes. Add the vegetables and stir-fry for 1 minute. Make a well in the center of the mixture, stir the sauce, and pour it into the well. Stir for 2 minutes, or until the sauce thickens and turns light brown.

4. Turn off the heat, transfer to a heated plate, and serve.

INGREDIENTS

4 cups Chicken Stock (page 54)

2 cups water

Duck giblets and bones from the Peking Duck (page 301)

1-inch-thick slice ginger, peeled and lightly smashed

1 teaspoon salt

1½ pounds Tianjin bok choy, stalks and leaves separated and cut on the diagonal into ½-inch-wide pieces

---

1. In a large pot, place the stock, water, giblets, and ginger, cover the pot, and bring to a boil over high heat. Lower the heat to a gentle boil and cook for 15 minutes.

2. Turn the heat to high, add the bones, and bring the soup to a boil. Lower the heat to medium, cover, leaving the lid slightly cracked, and simmer for 45 minutes.

3. Turn off the heat. Strain the soup through a fine-mesh strainer placed over a bowl. Discard the contents of the strainer. Return the soup to the pot, add the salt, and bring to a boil over high heat. Add the bok choy stalks, stir, and allow the soup to return to a boil. Lower the heat to medium and cook for 5 minutes. Raise the heat to high, add the bok choy leaves, stir, and cook for 3 minutes more, or until the bok choy is tender.

4. Turn off the heat, transfer to a heated tureen, and serve.

MU SHU PORK

|| MAKES 12 FILLED PANCAKES, OR 6 SERVINGS ||

 This is another universally familiar classic, which originated in the kitchens of the imperial court in Beijing. Because of the precise, elaborate preparation of its vegetables, it is regarded as another of the court dishes that showed effort. It was also known as "shaved wood pork," to suggest that the pork was so finely sliced that it might have been shaved by a carpenter's plane. Happily, it has been one of those dishes that has translated well. Any mixture of vegetables can be used in its preparation, and it is generally made well in most restaurants.

1. To make the sauce: In a small bowl, mix together all of the ingredients and reserve.

2. To prepare the eggs: Heat a wok over high heat for 30 seconds. Add the peanut oil and, using a spatula, coat the wok with the oil. When a wisp of white smoke appears, add the beaten eggs and scramble them to a soft consistency. Turn off the heat, transfer to a small dish, and reserve.

3. Wipe the wok and spatula with paper towels. Heat the wok over high heat for 30 seconds. Add the peanut oil and heat to 350°F on a deep-frying thermometer. Add the pork and oil-blanch for about 1½ minutes, or until the pork loses its pinkness. Turn off the heat. Using a Chinese strainer, remove the pork from the wok and drain well over a bowl. Reserve.

4. Steam the pancakes for serving as directed in the recipe.

5. While the pancakes are steaming, pour off the oil from the wok and strain if needed to remove residue. Return 2 tablespoons of the oil to the wok. Heat the wok over high heat for 20 seconds. When a wisp of white smoke appears, add the ginger and garlic and stir briefly. Add the cabbage, stir to mix for 3 minutes, or until the cabbage softens. Add the scallions, bamboo shoots, cloud ears, tiger lily buds, mushrooms, and white pepper and stir-fry for 3 minutes, or until well mixed. Return the pork to the wok and stir-fry

INGREDIENTS

SAUCE

3 tablespoons hoisin sauce	2 teaspoons Shaoxing wine
2 tablespoons Chicken Stock (page 54)	3½ teaspoons sugar
	1 tablespoon cornstarch
2 tablespoons double dark soy sauce	¾ teaspoon salt

EGGS

4 large eggs, lightly beaten	1½ tablespoons peanut oil

3 cups peanut oil	2 tablespoons cloud ears, soaked in hot water to cover for 30 minutes, drained, rinsed, hard ends discarded, and left whole if small and broken up if large
1 cup julienned lean pork	
12 Pancakes (page 304)	
1 teaspoon peeled and minced ginger	
1 teaspoon minced garlic	40 tiger lily buds, soaked in hot water to cover for 30 minutes, drained, rinsed, hard ends discarded, and then halved crosswise
4 cups finely shredded green cabbage	
3 scallions, cut into 1½-inch lengths and white portions quartered lengthwise	5 Steamed Black Mushrooms (page 81), julienned
½ cup julienned bamboo shoots	Pinch of white pepper
	1 tablespoon sesame oil

for 2 minutes, or until all of the ingredients are well blended. Make a well in the center of the mixture, stir the sauce, pour it into the well, and stir-fry for about 2 minutes, or until the sauce thickens and bubbles. Add the scrambled eggs and mix well. Turn off the heat, add the sesame oil, and toss to mix.

6. Transfer the mixture to a heated plate and place the plate on the table. At this point, the pancakes will be steamed. Remove them, still in their steamer, to a plate, and set alongside the pork mixture. To fill each pancake, place about 3 tablespoons of the pork mixture in the center of it, fold up the bottom, fold in the sides, and leave the top open, then serve.

THE HOT POT

|| MAKES ABOUT 10 SERVINGS ||

A legacy of northern China, this communal dish is said to have originated among the northern nomads before spreading to Beijing and beyond. It was a traditional dish of the Muslims, who subsisted on mutton and vegetables and ate no pork. Often referred to as a Mongolian hot pot, it called for placing a vessel holding a substantial stock or soup in the center of a table and heating the contents to a boil. Pieces of raw meat and vegetables were slipped into the hot liquid, where they cooked quickly, and then were removed by diners with their chopsticks, dipped into an accompanying sauce, and eaten. Ideal for wintertime, it was a warming repast whose effect was heightened considerably by the consumption of sorghum alcohol along with the meal.

In Beijing, the hot pot became a grand and elegant dish that included mutton, beef, fish, bean curd, and vegetables. It was often referred to as *shuan yang rou,* a northern China colloquialism that means "to scald with water." Mutton in two forms, paper-thin slices and rolls, was always served as the centerpiece of the hot pot. Surrounding the pot were many small dishes of sauces and condiments into which the food cooked in the hot stock were dipped before they were eaten. This elaborate dish became known as mutton and chrysanthemum hot pot for two reasons: The flames under the pot flared out like chrysanthemum leaves and green mum leaves were customarily among the vegetables. The pot itself might be a sand clay pot, a round-bellied bronze pot with a long central chimney that held burning charcoal, or, later, a steel version of the bronze pot.

The hot pot tradition spread south from Beijing and was taken up throughout China. Some people retained the Muslim observance of no pork. Others used the boiling soup to cook whatever suited their fancy: shrimp, pork, noodles, and all manner of vegetables. In southern China, the hot pot often contained dried shrimp, peanuts, chiles, and tea leaves. No matter where it spread, and no matter what it contained, the name Mongolian hot pot was used to describe it, surely an obeisance to its beginnings, and also probably because the name lent a touch of romance, and that remains true today. Observant Buddhists have even originated a vegetarian hot pot, with the bubbling meat-based stock replaced by a vegetable one.

Not surprisingly, a hot pot etiquette has evolved, too. Individual diners use chopsticks to place their food choices in the stock and then remove them with tiny, long-handled strainers and dip the morsels into individually concocted sauces before eating. The hot pot is a long meal, meant to be eaten at leisure with family or friends. And often, when all of the prepared foods have been consumed, dinner concludes with everyone sipping the now-rich broth, sometimes with rice added.

The best pot to use for making a hot pot is the traditional round-bellied metal pot with a chimney, which can be purchased in Chinatown markets. In its absence, a wide and deep fry pan, such as a chicken fryer or a two-handled *sauteuse,* about 11 inches in diameter and 3 inches deep, will do nicely. It will hold 2 quarts of stock, the perfect amount for cooking the hot pot ingredients. For a heat source under the pot, I suggest a small, inexpensive electric or propane portable stove. I have even used an electric fry pan with success. Carefully arrange your sauces around the hot pot, let the stock come to a boil, and enjoy your communal feast.

What follows is an adaptation of a traditional Beijing hot pot.

INGREDIENTS

1½ pounds boneless lamb loin, half-frozen

1½ pounds boneless beef fillet, half-frozen

1½ pounds firm white fish fillets, such as sea bass or striped bass, half-frozen

8 firm fresh bean curd cakes (2 pounds total), frozen for 24 hours

2 bunches watercress

1 pound spinach

1½ pounds mum greens

8 cups iceberg lettuce leaves

4 two-ounce packages bean thread noodles

8 ounces fresh white button mushrooms

CONDIMENTS AND SAUCES

8 cubes red wet preserved bean curd mashed with ½ cup bean curd juice and 2 teaspoons sugar

6 tablespoons sugar

⅓ cup Chinkiang vinegar

⅓ cup sesame oil

¼ cup Hot Pepper Oil (page 55)

⅓ cup light soy sauce

⅓ cup Shaoxing wine

⅓ cup double dark soy sauce

¼ cup sesame seed paste mixed with 2 tablespoons double dark soy sauce

¼ cup minced garlic

⅓ cup finely sliced fresh coriander leaves

½ cup finely sliced scallions

2½ quarts Chicken Stock (page 54)

1. First, prepare all of the ingredients to be cooked in the stock. Cut the lamb and beef across the grain into paper-thin slices. (If they are half frozen, they are easier to slice.) Slice the fish into paper-thin slices. Arrange the meats and fish on platters. Remove the bean curd from the freezer and allow it to thaw for 30 minutes. Cut each cake along its length into ⅓-inch-thick slices. (Freezing solid and then thawing the bean curd is necessary for the proper texture. See note accompanying Tomato, Bean Curd, and Chicken Leg Mushroom Soup, on page 111, for an explanation of the technique.) Arrange the bean curd slices on a platter.

2. Leave the watercress sprigs whole. Separate the spinach leaves. Cut the mum greens in half crosswise. Tear the lettuce into 4-inch pieces. In a bowl, soak the bean threads in hot water to cover for 20 minutes, or until they soften. Drain well and cut into 6-inch lengths. Cut the button mushrooms in half. Arrange the vegetables and noodles artfully on platters.

3. Place the hot pot in the center of the table. Arrange the platters of meats, fish, vegetables, and noodles next to it. Put the sauces and condiments in individual bowls, place on a tray, and place the tray alongside the platters. At each place setting, put two pairs of chopsticks—one for putting the food into the boiling stock and removing it and one for eating—and two small bowls, both for mixing sauces. Also put out a large bowl for diners to pour off their used sauces, so they can use the bowls to mix new ones. (Although the small strainers mentioned in the introduction are part of the evolving etiquette of the hot pot, I prefer chopsticks for both introducing and retrieving foods.)

4. While you are arranging the table, in a pot on the stove top, bring the stock to a boil over high heat. Then pour 7 cups of the boiling stock into the hot pot and turn the heat on under it. Keep the remaining 3 cups of stock hot, to replenish the stock as it is absorbed by the foods. Now begin your feast (see note).

5. Invite diners to mix up any sauce they wish from the selection of sauces and condiments. Then they can select morsels of food, put them in the boiling stock, remove them, and dip them into the sauce and eat. Everyone continues to make sauces and cook morsels until the platters are empty. The rich stock is wonderful to sip at the end of meal. Have porcelain spoons on hand for those who wish to enjoy it.

NOTE: Different foods cook for different amounts of time. The meats and fish will cook almost immediately in the boiling stock. The bean curd will take about 1½ minutes, the mushrooms about 2 minutes, the watercress and mum greens about 1½ minutes, the spinach and noodles about 1 minute, and the lettuce about 45 seconds.

第三集 ﹦ 再談南地菜 ﹦ PART 3 ﹦ LESSON 5: A SECOND COOKING TOUR, NORTH TO SOUTH

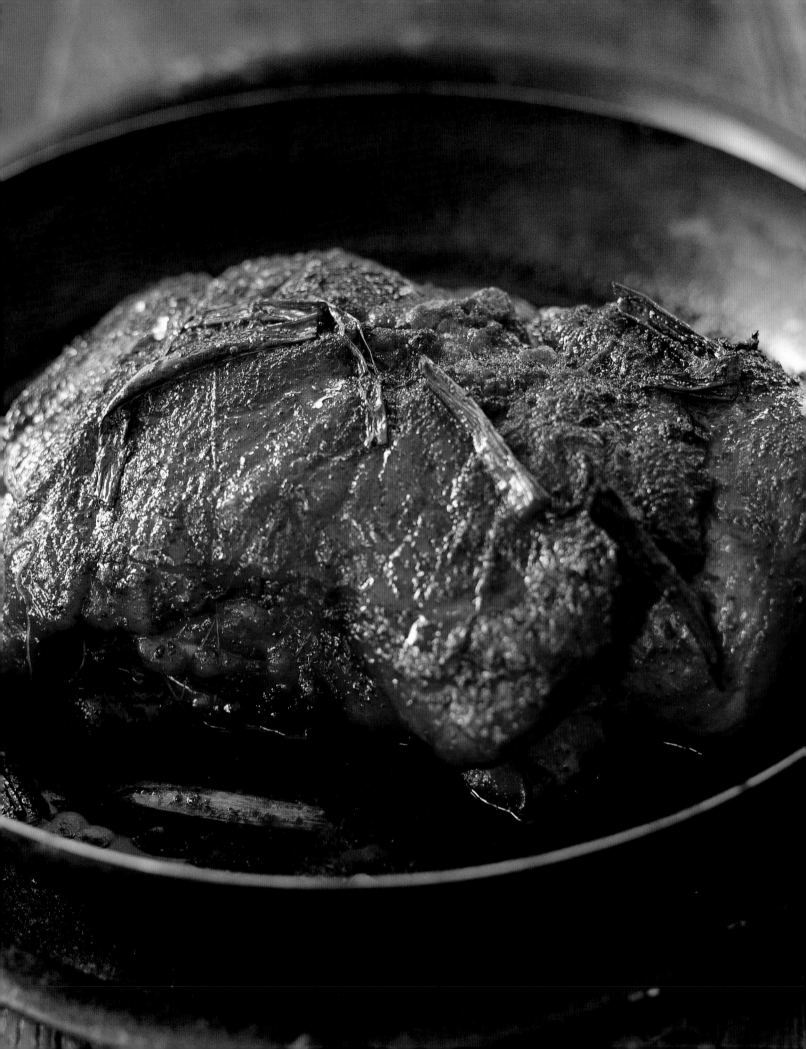

LONG-COOKED PORK SHOULDER

|| MAKES 10 TO 12 SERVINGS ||

上海焗蹄膀 This is a Shanghai classic, a dish of sweetened pork, so highly regarded that it is a must at family observances, feasts, religious occasions, and even funerals. Traditionally, a whole pork shoulder is blanched in boiling oil, then cooked in a large pot on the stove top for about 6 hours, until its meat is so tender it falls off the bone, thus its description as a long-cooked preparation. It is also known as a red-cooked dish because of its deep reddish-brown color, which comes from cooking it with powdered red rice.

I have remade this classic. I roast the meat slowly for many hours, instead of boiling it slowly in oil. The shoulder is also traditionally cooked with its outer skin and layer of fat intact. I pare the skin and fat off the shoulder before roasting. But I use all of the same ingredients, so what emerges is a dish identical in taste, texture, and color to the long-cooked shoulder of Shanghai tradition.

INGREDIENTS

1 bone-in pork shoulder, 9 to 9½ pounds, with skin and fat layer intact

¾ cup Shaoxing wine

¾ cup double dark soy sauce

1 tablespoon red rice, ground to a powder

1¼ cups sugar

½ teaspoon white pepper

4 eight-star anise, broken into pieces

3 cinnamon sticks, 1 inch long

4 scallions, cut crosswise into thirds

4 slices ginger, ½ inch thick, peeled and lightly smashed

1½ cups of boiling water

---

1. Preheat the oven to 400°F for 20 minutes. Meanwhile, rinse the pork shoulder under cold running cold water and dry well with paper towels. Place the shoulder on a cutting board and cut off the skin and fat. Transfer the shoulder to a roasting pan and rub the wine thoroughly into the meat. Then rub the meat vigorously with the soy sauce, coating it evenly. Sprinkle the powdered rice evenly over the shoulder and pat well so it will adhere. Next, sprinkle the shoulder evenly with the sugar, then rub it into the meat. Finally, sprinkle the shoulder evenly with the white pepper. Add the anise, cinnamon, scallions, and ginger to the roasting pan, scattering them evenly around the shoulder.

2. Place the roasting pan in the oven and roast the pork for 15 minutes. Lower the heat to 375°F and roast the pork for 30 minutes more. Baste the pork with the pan drippings. Roast for another 30 minutes, and baste again. Lower the heat to 350°F, baste the shoulder again, cover the shoulder completely with aluminum foil, and roast for another 30 minutes.

3. Remove the foil, turn the pork over, baste it, and add ½ cup of the boiling water to the pan. At this point, do not cover the pork completely with the foil. Instead, leave the foil open to reveal the meat, so that any fat on the shoulder will melt as the pork roasts.

4. Continue to roast the pork for 1 hour, basting it twice at regular intervals. Lower the temperature to 325°F, add another ½ cup of the boiling water, and allow the pork to roast for 3 hours longer, basting it once every hour and leaving the foil open. If the pork begins to dry out or burn, baste it well and seal the foil closed to cover the pork completely. The closed foil will help retain the moisture.

5. Lower the temperature to 300°F, add the remaining ½ cup boiling water, and roast the pork for 1 more hour. The pork shoulder is done when the meat separates easily from the bone. To test, insert a chopstick into the

Continued . . .

. . . continued

shoulder. If the meat does not immediately separate, roast for an additional 30 minutes and add an additional ¼ cup boiling water to the pan.

6. Remove the pan from the oven. The pork shoulder will glisten, its color will be a rich reddish brown, and its texture will be perfectly tender—just as if it had been prepared in the traditional manner. Transfer the pork shoulder to a cutting board, cut slices from the bone, and arrange the slices on a heated platter.

7. There should be 1 to 1½ cups of sauce in the roasting pan. Pour it through a fine-mesh strainer into a heated sauce boat, skim off any fat from the surface, and serve it with the pork slices.

NOTE: I have been asked if the powdered red rice can be left out of this recipe. You may do so, for the taste of the pork shoulder will be unaffected. But the color will be decidedly different, and for this Shanghai dish, its red color is important.

NINGBO PORK SHOULDER

‖ MAKES 6 TO 8 SERVINGS ‖

This recipe for cooking a pork shoulder is a regional variation of the Shanghai classic (page 311) from the nearby port city of Ningbo. The cooking of this neighbor is similar to Shanghai cooking in many ways, in many dishes. Both cities dote on stir-fried tiny shrimp, oil-browned bean curd dishes, and sweetened foods. But the people of Ningbo like their independence as well. For example, they enjoy their vegetables mashed or shredded, such as pumpkin mashed with salted egg yolks, crab mixed with shredded turnips, and beef cooked with mashed potatoes. They color their fish soups with powdered red rice, and they take pride in their traditional pork shoulder, which is quite different from Shanghai's famed version.

The shoulder is simmered first in a salt solution on the stove top and then finished in hot oil. I was introduced to this recipe in a private Ningbo restaurant in Hong Kong, actually a club for immigrants from the city. The skin of the pork shoulder is not removed before cooking, but is scrubbed thoroughly, a process Ningbo cooks believe ensures crispness. Actually it works only partially, but whatever skin is crisped is delicious indeed. Serve the pork with Fried Breads (page 168) and with Snow Pea Shoots Poached in Chicken Stock (page 89) for a complete meal.

INGREDIENTS

1 bone-in pork shoulder, 6 pounds, with skin and fat layer intact

3 quarts water

5 tablespoons salt

3 quarts peanut oil

---

1. Rinse the shoulder thoroughly under running cold water. Scrub the skin thoroughly to clean it.

2. Place the water in a very large pot. Add the salt and stir until it dissolves. Add the pork shoulder and bring the water to a boil over high heat. Lower the heat to a gentle boil, cover the pot, leaving the lid slightly cracked, and cook the shoulder for 1½ hours, skimming off any residue as it rises to the surface. Turn the pork over, re-cover as before, and continue cooking for 1½ hours, again skimming any residue as it rises to the surface. After 3 hours, turn off the heat, cover the pot tightly, and let the pork cool to room temperature.

3. Remove the pork to a rack placed over a bowl and let drain for 1 hour. Discard the cooking water. Dry the pork shoulder thoroughly with paper towels. This initial simmering process seals, cooks, and tenderizes the meat.

4. Rinse and dry the pot. Heat it over high heat for 1 minute. Add the peanut oil and heat to 375°F on a deep-frying thermometer. Place the shoulder in a deep-fry basket and lower it into the hot oil. The oil temperature will immediately drop slightly. Deep-fry the pork for 15 minutes, then turn the pork over and deep-fry for another 15 minutes. Throughout this time maintain an oil temperature of 350°F. The shoulder is done when the skin is deep brown.

5. Turn off the heat and remove the basket with the shoulder to a large bowl. Allow the oil to drain off and the shoulder to rest for 10 minutes. Then transfer to a cutting board, slice, and serve on a heated platter.

TEA-SMOKED DUCK

|| MAKES 6 SERVINGS ||

Throughout China, fowl are smoked, often over fragrant woods, more often over tea leaves. It is thought that smoking ducks and other fowl originated in Fujian, a region known for its cultivation of many different types of tea. The dish, however, has long been called camphor-smoked duck, despite the fact that tea, not camphor, was, and is, used. In Sichuan, chicken is often smoked over tea leaves flavored with jasmine flowers, over cypress wood, or over both. But the most highly regarded version of smoked duck is the one prepared with the green tea leaves of Hangzhou. The tea, Long Jing, or Dragon Well (see page 259), is one of China's most famous, and its use in this preparation is a tradition of many centuries. As the tea leaves smolder, the duck is flavored. The dish is notable as well because it employs four different cooking processes: steaming, smoking, roasting, and deep-frying.

INGREDIENTS

1 duck, 5½ pounds, preferably freshly killed, head and wings intact and feet removed	3 eight-star anise
	3 slices ginger, ½ inch thick, peeled
½ cup Shaoxing wine	⅔ cup Long Jing tea leaves
1 tablespoon salt	6 cups peanut oil
1 tablespoon sugar	Fried Breads (page 168)
3 cinnamon sticks, 2 inches long	Sichuan Peppercorn Salt (facing page)

---

1. Clean the duck as directed for chicken on page 54, then rinse and dry well with paper towels.

2. Place the duck, breast side up, in a steamproof dish. Rub the duck, inside and out, with the wine. Sprinkle the duck with the salt, again inside and out, covering evenly. Repeat with the sugar. Place 1 cinnamon stick, 1 eight-star anise, and 1 ginger slice in the cavity. Then place 1 cinnamon stick, 1 eight-star anise, and 1 ginger slice on each side of the duck in the dish. Place the dish in a steamer, cover, and steam the duck for 1 hour. Turn off the heat, remove the duck to a dish, and allow it to cool.

3. Preheat the oven to 350°F. While the oven is heating, smoke the duck. Place the tea leaves in a dry wok over high heat for 1½ to 2 minutes, or until the leaves begin to smoke. Reduce the heat to medium-low, place a rack over the leaves, and place the duck on the rack. Cover the wok, then place a wet cloth around the seam where the cover meets the wok to seal it. Smoke the duck for 7 to 10 minutes. If the smell of burning leaves is detected, reduce the heat to low. Turn off the heat and set the duck aside. Discard the tea leaves and wash and dry the wok.

4. Place a rack in a roasting pan, place the duck, breast side up, on the rack, and pierce its skin randomly all over with a cooking fork. This will allow the fat to run off as the duck roasts. Place the pan in the oven and roast the duck for 1 hour, or until the duck has rendered its fat. If very crisp skin is desired, turn the duck over halfway through the roasting. Turn off the heat, remove the duck from the oven, and let it cool.

5. Heat the wok over high heat for 1 minute. Add the peanut oil and heat to 400°F on a deep-frying thermometer. Place the duck on a Chinese strainer, and lower it into the oil. Fry the duck on one side for 5 minutes, carefully ladling hot oil over the top. Turn the duck over and fry, continuing to ladle hot oil over the top, for 5 minutes longer, or until the duck is a deep golden brown. Using the strainer, remove the duck from the oil and drain it over a bowl for 10 minutes.

6. Cut the duck into bite-size pieces and serve it with the breads and flavored salt.

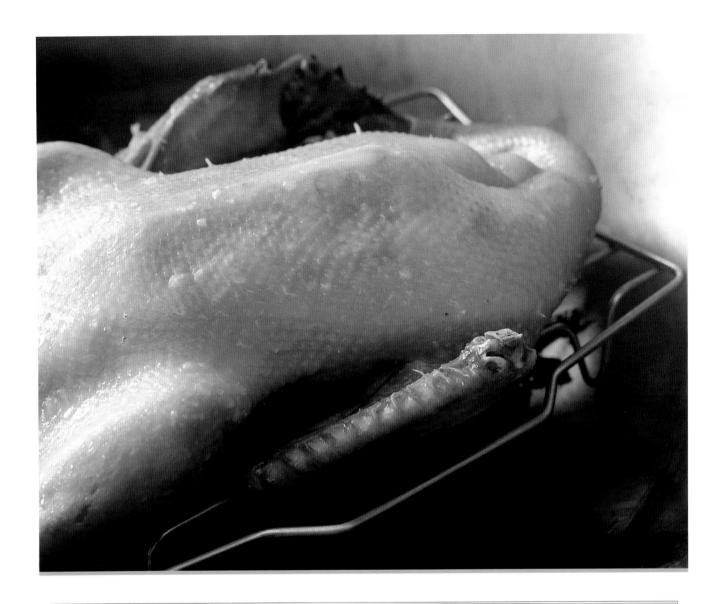

‖ **SICHUAN PEPPERCORN SALT** ‖

This flavored salt is a fine, subtle use of Sichuan peppercorns. It complements not only tea-smoked duck, but also almost any fowl and many meats and seafoods.

1 teaspoon Sichuan peppercorns

3 tablespoons salt

Heat a dry wok over high heat for 20 seconds. Add the peppercorns and stir continuously for about 1½ minutes, or until they turn deep brown and release their aroma. Turn off the heat and let cool

SICHUAN
PEPPER-
CORN
SALT

to room temperature, then grind to a powder in a spice grinder.

Place the dry wok over high heat for 20 seconds. Add the salt and stir continuously for about 2 minutes, or until very hot. Add the ground peppercorns and stir constantly for 30 seconds, or until thoroughly combined with the salt.

Turn off the heat and transfer to a dish. Use immediately, or transfer to a tightly sealed jar and store at room temperature. The salt will keep for 2 to 3 weeks, though its intensity will fade.

GENERAL TSO'S CHICKEN

‖ MAKES 4 TO 6 SERVINGS ‖

左宗鷄

If there is anyone who has not heard of General Tso's chicken, I have yet to meet him or her, for it is as famous and ubiquitous as any Chinese dish in or out of China. Like many traditional preparations, the history of this small piece of Hunanese cooking is a fanciful mix of history, myth, and folklore. I have seen it on the English menus of Chinese restaurants not only as the chicken of General Tso, but also of General Tsao, Taso, Toa, Cho, Gau, Ching, Kung, Yseng, Zuo, and Ciao—generals all, perhaps. Actually, no general's name is customarily attached to it in Hunan.

In fact, this popular dish has been cooked in that region of China's near west for much longer than any general's name has been associated with it. It was originally a simple dish of boned dark chicken meat, cooked in a sauce hot with chiles. Later, it was referred to as *zongtang ji,* or "ancestral meeting place chicken," and still later as *Zuo zontang ji,* translated as "Tso ancestral meeting place chicken." Somehow the general's name became connected with the dish, and soon countless chefs were claiming its authorship, in honor of a General Tso. There was indeed a General Zuo Zongtang (or Tso Tsung Tang, in Cantonese) in nineteenth-century Hunan, and by all accounts, he was a brave fellow and deserving of having a dish named after him.

But the naming, it turned out, was largely in the West, not in Hunan, where the dish is still called ancestral meeting place chicken. But more important, in those places where the general's name rides high on menus, his eponymous dish is seldom prepared correctly. To be authentic, this classic dish must be made with cubed drumstick and thigh meat, not chicken breast meat, ground chicken, or anything else.

What follows is how the dish is properly made in Hunan.

INGREDIENTS	
2 large whole chicken legs (thigh and drumstick), 12 ounces each	¼ teaspoon salt
	Pinch of white pepper
1 large egg, lightly beaten	2 tablespoons cornstarch

SAUCE

1½ tablespoons double dark soy sauce	½ to ¾ teaspoon Red Oil (page 149), to taste
1½ tablespoons hoisin sauce	1½ teaspoons minced garlic
2 teaspoons white rice vinegar	1 tablespoon peeled and minced ginger
2 teaspoons Shaoxing wine	2 teaspoons sugar

3½ cups peanut oil	4 to 5 white portions scallions, cut crosswise into ½-inch-thick pieces (¼ cup)
3 tablespoons cornstarch	
8 small dried chiles, preferably Thai	

1. Skin and bone the chicken legs, remove any fat and membranes, and rinse well. Cut into 1-inch cubes. (You should have about 1 pound meat. Alternatively, buy boneless, skinless thighs and cube the meat.) In a bowl, mix together the egg, salt, white pepper, and cornstarch. Add the chicken cubes, toss to coat them well, and let rest for 15 minutes.

2. To make the sauce: In a small bowl, mix together all of the ingredients and reserve.

3. Heat a wok over high heat for 40 seconds. Add the peanut oil and heat to 350°F on a deep-frying thermometer. While the oil is heating, spread the cornstarch on a sheet of waxed paper. Place the chicken cubes in the cornstarch and toss until they are well coated.

4. When the oil is ready, shake off the excess cornstarch from the chicken cubes, place the cubes in a Chinese strainer, and lower them into the hot oil. Deep-fry for 2 to 3 minutes, until the cubes are browned and crisp. Turn off the heat. Using the strainer, remove the chicken cubes from the oil and drain them over a bowl.

5. Pour off all but 1½ tablespoons of the peanut oil from the wok.

6. Heat the wok over high heat for 20 seconds. When a wisp of white smoke appears, add the chiles and stir them for 15 seconds. Add the scallions and stir-fry for 30 seconds. Add the chicken cubes and stir-fry for 1 minute, or until well blended with the scallions and chiles. Stir the sauce, pour it into the wok, and stir-fry for about 1½ minutes, or until the chicken cubes are evenly coated with the sauce.

7. Turn off the heat, transfer to a heated plate, and serve.

SOUR-AND-SWEET TIANJIN BOK CHOY

|| **MAKES 6 TO 8 SERVINGS** ||

 Essentially a salad of Tianjin bok choy, this popular preparation can be found from Beijing west to Sichuan and Hunan. Often prepared with hot chiles, it is just as often subtly flavored with Sichuan peppercorns as its prime taste.

INGREDIENTS

2¾ pounds Tianjin bok choy, outer leaves removed, to yield 2½ pounds	3 tablespoons peeled and shredded ginger (see Cleaver discussion, page 45)
2½ teaspoons salt	3 tablespoons white rice vinegar
1½ tablespoons peanut oil	2 tablespoons sugar
¼ teaspoon Sichuan peppercorns	1½ tablespoons sesame oil

1. Separate the individual stalks of bok choy and cut them crosswise into ⅓-inch-wide pieces. Place the bok choy in a large bowl, add the salt, and toss well. Let the bok choy rest for 2 hours, then drain off the water, and squeeze the bok choy pieces to rid them of any remaining moisture. Return the bok choy to the bowl.

2. Heat a wok over high heat for 20 seconds. Add the peanut oil and, using a spatula, coat the wok with the oil. When a wisp of white smoke appears, add the peppercorns and stir briefly. Add the ginger and stir for 45 seconds to 1 minute, or until it browns lightly. Turn off the heat and pour the peppercorn mixture over the bok choy.

3. Add the vinegar, sugar, and sesame oil and mix thoroughly. Cover and refrigerate for at least 4 hours or up to overnight to allow the flavors to blend before serving.

4. Transfer to a serving bowl and serve. The dish tastes best served cold or cool. Or, store in an airtight container in the refrigerator for up to 1 week.

SHANGHAI BOK CHOY POACHED IN MILK STOCK

|| MAKES 8 SERVINGS ||

奶湯灼白菜

This is an unusual dish from Shanghai, where the bok choy is customarily served moistened with a little of the poaching liquid. Whenever I eat this dish there, I ask for the liquid to be poured into a small bowl for me to drink. When I cook it, I prefer to serve it as a soup because I like the mingled tastes of the stock and the bok choy. I also suggest serving it at the midpoint of a larger meal or banquet, but it is enjoyable no matter where it is placed.

INGREDIENTS

2 pounds Shanghai bok choy (8 heads)	1 tablespoon salt
2 quarts water	1 teaspoon baking soda (optional)
1-inch-thick slice ginger, peeled and lightly smashed	

4 cups Milk Stock (page 146)	1 tablespoon fried garlic from Garlic Oil (page 56)
1 teaspoon salt	
1½ tablespoons Garlic Oil (page 56)	

1. To water-blanch the bok choy, first remove all of the outer leaves so only the pointed central bulb remains, then quarter each head lengthwise. Wash the pieces well under cold running water to remove any sand and grit. Repeat twice, then drain well. (I have included specific washing directions here because the shape of the vegetable and its dense character can cause grit to cling.)

2. In a pot, bring the 2 quarts water to a boil over high heat. Add the ginger, salt, and baking soda (if using). When the water returns to a boil, add the bok choy and blanch for 1 minute. Immediately turn off the heat and plunge the bok choy into ice water to halt the cooking. Drain well and reserve the bok choy and discard the ginger.

3. Rinse and dry the pot. In the pot, place the stock, salt, garlic oil, and fried garlic and bring to a boil over high heat. Add the bok choy, stir well, and allow the stock to return to a boil. Lower the heat to medium and cook the bok choy for 3 to 4 minutes, or until tender.

4. Turn off the heat and transfer the bok choy and its soup to a heated tureen. Ladle into individual bowls to serve, placing 4 pieces of bok choy in each bowl.

MAPO DOUFOU

‖ MAKES 4 TO 6 SERVINGS ‖

麻
婆
荳
腐
There is no suitable name in English for this superb Sichuan dish. The Chinese translates literally as "pockmarked old woman's bean curd." In Hong Kong, however, where it is known in Cantonese as *mah pao dau fu*, "grandmother" is used as an honorific in place of "old woman." In both cases, the dish is a direct, intense mix of bean curd, pork (or sometimes beef), and hot chiles, with its own particular story. Many years ago, an elderly woman whose face showed the effects of smallpox opened a restaurant in Sichuan, and among the dishes that she became known for was this preparation. It became so famous that people would travel for days, or weeks, to eat it at the old woman's restaurant. But it had no name, so it became known as *mapo doufou*, in acknowledgment of the cook who created it. As with other special dishes of China, it often suffers in translation. I have seen it referred to with authority in a most august journal as "the bean curd of Mrs. Paul," as if it were some variation on a fish stick. Never mind. Cook it as it is cooked in Sichuan, or order it in restaurants, but always ask for it by its Chinese name.

INGREDIENTS	
4 ounces ground pork	⅛ teaspoon salt
1½ teaspoons sesame oil	

SAUCE

5 tablespoons ketchup (page 75)	1 tablespoon Sichuan Peppercorn Paste (page 211)
¼ cup Chicken Stock (page 54)	1½ teaspoons double dark soy sauce
1½ tablespoons oyster sauce	1 teaspoon sesame oil
1 tablespoon Chinkiang vinegar	1 tablespoon cornstarch
1 tablespoon Shaoxing wine	2 teaspoons sugar
	¾ teaspoon salt

2 tablespoons peanut oil	3 or 4 scallions, cut on the diagonal into ¼-inch-thick slices, white portions (¼ cup) and green portions (½ cup) separated
4 fresh Thai chiles, minced, with seeds	
1 teaspoon peeled and minced ginger	4 firm fresh bean curd cakes (1 pound total), cut into ½-inch cubes
1½ teaspoons minced garlic	

1. In a bowl, combine the pork, sesame oil, and salt. Toss to mix well and let rest for 20 minutes.

2. To make the sauce: In a small bowl, mix together all of the ingredients and reserve.

3. Heat a wok over high heat for 30 seconds. Add the peanut oil and, using a spatula, coat the wok with the oil. When a wisp of white smoke appears, add the chiles, ginger, and garlic and stir to mix well for 30 seconds, or until the chiles begin to turn black. Add the pork and break it up with the spatula. Add the white portions of scallions and stir-fry for 45 seconds, or until the pork begins to turn white. Add the bean curd and stir-fry together for 3 minutes, or until the mixture is hot. Make a well in the center of the mixture, stir the sauce, and pour it into the well. Stir and mix for about 2½ minutes, or until the sauce thickens and bubbles. Add the green portions of the scallions and mix well.

4. Turn off the heat, transfer to a heated plate, and serve.

SHREDDED CHICKEN IN RED OIL

‖ MAKES 4 TO 6 SERVINGS ‖

 This Sichuan preparation is unusual. Although it is flavored with two Sichuan staples, hot red oil and Sichuan Peppercorn Paste, neither is used in the actual cooking of the chicken. Rather, these intense flavorings are used to dress the dish, which is always served at room temperature. The presentation is dramatic as well, with the chicken served atop Deep-fried Rice Noodles—perfect banquet fare.

INGREDIENTS

SAUCE

1½ tablespoons Shaoxing wine	1½ teaspoons peeled and minced ginger
1 tablespoon red rice vinegar	3½ teaspoons Sichuan Peppercorn Paste (page 211)
1 tablespoon light soy sauce	2½ tablespoons sesame seed paste
1½ teaspoons sesame oil	2½ teaspoons sugar
1½ teaspoons Red Oil (page 149)	½ teaspoon salt
3 tablespoons finely sliced scallions	

½ cup raw peanuts	Deep-fried Rice Noodles (page 143)
½ Roasted Chicken (page 152)	

---

1. To make the sauce: In a large bowl, mix together all of the ingredients, stirring until smooth. Reserve.

2. To dry-roast the peanuts, heat a dry wok over high heat for 30 seconds. Add the peanuts and stir for 1 minute. Lower the heat to medium-low and continue to stir for about 15 minutes, or until the peanuts are browned. Turn off the heat. Transfer to a small dish and let cool. Reserve.

3. Remove the meat from the chicken half, discarding the skin and bones. Place the meat on a cutting board and pound it with the side of a cleaver blade to break its fiber, then shred it by hand. You should have 2 cups. Reserve.

4. Deep-fry the noodles as directed, let cool, and spread into a bed on a platter. Set aside.

5. Add the shredded chicken and the peanuts to the sauce in the bowl and mix well. Spoon the chicken and peanuts and their sauce over the bed of rice noodles and serve.

BUDDHA JUMPS OVER THE WALL

|| MAKES 6 SERVINGS ||

 The city of Fuzhou, in Fujian Province, is home to this celebratory preparation. It is a feast of many dishes, which are first cooked individually, then assembled and heated in a rich broth. It is a complicated presentation, often made up of as many as twenty to thirty ingredients: meats, seafood, or vegetables, or a combination, depending on the ambitiousness of the cook. This traditional dish comes with a story more than a century old.

It is said that a rich merchant of Fuzhou, desiring to impress a mandarin whom he had invited to his home, asked his cook and his wife to concoct something special. They decided that they would immerse various meats and fowl in rice wine in an earthenware crock and cook them. The creation was such a success that the mandarin, on returning home, asked his own cook to duplicate it. But the cook failed. However, a subsequent joint effort by the two cooks was successful, the dish became celebrated, and the merchant's cook, Jang Chun Fat, opened his own restaurant in Fuzhou.

There are two versions of what happened next. One is that the new restaurateur convened a collection of colleagues and asked them to name his dish. The other credits a scholar who named it after eating it. Whether by chef or scholar, the dish was named *fo tiao qiang,* or "Buddha jumps over the wall." Why? Because even Buddha, who cared nothing for anything worldly or sensual, was unable to ignore the aromas of the dish and would come running, jumping over a wall, simply to have a taste.

This version, consisting of uncommon, festive seafoods, is one rendering of this Fujian feast. You will have prepared virtually all of its ingredients during earlier lessons in this book. What remains is the assembly.

INGREDIENTS

2 whole sea cucumbers (4 ounces total), soaked, cleaned, simmered, cooled, and each cut crosswise into 3 pieces (see page 243)

6 whole canned winter bamboo shoots, cut in half

6 whole abalones, prepared and cooked through step 3 in Braised Abalone (see page 255)

18 Braised Mushrooms in Oyster Sauce (page 98)

4 ounces dried shark's fin strands, prepared through step 2 in Shark's Fin Soup (page 246)

6 Steamed Sea Scallops (page 83), left whole

2 slices ginger, 1 inch thick, peeled and lightly smashed

8 scallions, white portions only, lightly smashed and cut in half crosswise

¾ cup Shaoxing wine

3 cups Superior Stock (page 145), or as needed

1. Place a rack at the bottom of a sand clay pot. Place the sea cucumber pieces in a single layer on the rack and the bamboo shoot halves in a layer on top of the sea cucumbers. Top with the abalones in a single layer and then with the mushrooms. Layer the shark's fin on top of the mushrooms, followed by the scallops in a single layer. Place 1 ginger slice on each side of the top layer. Lay the scallions in a layer on top of the scallops. Drizzle the wine evenly over the layers, then pour in the stock just to cover. If it doesn't cover the layers, add more as needed. If there is an excess of stock, set it aside and keep it hot to add if needed during cooking.

2. Cover the clay pot. Place it on the stove top, turn on the heat to medium, and bring the stock to a boil. Lower the heat to a gentle simmer and cook for 1 hour, or until all of the foods are heated through and their flavors have blended. As the pot simmers, uncover it from time to time to check the level of the stock. If it drops, replenish it with boiling stock.

3. Turn off the heat. Place the clay pot on the table and ladle some of each of the ingredients into individual bowls. There will be a delicious broth left in the pot to drink along with the meal.

THE COOKS OF SUN TAK YUEN

順德師傅

In the Chinese cooking universe, there are many practices, adages, habits, and even sayings regarded as truisms. They range from beliefs and practices derived from the Analects of Confucius, which not only dictate precisely how to cut foods before cooking and in which order to serve the foods for maximum enjoyment, but also the unchanging culinary beliefs and techniques of chefs. Two of the more famous of these beliefs concern Guangzhou.

First, it is said that a happy life in China is assured if you live in Hangzhou, a beautiful city of lakes and pavilions; marry in Suzhou, the city with the most beautiful people; dine in Guangzhou, home to the country's best food;

and die in Liuzhou, where the wood used for coffins is the most fragrant. It is also said that if you are born in Sun Tak Yuen, which lies just outside of Guangzhou, you are born to cook. You need only mention—one cook to another, one gastronome to another—that you are from Sun Tak Yuen, and a knowing smile appears, quickly followed by the words "you must be a cook." I was born in Sun Tak Yuen, and I know I was born to cook.

This is by way of introducing two fine preparations from Guangzhou, a pair of elegant banquet dishes that embody the Cantonese standards of impeccable freshness and unalloyed flavor.

STEAMED HAIRY MELON SOUP

‖ MAKES 6 SERVINGS ‖

This classic preparation of Guangzhou is gradually disappearing, the victim of impatience. When prepared traditionally, the zucchini-like hairy melons, with their fuzzy skins, are steamed to become individual tureens of soup. The melons themselves are versatile and can also be baked, boiled, fried, or stuffed. They are small, about a foot long, and slender. For this preparation, they should be used as soon as possible after they are harvested from their vines. In fact, in the past, many Guangzhou chefs would ask growers to

leave their hairy melons on the vine so that they would turn a lovely bronze and thus look more dramatic when cooked. Unfortunately, these days fewer chefs are taking the time to make the small tureens. Instead, they are cutting the melons into chunks or large slices and cooking them in the soup. I urge you to cook them in the classic way. Hairy melons are widely available in Chinatown markets, but if you can't find them, cucumbers can be used in their place. Either vegetable creates a visually spectacular presentation.

Continued . . .

中國調煮實習菜譜

MASTERING THE ART OF CHINESE COOKING

. . . continued

INGREDIENTS

3 hairy melons, 12 inches long and 3 inches in diameter

3 fresh water chestnuts, peeled and minced

3 dried black mushrooms, 1½ inches in diameter, soaked in hot water to cover for 30 minutes, drained, rinsed, squeezed dry, stems discarded, and caps cut into ⅛-inch dice

¼ cup fresh or thawed frozen green peas

6 tablespoons ⅛-inch-dice Salt-Cured Ham (page 150)

6 tablespoons fresh-cooked crabmeat

6 tablespoons ⅛-inch-dice Roasted Duck meat (page 153)

3 cups Superior Stock (page 145)

---

1. Cut each melon in half crosswise. Then, with a grapefruit knife, scoop out the seeds and the center core from all 6 halves. Wrap the base of each half in a cloth, and set each half in a small, heatproof dish, such as a Pyrex custard cup, making sure it stands firmly upright and does not move.

2. Divide all of the remaining ingredients evenly among the 6 melon halves. Place the halves, in their dishes, in a steamer, cover, and steam for 1½ hours, or until the melon halves are soft when tested with the tip of a chopstick but have not lost their shape.

3. Remove the melon halves in their dishes from the steamer and serve with small spoons, so the flesh of the melons can be shaved off and eaten with the broth and its fillings.

FRIED BEAN CURD

‖ MAKES 4 TO 6 SERVINGS ‖

 This simple dish, of Chiu Chow origin, was eagerly adopted by Guangzhou. It is simplicity that becomes elegant. I first ate this preparation in a tiny restaurant in Kowloon City, a small enclave at the outside edge of Hong Kong where many Chiu Chow immigrants first settled. Bean curd is cooked twice, then served with a cool, unadorned dip of salt water, which is simultaneously basic and odd and a way that the Chiu Chow believe perfectly balances the heat imparted to your system by the fried bean curd.

INGREDIENTS

6 cups water	4 firm fresh bean curd cakes (1 pound total), cut into slices 2 inches long and ½ inch thick (24 slices)
2 teaspoons salt	

SALTED WATER DIP

3 tablespoons boiling water	2 tablespoons finely chopped fresh Chinese chives
½ teaspoon salt	

3 cups peanut oil

1. Place the water and salt in a large pot, cover, and bring to a boil over high heat. Add the bean curd and allow the water to return to a boil. Turn off the heat. Using a Chinese strainer, remove the bean curd and drain well over a bowl. Dry the bean curd slices thoroughly with paper towels.

2. To make the dip: Mix together all of the ingredients in a small bowl, stirring until the salt is dissolved. Let cool, then divide among sauce dishes and reserve.

3. Heat a wok over high heat for 45 seconds. Add the peanut oil and heat it to 350°F on a deep-frying thermometer. Turn off the heat. Place 6 bean curd slices in the oil and deep-fry for 30 seconds. Turn on the heat to medium. The slices will rise to the top of the oil. Allow them to cook for 1 minute longer, or until they become golden. Using the strainer, remove the slices from the wok and drain on paper towels. Each slice should be crisp on the outside and soft on the inside. Deep-fry the remaining slices in 3 batches, 6 slices in each batch, the same way, adjusting the heat as needed to keep the oil at 350°F.

4. Arrange the hot bean curd on a heated plate and serve with the dip. To eat, dip a crisp bean curd slice into the dip, scooping up bits of the chopped chives at the same time.

OLD WATER DUCK

|| **MAKES 10 SERVINGS** ||

 In this classic of the Chiu Chow kitchen (see page 218), a simple dish is made elegant by its master sauce, known by the Chiu Chow as *lo soi,* or "old water." This preparation is handed down from generation to generation, and in the many Chiu Chow restaurants throughout Hong Kong, it is known as *lo soi* among the Cantonese as well.

It is one of the great dishes of the Chiu Chow table that begins with a basic stock, and though duck is simmered in the *lo soi* here, goose or chicken can be cooked the same way. It takes a first cooking with duck or other poultry to create the *lo soi.* Once it has been made, it goes on and on.

INGREDIENTS

LO SOI

3 cinnamon sticks, 3 inches long	4 pieces sand ginger, each 2 inches long, unpeeled, lightly smashed
5 eight-star anise	
1 teaspoon Sichuan peppercorns	4 pounds boneless pork butt, in one piece
¼ teaspoon whole cloves	3½ quarts water
2 teaspoons fennel seeds	2½ cups double dark soy sauce
1 whole *cho guor*	
8 pieces licorice root	1½ cups light soy sauce
3-inch-long piece ginger, unpeeled, lightly smashed	½ cup Mei Kuei Lu Chiew (see Wines, page 41)
	1 pound rock sugar or light brown sugar

1 duck, 5 pounds, preferably freshly killed, wings intact and head and feet removed

1. To make the *lo soi:* Place the cinnamon sticks, star anise, Sichuan peppercorns, cloves, fennel seeds, *cho guor,* licorice root, ginger, and sand ginger on a length of cheesecloth, and sew it closed. Wrap the pork in cheesecloth and sew the cloth closed.

2. Place the water, the spice bundle, and the wrapped pork in a large stockpot, cover, and bring to a boil over high heat. Lower the heat to medium, adjust the lid to leave it slightly cracked, and simmer for 3 hours. Turn off the heat, remove the pork, and reserve for another use.

3. Add the dark and light soy sauces, the *chiew,* and the sugar to the pot. Turn on the heat to high and bring to a boil uncovered. Stir until all of the ingredients are well blended and the sugar has dissolved. Turn off the heat. The *lo soi* is now ready to use. You should have about 3 quarts. Remove the spice bundle and reserve.

4. Place a rack at the bottom of a large pot. Place the duck, breast side up, on the rack. Pour in the *lo soi* and add the spice bundle. (Because you are cooking the duck in a new *lo soi,* you need to add the spice bundle to the pot. After you have completed this recipe, however, you should discard the spice bundle.) The liquid should cover the duck completely. Cover the pot, turn the heat on to high, and bring to a boil. Lower the heat to medium, adjust the lid to leave it slightly cracked, and simmer the duck, turning it several times as it cooks, for 1¾ hours. It should be very tender.

5. Turn off the heat and cover the pot. Allow the duck to rest in the liquid for 30 minutes.

6. When the duck is ready, transfer it to a cutting board, cut into bite-size pieces (see page 154), and arrange on a heated platter. Reserve the *lo soi* for future use.

NOTE: Serve the duck with a simple ginger-vinegar dip. In a small bowl, mix together 2 teaspoons white rice vinegar, 2 teaspoons peeled and grated ginger, ½ teaspoon sugar, 4 teaspoons water, and a pinch of salt, stirring until the sugar and salt are dissolved. Divide among small sauce dishes to serve.

LO SOI

老水

LO SOI

Once a chef makes *lo soi,* it is never removed from its pot because it is always in use. If a chef leaves one restaurant, he takes his *lo soi* pot with him. Each time some of the *lo soi* is used to cook a duck or other fowl, whatever liquid remains is added back to the original pot. Simply put, it is an always-replenished master sauce. One Guangzhou chef is said to have used his sauce for fifty years, willing it to a favored assistant on his death.

For the rest of us, *lo soi* should be stored in a tightly closed container in the refrigerator. Remove it each month, boil it for 5 minutes, then allow it to return to room temperature and refrigerate it again. (If you have cooked a bird in the *lo soi* at any time during a month, there is no need to boil it.) Cared for this way, it will keep for up to a year. Until the *lo soi* is used the first time, the spice bundle should remain in the sauce, then it can be discarded. Also, each time you use the sauce, taste it. You may want to replenish spices or add more *chiew,* soy sauce, or sugar.

For authenticity, I strongly suggest you seek out both sand ginger and *cho guor* for this sauce. They add immeasurably to its success. Both are available in Chinatown markets. Remember to bring photocopies of the Chinese characters with you to ensure you buy the correct items.

When you make *lo soi,* you are rewarded with a bonus: the sewn-up cooked pork butt. I suggest slicing it and serving it at room temperature or cooled with the same dip you serve with the duck.

SALT-BAKED CHICKEN

|| **MAKES 6 TO 8 SERVINGS** ||

 The nomadic Hakka have long prepared dishes that reflect their ability to create, and eat, in transit. One of their most famous preparations is chicken baked in a crust of salt, originally cooked over stones set in a hollow dug into the ground. When they settled in Guangdong, the top of the stove replaced the hole in the ground, and the chicken was baked in a wok.

The salt that surrounds the chicken becomes the oven, sealing in heat and flavor as the chicken bakes. Yet the chicken does not become overly salty. It is a fine dish, both as originally cooked in a wok and later in an oven. I have cooked the chicken both ways with success. Unfortunately, salt-baked chicken is another of those classics that has not been treated well in translation. What is often served in restaurants these days as salt-baked chicken is not baked at all, but instead simply poached in a salt solution. What follows is the recipe of tradition, prepared in the classic manner.

INGREDIENTS

1 whole chicken, 3½ pounds

¾ teaspoon sand ginger powder mixed with 2 tablespoons Mei Kuei Lu Chiew (see Wines, page 41)

2 scallions, white portions lightly smashed and each scallion cut into 4 equal pieces

½-inch-thick slice ginger, peeled and lightly smashed

1 piece dried tangerine peel, 1 by 2 inches, soaked in hot water to cover for 20 minutes, or until softened (see Old Skin Beef, page 209, for discussion of dried peel)

5 pounds kosher salt

2 lotus leaves, soaked in hot water to cover for 20 minutes until pliable, drained, rinsed, and damp-dried

DIPPING SAUCE

3 tablespoons grated ginger

4 tablespoons Scallion Oil (page 56)

1 teaspoon salt

1. Preheat the oven to 375°F for 20 minutes. If the neck and giblets are included with the chicken, freeze them for another use. Clean the chicken as directed on page 54, drain well, and pat dry with paper towels. Rub the chicken thoroughly, inside and out, with the sand ginger mixture. Place the scallions, ginger, and tangerine peel in the cavity. Set the bird aside.

2. Place the salt in a roasting pan, spread it out, place the pan in the preheated oven, and heat for 30 minutes until the salt is very, very hot.

3. As the salt heats, wrap the chicken. On a clean work surface, place the lotus leaves, smooth side up. Because the leaves are ribbed like an umbrella, each one must be pleated in the center so it will lie flat. Once you have pleated them, stack them so they are overlapping slightly. Then, place the chicken, breast side up, in the center of the leaves, and fold the leaves up and over the chicken, overlapping the edges and covering the bird completely. The leaves are damp and soft, so they will stay in place without tying. When the salt is heated, remove it from the oven and keep it at hand.

4. Heat a wok over high heat for 1 minute. Add half of the hot salt and spread it to make a bed in the bowl of the wok. Place the wrapped chicken, breast side up, firmly into the salt. Pour the remaining salt over the chicken, covering the bird completely. Cover the wok, lower the heat to medium, and allow the chicken to bake for 1 to 1¼ hours. Baking the chicken for 1 hour is usually sufficient, though allowing it to bake for another 15 minutes will ensure it is tender. If you detect a faint burning odor, reduce the heat to low.

5. To make the dipping sauce: In a small bowl, mix together all of the ingredients. Divide among 6 to 8 individual sauce dishes and reserve.

6. When the chicken is ready, turn off the heat. Brush off the salt, unwrap the chicken, and remove it to a cutting board. Cut into bite-size pieces (see page 154), and transfer to a heated platter. Serve with the sauce for dipping.

LOBSTER IN BLACK BEAN SAUCE

❙❙ MAKES 4 TO 6 SERVINGS ❙❙

敢汁龍蝦 The lobsters in the South China Sea are long and large, without the huge claws of the North American lobster. In fact, the Cantonese call their native lobster *lung har*, or "dragon shrimp." In a banquet, a lobster dish symbolizes strength. Lobsters from North America are now available in China, where they are called Canada lobsters. For this traditional dish, which customarily would use native lobsters, I prefer the North American lobster because the meat is smoother, more tender, and sweeter.

INGREDIENTS

¼ cup fermented black beans, rinsed twice and well drained	4 large garlic cloves, lightly smashed

SAUCE

1 tablespoon Shaoxing wine	1 teaspoon sesame oil
1 tablespoon oyster sauce	1½ teaspoons cornstarch
2 teaspoons double dark soy sauce	⅛ teaspoon white pepper
2 teaspoons light soy sauce	½ cup Fish Stock (page 147)

1 live lobster, 2 pounds	3 tablespoons Shaoxing wine
5 tablespoons cornstarch	
6 cups peanut oil	3 tablespoons Fish Stock (page 147), if needed
1½ tablespoons peeled and minced ginger	

1. Place the fermented black beans and garlic in a small bowl. With the handle of a cleaver, mash them into a paste. Or, use a mortar and pestle. Reserve.

2. To make the sauce: In a small bowl, mix together all of the ingredients and reserve.

3. Place the lobster on its back on a cutting board and plunge a sharp boning knife into its head and then pull it down through the body into the tail. (This will kill the lobster instantly. It is infinitely more humane than killing a lobster by boiling it. Or, have your fishmonger kill the lobster for you.) Pull open the lobster to butterfly it. Devein it. With the cleaver, cut the lobster in half from head to tail. Remove the spongy white strands from the head and the green tomalley and discard, and reserve the red coral (undeveloped roe) if present. Cut off the claws and feelers and set aside. Cut the lobster head and body into bite-size pieces. Still using the cleaver, cut the feelers at the joints. Smash the claws with the flat side of the cleaver blade to break the shells, then cut crosswise into bite-size pieces. Once the lobster is completely cut up, coat the pieces thoroughly with the cornstarch.

4. Heat a wok over high heat for 1 minute. Add the peanut oil and heat to 375°F on a deep-frying thermometer. Place all of the lobster pieces in a large Chinese strainer and lower them into the hot oil. Oil-blanch the lobster for 2 minutes, or until the shells turn red. Use a ladle to keep the lobster pieces separated. Turn off the heat. Using the strainer, remove the lobster pieces from the wok and drain well over a bowl. Reserve.

5. Pour off the oil from the wok and strain if needed to remove residue. Set aside 3 tablespoons. Reserve the remaining oil for another use. Heat the wok over high heat for 30 seconds. Add the 3 tablespoons oil and, using a spatula, coat the wok with the oil. When a wisp of white smoke appears, add the reserved black bean paste and the ginger and stir for 45 seconds, or until the black beans release their fragrance. Add the reserved lobster pieces and stir-fry for 1 minute, or until very hot. Drizzle in the wine, adding it along the edge of the wok. (This will create steam.)

6. If there is no moisture in the wok at this point, add the stock, drizzling it in along the edge of the wok, and then stir to mix for 1 minute. Make a well in the center of the mixture, stir the sauce, and pour it into the well. Stir-fry for about 2½ minutes, or until the ingredients are mixed and the lobster pieces are well-coated.

7. Turn off the heat, transfer to a heated platter, and serve.

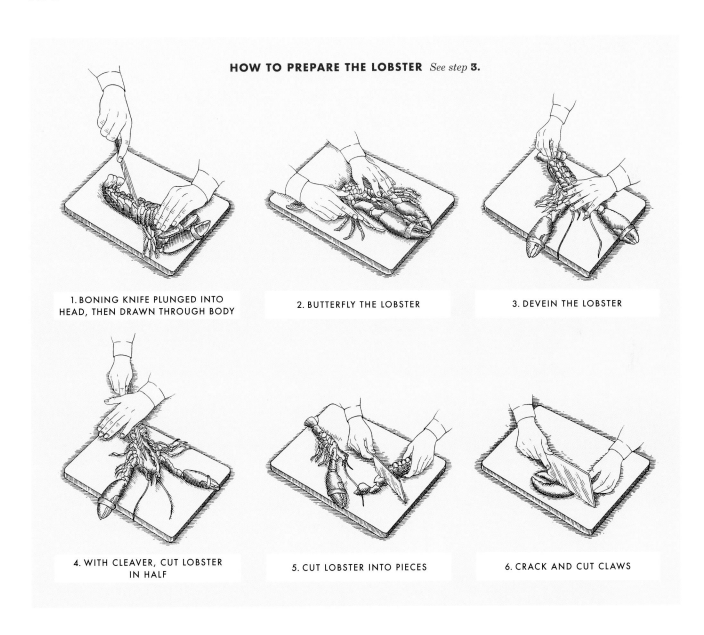

HOW TO PREPARE THE LOBSTER *See step* **3.**

1. BONING KNIFE PLUNGED INTO HEAD, THEN DRAWN THROUGH BODY

2. BUTTERFLY THE LOBSTER

3. DEVEIN THE LOBSTER

4. WITH CLEAVER, CUT LOBSTER IN HALF

5. CUT LOBSTER INTO PIECES

6. CRACK AND CUT CLAWS

HONG KONG

We move from the inland farms and historic walled villages of the Hakka to urban Hong Kong, where newness and a willingness to experiment with once-unfamiliar foods are prized as much as culinary tradition. In Hong Kong, you will find countless examples of authentically precise classic recipes and of contemporary creations. What follows are examples of both.

XO CAULIFLOWER

‖ MAKES 4 TO 6 SERVINGS ‖

This recipe is an example of Hong Kong innovation. The cauliflower, which likely originated in Asia Minor and was later grown throughout the Middle East, moved eastward to China, where its Chinese name translates to "cabbage flower," both a descriptive and an accurate name for this member of the cabbage family. It remained for Hong Kong chefs to remove this import from a pot of boiling water to this intensely flavored dish, made with the territory's own XO sauce.

INGREDIENTS

6 cups water	4½ cups tightly packed small cauliflower florets (1 pound)
1 tablespoon salt	
1 teaspoon baking soda (optional)	
2 tablespoons peanut oil	3 tablespoons XO Sauce (page 157)
2 teaspoons peeled and minced ginger	2 tablespoons Chicken Stock (page 54), if needed
¾ teaspoon salt	

1. To water-blanch (see page 63) the cauliflower, in a large pot, bring the water to a boil over high heat. Add the salt and baking soda (if using). When the water returns to a boil, add the cauliflower and blanch for 1 minute. Immediately turn off the heat and plunge the cauliflower into ice water to halt the cooking. Drain well and reserve.

2. Heat a wok over high heat for 30 seconds. Add the peanut oil and, using a spatula, coat the wok with the oil. When a wisp of white smoke appears, add the ginger and salt and stir briefly. Add the XO sauce and stir to mix well. Add the cauliflower and stir-fry for 2 minutes, or until well coated with the sauce. If no liquid is visible in the wok, add the stock. Stir and cook for another 2 minutes, or until the cauliflower is tender and very hot.

3. Turn off the heat, transfer to a heated plate, and serve.

WHITE RICE FISH

|| MAKES 4 SERVINGS ||

These tiny, milk-white fish, also known as whitebait, are pulled in by the millions in fine nets from the waters of the South China Sea. Cousins of the anchovy, the slender fish, ranging from about 1½ to 3 inches long, were historically used as bait by Chinese fishermen. Hong Kong decided to cook them. These days, they are served mounded on plates as a welcoming food in restaurants, to be nibbled on as you peruse the menu, or as small, elegant dinner introductions to whet the appetite, no more than two or three to a plate. It is a new custom that has traveled beyond Hong Kong as well. Look for these fish frozen in 1-pound boxes in Chinatown markets. They are imported from China and usually labeled "silver fish" and "wild caught." Even whitebait found loose in fish markets are simply these same imported fish that have been thawed. They are simple to cook, but demand attention to detail to turn out well.

INGREDIENTS

8 ounces frozen whitebait (see headnote)

3 cups peanut oil, plus ¾ cup if needed

5 tablespoons cornstarch

¼ to ½ teaspoon Sichuan Peppercorn Salt (page 315)

1. Allow the fish to thaw, then place them in a bowl and rinse with cold water. They are quite tender and fragile, so rinse them gently. Remove them to a strainer and drain over a bowl until dry.

2. Heat a wok over high heat for 1 minute. Add the 3 cups peanut oil and heat to 325°F on a deep-frying thermometer.

3. While the oil is heating, spread the cornstarch on a sheet of waxed paper. Place the fish in the cornstarch and toss until they are well coated.

4. When the oil is ready, shake off the excess cornstarch from the fish, place them in a Chinese strainer, and lower them into the hot oil. Deep-fry the fish, loosening them with a ladle, for 2 minutes, or until they turn off-white. Take care to regulate the heat. If the oil is too hot, the fish will clump together. If they begin to stick to one another, pour in ¾ cup room-temperature peanut oil. This will immediately cool the oil and the fish will separate. After 2 minutes, turn off the heat, remove the whitebait with the strainer, and allow to drain over a bowl until cool. Leave the oil in the wok.

5. Heat the oil again over high heat to 350°F. Place the fish in the strainer and lower them into the hot oil. Deep-fry for 2 minutes, or until they are light brown. Turn off the heat. Using the strainer, remove the whitebait and drain briefly over a bowl.

6. Transfer the fish to a heated plate, sprinkle with the flavored salt to taste, and serve.

TYPHOON SHELTER CHILI CRAB

|| MAKES 4 SERVINGS ||

 For most of a century, the waterfront of Hong Kong's Causeway Bay was a floating neighborhood of Chinese junks, sampans, and tenders that serviced the merchant ships in the territory's harbor. This curving, protected bay was also a perfect place of refuge during the typhoon season and came to be known formally as Bei Fung Tong, or Typhoon Shelter. Gradually, it also became home to a small fleet of floating restaurants, to which diners were ferried for the particular dishes of these boat people, such as salted pork with chive flowers and a special congee of pork innards. The best-known dish of this floating enclave, however, was chili crab, cooked on the small kerosene stoves of the boats.

Over the years, as the harbor began to be reclaimed and filled in, the international freighters started to anchor outside of the harbor proper, and the moorings of the boating marina multiplied, the boat people were forced to move out, and the Typhoon Shelter ceased to exist as a residential neighborhood. But its cooking remained. Many people left their boats for the shore and opened small restaurants close to the waterfront, where they prepared, and still do, their traditional foods. Quite a few serve chili crabs, cooking giant, big-clawed crustaceans imported from Vietnam. The closest we have to these crabs in the United States are the Dungeness of the West Coast, and they are quite good indeed. Here is how to make your own Typhoon Shelter chili crab as it is made in Hong Kong.

INGREDIENTS

7 cups peanut oil

¾ cup minced garlic

1½ tablespoons fermented black beans, rinsed twice and well drained

1 live Dungeness crab, 2½ pounds

¼ cup all-purpose flour

½ cup double dark soy sauce

2 teaspoons hot pepper flakes (page 55)

2 tablespoons ¼-inch-dice onions

6 scallions, white portions lightly smashed and white and green portions cut into 2-inch lengths

1 teaspoon sugar

---

1. Heat a wok over high heat for 30 seconds. Add 1 cup of the peanut oil, then immediately add the minced garlic and black beans. Stir to mix for 3 to 4 minutes, or until the garlic turns light brown. Turn off the heat. Ladle the garlic–black bean mixture into a fine-mesh strainer and drain over a bowl. Reserve the garlic–black bean mixture and the oil.

2. Rinse the crab well and pat dry. Place on a work surface, shell side up. With the eyes of the crab facing you, place the fingers of both hands at the edge of the shell and pull it away from the body. This will reveal the feathery, grayish gills and the pale yellow viscera, also known as crab butter. Pull off the gills and discard them. They are the only part of the crab that is inedible. Often the viscera are removed as well, but I do not suggest this. They are a delicacy and should be left intact. Drain off the liquid inside the body and the shell, also called the carapace, and discard it. Pat the body, shell, claws, and legs dry.

Continued . . .

. . . continued

3. With a cleaver, cut the body in half lengthwise. Then cut off the claws. With the blunt edge of the cleaver blade, crack the shells of the claws, then cut the claws at the joints to separate them into pieces. Cut each half of the body crosswise, with the legs attached, into 4 pieces, creating 8 pieces. Always keep the crab pieces dry by patting them with paper towels. They will continue to exude small amounts of moisture. When you have finished cutting up the crab, pat all of the pieces dry again, including the shell.

4. Heat a wok over high heat for 1 minute. Add the remaining 6 cups peanut oil and heat to 325°F on a deep-frying thermometer. While the oil is heating, spread the flour on a sheet of waxed paper and dredge the crab pieces and shell in the flour, coating them evenly.

5. When the oil is ready, shake off the excess flour from the crab and place the crab claw pieces in the hot oil. Deep-fry, using a ladle to prevent the pieces from sticking together, for 1 minute. Add all of the remaining crab pieces, except the shell, and deep-fry for another 2½ minutes, or until the pieces turn red, continuing to move the pieces about with a ladle to prevent sticking. Using a Chinese strainer, remove the crab pieces from the wok and allow to drain over a bowl. Place the crab shell in the wok and deep-fry for 1½ minutes, or until it turns red and its interior cooks. Turn off the heat, remove the shell from the wok, add it to the other pieces of crab, and allow to drain. Pour off the oil from the wok and reserve. Wash and dry the wok.

6. Heat the wok over high heat for 30 seconds. Add half of the reserved oil and heat until it bubbles. Because it is still hot, it will begin to bubble in 30 to 45 seconds. Add the crab pieces and the shell, then immediately add the soy sauce and cook, ladling the oil and sauce over the crab to ensure it covers evenly, for about 2 minutes, or until the crab is a rich brown. Turn off the heat. Using the strainer, remove the crab and drain as before. Pour off the soy sauce oil into a heatproof bowl.

7. Return the wok to the stove, add 2 tablespoons of the oil reserved from deep-frying the crab, and heat the wok over high heat for 20 seconds. When a wisp of white smoke appears, add the pepper flakes and onions and stir to mix. Immediately add the scallions and stir-fry for 30 seconds. Add the sugar and stir to mix briefly. Return the crab and shell to the wok and stir-fry for 1 minute, or until well mixed with the scallions. Sprinkle the reserved garlic–black bean mixture over the crab, then stir-fry continuously for about 2 minutes, or until all of the crab pieces are well coated.

8. Turn off the heat, transfer to a heated platter, and serve.

‖ SAVING OIL ‖

储存油

SAVING OIL

You can save some of the oil used for cooking this dish and use it again. The oil reserved from cooking the garlic and black beans can be used as another garlic oil recipe (page 56). The mixture of oil and soy sauce used to color the crab can be kept to cook another crab. It is perfectly blended and will keep in a tightly covered container in the refrigerator for up to 2 months.

BIG BOWL

盤菜

For our final preparation in this tour of China, we conclude with a celebration, a banquet dish, just as we did with our first regional culinary journey. For it, we leave Hong Kong and return to the New Territories of the Hakka farmers.

BIG BOWL

‖ **MAKES 12 TO 14 SERVINGS** ‖

This feast is truly a banquet in a bowl, actually nine courses, cooked separately, then assembled in layers and heated slowly with stock so their flavors combine. It is not only called big bowl, or *poon choi*, but also *gau dai guai*, or "nine precious flavors." It is a celebratory meal of the Hakka people, and it is known by this latter name both among the Hakka and by the Cantonese who surround them. Its existence dates to the Song Dynasty in the thirteenth century, when the Mongols invaded China, and the imperial family, members of the court, many followers, and remnants of the emperor's army fled south. They duplicated the earlier route taken by the nomadic Hakka, who settled primarily in what is now Guangdong and Hong Kong's New Territories.

As the Song refugees traveled through Fuzhou and headed westward through Guangdong, the local Hakka farmers took it on themselves to create, as best they could, a meal sufficiently elaborate to please the emperor and his entourage and to thank the soldiers for their presence. When the emperor and his followers reached what is now the New Territories, scores of area farmers and people from the neighboring Hakka walled village were reportedly asked to give whatever they could to feed the emperor and his army. What emerged was a collection of "precious flavors" assembled in huge wooden tubs—tubs normally used for bathing—creating a series of "big bowls." Eating utensils were scarce. There were enough for the emperor and his party, but not for his soldiers, who were forced to eat communally from the same bowl.

This slice of culinary lore has become a recurring Hakka banquet, served at religious festivities, family observances, weddings, and harvest festivals. Among the traditional ingredients of the big bowl are roasted duck and pork, boiled shrimp, fried fish, fried pig skin, dried eel and scallops, eggs, bean thread noodles, and bean curd sticks. Every big bowl has some of these, but variations exist, depending on the season or the occasion. In February 2002, a small army of chefs in Shenzen, just over the border in China from the New Territories, cooked four thousand big bowls on more than 150 stoves and served the feast to forty thousand diners, who sat down at tables for ten.

Continued . . .

第三集 ‖ 再談南北菜 ‖ PART 3 ‖ LESSON 5: A SECOND COOKING TOUR, NORTH TO SOUTH

. . . continued

You may be more modest. The individual elements of this dish are simple, but assembling it requires time and effort. Several of the dishes that go into it are classics in their own right, and they have already been prepared in our previous lessons. Most of them can be made in advance and refrigerated until needed, though some of them must be made on the day of serving.

For this traditional version, the ingredients and individual recipes will be listed and prepared in the order they are layered, from the bottom of the bowl to the top. This big bowl has eleven individual parts, or layers, but it is still considered *gau dai guai*, or "nine precious flavors," because the first layer is lotus root, which is considered a base for the layers, and the top layer is *choi sum* stalks, a garnish. Taken together, all of the layers are considered a complete culinary treasure.

To cook the dish, you will need an 8-quart stainless-steel bowl with curved sides and a flat bottom, with the bottom about 6 inches in diameter and the top rim about 12 inches in diameter. Stainless-steel bowls of this size are commonly found in housewares stores.

INGREDIENTS

1 Long-Cooked Pork Belly (facing page)	Simmered Bean Curd Sticks (page 342)
½ recipe Barbecued Pork (page 103; 2½ pounds)	Water-Blanched *Choi Sum* (page 342)
2 recipes Baked Duck Breasts (page 155; 3 pounds total)	Oil-Blanched Sea Scallops (page 343)
Braised Mushrooms in Oyster Sauce (page 98)	Stir-fried Eggs with Bean Threads (page 343)
Six-Flavor Chicken (facing page)	1½ pounds lotus roots
Poached Shrimp (page 342)	5 cups Chicken Stock (page 54), or as needed

---

1. Prepare the Long-Cooked Pork Belly as directed, up to 4 days in advance. Just before using, cut off and discard the strings and any bones and cut each square in half.

2. Prepare the Barbecured Pork as directed, up to 4 days in advance. Just before using, cut crosswise into ½-inch-thick slices.

3. Prepare the Duck Breasts as directed, up to 3 days in advance. Just before using, cut into ½-inch-thick slices.

4. Prepare the Braised Mushrooms in Oyster Sauce as directed, up to 3 days in advance.

5. Prepare the Six-Flavor Chicken as directed, up to 2 days in advance.

6. Prepare the Poached Shrimp as directed, up to 1 day in advance.

7. Prepare the Simmered Bean Curd Sticks as directed, up to 1 day in advance.

8. Prepare the *Choi Sum* as directed, up to 1 day in advance.

9. Prepare the Oil-Blanched Sea Scallops as directed. The scallops must be prepared on the day of use.

10. Prepare the Stir-Fried Eggs with Bean Threads as directed. The eggs must be prepared on the day of use.

11. Cut the lotus roots crosswise into ¼-inch-thick slices and reserve. The lotus roots must be prepared on the day of use.

12. The Big Bowl is ready for layering. Have all of the ingredients at room temperature. Spread the lotus root slices on the bottom of the bowl, creating a bed about ½ inch thick. Lay the pork belly pieces on top of the lotus root, to form the first layer. Then top with, in order, the duck breast meat, the bean curd sticks, and the barbecued pork to create the second, third, and fourth layers. Next, set down the fifth layer, the braised mushrooms, followed by the chicken, the scallops, and the shrimp to make layers six, seven, and eight. Top with the scrambled eggs and bean threads, the ninth layer. Arrange the *choi sum* stalks around the perimeter of the bowl, following its curve.

13. Place the bowl on the stove top. In a pot, bring the stock to a boil. Pour the stock into the bowl to the level of, but not covering, the shrimp. You may not need all 5 cups. Turn on the heat to medium-low and bring the contents of the bowl to a boil. Allow to boil for 3 minutes to blend the flavors of the ingredients with the boiling stock. Turn off the heat.

14. Bring the Big Bowl to the table, and invite diners to serve themselves.

 LONG-COOKED PORK BELLY

3 pounds fresh pork belly, in 2 slabs, cut into 10 equal squares by the butcher	2-inch-long piece ginger, unpeeled, lightly smashed
7½ cups water	6 ounces sugarcane sugar, broken into pieces
8 scallions, cut in half crosswise	¾ cup double dark soy sauce
	¼ cup Mei Kuei Lu Chiew (see Wines, page 41)

1. Using kitchen string, tie each pork belly square both ways, as if tying a package, to create a bundle. Place the water and scallions in a large pot, then the pork belly bundles, skin side down, in a single layer. Add the ginger and sugar and bring to a boil over medium heat. Add the soy sauce and allow to return to a boil. Add the *chiew* and again allow to return to a boil. Lower the heat to a simmer, cover the pot, leaving the lid slightly cracked, and cook for 3 hours. Turn the bundles every 30 minutes to ensure they cook evenly.

2. After 3 hours, reduce the heat to very low, cover the pot, and cook for 1 hour more, turning the bundles once more. Turn off the heat and allow the bundles to rest for 10 minutes.

3. Transfer the bundles to a dish and let them cool. (There should be about 2 cups liquid remaining in the pot. Reserve for another use.) Cover the cooled bundles with plastic wrap, and refrigerate for at least overnight or for up to 4 days.

 SIX-FLAVOR CHICKEN

3 cinnamon sticks, 2 inches long	4 cups Chicken Stock (page 54)
4 eight-star anise	3-inch-long piece ginger, peeled and lightly smashed
3 pieces dried tangerine peel, 1 by 2 inches (see Old Skin Beef, page 209, for discussion of dried peel)	1 cup double dark soy sauce
10 whole cloves	4 ounces sugarcane sugar, broken into pieces, or ⅔ cup firmly packed dark brown sugar
2 whole *cho guor* or nutmegs	
6 bay leaves	¼ cup Mei Kuei Lu Chiew (see Wines, page 41)
4 cups water	3¾ pounds bone-in, skin-on chicken breasts

1. Place the cinnamon, star anise, tangerine peel, cloves, *cho guor*, and bay leaves on a length of cheesecloth and sew it closed. In a large pot, place the water, stock, ginger, and spice bundle and bring to a boil over high heat. Add the soy sauce and return to a boil. Add the sugar and return to a boil. Add the *chiew* and return to a boil. Add the chicken breasts and return to a boil. Lower the heat to a simmer, cover the pot, leaving the lid slightly cracked, and simmer

Continued . . .

. . . continued

for 12 minutes. Turn over the chicken and cook for 12 minutes more. Turn off the heat. Cover the pot tightly and allow the chicken to rest for 1 hour.

2. Remove and discard the ginger and the spice bundle. Remove the chicken and discard the skin and bones. Cut the meat into 1½-inch-thick slices. (Reserve the liquid for another use.) The chicken can be prepared 2 days in advance.

POACHED SHRIMP

1 pound extra-large shrimp (26 to 30 count per pound)	1-inch-thick slice ginger, peeled and lightly smashed
3 cups water	3 scallions, cut crosswise into thirds
2 teaspoons salt	

I suggest using "easy peel shell on" shrimp (see page 75), which are deveined with the shells intact. In a pot, place the water, salt, ginger, and scallions and bring to a boil over high heat. Lower the heat to a simmer, cover the pot, leaving the lid slightly cracked, and simmer for 5 minutes. Raise the heat to high and bring to a rolling boil. Add the shrimp and cook for 1½ to 2 minutes, or until they curl and turn pink. Turn off the heat. Using a Chinese strainer, transfer to a bowl. The shrimp can be prepared 1 day in advance.

SIMMERED BEAN CURD STICKS

8 pieces bean curd sticks (4 ounces)	2 cups Chicken Stock (page 54)

In a bowl, soak the bean curd sticks in hot water to cover for 20 minutes, or until elastic and pliable. Drain well and cut into 2-inch pieces. In a pot, place the stock and bean curd sticks and bring to a boil over high heat. Lower the heat to a simmer, cover the pot, leaving the lid slightly cracked, and simmer for 20 minutes. Turn off the heat and allow the sticks to cool in the liquid for 5 minutes. Drain the sticks and reserve. (Reserve the stock for another use.) The bean curd sticks can be prepared 1 day in advance.

WATER-BLANCHED *CHOI SUM*

20 heads *choi sum*	1 tablespoon salt
6 cups water	1 teaspoon baking soda (optional)

1. Strip off the outer leaves from each head of the *choi sum* and trim off the tough end of the stalk. Use only the top tender portion of each head, about 4 inches long.

2. Bring the water to a boil in a large pot over high heat. Add the salt and baking soda (if using). When the water returns to a boil, add the *choi sum* and water-blanch for 45 seconds, or until it turns bright green. Turn off the heat and immediately plunge the *choi sum* into ice water to halt the cooking. Drain well. The *choi sum* can be cooked 1 day in advance.

OIL-BLANCHED SEA SCALLOPS

---

12 sea scallops

6 cups peanut oil

5 tablespoons water chestnut flour

---

1. Cut the scallops in half horizontally to create 24 medallions. Heat a wok over high heat for 1 minute. Add the peanut oil and heat to 350°F on a deep-frying thermometer.

2. While the oil is heating, pat the scallops dry with paper towels. Spread the flour on a sheet of waxed paper and toss the scallops with the flour, coating evenly.

3. When the oil is ready, shake off the excess flour from the scallops, place them in a Chinese strainer, and lower them into the hot oil. Oil-blanch for 1 minute. Turn off the heat, remove the scallops from the oil with the strainer, and drain over a bowl. The scallops must be prepared on the day of use.

STIR-FRIED EGGS AND BEAN THREADS

3½ cups Chicken Stock (page 54)

2 (2-ounce) packages bean thread noodles

4 whole extra-large eggs, plus 3 extra-large egg yolks

½ teaspoon salt

Pinch of white pepper

5½ tablespoons peanut oil

---

1. Place the stock in a pot and heat until very hot. Turn off the heat. Immerse the bean thread noodles in the hot stock, loosen them, and allow them to soak for 20 minutes, or until softened. Drain the noodles, then transfer to a dish and cut into 3-inch lengths. (Reserve the stock for another use.)

2. While the noodles are soaking; in a bowl, beat together the whole eggs, egg yolks, salt, pepper, and 1½ tablespoons of the peanut oil until smoothly blended.

3. Heat a wok over high heat for 20 seconds. Add the remaining 4 tablespoons peanut oil and, using a spatula, coat the wok with the oil. Lower the heat to medium and allow the oil to heat for 10 seconds. Then add the bean thread noodles and stir-fry for about 15 seconds, or until well coated with the oil. Add the beaten egg mixture and stir-fry to a soft, fluffy scramble. This will take about 1 minute. Adjust the heat as needed to avoid overcooking the eggs or toughening the bean threads. Turn off the heat and transfer to a dish. The eggs must be prepared on the day of use.

THE BIG BOWL, DECONSTRUCTED

BIG BOWL DECON-STRUCTED

As noted in the introduction to the recipe, the unique character of this festive dish is in its melding of many individual preparations. But each element can also be enjoyed on its own, a few can be cooked to create a simple menu, or all of them can be cooked to create a multicourse banquet (page 362).

As you eat this Hakka feast, with all of its different tastes, you will want to have a bowl of rice at hand so you can spoon a little of the delicious sauce from the pot over it.

LESSON 6
A DISCUSSION OF SWEETS

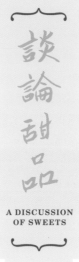

談論甜品

**A DISCUSSION
OF SWEETS**

I have reserved for our final lesson a taste of Chinese sweets. This is not only to conclude on a note of sweetness, but also to dispel the many widespread misconceptions about Chinese sweets. China, in its long culinary history, has a tradition of foods sweetened with honey and cane sugar that goes back to the time of the Han Dynasty, in 200 B.C. Han writings talk of a "white" honey of northern China that is superior to the honey of the south, and sweetened and candied fruits and vegetables, sweetened soups and drinks, and various candies have long existed.

Historically, there are no Chinese desserts, but there are sweet cakes and sweetened foods. Sugar beets arrived in China from the Near East in the seventh century, and the town of Yangzhou, south of Shanghai, became the country's sugar-refining center. Cakes made from wheat and rice flours were sweetened with this new sugar, then steamed or fried.

For several centuries, the teahouses of Yangzhou enjoyed an enviable reputation for their sweets. According to legend, a cake even led to the creation of the Ming Dynasty in the twelfth century. A monk, Zhu Yuanzhang, leading the rebellion against the Mongols, passed battle plans to his forces in filled cakes, a successful practice that helped the monk to rout the Mongols and install the Mings in Beijing. This event is celebrated each fall with the Mid-Autumn Festival and its moon cake, once a thin wheat flour dough encasing sweetened nuts and ham and now a cake filled with sweet lotus seed paste and duck egg yolks—the more yolks, the finer the cake.

Whether cakes were made of wheat flour or rice flour, were imperial or everyday, they were always teahouse pleasures, never desserts. Meals, both modest gatherings at family tables and imperial banquets, were concluded with fresh fruits. Sweets, though part of the great Chinese table for thousands of years, were enjoyed with afternoon tea in the country's many teahouses, were given as special gifts to relatives and friends, were a part of festive observances, or were temple offerings to ancestors. Although sweet soups and puddings were often included in meals, they were never considered the finale. Only fresh fruits played that role.

As we walk about the market streets of Chinatowns these days, we notice there is no shortage of so-called Chinese bakeries, which, to be perfectly accurate, are simply bakeries owned and/or staffed by Chinese. What they sell—icing-covered layer cakes, glazed doughnuts, frosted cupcakes, jam-topped pastries, muffins, even the egg custard tartlets so popular in today's dim sum restaurants—is not traditionally Chinese. There are Chinese adaptations of the specialties of Western bakers, a culinary practice that took root first in Shanghai, then in Guangzhou, where bakeries thrived in the foreign concessions. Some have suggested, and it is probably true, that even the almond cookie, long a staple in modern Chinese restaurants, first appeared in Shanghai.

Shanghai has also seen ornate, tiered Western wedding cakes become customary at the city's Chinese weddings. Plus, we now have what the Cantonese have added to the dim sum repertoire, including *mak sai gah bau*, or Mexican buns, which are round and sweet and covered with dense sugar icing; *bor law bau*, so-called pineapple buns, in which a design resembling a pineapple is etched into the icing; and *gai mei bau*, or cocktail buns, which are shaped like a frankfurter roll, filled with sweet custard, and covered with crushed peanuts—all of them inspired by Western baking. And while these bakeries also sell traditional Chinese *guk char siu bau* (page 280), the concept of a filled baked bun is carried forward to include "Chinese" jelly-filled doughnuts.

That such concocted pastries are often offered as desserts in Chinese restaurants is simply another aspect of the adaptation of Western sweets. And so we see layers of pastry folded around red bean paste, thick steamed sponge cakes, and rice-flour layer cakes, none of which are historically Chinese, but all of which have become standards of a new Chinese-Western sweets tradition. The fortune cookie is an interloper, too, for it has never existed in China.

The tradition of fresh fruit to conclude a meal was the direct influence of the culinary glory of China's tropical south. The south was always, and still is, bursting with fresh fruits of all varieties. Large markets such as Qing Ping in Guangzhou and others in Hong Kong and Shanghai are piled high with oranges, tangerines, pomelos, kumquats, loquats, persimmons, pomegranates, pears, apples, and the highly prized, large, flat-topped, pearl-white peaches. Alongside them are apricots, plums, cherries, wild strawberries, the red dates known as "jujubes," and all manner of melons, including cantaloupes, honeydew, casabas, and the much-sought-after small, hard, incredibly sweet *Hami guah* muskmelon that originated in Hami, in Xinjiang Province, and once appeared only briefly in the early summer, but is now available throughout the season.

All of these fruits found their way to the court of whichever emperor was in power in Beijing, where they were stored on huge blocks of ice that had been cut in the far north in wintertime, transported to the capital, and kept in icehouses.

There are also litchis, coconuts, the bananas and kiwifruits that once grew wild but are now cultivated, and the many imports that readily took to the vast southern orchard: papayas and peanuts, guavas and avocados, mangoes and pineapples. Some were eaten fresh, some were candied, others were pickled, and still others were preserved in salt. The tradition of drying and preserving foods and sweetening them with cane syrup has existed as long as fruits and vegetables have been cultivated in China.

When I was a child, the custom of festive sweets was important in our family house in Sun Tak Yuen, particularly in preparation for the Lunar New Year, when we put together gifts for our holiday guests. We made *chau mai bang*, which called for dry-frying rice kernels until they popped, spreading them out, covering them with a sugar syrup, allowing them to harden, and then slicing them into squares. We made *far suntong*, a hard, sweet peanut brittle, and both *sot kei mah*, syrup-laden strips of deep-fried wheat flour dough, and *dan san*, deep-fried bows of wheat dough glazed with honey and sugar. We made *jin dui*, using, once again, dry-fried rice kernels, but this time sweetening them and then covering them with a pliable rice dough and fashioning them into fish and fruit shapes. And we made *ling goh*, steamed cakes of rice flour and sugarcane sugar that carried the promise that the recipient would rise higher and higher each year.

All of these sweets would be arranged on a welcome table for our New Year's visitors. We also put out candied watermelon rind, lotus root, lotus seeds, ginger root, coconut chunks, and sweet potato squares; preserved and fresh dates; sugar-coated walnuts; dried and salted watermelon seeds and pumpkin seeds; and deep-fried peanuts. Other lacquer bowls were filled with dried apricots, pears, apples, and pineapples; candied orange peel; and

sweet and salty lemon rind. We served the sweets with our best teas, which we kept in a traditional multicompartmented lacquer tea caddy. This custom of sweets and tea service was repeated at betrothals, weddings, and birthdays.

Sweet soups of sweetened fermented rice, red beans, or various fruits, along with the grandest of all sweet soups, bird's nest, which we prepared in an earlier lesson (see page 249), are also part of the Chinese sweets tradition. They may be clear or pureed, cool, warm, or hot, but what they all have in common is a liquid base sweetened with rock sugar or sugarcane sugar. They are a specialty of Guangdong and Fujian and are known generically in Cantonese as *tong soi*, and in Mandarin as *tang shui*, or "soups of sugar water." Cooks often drop small glutinous rice flour balls filled with sweetened bean, black sesame, or peanut paste into sweet soups. The balls, known as *tong yeun* in Cantonese or *tang yuan* in Mandarin, which are easy to make and cook quickly, add to the enjoyment of the soups.

Fujian Province, and particularly its main city of Fuzhou, is famous for both its sweet soups and its sweets. For the New Year, the Fujianese add glutinous rice dumplings filled with ground peanuts, soybeans, and sugar to their sweet soups. They fry long crullerlike pastries and make custardlike puddings from cooked and mashed sweet potatoes, pumpkins, and lotus seeds. Farther north in Suzhou, near Shanghai, soft, chewy candies made from black sesame seeds, dates, plums, walnuts, almonds, licorice, and even the essences of roses and jasmine blossoms are traditional.

China's sweets tradition also extends to the streets, where hawkers pull carts laden with both sweet and sour dried plums, salted dry-fried broad beans, preserved lemons, red-dyed salted ginger, and preserved kumquats.

What follows are sweets that are truly Chinese. These are classics, not hybrids, enjoyed at the family table or at the teahouse.

SWEET WALNUTS

‖ MAKES ABOUT 4 CUPS ‖

 This traditional sweet is believed to have originated in Sichuan, where walnut trees from Persia were first planted in China. As with many Chinese foods, the walnut is imbued with symbolic meaning: It is believed to benefit the mind because the shelled nut looks like a brain lobe. Brain food or not, the walnut was a deliciously significant sweet long ago in Sichuan and western China. Reminiscent of halvah, mashed walnuts encased in a thin, flaky dough and covered with sugar syrup is a famed teatime dish and just one of many Sichuan creations based on walnuts.

In this recipe, walnuts go through four distinct cooking processes: They are boiled, reboiled, glazed, and finally deep-fried. Once a provincial sweet, they emanated outward from Sichuan many years ago, turning up in restaurants in Shanghai, Guangzhou, and Hong Kong, usually as appetite-whetting, premeal snacks and just as often as snacks to conclude a meal along with fresh fruit. They were quickly dubbed "honey walnuts," though they are glazed with sugar syrup. They began to appear in the West about forty years ago, with the onset of the popularity of Sichuan and Hunan restaurants. These days they are a standard offering.

One particularly attractive aspect of these crisp, sweet walnuts is that they do not become soft if stored properly. Packed in an airtight container and left at room temperature, they will keep for at least 1 week. They will keep for at least 6 months in the freezer, and when served directly from freezer to table, they will still be crisp. Although I do not recommend freezing them for an inordinate time, I did once leave them in the freezer for a year as an experiment. They were perfectly crisp and not at all stale. If you decide to make walnuts for storage, do not double the recipe, as the walnuts won't cook properly. Instead, make individual batches. Pecans can be prepared the same way.

INGREDIENTS

10 cups water; plus
6 tablespoons for glaze

12 ounces (about 4 cups)
walnut halves

6 tablespoons sugar

5 cups peanut oil

1. Place 5 cups of the water in a pot and bring to a boil over high heat. Add the walnuts and stir. Allow the water to return to a boil and boil for 3 minutes. Turn off the heat and run cold water into the pot. Drain the nuts thoroughly in a strainer. Return the nuts to the pot, add 5 cups of the water, and bring to a boil over high heat. Allow the nuts to boil for 5 minutes, then drain again and set the walnuts aside to dry.

2. This next step requires a wok that is completely free of oil. Place the 6 tablespoons water in the wok and bring to a boil over high heat. Add the sugar and stir to dissolve with a spatula. Bring to a boil and stir constantly for 2 minutes. Add the walnuts and continue to stir for about 8 minutes, or until the nuts are coated completely with the sugar syrup and the liquid in the wok has evaporated. As the walnuts become glazed with the syrup, take care to regulate the heat so neither the nuts nor the glaze burns.

3. Turn off the heat. Using a Chinese strainer, remove the walnuts and set aside on a plate. Wash the wok and the spatula with extremely hot water to remove the sugar residue and dry thoroughly.

Continued . . .

. . . continued

4. Place the peanut oil in the wok and heat it to 375ºF on a deep-frying thermometer. Place the walnuts on the strainer and lower them into the hot oil. Fry the walnuts, stirring with the spatula, for about 5 minutes, or until they turn a golden amber brown. Turn off the heat. Scoop the nuts from the oil with the strainer and allow to drain briefly.

5. Spread the nuts on a baking sheet and let cool completely. After 2 minutes, loosen the walnuts so they do not stick to one another. Serve the cooled nuts or transfer them to an airtight container and store as directed in the introduction.

EIGHT-TREASURE RICE

‖ **MAKES 10 SERVINGS** ‖

八寶糯米飯 This festive dish, hugely popular in Shanghai and once believed to have been created there, was actually first made in northern China. A mixture of glutinous rice steamed with candied, dried, and preserved fruits, it was a holiday tradition throughout the north and in Beijing, and then spread to Shanghai, Suzhou, and Nanjing. Today, it is common throughout all of China. Historically, the eight treasures were some fruits, cubes of citron, lotus seeds, almonds, red dates, and red bean paste, over which a sugar syrup was poured before serving.

Often called a cake, just as often a pudding, eight-treasure rice has evolved into a much desired dish that is to be typically served as the penultimate course of a banquet, just before the concluding plate of iced fresh fruit. It has become a recipe upon which cooks lavish attention, changing, adding, and subtracting treasures, usually ingredients indigenous to the region where it is being made. It has even, in miniature form, become part of Shanghai's dim sum repertoire. The only stipulation is that it must contain eight treasures.

It requires effort to make and is usually not made at home, but rather enjoyed in restaurants, where it must be ordered in advance. However, it is enjoyable to prepare. What follows is a traditional version, with but one change. I have left out citron, for I do not like the excessive sweetness and hardness of the skins of citron cubes, which I believe detract from the natural, intense sweetness of the other preserved and dried fruits. This dish is beautiful to present, delicious to eat. Enjoy the effort.

INGREDIENTS

2½ cups glutinous rice	⅛ cup (2 tablespoons) dried peaches
2½ cups water	
¼ cup dried apricots	¼ cup pitted dried dates
¼ cup dried pears	2 tablespoons raisins
¼ cup dried pineapple	4½ teaspoons peanut oil
¼ cup dried mangoes	1 cup red bean paste, or lotus seed paste

SYRUP (OPTIONAL)

¾ cup water	2 teaspoons tapioca starch mixed with 1 tablespoon water
½ cup sugar	

1. Place the rice in a large bowl and fill the bowl with water. Wash the rice by rubbing it between your palms, then discard the water. Do this 3 more times, then drain the washed rice well. Place the rice in a 9-inch cake pan and add the 2½ cups water. Place the cake pan in a steamer, cover, and steam for 30 to 40 minutes. The cooked rice will have a glaze and be translucent.

2. While the rice is steaming, cut all of the fruits, except the raisins, into ⅓-inch dice, and place in a large bowl. Add the raisins, mix well, and reserve.

3. When the rice is ready, turn off the heat. Scoop the rice from the cake pan into the bowl holding the fruit and combine the fruit and rice thoroughly.

4. Coat the interior of a 1½-quart steamproof bowl with 1½ teaspoons of the peanut oil, making certain its sides are well coated. Coat your hands with oil as well, so the glutinous rice can be handled easily. Pick up half of the rice-fruit mixture, coat it with the remaining 3 teaspoons

Continued . . .

349

. . . continued

peanut oil, and then pack it into the bowl, pressing it up against the sides to leave a hollow in the center. Place the red bean paste in the center of the rice, spread it slightly, then place the remainder of the rice-fruit mixture on top and press down gently.

5. Place the bowl in a steamer. If using a tiered metal steamer, remove the base of one tier so the bowl will nestle properly. Cover the steamer and steam for 45 minutes. During steaming, all of the fruits will combine well with the rice and the bean paste.

6. Turn off the heat, remove the bowl from the steamer, and allow to cool for about 5 minutes. Pass a blunt dinner knife around the rim of the bowl to loosen the rice. Invert a flat serving plate on top of the bowl and invert the bowl and plate together. Lift off the bowl. The molded rice should slip out easily.

7. To make the syrup: In a wok, bring the water to a boil over high heat. Add the sugar and stir to dissolve. Allow it to return to a boil and stir constantly for 1½ minutes. Stir the starch-water mixture, pour it into the wok, and mix quickly to prevent lumps from forming. Return the mixture to a boil; bubbles will form on top. Turn off the heat, transfer the syrup to a sauce boat, and pour it evenly over the molded rice. (You can serve the dish with or without a sugar syrup. I do not use the syrup because the various fruits, with their concentrated flavors, make the dish sufficiently sweet.)

8. Scoop the rice into individual bowls to serve.

RED BEAN SOUP WITH LOTUS SEEDS

|| MAKES 6 SERVINGS ||

Sweet soups have long been a tradition throughout China, but particularly in Fujian. They are based not only on fruits, but also on such sweetened vegetables, nuts, and seeds as mung beans, red beans, sweet potatoes, taro root, black and white sesame seeds, almonds, and walnuts. Of course, the court in Beijing demanded exotic sweet soups as well, made from such ingredients as the nests of Southeast Asian swifts or the ovaries of tiny snow frogs, both soups made with a base of coconut milk and sugar.

When I was growing up, this soup was a Lunar New Year must in our family. The inclusion of lotus seeds, called *lin jee* in Cantonese or *lian zi* in Mandarin, was to ensure the entire family would be rewarded with many children. The soup was also typically served at wedding banquets, where the lotus seeds brought the newlyweds the promise of a child each year. Equally propitious are red beans, called *hung dau* in Cantonese or *hongdou* in Mandarin, which are thought to build strength, making this the perfect soup for a New Year's wish.

1. Place the beans in a large bowl and fill the bowl with water. Wash the beans by rubbing them between your palms, then discard the water. Do this two or three more times, then drain the washed beans well. Return them to the bowl, add water to cover, and let soak for 1 hour. Drain the beans well.

2. Place the 7 cups water, the drained beans, the lotus seeds, and the tangerine peel in a large pot. Cover the pot and bring to a boil over high heat. Reduce the heat to low, adjust the lid to leave a slight crack, and cook for 1¼ to 1½ hours, or until the beans are tender and about half of them have split open and the lotus seeds have softened.

3. Add the sugar and stir well. If using sugarcane sugar, raise the heat to medium and cook for 5 minutes, or until the sugar has dissolved and blended fully with the other ingredients. If using brown sugar, simply stir well. The sugar will quickly dissolve, so there is no need to cook for 5 minutes.

4. Turn off the heat, transfer to a heated tureen, and serve.

INGREDIENTS

1 (14-ounce) package dried red beans

7 cups water

3 ounces (about ½ cup) lotus seeds, rinsed and well drained

1 piece dried tangerine peel, 1 by 2 inches, soaked in hot water to cover for 20 minutes, or until softened (see Old Skin Beef, page 209, for discussion of dried peel)

6 ounces sugarcane sugar, broken into pieces, or ¾ cup firmly packed dark brown sugar

---

SWEET WINE RICE SOUP

‖ MAKES 4 TO 6 SERVINGS ‖

This is a classic sweet soup from Shanghai, traditionally served to welcome a guest, usually accompanied with the excellent Dragon Well tea from nearby Hangzhou, or as a popular afternoon snack. It has evolved into a sweet that appears as the last course of a meal—whether simple or bountiful—and though once found only in Shanghai restaurants, it is now a standard sweet in the restaurants of Hong Kong as well.

It is served in two variations. In the first, a gently boiled, just-set egg is slid into a bowl and the soup is poured over it. In the second, eggs are beaten and added to the soup as it cooks, providing a texture reminiscent of an egg drop soup. I prefer the latter for both its appearance and texture. The small, chewy pieces of glutinous rice dough that cook quickly in the hot soup can be rolled into tiny balls, or they can be cut from a slender cylinder of dough into what I call nuggets. Again, I prefer the irregular pieces for their pleasing texture.

INGREDIENTS

1 cup glutinous rice powder (see sidebar)

½ cup hot water

2½ cups cold water

¼ cup sugar

⅔ cup Shanghai Sweet Wine Rice (page 182)

½ cup liquid from Shanghai Sweet Wine Rice (page 182)

1 large egg, lightly beaten

1. Place the glutinous rice powder on a work surface and make a well in the center. Gradually add the hot water to the well and use your fingers to combine it with the powder until it is absorbed. Knead into a dough, picking up any loose powder with a dough scraper. Continue to knead for about 7 minutes, or until the dough is firm and elastic.

2. Cut the dough into 4 equal pieces. Work with 1 piece at a time and keep the others covered with plastic wrap. Using your palms, roll the piece into a slender log 15 inches long. Cut the log crosswise into ½-inch nuggets. Repeat with the remaining dough pieces. You should have 120 nuggets. Sprinkle them lightly with rice powder to prevent sticking.

3. Place the cold water in a pot and bring to a boil over high heat. Add the sugar and stir until it dissolves. Shake any excess rice powder from the nuggets, add them to the pot, and stir to ensure they do not stick to one another. Allow the liquid to return to a boil, then lower the heat to medium and cook the nuggets for 2 to 3 minutes, or until they rise to the surface. Add the wine rice and the wine rice liquid, stir to mix well, and allow the soup to return to a boil. Slowly add the beaten egg while stirring constantly with a cooking fork. The egg will cook into strands.

4. Turn off the heat, transfer to a small heated tureen, and serve.

‖ **GLUTINOUS RICE POWDER** ‖

GLUTINOUS RICE POWDER

To make this powder, or flour, glutinous rice is first soaked and allowed to dry. Then, while just slightly moist, it is milled into a flour. This flour, commonly referred to as a powder, is used occasionally in dim sum, for dumpling wrappings; in cakes in China and Southeast Asia; and for tiny dumplings in sweet soups. It comes in plastic sacks in Asian markets, imported from China and Thailand. Store it as you would any flour.

NOU MI TANG YUAN

This special sweet has no equivalent name in English. In most of China, it is called *nou mi tang yuan*; in southern China and in Hong Kong, it is *nor mai tong yeun*. Both translate as "glutinous rice soup round," to describe a round glutinous rice dumpling with a sweet filling that is cooked in a *tong soi*, or a sweet soup of sugar and water. If you ask simply for *tangyuan* or *tong yeun*, you will be served these sweet dumplings in soup.

The dumplings are popular foods for festive Lunar New Year meals and for weddings, birthdays, family gatherings, and feast-day observances. Because they are round and sweet, they symbolize the endlessness of the family and the wish for the family's good fortune to go round and round and never depart. Traditionally, they were made with pieces of sugarcane sugar wrapped in glutinous rice flour dough, but they have evolved into dumplings of many different fillings, such as roasted white sesame seeds mixed with crushed roasted peanuts and sugar; sweet bean paste; or black sesame seed paste and brown sugar.

The sweet soup is equally traditional. I have already mentioned that sweet soups have been part of Chinese cooking for many centuries and that many of them are based on fruits and vegetables. But clear *tong soi*, occasionally with other ingredients added, have the longest history. They have traditionally been made of sugar dissolved in water, to which white tree fungus, cloud ears, lotus blossoms, cassia flowers, chrysanthemums, or even raisin stems or hawthorn berries are added. One *tong soi* calls for slices of a dough made from glutinous rice and wheat kernels. The soups are served hot or cold, but they are always sweet and are said to make the body "clean and clear."

The *tangyuan* that follow are believed to be from Shanghai, though dumplings similar to these are found throughout China. Wherever their provenance, they are a delightful sweet, gratifying to make and to serve.

INGREDIENTS

FILLING

½ cup black sesame seed powder (see sidebar, page 354)

½ cup firmly packed dark brown sugar

3 ounces lard, melted and kept hot (½ cup)

DOUGH

1½ cups glutinous rice powder (page 352)

¾ cup boiling water

3½ cups cold water

½ cup white sugar

1. To make the filling: In a bowl, place the sesame powder and brown sugar and mix well. Add the hot melted lard and mix well with chopsticks until the ingredients are combined. Refrigerate, uncovered, for at least 2 hours or up to overnight.

2. To make the dough: Place the rice powder in a bowl. Slowly pour in the boiling water with one hand while mixing with chopsticks with the other hand. Continue to mix for about 2 minutes, or until the dough is cool enough to knead. Transfer to a clean work surface and knead, incorporating any dry powder that may drop off with a dough scraper, for about 7 minutes, or until the mixture begins to become resilient.

Continued . . .

. . . continued

3. If the dough is sticking to your hands, wash them thoroughly. Sprinkle the work surface with glutinous rice powder and knead the dough for 3 to 4 minutes longer, or until it becomes elastic. Using your palms, roll the dough into a log 15 inches long. Cut the log crosswise into thirds. Work with 1 piece at a time and keep the others covered with plastic wrap. Again using your palms, roll the piece into a log 10 inches long. Cut the log crosswise into 10 equal pieces. Repeat with the remaining 2 pieces. You should have 30 pieces total. Sprinkle them lightly with rice powder to prevent sticking.

4. Remove the filling from the refrigerator. Roll 1 piece of dough into a ball, then, using your thumbs and fingers, shape it into a cup. Place 1 teaspoon of the filling into the hollow of the cup, close the dough securely over the top, and then roll it into a ball and set aside on a baking sheet. Repeat until all 30 dumplings are made. Sprinkle the dumplings lightly with rice powder as you make them to prevent sticking.

5. In a pot, place the cold water and white sugar and bring to a boil over high heat, stirring to dissolve the sugar. Add the dumplings and stir with a wooden spoon to prevent sticking. Allow the water to return to a boil, then reduce the heat to medium-low and simmer the dumplings for 5 to 7 minutes, or until they rise to the surface. Turn off the heat.

6. The "skins" of the dumplings should have a pleasant, chewy bite, the filling should be sweet and a bit grainy, and the soup should be faintly sweet to complement the dumplings. You can add more or less sugar to taste when you make the soup.

7. To serve, place 5 dumplings and about ½ cup of the soup in each bowl.

⊣ BLACK SESAME SEED POWDER ⊢

黑芝蔴粉

BLACK SESAME SEED POWDER

Traditionally, this dumpling filling was made with black sesame seeds that cooks roasted and then crushed. In recent years, black sesame seed powder, which is simply seeds that have been roasted and finely ground, was developed to eliminate that step. It is used not only to make a sweet dumpling filling, but also for various dim sum and pureed soups. The powder comes in plastic packages labeled "black sesame powder," usually from Taiwan, and its pronounced sesame taste is quite good.

Avoid buying boxes that are labeled "instant sesame powder mix," which is black sesame powder to which sugar, salt, potato starch, and often bits of peanuts have been added.

MANGO SOUP WITH TAPIOCA PEARLS AND POMELO

‖ **MAKES 4 SERVINGS** ‖

芒菓西米露 Here is perhaps the ultimate sweet fruit soup, a modern classic born in Hong Kong, the most recent in the long heritage of such sweets. I have told the story of sweet soups in China, of how they have been based on virtually every fruit grown in the country, from northern apples to southern litchis, and sweetened with sugarcane sugar, rock sugar crystals, brown sugar, or beet sugar. And I have explained how China welcomed fruits from elsewhere in Asia, the Middle East, and the Americas: finger-length bananas, star-shaped carambolas, sweet pineapples no bigger than a child's clenched fist, mangosteens, durians, jackfruits, rambutans, pomegranates, figs, papayas, guavas, and passion fruits. All of them have found their way onto the Chinese table, either cooked and sweetened, made into soups, or fresh as part of an elaborate fruit basket served at the end of the meal.

Of particular note among these imports is the mango, a native of India that came to China by a circuitous route. It was collected in India, probably in Goa, by Portuguese explorers, who carried it to Brazil, where it was cultivated. Later, the Portuguese introduced the mango to China through their colony of Macau. The oval, fleshy, sweet fruits were enthusiastically embraced by the Chinese, who ate them fresh or dried them for snacks. They also preserved small unripe mangoes in salt or pickled them with sugar, salt, and white rice vinegar. In Guangzhou, mangoes were stir-fried with chicken, and in Hong Kong, they were added to salads.

It was also in Hong Kong that this sweet soup was born, a combination of mangoes, pomelo, and tiny, white tapioca pearls. It is a lovely cold soup, with several contrasting textures and flavors,

including grapefruitlike pomelo and rich coconut cream. I consider it the most modern manifestation of the Chinese way with sweetened foods.

INGREDIENTS

2 tablespoons tapioca pearls	2 small ripe mangoes, peeled, pitted, and pureed (1 cup)
⅓ cup water for soaking tapioca	5 tablespoons coconut cream (see note)
⅔ cup plus 1 tablespoon water	3 tablespoons broken-up pomelo pulp (pulled apart by hand)
2½ tablespoons crushed rock sugar	
⅔ cup plus 1 tablespoon milk	3 tablespoons ¼-inch-dice mango

---

1. In a small bowl, place the tapioca pearls and the ⅓ cup water. Allow the tapioca pearls to soak for 30 minutes, or until doubled in size. Drain the tapioca pearls and reserve.

2. In a pot, place the ⅔ cup plus 1 tablespoon water and the rock sugar and bring to a boil over medium heat, stirring constantly until the sugar dissolves. Add the tapioca pearls and, while stirring constantly, allow the mixture to return to a boil. Lower the heat to a gentle boil and continue to stir for about 7 minutes, or until the tapioca pearls become translucent and the liquid thickens.

3. Turn off the heat. Add the milk and stir well. Add the mango puree and stir well. Add the coconut cream and stir to combine thoroughly. The soup will be creamy, colored yellow from the mango, and thickened. Pour into a bowl, cover, and refrigerate for 8 hours. The soup will thicken further as it chills.

4. Remove the soup from the refrigerator. Add the pomelo pulp and diced mango and stir to combine thoroughly. Divide evenly among individual bowls and serve chilled.

Continued . . .

. . . continued

NOTE: For coconut cream, purchase a can of coconut milk (liquid extracted from the grated flesh of mature coconuts), and open the can without shaking it. A layer of thick cream will have settled on top. Skim off the cream to use in this recipe. Do not purchase canned sweetened coconut cream, sometimes labeled "cream of coconut," which is used primarily for tropical drinks and some desserts.

‖ TAPIOCA PEARLS ‖

TAPIOCA PEARLS

These small, white balls are formed from the starch of the cassava root. They are used decoratively and for their ability to thicken liquids in sweets and sweetened fruit soups. When cooked, they resemble tiny, clear marbles and have a slightly chewy texture.

Tapioca pearls come in 1-pound plastic packages in two sizes. The smaller pearls are no larger than the ball of a tiny dress pin. The larger pearls are about the size of a small pea. I prefer the smaller ones because of their more elegant appearance and texture. There are many brands of tapioca pearls, but my choice is Tapioca Pearls Phayanak, from Malaysia. On its label, Chinese characters indicate it is Three Dragon brand.

You will also find almost identical small, white balls labeled "sago pearls" in Chinese and other Asian markets, though they are less common. They are made from a starch extracted from the pith of the sago palm tree; come in various sizes, from tiny balls to full-grown peas; and are often tan. Chefs in China use sago pearls and tapioca pearls interchangeably, calling both of them *sai mai* in Cantonese or *xi mi* in Mandarin, and they are often quite careless with their nomenclature. However, tapioca pearls are slightly starchier than sago pearls, and in the case of the mango soup they result in a creamier soup, so be certain to buy tapioca pearls for this recipe.

With this lovely, cool sweet, our cooking lessons are concluded. I have given you all that you need to know in order to cook authentic Chinese food well. You have the kitchen tools, which are few. You have the techniques and processes, which are varied but basically simple and no longer mysterious. You know how to shop for the foods you will need—foods once strange but now familiar. As you shop, I know you will keep in mind the axiom of my father: There is no substitute for quality and freshness, and select foods with as much care as you would a son-in-law or daughter-in-law. You know how to organize your ingredients with precision before you ever switch on the stove. You also know there are no shortcuts to cooking well, but that your efforts will bring great joy. You are now ready to cook.

The more you cook, the more skillful you will become, the more knowledgeable you will be. Never despair when you make an error, for you will. Mistakes are merely circumstances of learning. Cook, and then cook again. You will know when what you have done is right. When you have confidence in your skills, you will not only please those for whom you cook, but also yourself. When you dine in a restaurant, you will know how the chef prepared a dish and whether or not it is authentic. Cooking good food and eating it satisfies on many levels, and in good food, I believe, lies longevity.

Ho ho sik, as my family used to say—"Good eating."

LESSON 7
CREATING MENUS
IN THE CHINESE MANNER

設計中國菜單

CREATING
MENUS
IN THE
CHINESE
MANNER

Much of the enjoyment from Chinese cooking lies in devising a group of dishes that will come together in a meal that is balanced in terms of taste, variety, and nutrition. When planning meals, careful Chinese cooks instinctively do this. For example, I learned early from my parents and my grandmother that in a meal designed to both please and nourish, a dish considered mild, or cooling, should precede one perceived to be warmer, which should followed by another dish that is even warmer.

Larger meals of many courses, such as banquets, usually escalate upward from mild to intense, then back down again to mild, satisfying the palate and ensuring balance. These large meals are also driven by a variety of traditions.

Unlike Western meals, soups are never first courses. Rather they are typically placed midmeal, where they are enjoyed not only for their flavor but also to cleanse the palate. Meats are rarely final courses, as in most Western meals. They, too, are served at a midpoint in the banquet. Traditionally, such meals come to a conclusion first with noodles, in the case of a birthday-feast wish for longevity, or with fried rice, then finally a fish, usually whole, so that diners finish with the real taste of the sea. The arrival of the fish symbolizes a meal that has been both smooth and abundant from the beginning and is peaceful at the end.

As I have previously stressed, sweet desserts are not a Chinese tradition. Fresh fruits are eaten at the end of a meal. Sweet dishes are often served at banquets, however, usually at the conclusion, but they are never considered desserts. A good example of this is Eight-Treasure Rice (page 349). It is definitely sweet, and it could—and does—easily conclude a meal, but it is regarded as a rice dish.

What follows are six menus I have devised. All of them should be regarded only as examples, to be altered according to your taste, always keeping in mind the concept of balance. I start with three five-course menus, each one corresponding to the lessons in Parts 1, 2, and 3, respectively. These are followed by a vegetarian menu, and then with what I call a modified banquet menu, which includes fewer than the typical ten courses, but is still what I consider a grand meal.

Finally, I have presented a banquet menu that clearly illustrates the idea of tastes that escalate upward in intensity, peak, and then travel downward.

Some of the dishes you have learned that are complicated, that require more than one cooking process, can be miniature banquets on their own. This includes The Hot Pot (page 308), Big Bowl (page 339), Buddha Jumps over the Wall (page 323), and Tea-Smoked Duck (page 314), to name only a few. When you cook these, regard them as extra special and make just one or two simple dishes to accompany them, such as *Choi Sum* with Oyster Sauce (page 65) or Stir-fried Chives with Scrambled Eggs (page 71).

Finally, if you want to serve your meals in the Chinese manner, you will want to observe a few rules. At the table, whether it is round or square, you, the host, will sit with your back to the door, with the guest of honor facing you and with other diners arranged at will. (In China, these others would be seated, in descending order of importance, from the seat of the guest of honor.) If you are joined by a second host, you will sit as a pair with your backs to the door. Other couples should be seated together around you, with males to the left of their female companions.

At larger meals, foods are generally presented on communal platters, with diners serving themselves. Outfit each diner with two sets of chopsticks, one for serving and one for eating. To avoid embarrassing your guests who may still be mastering chopsticks, place forks and porcelain spoons at each place as well.

LEFT TO RIGHT: CHICKEN WITH CHICKEN LEGS; FRIED RICE WITH XO SAUCE

MENU ONE

|| SERVES 4 TO 6 ||

Braised Mushrooms in Oyster Sauce (page 98)

Barbecued Pork (page 103)

Fresh Bean Curd and Green Pea Soup (page 112)

Chicken with Chicken Legs (page 68)

Singapore Fresh Rice Noodles (page 126)

NOTES: I recommend serving plain cooked rice with the braised mushrooms and the chicken dish. The mushrooms and barbecued pork can be prepared in advance. With this meal, the tastes begin at a high with the directness of the mushrooms, decrease in intensity with the soup at midmeal, then increase again, to the spice of the noodles. I suggest a selection of melons for dessert.

MENU TWO

|| SERVES 4 TO 6 ||

Squash Pancakes (page 222)

Baked Duck Breasts (page 155)

White Soup with Two Bean Curds (page 206)

Veal in Black Pepper Sauce (page 228)

Fried Rice with XO Sauce (page 190)

NOTES: The duck breast recipe can be made in advance. I would not serve any plain cooked rice with this menu because a rice course is included. The menu begins with mild dishes, the meal's intensity gradually increases with the black pepper–sauced veal, and then another step up to the spice of the XO sauce mixed with the fried rice. Finish the meal with litchis and longans.

LEFT TO RIGHT: STEAMED HAIRY MELON SOUP; TOMATO, BEAN CURD, AND CHICKEN LEG MUSHROOM SOUP

MENU THREE

‖ SERVES 4 TO 6 ‖

White Rice Fish (page 335)

Water Dumplings (page 276)

Mapo Doufou (page 319)

Steamed Hairy Melon Soup (page 324)

Lobster in Black Bean Sauce (page 332)

NOTES: The soup can be steamed up to 2 hours in advance, then steamed briefly to reheat. The dumplings can be frozen for up to 2 months. Make them, boil as directed in the recipe, then cool completely and freeze. To serve, allow to come to room temperature, then steam for 5 minutes. Cooked rice will go nicely with both the spicy bean curd and the lobster. This meal's tastes go up and down: Salty deep-fried whitebait and down to subtle water dumplings, then up to spicy bean curd and down again to the steamed soup, and finally up to the assertiveness of the fermented black beans with the lobster.

A VEGETARIAN MENU

‖ SERVES 4 ‖

Roast "Goose" (page 295)

Tianjin Bok Choy with Braised Mushrooms (page 99)

Tomato, Bean Curd, and Chicken Leg Mushroom Soup (page 111)

Long Beans with Roasted Sesame Seeds (page 66)

Stir-fried "Beef" with Broccoli (page 296)

NOTES: The seasonings in this all-vegetable meal deliver a selection of direct tastes. The "goose," of course, is bean curd sheets, and the "beef" is the pressed bean curd so beloved by Buddhists. The bok choy dish can be prepared up to 2 hours in advance and kept at room temperature. The soup can be prepared up to 1 hour in advance and kept at room temperature. Reheat both dishes before serving. Use Vegetable Stock (page 53) in place of the chicken stock in the soup. The crispness of apples and pears is a good finish to the meal.

A MODIFIED BANQUET MENU

‖ SERVES 6 TO 8 ‖

Cook and Sell Dumplings (page 273)

Salt-Baked Chicken (page 331)

Spinach, Shrimp, and Bean Thread Noodle Soup (page 127)

Fried Rice with Duck (page 189)

Steamed Sea Bass with Shredded Pork (page 85)

Red Bean Soup with Lotus Seeds (page 351)

NOTES: A banquet in China is always a meal of at least ten courses and occasionally more. Such a meal can be daunting to prepare, yet I think this meal of six courses, with an elaborate, traditional festive dish, the chicken, as the focus, is sufficient to be deemed a banquet. It is an even-flavored meal of subtle changes of taste: the shrimp and pork of the dumplings, the slight saltiness of the chicken, and the essential mildness of the soup, the rice and the steamed fish glide effortlessly into one another and into the sweet soup. The dumplings, the salt-baked chicken, and the red bean soup can be made in advance. Make the dumplings and cook as directed in the recipe, then cool completely and freeze for up to 2 months. To serve, thaw and allow to come to room temperature, then steam for 5 minutes to heat through. The soup can be prepared up to 3 hours in advance and kept at room temperature. Before reheating, check to see if it has thickened and thin with water if needed. The chicken can be made 1 hour in advance. It will keep warm nested in the salt until serving. I recommend cold melon wedges, such as honeydew and cantaloupe, and sliced mangoes with this small banquet.

MENU FOR A LUNAR NEW YEAR BANQUET

‖ SERVES 10 TO 12 ‖

For the Chinese, a banquet at the beginning of the year is more than a meal. What is eaten is food, of course, but a New Year's menu is a collection of symbols and omens as well. What follows is a New Year banquet meal of the kind I experienced as a young girl growing up in Sun Tak Yuen. It might have been on New Year's Eve, marking the end of an old year, or the second day of the New Year, to welcome spring and the beginning of a new year.

Sweet Walnuts (page 347)

These sweet nuts, like all sweet foods, represent the essential sweetness of life.

Sour-and-Sweet Tianjin Bok Choy (page 317)

This course opens the palate and whets the appetite.

Live Shrimp Poached in Rose Petal Dew (page 87)

The Cantonese word for shrimp is har, *which sounds like happy laughter.*

Clams Stir-fried with Black Beans (page 77)

When clams open, they symbolize prosperity.

Shark's Fin Soup (page 246)

Serving this soup demonstrates the wealth of the host.

Ningbo Pork Shoulder (page 313)

For the Chinese, meat equals pork and symbolizes plenty.

Eggplant with Garlic Sauce (page 169)
served with Fried Breads (page 168)

Bread is considered a living food and thus gives life.

Yellow Croaker with Sweet Wine Rice Sauce
(page 205)

A whole fish is smoothness, ever moving, eternal, and never ending. Fish is yu, a homonym for growth and surpluses, and its presence ensures that one's fortune will continue to increase. Its constant swimming motion connotes that good fortune will never stop. The Cantonese saying Mon sui yu e, *or "A million things will go smoothly," is a wish for world peace as well. All of this was expressed by my grandmother, who presided over our New Year meal.*

Eight-Treasure Rice (page 349)

These eight precious treasures, or baht bo, *in one dish are the essence of the New Year.*

Oranges and Tangerines

Oranges are sweet and their seeds symbolize the birth of many children. The Cantonese word for tangerines is gut, *which translates as "good luck."*

NOTES: Many of the recipes for this banquet can be prepared in advance, including the walnuts, the bok choy, the soup, and the pork shoulder. The bread can be steamed ahead of time and then fried just before. The rice can be steamed, mixed with its eight treasures, and then steamed just before serving.

{ PART 3 }

LESSON 8
SERVING WINES, EAST AND WEST, WITH CHINESE FOOD

中西名酒和中餐

SERVING
WINES,
EAST AND
WEST

The first time I ever drank alcohol was when I was ten or eleven years old, growing up in Sun Tak Yuen, and an uncle offered me a sip of a white rice wine. It burned my throat. The first time I had wine with food was later, after I went to Hong Kong, when I tried a sip of the strong spirit known as *ng ga pei*. I did not like it. Not long after that, I tried various rice wines of different ages and breeding, and because I was not used to them, I generally found them not to my taste.

But as I grew older, I learned to appreciate many Chinese wines and spirits, both as beverages and, more important, as ingredients in cooking.

The Chinese have always consumed wines and other spirits with their food. In the north, they were typically strong flavored and made from fermented sorghum, millet, or wheat. In the south, glutinous rice was the base. Throughout the country, spirits flavored with pears, dates, rose petals, and other foods and aromatics were made. The elegant sorghum-based Mei Kuei Lu Chiew, infused with rose petals, is a prime example.

The Shaoxing region, which lies south of Shanghai and east of Hangzhou, is home to China's best traditional wines, all based on rice. They are meant, as are all fine wines, to be drunk with food, and they should be served pleasantly warm to the touch and the tongue. Several of the best of these wines can be found in Chinatown wine shops. They should be bought by their labels. Here are three good choices.

SUPREME HUA TIAO CHIEW. This yellow to amber wine is sold in a long-necked bottle, with a blue label and a red seal displaying its name. I drink this sparingly, and I cook with it.

HUA TIAO, STATE BANQUET OR PEOPLE'S CONGRESS. Aged eight to ten years, this is regularly served at state banquets at Beijing's Diao Yu Tai Guest House, and at sessions of the People's Congress. Its label is gold.

HUA TIAO VINTAGE. Aged five to eight years, this wine is usually bottled in decorative ceramic crocks that are sold nestled into brocaded gift boxes. It tastes similar to a medium sherry. Hua Tiao Calabash, bottled in a gourd-shaped crock, is also available. It is slightly sweet and favored either as an aperitif or for serving at the end of a meal.

Another Shaoxing wine, which is both good to drink and good to cook with, is not from Shaoxing. The wine is made in Taiwan, but the bottle is labeled "Shao Hsing V. O. Rice Wine," and its box is labeled "V. O. Shao Hsing Chiew." It is ten years old, thus its V. O. designation; is mild and smooth; and has a taste of sherry similar to Hua Tiao Vintage. As a cooking ingredient, it especially enhances fish and shellfish. The wine, which comes in a four-sided bottle that reminds me of a classic square-sided Scottish whisky bottle, is widely available in shops that stock Chinese wines and other spirits.

There are many other varieties of Shaoxing wine, from pale yellow to deep brown, some in special bottles of etched glass and others in brown earthenware or porcelain crocks. I have tasted them all and cooked with them all, and I prefer the first two Hua Tiao wines I have described over all of the others.

These days, however, more and more Western wines are available in Asia in general and in China in particular. Growers from France and other European countries and from the Americas have been invited to China to grow and harvest grapes and to make wines in the Western manner. Chinese growers and wine specialists are becoming ever more knowledgeable about Western wine varieties and their compatibility with the climates and soils of different parts of China. Wine-appreciation societies have sprung up in Shanghai, Beijing, Guangzhou, Hong Kong, and other Chinese cities, and wine courses and wine tastings are now commonplace. In the past, Western wines served at a Chinese table were invariably mixed with ginger ale or cola. That is no longer the case.

Major hotels in Asia have extensive wine lists and periodically convene dinners at which great wines are matched with Chinese food and diners are treated to lectures from winemakers. Such interest has fueled a strong demand for fine Western wines. A uniquely Chinese example of this is Hong Kong's Fook Lam Moon, which I consider the finest Chinese restaurant in the world. Its owner, Chui Wai-Kwan, employs a so-called Emperor of the Fish, who accepts or rejects fish for his restaurant. He specifies particular fins from particular sharks, and insists on crabs caught off the coast of a small South China Sea island at the confluence of salt and fresh waters because they yield a sweet yellow oil when steamed. When Mr. Chui decided that he would have wines in his restaurant, he sought out experts who drew up lists of the best first- and second-growth Bordeaux, which he promptly bought at a cost of hundreds of thousands of dollars. They are what he serves, only.

Over the years, I have been asked to create menus matching Chinese foods with Western wines. I have done food and wine banquets for California winegrowers and wine-tasting groups, for Les Dames d'Escoffier and other American gastronomic societies, for wineries in Germany and on Long Island, and for individual winemakers, such as Angelo Gaia from Italy's Piedmont region. They have generally been successful, so long as care was taken to be precise about the Chinese foods to be paired. I am particularly proud of two such food and wine weddings.

The first was a wine and food banquet to benefit a national charitable effort of Cancer Care. This dinner for twelve fetched a successful auction bid of fifteen thousand dollars.

The second banquet, the memory of which is dear to me, was arranged for the New World of Food and Wine Festival in Singapore, for which I created a menu to accompany only various Moët & Chandon's Champagnes, including Dom Pérignon. I spoke with the winemaker in Reims, giving him the dominant flavors in my proposed dishes, and together we decided on the Champagnes.

=== BANQUET 1 ===

Sweet Walnuts (page 347)
Bollinger Grande Année Champagne, 1992

Chicken with Melon Salad
Chalone Pinot Blanc

Drunken Shrimp in Mei Kuei Lu Chiew
Prager Riesling Federspiel Steinriegl

Vegetarian Oysters
Chalk Hill Estate Vineyard Select Pinot Gris

Grated Winter Melon Soup with Lobster
Chalk Hill Estate Vineyard Select Pinot Gris

Soft-fried Noodles with Scallops
Te Mata Estate Woodthorpe Sauvignon Blanc

Sweet-and-Sour Swordfish
Léon Beyer Gewürztraminer Comtes d'Eguisheim

Beggar's Chicken (page 201)
Joseph Drouhin Beaune Clos des Mouches

Veal in Black Pepper Sauce (page 228)
Jean-Luc Colombo Les Méjeans Cornas

Green Tea Ice Cream and Fresh Fruit
Nino Franco Prosecco Rustico

=== BANQUET 2 ===

Shrimp Marinated in Mei Kuei Lu Chiew and Sesame Oil
Cuvée Dom Pérignon, 1990

Salad of Barbecued Duck and
Fresh Cantaloupe Melon with Crisp Vegetables
Scallops and Yunnan Ham Steamed and
Scented with Scallion Oil
Sweet Eggplant Stuffed with Pungent Ginger Pickle and
Sweet Onion, Coated and Fried
Fresh Sliced Fish and Spinach in Superior Stock
Moët & Chandon Brut Impérial Rosé, 1993

Aromatic Smoked Chicken with
Litchi Black Tea and Rice, served with Steamed Buns
Buddhist "Squab" of Minced Soybean Cakes,
Flavored with Anise and Cinnamon, Brushed with
Hoisin Sauce, Wrapped in Lettuce Leaves
Moët & Chandon Brut Impérial

Medallions of Veal Marinated in Shallot Oil,
Sautéed in Crushed Black Peppercorns
Fried Rice with Piquant Sun-dried Tomatoes,
Broccoli Stems, and Coriander
Poached Fresh Pears and Raisins, Scented with
Honey and Lemon Balm
Moët & Chandon Nectar Impérial

Chinese Petit Fours
Selection of Chinese Teas

Over the years, I have come to favor certain Western wines with Chinese foods. Champagne is perhaps the most successful pairing. For more than twenty-five years, my husband, an officer in L'Ordre des Coteaux de Champagne, and I have celebrated Christmas Day with a buffet banquet of Chinese foods and French Champagne, to the delight of our recurrent guests and ourselves.

I prefer white wines to reds with Chinese foods, despite the grandeur and success of Fook Lam Moon. In addition to Champagne and its sparkling Italian counterpart, Prosecco, I serve whites with only slight acidity and with the flower of fruit. I particularly like the wines of Alsace, Rieslings with poached seafoods and with steamed fish, Pinot Blancs with chicken alone and in stir-fries with various vegetables, and lovely Gewürztraminers with dishes in which the flavors of garlic and ginger are pronounced.

I have had success pairing Spain's Albariños with dim sum dumplings and Pinot Gris with clams with black beans and with stir-fried noodles. I have also found Sauvignon Blancs from France and South Africa and some Rieslings from New York state pleasant to some degree. New World wines from New Zealand and Australia, particularly New Zealand Sauvignon Blancs, are highly drinkable with Chinese foods. I stay away from American Chardonnays, especially the heavily oaked ones that are so fashionable these days. These wines tend to be overbearing and will destroy any attempt at a happy union of tastes. Nor do excessively sweet wines complement Chinese foods.

Red wines are generally questionable with Chinese food. A big Bordeaux or Burgundy is wasted on foods seasoned subtly with the flavors of soy sauce and curry powder, bean paste and ginger. Tannic Cabernet Sauvignons often flatten out and become bitter with Chinese spices. But I have successfully matched Pinot Noirs from Oregon and the Côte de Beaune with my veal in a sauce based on cracked black peppercorns and with my chicken crusted with roasted garlic.

Keep in mind that the wines cited are those I personally favor and have served successfully. Pairing Chinese foods with Western wines should be regarded as an adventure in progress. I suggest you try some small weddings of your own. Who can predict what may emerge?

目錄

INDEX

中國調煮實習菜譜

MASTERING THE ART OF CHINESE COOKING

中國調煮實習菜譜

MASTERING THE ART OF CHINESE COOKING